DERRY CITY

DERRY CITY

Memory and Political Struggle

in Northern Ireland

MARGO SHEA

University of Notre Dame Press
Notre Dame, Indiana

Published in the United States of America

Library of Congress Cataloging-in-Publication Data

Names: Shea, Margo, 1970- author.
Title: Derry City : memory and political struggle in Northern Ireland / Margo Shea.
Other titles: Memory and political struggle in Northern Ireland
Description: Notre Dame, Indiana : University of Notre Dame Press, [2020] |
Includes bibliographical references and index.
Identifiers: LCCN 2020007551 (print) | LCCN 2020007552 (ebook) |
ISBN 9780268107932 (hardback) | ISBN 9780268107963 (adobe pdf) |
ISBN 9780268107956 (epub)
Subjects: LCSH: Derry (Northern Ireland)—History—20th century. |
Christianity and politics—Northern Ireland—Derry. | Catholics—Political activity—
Northern Ireland—Derry. | Religious tolerance—Northern Ireland—Derry. |
Nationalism and collective memory—Northern Ireland—Derry. |
Group identity—Northern Ireland—Derry.
Classification: LCC DA995.L75 S54 2020 (print) | LCC DA995.L75 (ebook) |
DDC 941.6/21082—dc23
LC record available at https://lccn.loc.gov/2020007551
LC ebook record available at https://lccn.loc.gov/2020007552

CONTENTS

FIGURES

ACKNOWLEDGMENTS

This book had its beginnings in another book. I first read Seamus Deane's *Reading in the Dark* in 1998, while on vacation in New Mexico with Britt Anderson, who has the gift and talent of making space for seemingly disparate things. Having spent a summer in Fermanagh many years earlier with American Field Service (AFS) and its affiliate organization Intercultural Educational Programmes (IEP), I was compelled to go to Derry after reading Deane. I was fortunate to be offered a visiting fellowship at Magee College of the University of Ulster. That first sojourn in Derry was a formative one, and it led me eventually to pursue this project on memory and cultural nationalism in Derry City.

I remain appreciative of the work that my academic mentors did to support the original project, from which this current work eventually emerged. David Glassberg, Dermot Quinn, Max Page, and James Young encouraged the project and made it better through their questions, critiques, and suggestions. I am particularly grateful to Dermot Quinn, who helped me get to Derry in the first place, and then guided, encouraged, and challenged me as I tried to learn about and understand Derry's history as an outsider. I am profoundly grateful to the reviewers who offered constructive critique, suggested new avenues of inquiry, and pointed out the strengths and the flaws of manuscript drafts. Special appreciation is due to Eli Bortz at University of Notre Dame Press and to the production team.

Thanks go to many who have read chapters, discussed the work over the years, and contributed in innumerable ways to the arc of ideas included herein, including John Fahey, Elizabeth Cahn, Bryonie Reid, Simon Jolivet, Jon Olsen, Andrew Dausch, Denise Meringolo, Cathy Stanton, Cheryl Harned, Billy Scampton, Richard Wilkie, Jennifer Heuer, Kate Preissler, Andrew Darien, Anna Sheftel, Stacey Zembrzycki, Marla Miller, and the late Diana Colbert. Holly White shared in this Derry story from the outset and has been a valued fellow traveler through life and academe. Bruce Laurie was a formative influence on my history education, and Ira Harkavy instilled in me a sense that scholarship should matter, which has always guided my public history work in Derry. The late Eric Schneider mentored and supported me, introduced me to E. P. Thompson, taught me the power of discipline, and championed my growth from the earliest days of my undergraduate career until his death in 2017. I only hope that his intellectual legacy is visible in these pages.

My colleagues at Salem State have been extremely supportive, and Alex Kyrou, Annette Chapman-Adisho, Brad Austin, Gayle Fisher, Dane Morrison, and Michele Louro have read chapters, participated in writing groups, and provided practical support, encouragement, and advice. Erik Jensen has done all of this and more as officemate, confidante, and ally in all things. A grant from Salem State's School of Graduate Studies' Scholarship Support Grant Program supported a research trip to Derry. I am grateful to the Salem State University History Department and the Center for Research and Creative Activities for supporting my attendance at conferences so that I could present work and gain valuable feedback.

Many people in Northern Ireland supported this project by offering direction, granting access to archives, agreeing to be interviewed, and suggesting sources and resources. I am grateful to have had a place at the Academy for Irish Cultural Heritages at Magee College of the University of Ulster as a practical and logistical site of operations during the early days of this project. I would like to thank Dr. Billy Kelly, formerly of the University of Ulster, for leading me towards the questions that needed to be asked and teaching me to read between the lines in seeking their answers. Phil Cunningham's work introduced me to a Derry rarely seen in the official sources, and the late Bishop Edward Daly's and Bernard Canning's work illuminated previously opaque avenues of research. Special thanks also go to Louis Childs of the University of Ulster Magee Campus Library; Linda Ming, Jane Nichols, and other reference staff at the Derry Central Library; staff at the Linenhall Library's Northern Ireland Political

Collection; the Heritage and Museum Service of Derry City Council's archives staff; staff at the Public Records Office of Northern Ireland; and Adrian Kerr and John Kelly of the Museum of Free Derry for leading me to and granting me access to useful sources. Local historians Sean Mc-Mahon, Michael McGuinness, Ken McCormack, and Brian Mitchell provided extremely useful information, as did Sara Cook, Eamon Deane, and Maureen Hetherington of the Junction, a community relations and peace-building organization. I am especially grateful to the late Bishop Daly and Frank Curran for agreeing to be interviewed, and to Daly for his generosity in working with me in the diocesan archives. Inordinate thanks go to Pamela Kelly and Madeleine McCally for the generosity and knowledge they shared in their interviews.

Paul Gillespie, a columnist for the *Irish Times*, suggested in 2007 that animating the concept of "through-otherness" might be the way forward for Northern Ireland. The idea had arrived to him upon recollection of a talk Seamus Heaney had given at the University of Aberdeen in 2001, in which he'd invoked the minister-turned-poet W. R. Rodgers. Heaney had observed that Rodgers's life exemplified the triple heritage of Irish, Scottish, and English traditions that "compound and complicate the cultural and political life of contemporary Ulster."[1] As Heaney had explained, for Rodgers, it "wasn't a question of the otherness of any part of his inheritance, more a recognition of the through-otherness of all of them."[2] He went on to define the term, remarking that "'through-other' is a compound in common use in Ulster, meaning physically untidy or mentally confused, and . . . it echoes the Irish-language expression, trí na chéile, meaning things mixed up among themselves."[3]

The cover image for this book, *The City Walls, Walker's Monument, Fahan Street and Nailor's Row, 1945*, painted by John Hunter, is an example of that through-otherness. The original painting hangs in the Chapter House of St. Columb's Cathedral, Londonderry, and is used here with generous permission of St. Columb's Cathedral and its representative Ian Bartlett. Hunter, a Presbyterian artist, painted the work, the original of which hangs in the Church of Ireland Cathedral and is used here through the generosity of St. Columb's Cathedral and its stewards, thus fronting the cover of a book about Derry's Catholics—through-otherness in the most Derry way possible. I am grateful to Andy Shears and Muncie Map Company for creating the book's beautiful maps.

Thanks go to Monica Mason Perkins and Barbara Burke, who were there from the very beginning. I would especially like to thank Patrick McGuinness, Pamela Kelly, Billy and Ellen Kelly, Elizabeth and Aubrey Fielding, Stephen and Julia Fielding, Bryonie Reid and Craig Sands, Siobhan Downey, and Billy Scampton for their open doors and open hearts. They have helped me to understand the many faces of Derry and Northern Ireland and made me feel at home. Particular thanks goes to Myra Canning, whose fierce and indomitable spirit, poetic sensibility, and insight into Derry guided me throughout the long process of writing this book.

My late mother, Janice Shea, was an ardent supporter of this project, and my father, William T. Shea, continues to be. My sister, Mary Shea, provided financial support at critical points to enable me to conduct research in Northern Ireland. Saving the best for last, my husband, Matthew Barlow, has encouraged and loved this project and my commitment to it from the day we met and has lived with it for as long as he has known me. It is hard, in a marriage of both hearts and minds, to know where one's ideas end and one's partner's ideas begin and that is very true in the case of this book. He has read and reread these pages, asked the right questions, and corrected footnotes and assumptions alike. As the Irish saying goes, "Two shorten the road," and because of Matthew, the long road towards this project's completion has seen more laughter than tears, more excitement than frustration, and all kinds of love.

MAPS

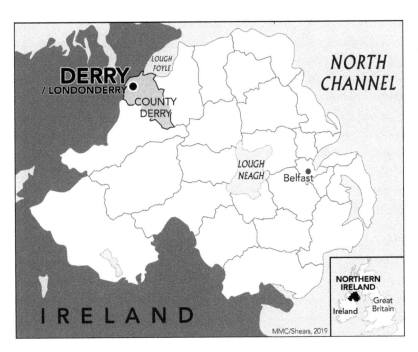

Map 1. Location of Derry within Northern Ireland, Ireland, and the British Isles

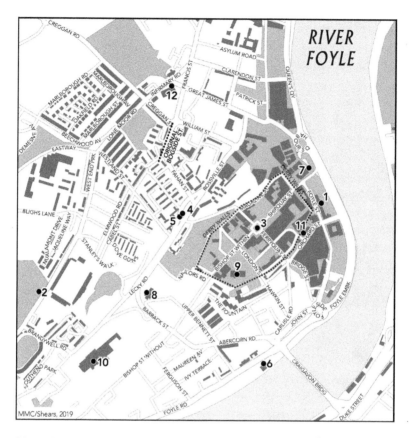

Map 2. Derry City sites of interest and memory

Points of Interest

1. Ancient Order of Hiberians Hall
2. Derry City Cemetery
3. The Diamond
4. Foxes Corner
5. Free Derry
6. Great Northern Railway Station
7. Guildhall
8. Longtower Catholic Chapel
9. St. Columb's Cathedral
10. St. Columb's College - original campus
    (currently Lumen Christi College)
11. St. Columb's Hall
12. St. Eugene's Catherdral

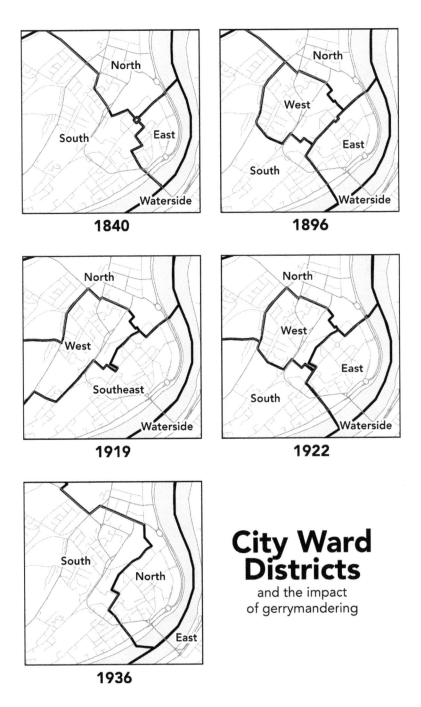

1840

1896

1919

1922

1936

City Ward Districts
and the impact
of gerrymandering

Map 3. Ward redistricting maps, 1840–1936

INTRODUCTION

Barney McMonagle was twenty-four years old and an aspiring amateur photographer when the civil rights movement got under way in Derry, Northern Ireland, in the late 1960s. Looking back on his experiences of documenting the movement and the outbreak of the Troubles, he said, "What a heady sense of change there was then in the trembling Derry air, what a tumult of ideas and bright-seeming glimpses of a different future beckoning. What was said then was, 'Everything's changed. Nothing will ever be the same again.'"[1] To explain this sense of overwhelming rupture, McMonagle recounted Derry Catholics' sense that something perceptible had shifted in the city's political culture after decades of stalemate. A space opened; from it poured pent-up frustrations at city authorities whose policies had long marginalized the political voices of the city's Catholic and nationalist majority. In August 1969, the Battle of the Bogside between the Royal Ulster Constabulary (RUC), B Specials, and local Catholics saw the stalemate end in a torrent of unrest: "There's a story, probably made up but possibly true, of a ten-year-old girl hurling a stone down Rossville Street at the RUC and shouting, 'I've waited 50 years for this!' Everybody will have known what she meant."[2]

When I started this project, I found myself drawn to McMonagle's story and to the image of a little girl with a big memory. It struck me that it didn't much matter if the tale about her was true; its persistence as community lore made it compelling. The girl on Rossville Street beckoned me, suggesting that ordinary people's engagements with the past were embedded everywhere in Catholic Derry. The community's histories and memories were rooted in the streets inhabited by its residents, in their activities and their voices. Catholics performed memory—told stories, sung songs, gathered, played out the past—more than they wrote about it or imprinted it on the urban landscape. Documented histories, formal

1

memorial narratives, written reminiscences and commemorations were simply the visible tip of a hulking iceberg of cultural memory that was expressed persistently and ubiquitously through words and deeds, through "ephemeral social practices, gestures and ritual."[3]

The story of the stone-thrower on Rossville Street also suggested that studying remembrance might reveal previously opaque or hidden histories. Northern Irish Catholics were underdogs and largely invisible in public life before adherents of the Home Rule movement in the late nineteenth century demanded that governance of Ireland be returned from Westminster to a domestic parliament in Ireland. Following Partition and the creation of Northern Ireland in 1921, Catholics faced legal restrictions that stunted cultural and political expression. This absence of overt expression has led historians to view quiet on the political front as apathy and disengagement with questions of cultural and national identity. The apocryphal tale of the stone-throwing girl, though, suggested that underneath the placid surface of public life, Catholics possessed more trenchant attitudes and stances concerning the politics of Irish identity. There is more to the story of the cataclysm of civil rights and the early Troubles than a seething Catholic acquiescence to the Northern state that erupted on the streets in the heady days of 1968.

From the Home Rule campaign to the onset of the Troubles and beyond, Derry Catholics' community identity—its sensibilities and aspirations—sought nourishment from acts and expressions of memory. Drawing on the past, a diverse set of Derry residents animated and articulated a distinct Irish Catholic identity in the city with striking continuity up to and through the early Troubles. Indeed, when Catholic bishop Neil Farren was asked to provide a statement for the Cameron investigation into the violence at Duke Street in October 1968, he didn't begin in the 1960s, 1921, or even 1801. His response was tied to memory of an Irish and Catholic Derry standing alongside the city that was planted and planned in 1614 as part of the English colonial project in Ireland. For the bishop, the turmoil of the late 1960s was inextricably tied to his understanding of Plantation and the world that it replaced:

Derry was founded in the year 548 by St. Columba and his monks and Londonderry was established almost 1000 years later by royal charter of King James I. Although these events are now only history, the problems they created are what perplex the city today. The principal task entrusted with the Irish Society in 1612 was, I quote, "the Petition of Sir Thomas Phillips—the Avoiding (removing) of the NATIVES and planting wholly with BRITISH."[4]

In Derry, Catholics simultaneously invoked, drew on, and constructed the past through memory work—the conscious and subconscious staging of memory through discussions, writings, displays, commemorations, festivals, protests, religious celebrations, memorials, oral histories, personal accounts, and community conversations.[5] Paying attention to memory reveals how Catholics drew selectively and instrumentally from the past to construct and negotiate cultural, social, and political identities from 1896 to 1969. These years are not arbitrary—1896 saw the city's first political gerrymander, ward redistricting, to achieve unionist political objectives as the Home Rule movement and the Gaelic Revival took on steam; 1969 saw not only the start of the Troubles and arrival of British troops in Northern Ireland but also the dissolution of the Londonderry Corporation, which marked the end of the era of political gerrymander and the decline of unionist political power in the city.

Mapping memory work and historical consciousness illuminates a deep reservoir of a community's experience and makes visible battles that were waged quietly, out of the limelight over long periods of time.[6] As such, this investigation of Catholic and nationalist memory in Derry contributes to broader histories of Ireland and Northern Ireland by inviting a reconsideration of the decades between Partition and the Troubles. At the same time, it offers insight more broadly into the gestures, discourses, and rituals communities draw on to weave threads of historical consciousness out of their experiences, aspirations, and fears.

Scholars and politicians have long lamented an Ireland imprisoned by its history. Interpretation of the past has played a part in political conflict, presiding over ongoing disputes that center around claims to national identity and its socioeconomic, spatial, territorial, political, and cultural manifestations. Derry has been a poignant example of this process at work; its history is in many ways an unfolding story of "dissonant heritages" and their effects.[7] When John Lees came to Derry in 1968 to write a story for the *New York Times*, he observed that Derry was the epitome of conflict in Northern Ireland. Of the divided city, he observed, "Its problems are in a real sense . . . deeper and more hurtful because the city's special place in Northern Ireland's history has made it a talisman of prejudice on either side."[8] Brian Keenan also observed this phenomenon: "Nowhere are people more aware of their heritage whether recent or distant; nowhere are they more conscious of their ancestors' triumphs and sufferings. There, people experience ancient antagonism; there, they also are struggling to find ways to accommodate each other's differences. To those who view 'Londonderry' as a microcosm of Northern Ireland, there is a sense that current 'troubles' began in Derry, and a sense that Derry also might point the way to resolution."[9]

In the context of Northern Ireland, the presence of the past is not so much a divided narrative as much as it is (at least) two separate ones.[10] "Protestants and Catholics," Henry Glassie observed, ". . . begin at different points, follow different routes, embrace different personalities . . . history is not so much a weapon between groups but a means to consolidate one group."[11] In addition, Protestants and Catholics alike have felt historic sensibilities of marginalization and victimization. As a result, members and representatives of both communities have encouraged interpretations of the past that have not only explained patterns of division but have helped to perpetuate them.

For Ulster's Protestants, remembrance was woven into official histories and mapped onto the physical landscape. Often a very public process, memory work was accompanied by pageantry and ritual that claimed physical space and reaffirmed authority in the present through references to the past. Londonderry is the "Maiden City," besieged but undefiled during the Glorious Revolution of 1688–89; the survival of the small community of supporters of the Protestant king William of Orange made possible his ultimate victory at Drogheda's Battle of the Boyne in 1690, shaping Irish history (and that of the "three kingdoms") for the next several centuries.[12] As early as 1789, the siege became the subject of annual commemorative attention.

The events of the Siege of Derry and its commemorative resonances were themselves motivated by remembrance of events associated with the Irish Rebellion in 1641, when thousands of Protestant settlers were killed, exacerbating fear and kindling animosities between Protestants and Catholics. Derry, with its walls and loyal citizenry, became a figurehead for the province's Protestants from the eighteenth century onward, the events there gradually enshrouded in a sanctified memory and made an official part of the province's historical narrative after 1921.[13]

Londonderry's Protestants have taken strength from unionism and motivation from the memory of their forefathers' righteous vulnerability to establish traditions that reaffirmed their identity in order to overcome anxieties accompanying minority status on the island of Ireland and, later, anxieties that the United Kingdom would not support their status as members of the Union. The city's official history dovetailed for centuries with many aspects of Anglo-Protestant experience; indeed, many considered Derry the "chief city of ascendancy in Ulster."[14] From the city walls themselves to the parades around their perimeters, rites and expressions of memory served that history and affirmed it. When the Troubles began in 1969, one journalist put it this way, "Sanctified as it is by the mythology of the past, Derry is seen by many nervous Protestants as the key to the survival of their state and their society."[15]

To Irish Catholics, Derry is associated with the ancient oak grove for which the city was originally named and with Columba, also known as Colmcille, the city's patron saint who founded a monastery there in the sixth century. As the Derry annals would have it, the stones of the ruins of a once great church, the Tempul Mor, were carted away to build the city walls and ramparts in the early seventeenth century, colonialism bringing creative destruction in material form.[16] In the 1960s, Derry was home to a broad-based civil rights movement that turned violent and brought soldiers onto Northern Ireland's streets at the same time that governmental "business as usual" was suspended and life in the city and the province changed dramatically. Site of 1972's Bloody Sunday, the city saw thirteen unarmed and peaceful civil rights protestors shot and killed by British paratroopers. Official British government apologies in 2010 notwithstanding, Bloody Sunday continues to loom traumatic in collective memory. In fact, Bloody Sunday itself carried within it echoes of fierce street conflicts in the city in 1920 that saw more than twenty local Catholics shot and the community ripped apart in the wake of looting and arson.

In public consciousness and also within scholarly histories, a long gap stretches between the days of the sainted grove and the turbulent period of civil rights and the early Troubles. For much of this time, Derry's Catholics represented a world apart; their culture reflected complicated identities. Long before the establishment of the border between Northern Ireland and the Irish Free State, they were seen as "other" by Protestant settlers who developed and laid claim to Londonderry from the Plantation period onward. Independence and the establishment of the Free State only three miles from Derry's city center ruptured ties with nearby County Donegal, the place where many Derry Catholics had roots, and had created and nurtured an urban Irish Catholic culture from these experiences of difference. Although they held a demographic majority since 1850, Catholics' political representation was steadily reduced through periodic and strategic use of gerrymander from 1896 until the dissolution of the Londonderry Corporation in 1969, constraining opportunities for political voice, geographic mobility, higher education, and public employment. Largely divorced from traditional politics for much of this time, many Catholic nationalists in Derry shaped and framed identity through relationships to home, church, and neighborhood; they only episodically participated in explicitly public and political realms; thus, the city's twentieth-century cultural history of nationalism and resistance has been largely overlooked. Yet, this history is crucial for understanding "the interwoven politics of community, struggle and power" that shaped nationalists' perceptions of and commitments to civil rights and ultimately ushered in the era of conflict the world came to know as the Troubles.[17] More broadly, it also invites a rethinking of the long-standing trope of an Ulster Catholic "culture of grievance" that has been used by historians for decades to describe, and indeed define, Catholic attitudes towards public life in Northern Ireland.[18]

This book examines how and under what circumstances Catholic Derry emerged and evolved from the turn of the twentieth century, when it was first incorporated as a city and experienced its first political gerrymander, to the end of the 1960s—which saw a suspension of local government, the rise of paramilitary activity, and the introduction of British military presence. A focus on this period resituates the civil rights movement and the Troubles by highlighting the ways urban development and community life intersected with larger social and political issues and events for Catholics who understood themselves to be Irish both before and after Partition.

Here, we trace the past through remembrance itself, honing in on Catholic Derry's history through the lens of the memories its inhabitants cultivated and nurtured and also through the versions of the past Catholics and nationalists contested. In their engagements with one another, with Protestant unionists and with those across the Irish border, the concerns and hopes of Catholics and nationalists in Derry were often expressed through memory work. As they sought recognition locally, worked to influence broader debates over political, social, and economic issues, and endeavored to maintain an Irish cultural identity, Derry Catholics drew on the past to sustain their communities, to reflect their experiences, and to change their fortunes.

My focus on memory and historical consciousness draws this book into a lengthy and lively conversation about the influences of memory on Irish history. History and memory have been understood in opposition to one another, and many historians of Ireland have argued that history—with its tests for veracity, its impartiality, its complexity—engages in pitched battle with the "feel-good happy-clappy therapeutic refuge" of popular memory. The dangers of memory could be seen in overly simplistic, essentialist, and essentializing rhetorics that, by invoking the past instrumentally, served to exaggerate difference, reify sectarian divides, and exacerbate conflict over much of Ireland's modern history. It has been argued that Irish nationalism itself fed on inventions in the form of memory, and ultimately led political leaders to codify those memories as popular history.[19]

This focus on the dangers of popular history and memory may, of course, elide the processes through which those particular interpretations became useful and, indeed, popular. George Bernard Shaw famously wrote that critiques of nationalism are luxuries for those whose national identity is not in jeopardy: "Nationalism stands between Ireland and the light of the world. Nobody of any intelligence likes Nationalism any more than a man with a broken arm likes having it set. A healthy nation is as unconscious of its nationality as a healthy man is of his bones. But if you break a nation's nationality, it will think of nothing else but getting it set again."[20]

Aspects of British colonial involvement in Ireland, particularly era-
sures of the Irish language, shrunk the scale and scope of understanding
of the island's history. Depopulation in the nineteenth century through
famine and emigration meant the further loss of cultural inheritances.
Meanwhile, official histories celebrated the union of Ireland and Britain,
masked the subordinate role of Ireland and de-emphasized perspectives
on the past that did not highlight the benefits of both Anglicization and
modernization.

In response, countermemories emerged. Often locally specific, frag-
ments embedded in songs, stories, folklore, the Irish language, and quotidian performances and rituals, countermemories kept alternative narratives alive throughout the eighteenth and nineteenth centuries.[21] As Joep
Leerssen points out, "The balladeers and historians of Gaelic Ireland,
the Gaelic-speaking priests writing anti-English history on the Conti-
nent, the known or anonymous authors of Jacobite-Messianist aisling poetry, the seanchaí-based village scholars" took snippets from the past and
formed the bedrock of a Gaelic-identified Irish cultural identity that was
then adopted and adapted in the nineteenth century as a way of creating
a "shared sense of us-ness" that shaped nationalism from the Young Ireland period onward.[22] By the Gaelic Revival era at the turn of the twentieth century, remnants from the Gaelic, Catholic Irish past had been knit
together to achieved a sense of continuity and comprehensibility that nationalists harnessed quite intentionally for the purposes of state-making.

Claims of invention overlook the project of repair so central to the
nationalist histories of this period. Fashioning a usable past from available
remnants and traces became part of the national project. As revolutionary
and romantic nationalism coalesced in the early years of the twentieth
century, a patchwork of rescued stories, collected memories, and refash-
ioned "found" narratives fused to form Ireland's new official history that
could be utilized to marshal support for the emergent state and to present
cohesion in the past as a salve for a fractured Ireland. This history portrayed the Irish past from the Norman period onward as a long, undiffer-
entiated, and uninterrupted story of struggle that excluded characters and
events that deviated from a script that simplified Irish "freedom" and
framed it as a goal at once "timeless and perennial."[23]

It was during this time of revolutionary foment, simultaneously and paradoxically both formative and destructive, that the familiar tropes of Irish nationalist popular history were codified. The story went something like this: An unspoiled, uncorrupted past characterized by a unified, Celticized Irish island-wide culture dating to pre-Christian times met rupture in the form of 700 years of English misrule, until Ireland achieved independence and democracy, both of which were universally desired, achieved, and celebrated. At the same time, Ulster's politicians and writers were narrating an alternative history in which Anglo-Norman settlement and the British presence were responsible for civilizing and organizing the chaotic, illegible backwaters of unruly Ireland. In these unionist narratives, Ulster had been the exception to the historical rule since the pre-Christian era.[24] It had emerged thus as a homogeneous, industrious Protestant region. Analysis of current events and arguments for independence on the one hand and for Partition on the other relied increasingly on an understanding of Irish history punctuated and thus shaped by these interpretative divides.

The early years of Irish independence saw the cementing of narratives on either side of the new border, but over the following decades, the scholarly study of Irish history underwent revision and embraced the many "varieties of Irishness," exploding the myth that Irish identity could be understood in terms of a monolithic political affiliation, or any political affiliation at all, for that matter.[25] The tidiness of previous interpretations was revisited and complicated. Multiplicity was the watchword of the moment. Binaries were deposed and narratives too centered around Irish nationalism or British colonialism were castigated for toying with history.

The political climate in Northern Ireland also shaped the way historians viewed memory and thus how they chronicled the past. After 1969, historians became ever warier of attributing nationalist intentions to their Northern Catholic historical subjects. The belief that nationalist mythology had contributed to radical militant republicanism in Northern Ireland motivated historians to reassess their participation in public discourse about the past. Echoing Yeats after the Easter Rising, Nancy Curtin suggests that historians felt culpable for sending out a new generation of men whom "the English shot."[26] Feeling queasy about their possible collusion with militant republicanism, historians wondered if "an uncritical nationalist republican history affirm[ed] the men of violence and polarize[d] the two communities in the north beyond reconciliation?"[27]

Under these circumstances, identifying and highlighting the importance of widespread nationalist sentiments in the North prior to the Troubles looked dangerously like aiding and abetting terrorists. John Regan argues that this had its own dramatic effect on the production of historical knowledge about Ireland. When historians assumed "a causal relationship between art and politics on the one hand, and historiography and violence on the other," a moral crisis within the Irish academy ensued. Hardly dismissive of their power, critics attacked popular interpretations of the past precisely because of their explosive effects. Underlying many of these critiques lay an assumption that memorial discourses fueled the conflict as much, if not more than, the conflict itself encouraged particular kinds of memory work. Historians, Regan argues, responded by producing "counterinsurgency narratives" that aimed, consciously or not, to defuse republicanism.[28]

Debates over revisionism and the limits of historical objectivity have been covered masterfully elsewhere.[29] Here, it is sufficient to acknowledge historians who have insisted that a reckoning with "the burden of the past" in Irish history is a requisite for any meaningful communication about it. Contending with the complexities of memory is possible, they illustrate, without reducing it to lie, manipulation, or delusion. Brendan Bradshaw made a salient observation when he pointed out that efforts to remedy the anachronistic projections of nationalist ideology that had been foisted on the past had only succeeding, in fact, "in extruding the play of national consciousness."[30] Leaving Ireland a place with a fragmented and disfigured past characterized only by discontinuity, he argued, destroyed the community's resource—a past that might enable them to understand themselves better. If "the Irish had clung tenaciously to their nationalist heritage," what right had historians to take it away?[31]

Certainly, Derry is illuminative in this respect. This study of memory work in a corner of Ireland far from the state-making crafters of nationalist history in Dublin, as Beiner's work on 1798 and William Kelleher's study of the eponymous Ballybogoin or Henry Glassie's exploration of County Fermanagh have also done, illustrates that Irish memory practices have operated from the bottom up as much as from the top down.[32] As John Bodnar explained so persuasively in the context of the United States, strands of vernacular and official memories are difficult to tease apart.[33] In Ireland, threads of folklore, performances of traditions passed down through generations, and elaborate festivals around Catholic saints and holy days all complicate the arguments that Celticized, Catholicized historical memory was artificially imposed by the state-makers. Although not specifically about memory, William Payne's *I've Got the Light of Freedom*, documenting the early civil rights struggle in Mississippi, and William Hinton's *Fanshen: A Documentary of Revolution in a Chinese Village* illustrate the power of the local study to illuminate patterns and connections that a more traditional research model might overlook.[34] Indeed, as other scholars have noted, there are parallels to be drawn between the long arc of African American struggles for freedom and equality in the United States and the Northern Irish civil rights movement, and this book provides a deeper context for this kind of analysis.[35]

Revisionist perspectives still infuse academic thinking in Irish scholarly discourse about the presence of the past and bolster the notion that revisionism made it possible for Irish historical studies to eschew the vagaries of memory in order "to reach a new level of impartiality and professionalism."[36] The idea that memory is invariably and crudely instrumental is deeply embedded in these assertions, as is a dismissal of memory in favor of more reliable history. Christopher Norton recently asserted that "in Ireland . . . memories are frequently called upon to defend entrenched political positions and nearly always to present a fatalistic vision of the past." In holding up his own work of historical scholarship as distinct from the vagaries of memory, he quoted Pascal Bruckner's assertion that "memory intimidates, condemns, blasts; history desacralizes, explains, details. One divides, the other reconciles."[37] This continued polarization at once valorizes history and chastises memory without considering the limitations of the former and the affordances of the latter. Of course, historical production itself is complicated by issues of power, inequalities in both the production of and access to the archive, notions of what constitutes historical knowledge in the first place, and which social actors ultimately have the resources to become reputable chroniclers of the past.[38] The continued insistence on memory as an unreliable narrator obscures the problematic notion that professional history is by definition always rational, verifiable, mature, methodical, and correct.

Remembrance can be telling on its own, not simply as a foil for history or a scoresheet on which to mark where popular historical consciousness gets it wrong. Remembering is a creative act, one of invention as much as of retrieval. Gaining insight into a community's experiences requires "taking seriously their ways of structuring experience, their popular narratives, the distinctive manner in which they frame the social and political realities which affect their lives."[39] Indeed, it is useful to conceive of memory as both "a source and a subject" for historians. Through interpretation, studies of memory help us to identify why and "how a certain view of the past is incorporated, sustained or alternatively eclipsed."[40] Understanding context is critical for all remembrance; our social worlds constitute the scaffolding for memories. A study of social frameworks—the environments and situations within which the past is drawn forth—is as necessary as memories themselves for deepening insight into historical consciousness, for "it is in society that (people) recall, recognize, and localize their memories."[41] The memories we hold closely as ours alone, in fact, emerge and remain tenacious only in dialogue with the social worlds we inhabit: "Individual memory takes place in an intersubjective nexus that is at once social and collective, cultural and public."[42] In other words, memory is a social process. The knowledge, values, and perceptions a community or society considers important and necessary are reiterated and upheld through memory work.

Folklorist Henry Glassie distills the social power of remembrance and telling when he explains that in Northern Ireland stories about the past have served to coordinate "multiple responsibilities to time, to the past event, the present situation and the future of the community."[43] This, of course, is why historians hold suspicions about memory, arguing multiple responsibilities yield plural masters and, thus, memory elides, masks, and contorts as much about the past as it reveals. Ultimately, it is not useful to compare history to memory, using the former as the scorecard on which to measure the latter. Memory is dynamic, fluid, subjective, and extremely impressionable. Though memory may indeed have complicated allegiances, it operates fluidly and according to a pragmatic sensibility: "It only accommodates those facts that suit it; it nourishes recollections that may be out of focus or telescopic, global or detached, particular or symbolic."[44] Far from being unconcerned with the truth, memory digs in deep, seeking a different truth. Molding and recasting what novelist Elena Ferrante calls the "disjointed, unaesthetic, illogical shapeless banality of things," memory goes to work on the past. It distills experience, putting some things into sharp relief while abandoning others, constantly framing and reframing past events to make sense of the present and the future.[45]

Indeed, interpretations of the past are more than merely discursive exercises. Memory's ability to do more than recall—to actually *construct* pasts—is essential to identity, as many scholars have argued.[46] By conjuring up a usable past, communities make use of memory to explain themselves into being just as much as they explain how they came to be.

By denying memory its own history, we run the danger of erasing the contexts, events, patterns, and experiences out of which memories emerge, establish ground, and gain traction. This robs memory of its own process, its own story. It belittles those who hold it and make it. Memory may be influenced by invention, but the invention itself must be historicized. As Kevin Whelan argues, it is the responsibility of the historian to piece together the collective and collected memories of those who peopled the past.[47]

This book carefully historicizes memory and historical consciousness in an effort to reframe discussions of the problem of Irish memory. Circular debates about the utility and nature of history versus memory cease when we place collective remembrance within an historical context.[48] Here, the concrete discussion of actors, agency, participation, and the back-and-forth between cultural production and reception by a broad range of citizens makes memory a part of history instead of its delusional twin. If memory is *always* strategic and responsive to contemporary concerns, this does not render remembrance trivial or insignificant. Rather, the discursive qualities within expressions and practices of memory help us to understand the worldview of ordinary men and women and also of cultural and political leaders. Further, contextualizing memory work and relating it to the social, political, economic, and spatial processes that surround, forge, and inform it illustrate how collective remembrance shapes community identity. Excavating the quarries of remembrance reveals beliefs, assumptions, and desires held by people who otherwise might leave only vague historical footprints of their cultural and intellectual experiences. At the same time, history itself can appear quite differently once memory is given its due, making visible battles that were waged quietly and out of the limelight over long periods of time. Not only does memory have a history, it also makes history.

Mapping historical consciousness also upsets the accepted historiography of the Troubles, which generally frames civil rights and social and political unrest in Northern Ireland within the tumult of the global 1960s. Historians of the Irish civil rights movement have identified its causes, namely, a newfound sense of entitlement in the wake of postwar affluence and higher education, concern over a host of bread and butter issues, inspiration gleaned from television sets broadcasting civil rights' struggles around the world, and/or the agitation of frustrated young bucks of the baby boomer generation keen on upending the status quo. In so doing, they have overlooked the organizations and cultural practices that built a foundation for the civil rights movement out of a long history of political frustration, Irish cultural identity, and community strength.

There are three major complications when it comes to studying memory in Northern Ireland. One is the way the Troubles haunt other memories. Examinations of the memorial imaginary for the nationalist community in Derry, particularly, have centered on events of the early Troubles. For many Irish Catholics in the North, the Republic of Ireland, and the diaspora, Bloody Sunday came to encapsulate and symbolize the inequalities and injustices that many believe fueled the fury that ignited the modern Troubles.

As a result, historians have often described the beginnings of the Troubles in incendiary terms. "Five decades of frozen politics" were over.[49] Violence "erupted," the result of a "highly explosive mix" of circumstances and communal disturbances "erupting without plan or premeditation." Battle lines led to "insurrection." One historian refers to the late 1960s simply as the time "the whirlwind struck." In *Making Sense of the Troubles*, David McKittrick and David McVea refer to post-Partition Northern Ireland as an utterly "static society," which obscures the very real transitions and transformations therein.[50] These interpretations of the start of the Troubles have not only obscured subtler genealogies of the conflict; they have also rendered the years between the establishment of Northern Ireland and 1968 as a preface to the "real story" instead of as an important historical period in its own right. As a result, there is a dearth of work that examines Catholic and nationalist community identity and the ways memory forged that identity in the decades before the Troubles began.

The second complication is that historians have tended to frame Northern nationalism in purely political terms. Drawing on a framing of nationalism that dates back to early twentieth-century notions of resistance to British rule in Ireland articulated by Cumann na nGaedheal and Sinn Féin, followed by de Valera's republican vision of a united and independent Irish nation, nationalism was equated with republicanism, or indeed with physical force republicanism. Using this gauge, they have asserted that Northern Catholics' sense of Irish nationalism was on life support by the late 1950s. Historians argue that the IRA Border Campaign of 1957–62 failed largely from lack of grassroots support; they further suggest that the idea of a united Ireland simply failed to incite Northern Catholics or to ignite their imaginations.

In terms of historicity, fears that any kind of nationalist sympathy would be read as an avowal of violence during the Troubles shaped the ways scholars, politicians, and even ordinary people talked about civil rights, underscoring bread-and-butter issues and underplaying cultural or political identity. Consider this Derry resident's 1979 reflection on the civil rights movement and his insistence that the protests were not fomenting violence: "I took a fairly active part as a steward in the civil rights. I think, in those days, republicanism wasn't mentioned, even a United Ireland wasn't mentioned. What we marched for was equality, jobs, houses, etc. things like that."[51]

This was exacerbated by British journalists' direct linkage of Irish nationalist histories and IRA recruitment. The Irish Republican Army, or IRA, was formed in 1917 as a paramilitary organization dedicated to the idea that all of Ireland should be an independent republic free from British rule. Those members opposed to the treaty leading to the partition of Ireland continued the organization after 1922. In 1969, after an internal disagreement over abstentionism, the Provisional IRA was formed after a split with the "official wing" and formed the PIRA, or "Provos."[52] In Peter Taylor's 1989 documentary *The Volunteer*, Derry's Christian Brothers Primary School history teachers served up to their students a "romantic diet of Irish history" and led Shane Paul O'Doherty to join the Provisional IRA. Presenting the IRA's first leaders in 1917 as the "fathers of the nation" drove young men to the cause because "the whole meaning of life could be contained in that fight for Irish freedom."[53] Conflating nationalism, Irishness, and republican violence made people wary of being branded terrorists if they appeared overtly interested in anything to do with Irish political identity. Hence "nationalism" has tended to not appear in the archives unless political intent is understood.

Third, there is a deep and important preoccupation with the issue of divided and divisive memory in postconflict Northern Ireland. Memory work has been framed problematically as articulating parallel, opposi-tional narratives about the past for Catholics and Protestants, calcifying difference and providing safe cocoons for separateness, nurturing polari-ties instead of facilitating convergences. As Marie Breen Smyth suggests, within the Northern "culture of blame" that accompanied the Troubles and their aftermath, motivations for memory remain mixed.[54] Just as people look to remembrance as a way "to mitigate loss, honor the dead, affirm identity, resolve justice issues and unfinished business, get answers to unanswered questions, learn the lessons of the past and achieve new understandings," they also find it useful as a way to shame enemies, as-sert moral superiority, and justify future behavior.[55] Conceived as such, memory is a barrier to a postconflict public culture that makes room for difference. This view of memory incorporates many of the critiques new revisionists lodged against what they have called popular historical narratives.

Gerry Slater of the Public Record Office of Northern Ireland recently echoed a widespread misconception that contemporary historical con-sciousness is somehow exceptional: "The present-day reality is that the two communities have projected versions of history that strengthen com-munity identity at the expense of reinforcing stereotypes and myths of 'the other side.'" By implication, creating and projecting different versions of the past is an artifact of the Troubles, not a reason for them in the first place. These pesky projections stand in the way of equality, compassion, shared understanding—a shared public culture. Jonathan McMaster of the Irish School of Ecumenics critiqued the role of memory:

Must the remembering forever divide us? Must we live forever with the sectarianization of memory, the exclusivity of commemoration? Or can we find ways of inclusive remembering, of entering into each other's chosen traumas, of walking through history together? . . . Can we move beyond our victor/victim categories, our zero-sum politics . . . into a different future, a shared future based on compassion, justice, equality, diversity, interdependence and peace?

Understandably, there has been skepticism about single-identity research about Northern Ireland and impassioned cries for historical research that does not partition the island or its communities despite recognition that there can be no "national shared strategy for remembrance," at least not yet.[56] These critiques mirror some of the trenchant debates about Irish history writing more generally. Some critics assert that articulating difference and division performs it: by saying it, one exacerbates it, reifies it, and perhaps even celebrates a green and orange version of the past instead of identifying and exploring meanings of the many shades of gray. Others argue that understanding each community's history from the inside is necessary before seeking to understand across the cultural, religious, and ethnopolitical divides. Pretending the divisions were not engrained and experienced does not erase their valence in daily life in Northern Ireland for much of its history. When asked about the significance of using political and religious terms interchangeably and creating Catholic/Protestant categories with associated political identities, Derry's Eddie McAteer observed in 1964, "Whether the political theorists like it or not, the facts of life are [that] these descriptions are interchangeable for 99% of the population."[57]

If we assume Brian Keenan is right that Derry is a good starting place in the quest to build a multicultural and peaceful future, then this history of Catholic, nationalist Derry serves two important purposes. First, it returns to the city's Catholic and nationalist citizens a fuller twentieth-century cultural history that they can examine, debate, refute, and build upon. In the face of Brexit, the prospect of a hard border between Northern Ireland and the Irish Republic has reawakened violence and revealed the flaws of the two Northern standbys, "whataboutery" and "letsgetalong."[58] In the wake of the murder of journalist Lyra McKee by those who identify as dissident Irish republicans in Derry in 2019, the need to understand the full history of the city is more important than ever. Although most efforts to transcend Northern Ireland's painful histories recognize the significance of memory, this work faces significant challenges. Before a shared historical consciousness can emerge in Northern Ireland, citizens must first *share* their historical consciousness.

At the same time, the long history of Derry as a Catholic and nationalist city still matters in discussions of economy, opportunity, and growth. Derry, as journalist Steve Bradley explains, remains at "the bottom of the prosperity pile" more than twenty years after the Good Friday Agreement (1998), and suffers from both financial and social deprivation.[59] The histories of Partition, discrimination, underinvestment, and a general orientation towards Belfast and Coleraine for development initiatives have all shaped the challenges currently facing the city. These challenges, in turn, may have the effect of making militant republicanism look like a solution to those without prospects or purpose.

Finally, looking beyond Derry, this history of the performance of identity through expressions of memory can be instructive beyond its particularities. Here, the details yield a better understanding of how the categories such as "Protestant" and "Catholic" come to be constituted, understood, and calcified. As we grapple with the limits and affordances of nationalism within increasingly multiethnic, diverse societies, observing closely the ways memory work and other symbolic practices can shape identity is important. Identity, like memory, is a process. Reactive and iterative, concrete and elusive, situated and imagined as it may be, it cannot be fully understood if it is alienated from its history.

In Derry, people practiced remembrance, simultaneously invoking, drawing on, and constructing the past. Expressions of memory were embedded in speeches, newspaper accounts, travel writings, oral accounts of familiar ghost stories, children's rhymes, a plethora of commemorative events, letters to the editor, souvenir booklets, church sermons, street festivals, protests, religious celebrations, documentary films, féisanna, memorial constructions, oral histories, personal accounts, and radio programs. Practices such as harvesting shamrocks along the banks of a local river in preparation for St. Patrick's Day, rehearsing Gaelic songs and stories months before an annual féis, preserving and rebuilding an ancient

Celtic ruin, or utilizing obituaries to teach powerful community lessons nourished Derry's Irish sensibilities and aspirations from before Partition to the onset of the Troubles and beyond.

Here, memory is both "a perpetually actual phenomenon, a bond tying us to the eternal present" and a way of calling on and representing the past for the sake of the present and the future.[60] Often fleeting, fluid, performative, and embodied, the activities of memory described here do not inform on their own so much as they stand together, each a small dot in a constellation of Catholic Derry's cultural and political experiences. Public history—with its attention to local history writing, oral history and storytelling, experiential practice, material culture, performance studies, and landscape analysis—offers a way into Derry's history that traditional archival sources miss.

Catholics utilized collective remembrance before and after the establishment of the border to nourish a shared sense of Irish national and cultural identity. Remembrance work changed over time, as Derry's Catholics recrafted their ways of understanding themselves in response to social change—both within their community and beyond it. Though often depicted by both journalists and scholars as isolated, passive, reactive, self-deprecating, and politically myopic, the Catholic community in Derry had long created outlets for expressing and constructing identity by invoking memory.[61]

Reaching deep into the history of community memory provides opportunities to understand Derry's past, present, and future. By examining memory work from the period before Partition to the beginning of the Troubles, one finds continuities that more traditional historical investigations have overlooked. Here, one example proves telling. The well-studied civil rights movement of the late 1960s saw Catholics and nationalists physically claiming their rights to the city. As the first large-scale march culminated at the ceremonial center of the city, the Diamond, John Hume took the megaphone and declared, "We are within the Walls and we will stay here. We have the force of the like of which has never been seen in the city before. . . . I am not a law breaker by nature, but I am proud to stand here with 15,000 Derry people who have broken the law. . . . I invite Mr. Craig to arrest the lot of us."[62]

This was new, and at the same time, it was anything but. Seventy-five years earlier, in 1896, Derry Catholics and nationalists had claimed their

electoral rights, for the first time voting in a slate of Nationalist councillors to the City Corporation. In celebration of their inauguration, an article ran in the *Derry Journal* declaring, "(we) are inside the Walls, on the
Walls, and without the Walls, going and coming as . . . duties, business,
pleasure calls, no man daring to make (us) afraid."[63] Both Hume and the
Derry Journal echoed the language of official bans that prohibited Catholics from processing "within or upon the walls."[64] In both eras, the symbol
of the walls as a space that excluded Catholics both by law and by their
association with the long-ago Siege resonated with Catholics. Memory
of the penal laws, forbidding them from the walled city, remained reso-
nant despite the fact they had been defunct since the early nineteenth
century.

Historians have generally tended to track remembrance of major historic events over time. Year after year, they chart how memory is deployed
in response to changing exigencies. Examining expressions of memory in
their own right illuminates unexpected historical issues and patterns. By
contextualizing how expressions of memory fostered internal community
cohesion, protected and nourished an Irish cultural identity, and amplified political claims within the broader context of Derry life, this book
adds depth and complexity to the tropes of Catholic memory and sheds
light on issues that have been understudied. It also destabilizes histories
of Northern Ireland that begin with the border. Viewed through the lens
of Derry Catholics' memory work, no border ran through their past. They
never stopped identifying as Irish or aspiring to inclusion within Ireland.
At the same time, it reframes the events of the Troubles and suggests an
unsettling in the folds of memory that have shaped Derry's story since the
turbulent late 1960s and '70s.

This book examines an array of cultural productions and political
machinations that could be construed simply as "events," or unnote-
worthy aspects of Catholic Derry's quotidian community life, things such
as a féis, a concert, a religious procession, a political campaign, a riot, or
even a warning about a haunted fairy bush passed down from generation
to generation. Framing these as acts of remembrance instead of dividing
them into discrete categories—acts of resistance, demonstrations of religious faith, family and neighborhood rituals, for example, I argue here

that Derry's Catholic community forged threads of connection and continuity that animated an Irish cultural identity up until the beginnings of the Troubles. At that point, memory work changed radically. It became part of a complex process of bonding and fragmentation in a community increasingly dislocated geographically and divided by class, religious commitment, and positions on political violence.

Chapter 1 contextualizes and introduces turn-of-the-century Derry, outlining key social and political factors that influenced community life and shaped sectarian struggles during the turbulent period before Irish independence and the establishment of the Northern Irish state. For those unfamiliar with Irish history, it offers a short historical summary that will help readers understand the sources of some conflicts that have troubled Northern Ireland. Chapter 2 examines how Derry Catholics looked to the past in an effort to orient themselves politically to a tumultuous present and an uncertain future during the period that culminated with Irish independence, the formation of Northern Ireland, and the establishment of the border. Memory work enabled Catholics to hold their ground politically within Derry, gain political leverage through electoral adjustments, and develop a set of cultural traditions to rival and parallel the robust historical consciousness of the Protestants' Maiden City.

Chapter 3 finds Catholic Derry unsettled by the new border. When the Northern state was established in 1922, most Catholic nationalist residents of Derry continued to hold out hope that a boundary readjustment would locate the west bank of the Foyle in the newly formed Irish Free State. They endeavored and failed to have the boundary lines redrawn. Memory work helped to stabilize Catholic life during an era of political invisibility and economic impoverishment in the 1920s and '30s. During the anxious years of the Boundary Commission's deliberation, the quiet years of political abstention, the hungry years of financial deprivation, and the struggles accompanying World War II, memory work proved steadying. As politicians stepped to the sidelines of the public stage during the years of nationalist abstention, the *Derry Journal* and the Catholic Church played increasingly important roles, even as families retreated to their homes and streets as Irish and Catholic havens. The memory work of women and children, woven as it was into ritual, story, games, and songs, nestled Irish cultural identity into the fabric of family and community life, particularly important as male family members traveled more frequently to England and Scotland for work.

In Chapter 4, Derry Catholics emerged from World War II ready to protest Partition and challenge unfair political practices in the city. The years between World War II and the beginning of the civil rights movement accompanied the slow demise of "old Derry" as the city's physical landscape changed and the institutions and values that framed Catholic life lost some of their capacity for cultural cohesion. Political leaders in Northern Ireland were intent on creating a portrait of a unified and British province and clamped down on expressions of Irish identity, but Derry Catholics challenged the image of a unionist and Protestant North and fought for the right to fly the Irish Tricolour, taking inspiration by looking to the past. As the pre-Partition generation died, writers in the *Derry Journal* and elsewhere drew on history to educate those who had only ever known the border. This chapter reexamines and ultimately refutes the prevailing historical interpretation that nationalism in the North faded out during in this period.

Chapter 5 takes a close look at how local Catholic nationalist leaders understood, performed, and articulated memory during the period immediately leading up to the civil rights era and explores how their memory work operated in dialogue with Derry's rank-and-file Catholics. Although the creation of the social welfare state did ease some of the worst instances of poverty in the city, the postwar focus on building and infrastructure development impressed upon Derry Catholics the ways the city was consistently overlooked when the eastern regions of the province were targeted for growth. Protesting ongoing gerrymanders, poor housing conditions, and meager employment and educational opportunities, Derry Catholics' memories of past injustices fueled frustration and heightened resolve.

During this period, Catholics drew from a deep well of memory to nourish nationalist sensibilities. At the same time, people, places, rituals, and celebrations mattered to Derry residents and lent them a sense of community identity that maintained continuity with a long Irish past. In an effort to contextualize this period more deeply, chapter 5 explores the civil rights movement and the beginning of the Troubles in Derry through some of the memories that captivated people during those tumultuous years. I argue that the leaders of the civil rights movement in Derry may not have been motivated specifically by an historical consciousness of injustice, but ordinary Catholics framed their support for civil rights through a long historical lens.

Chapter 6 treats the explosion of citizens onto the streets in 1969 by examining how participants utilized the past to comment on the present and forge a different kind of future. Historical consciousness of past injustices motivated local Catholics to support and eventually to participate in the early civil rights movement. Housing became a rallying issue in Derry precisely because it was the concrete by-product of an entire set of social, political, and economic relations that had always been tacitly understood but not often articulated or externalized in Northern Irish life. A direct outcome of the long history of gerrymandering in the city, the acute shortage of safe and affordable housing became a potent symbol of the effects of unionist intransigence on the city's Catholic and nationalist population. The issue held both tangible and symbolic meaning and therefore attracted local residents' attention. Precisely because it attacked the housing problem and, as such, drew from a deep historical consciousness in Catholic Derry, the civil rights movement was broader, more diverse, and more deeply connected to local community networks than it has been given credit for.

As my conclusion illustrates, even when those involved in the tumult and violence of the late 1960s were not thinking about the past, they continued to draw from it. During the tumultuous days and weeks that followed the Battle of the Bogside, Catholics performed memory work through their approach to problems and solutions alike. Their struggle for a better future was built on deep foundations: the intimate geographies, extended families, long-held associations, customs, and values of Catholic Derry. As the heady days of the civil rights movement evolved into heated altercations with members of the police force and ultimately the British army, Derry Catholics still formed a coherent community with a long "history of holding together."[65] Civil disturbances in the early years of the Troubles saw many Catholics, instead of working against history, drawing on their shared history in order to mobilize for social and political change.

Chapter One

_____

SITUATING THE PAST
IN DERRY

A busy port city marked by steep hills that spilled down onto the banks of the Foyle River, Derry was a center for trade and industry in the northwest of Ireland when our story begins in the last years of the nineteenth century. With a large and growing Catholic Irish population that threatened the city's political unionism and upset the Protestant culture of the city, continuity and change wrestled at the turn of the twentieth century just as it had for the previous three hundred years. The Londonderry Improvement Bill of 1896 incorporated Londonderry as a city and established its first gerrymandered political boundaries. These two events would shape the city's political geography for decades to come, but they also reflected a much longer and deeper history.

Before delving into twentieth-century memory practices in Catholic Derry, I provide a brief overview of the city's history and a glimpse of the key social, spatial, and political factors that influenced Catholic community life and memory work. I highlights events that would come to affect Derry during the period between 1896 and 1969. This review is by no means exhaustive; in fact, it is anything but. However, for readers with little background knowledge of Ireland and Northern Ireland, I lay out how settler colonialism, the Great Hunger, industrialization, and episodic contests over the politics of urban space shaped Derry's sectarian geographies and cultural politics.

Derry. Londonderry. The city's double name hints that the place's history is anything but straightforward. In fact, it has had several names, each simultaneously a reflection and a harbinger of political and cultural change. Originally called *Doire*, Gaelic for "a stand of oak trees," its location was significant as a place of convergence of the territories of the Cenél nEgan and the Cenél Conaill. It was also referred to as Doire Calgalch, after the ancient warrior and Caledonian leader who claimed much of northwest Ulster and northern Scotland as his territory.[1] Originally an island in the midst of the Foyle River, it was, according to John Toland, an educational center of Druidism. In the sixth century, the island of Derry became the site of an early Christian monastery associated with Colmcille, or St. Columba; its name was changed to Derre (Doire) Colmcille to honor its patron saint, whose writings suggested a deep and abiding love for the place. Derry remained an important monastic site until the middle of the thirteenth century and was briefly the diocesan seat. By this time, it was an active community, home to a major church, the Tempul Mor, built in 1164, and an Augustinian monastery. In addition, the O'Doherty clan built a tower house here for their overlords.

Towards the end of the sixteenth century and in the midst of a long strategic and military conflict with Hugh O'Neill, Second Earl of Tyrone and reigning leader of Ulster, Derry caught the attention of Elizabethan forces—it appeared to be strategically positioned for undercutting the Gaelic stronghold in Ulster. A short-lived garrison was established in Derry in 1566 but dismantled after an accident when the troops' own explosives the following year burned much of the settlement to the ground. Its first charter, granted in 1604 by James I, created the city of "Derrie." The charter's language offered clues to an emerging vision of the Ulster plantation and the broader colonial project in Ireland. Its newly appointed governor, Sir Henry Dowcra, was charged to "repossess, repair, and re-people" the city in order to "plant a colony of (the) civil and obedient."[2] Dowcra departed in 1608, after only four years, dismayed by a lack of support for the new settlement by the Irish administration generally and by Charles Blount, Lord Mountjoy, specifically.

After defeat in the Nine Years' War, the Flight of the Earls in 1607 saw the departure of Hugh O'Neill and many Gaelic chiefs of Ulster. Plantation efforts began in earnest.[3] Even after the O'Doherty clan attacked the settlement at Derry and destroyed many of its buildings in 1608, it was earmarked as a critical site for the Plantation initiative. However, the earthen ramparts and timber of the early fortifications at Derry were deemed too weak to withstand innovations in artillery fire. The ruins of the Tempul Mor and abbey buildings were dismantled, and, according to folklore as recounted by Daly and Devlin, their stones were used "to build the walls and ramparts of the City."[4] The durable walls spoke to the intended permanence of the Plantation.

Londonderry's founders envisioned the city as a tabula rasa. Virtually all of the settlement's standing structures were demolished to make room for a fully planned city, the first product of urban planning design in Ireland.[5] In 1613, King James I suggested or demanded that London's trade companies and guilds invest in the Plantation enterprise. The City of London's Court of Common Council formed a joint-stock company to finance fifty-five livery companies' colonial enterprise in Ulster, "The Society of the Governors and Assistants of London of the New Plantation of Ulster within the Realm of Ireland." The company became known as "The Honourable The Irish Society."[6] In the process of creating the Irish Society, the Court of Common Council also changed the city's name from Derry to Londonderry to indicate ties to its new sponsor.[7]

The broad outlines of the struggle that would episodically consume inhabitants of the north of Ireland were drawn in the century that followed the settlement of the Ulster Plantation, the consequent establishment of Londonderry, and sporadic violence that resulted in sieges of the walled city in 1641, 1649, and, most famously, the Siege of Derry in 1688–89. In a region that had until that time been largely independent from English oversight, Crown administrators redistributed land as the native Irish aristocracy was persuaded to sell or eventually forced to turn over their property to English and Scots settlers.

The task for the new arrivals, from the Crown's perspective, was to protect the region from foreign invasion and native Irish insurgence while at the same time rendering it geopolitically legible and economically productive. Not just the first walled city of Ireland, Derry became synonymous with the Protestant struggle for religious and political self-determination. This was brought home in 1789, when the Londonderry Corporation celebrated the centenary of the Relief of Derry that ended the Siege by building new ceremonial entries to the walls of the city; their architecture was designed to incorporate the stories of the Siege of Derry and the Battle of the Boyne into the urban fabric. A century later, in 1884, the *Belfast News Letter* would note the entangled associations between Protestantism, unionism, and the walls themselves: "The Walls of Derry are to the Protestants of Northern Ireland what the trophy of Marathon was to the Athenians."[8]

Newcomers to Ulster in the seventeenth century generally found their Irish neighbors unsavory. They viewed Donegal natives, many of whom would eventually migrate to Derry City, as "'a rude people,' 'a most bigoted and superstitious race,' 'a lawless and turbulent body,' 'ill-disposed,' 'uncivilized,' 'outrageous,' even 'evil.'"[9] For their part, many who called Donegal home until settling in Derry City in the nineteenth century found that the political history of colonization also possessed a geography. Rich and fertile lands were procured by colonists. Hugh Dorian, who wrote a ground-level report of life in rural Donegal during and after the Famine, observed that "the horrors of the past [were] inscribed on the landscape made up of 'rich lands of the plantation' while 'the mountain, the bog and the seashore' were inhabited by 'the Celt.'"[10]

Most Irish stayed on in Ulster as this new society took root and strived to adjust to a vastly changed physical, political, and social landscape. Upheavals were myriad. If the average inhabitant of Irish Catholic ancestry did not experience a fundamental shift in material fortunes, the loss of their social leaders (a landowning class that might have served as equal arbiters in ongoing social relations with the settlers) jolted cultural, social, and economic life.[11] As Edward Daly and Kieran Devlin put it, if the native Irish Catholics were not threatened with physical violence or intimidation, "their cross was the injustice they had to accept from day to day."[12]

By the eighteenth century, the region's populations aligned themselves into several distinct groups, differing in political allegiance, religious practice, cultural values, and interpretations of the past. Native Irish, predominantly Catholic, believed that they had been victims of theft when their land was expropriated. Conscious of this and apprehensive about it—albeit incredulous that such an unsystematic, illegible, and unrooted utilization of land and livestock could have ever amounted

to proper use of Irish land—Protestants gradually forged a loosely coherent political and cultural identity out of myriad denominational, cultural, historical, and regional differences over the course of the nineteenth
century.

The major events that came before and after the settlement of the
Ulster Plantation were thus framed within two very different paradigms,
simultaneously reflecting and shaping disparate cultural and, eventually,
national identities. The influx of residents from Scotland and England
who had arrived in the seventeenth century and the hold of The Honourable The Irish Society over the bulk of city assets until the mid-1800s
shaped Derry's streetscapes, economic and political makeup, and culture.[13]

After 1690, laws were enacted as a "reasonable precaution taken by
the State against a selection of citizens who surrendered themselves to the
guidance of foreigners and played the part of enemies to the Constitution."[14] Designed in accordance with Anglican doctrine, penal laws were
designed to make the Church of Ireland the official religion of Ireland
(the counterpart of the Church of England) and curtailed Catholic and
also dissenting Presbyterian religious expression.[15] As a result, Catholics
worshipped privately or outdoors at Mass rocks and under the protection
of trees until the latter half of the eighteenth century, when restrictions
that had outlawed public worship loosened, enabling them to become
more visible as a community.[16] Writing in 1731, the Anglican bishop of
Derry identified this as a problem: "We are infested with strolling friars
and regulars who say Mass from parish to parish as they pass in the open
fields of mountains and gather great numbers of people about them."[17]

In 1783, the Londonderry Corporation donated £50 towards the
construction of a Catholic chapel, St. Columba's Church, referred to locally as the "Long Tower" in reference to an Irish round tower on the
grounds of the church; local lore had it that this was the site of the me-
dieval Tempul Mor, or "Great Church," of the city. The Long Tower became the site and keeper of Catholic Derry's traditions. One of its original
chalices is believed to have been made at the request of Father Matthew
McKenna in 1749 and the other was a gift from "the pious ladies of Tem-
plemore," circa 1845.[18] Local parish priest John Lynch printed a public
notice of gratitude in the *Londonderry Journal*, noting that the Common
Council had generously taken into consideration "the hardships their

Roman Catholic neighbors have labored under by being exposed to the inclemency of the weather during public worship."[19] Sanguine relations between Catholics, Protestants, and Dissenters appeared to be the norm at this time. The 1798 Irish Rebellion, organized by the United Irishmen, did not see much action in Derry, though mid-Ulster towns such as Maghera, Magherafelt, and Coleraine had intense guerilla activity; County Tyrone and other areas of south Ulster had active Defender movements born out of a radical agrarian secret society that allied with the United Irishmen in the early 1790s.[20] In fact, Derry was believed to be the only city or town in Ulster without guerilla activity.[21] Peace did not mean mutual understanding or parity, however. In 1792, an author calling himself "A Citizen of Londonderry" drew from devotional texts to explain why Catholics, vested as they were in rule from Rome, "were not sufficiently *enlightened* to be emancipated" politically.[22]

Skepticism about Catholics ran deep in Derry. When the Catholic clergy, through a Protestant proxy buyer, secured a building inside the city walls on Pump Street in 1841, there was outrage among local Protestants that they were "about to plant a seminary for the inculcation of Popish errors and to erect a temple for the worship of their wheaten idol in a spot which was once the stronghold of Protestantism."[23] The *Derry Standard* called this announcement of the "surrender" of the Kings Arms Hotel property "the most disagreeable announcement it ever had to make," even then drawing on imagery of the Siege.[24] The Sisters of Mercy took over the premises on Pump Street in 1848 and established the first convent there since at least the fifteenth century.[25]

The Famine (1845–52) years in Derry were marked by movement. The port city was an important point of departure for many traveling to Great Britain, the United States, and Canada. The prospect of finding work building new rail lines also drew people to the city, as did hope for relief and survival at the city's workhouse. Fever killed many more in the city than starvation, most likely because Derry had a richly diverse agricultural economy; chief agricultural exports from the city included beef, pork, eggs, oatmeal, and butter.[26]

In the nineteenth century, Catholics appeared rarely in public life. Their status precluded them from engaging in politics locally or at Westminster. The £10 franchise was introduced in 1884, making voting a possibility for most men; by 1885, the Irish electorate had grown from 226,000 to 738,000.[27] There were no standing Catholic representatives in city government until the elections of 1896.[28]

The geography of the city's political wards was first established in 1840, and generally strict voting requirements across Ireland blocked most Catholics from the electoral process at the local level. That year, Parliament passed the Municipal Corporations Act in order to reform the municipal borough system in Ireland and to upgrade royal charters such as Derry's. With its population at 16,000, Derry was broken into three electoral wards. Ward boundaries, coupled with property restrictions on voting, yielded a local government with no Catholic representatives. In 1876, the Derry Catholic Registration Association had 713 Catholic voters listed as registered in the city.[29] Those who could vote backed liberal Protestants standing for election because they could generally be counted on to support the repeal of the Act of Union (1801) and were in the main responsive to their Catholic constituents.

The success of grassroots politics across Ireland affected Derry. In 1832, laws prohibiting public political demonstrations of all kinds in Ireland were passed in response to the success of Daniel O'Connell's monster meetings, at which tens of thousands of Irish Catholics appeared to hear O'Connell speak and to show support for the Catholic Association and for repeal of the Act of Union. Though the letter of law applied to all groups, in Derry, the legislation tended to be enforced specifically in relation to Catholic events. Customary commemorations of the 1689 Siege of Derry and Lundy Day, when an effigy of Robert Lundy is burned, carried on as usual.[30] Lundy was the governor of Derry who opened the city gates to King James's forces in 1688, achieving infamy as a traitor to the Protestant cause.

Catholics responded by turning inward and strengthening their own community. Building churches throughout the city was a priority; houses of worship simultaneously accommodated and broadcast Catholic Derry's burgeoning growth and steady advance.[31] Contending simultaneously with migration into the city and mass emigration from its port in the years following the Famine, Catholic organizations under the leadership of Bishop Francis Kelly—including the Sisters of Mercy, the Christian Brothers, and the Society of St. Vincent de Paul—provided needed social services and mutual support, offered charity, and increased educational and social opportunities for Derry's Catholic residents.[32] In 1879, St. Columb's College opened to prepare boys from the diocese for the priesthood. According to stipulations laid out at the Council of Trent in the sixteenth century, every Irish diocese was supposed to have such a school; in Derry this had been postponed "for effectively three centuries."[33]

THE BURGEONING CATHOLIC COMMUNITY OF DERRY

Like its cathedral, St. Eugene's, Derry's Catholic community had come into its own bit by painstaking bit over the course of the nineteenth century. In 1838, the original building committee convened to plan for St. Eugene's construction in anticipation of Derry's growing Catholic population. However, the church's foundation was not laid until 1851, after the worst of the famine years had passed. Then, over twenty years the cathedral was built incrementally as "stone was laid upon stone until the building rose with the growth of the Catholic people."[34]

Opened in 1873, St. Eugene's stood as a symbol of sturdy optimism that had been built on hard work and sacrifice by a community described at the time as "the reverse of opulent."[35] As *Derry Journal* editor William Roddy declared later, "Do not let us forget that this is a Cathedral built out of the pennies of the poor, the sixpences of those not quite so poor and the shillings of those who were better-to-do."[36] The church, like the community it would serve, remained a work in progress. Plans for intricate stained-glass panels, bells, and an imposing spire that might raise St. Eugene's high as a sign of Catholic strength in Derry had to be deferred an additional twenty-five years until members of the community could raise sufficient funds. When the bells finally arrived in 1902, they were tested for quality and sound; Derry echoed with Irish favorites, including "The Minstrel Boy," "The Wearing of the Green," and the popular elegy to the United Irishmen's Uprising, "Who Fears to Speak of '98?"[37] After that, the bells rang out twice daily, reminding Catholics to recite the Angelus.[38] For many Derry Catholics, the cathedral bells were a welcome addition to the city's soundscape; at the turn of the century, bells pealed from the Church of Ireland's St. Columb's Cathedral twice each day in memory of the century after Plantation, when Catholics were only allowed inside the area within the walls between 7:00 a.m. and 9:00 p.m.

The city's Protestant community had mixed reactions to St. Eugene's, as they did to Catholic Derry as a whole, which by this time was more than half of the city's population. City guides often pointed it out to visitors, calling attention to the empty space in the skyline where the spire was supposed to grace the building, citing it as an example of Catholic laziness and inability to get the job done.[39] Yet, they also viewed the church design as boastful and triumphalist, a grand architectural statement at discomfiting odds with their sense of Catholics' status in the city. It was, after all, taller than their own venerable cathedral, built in 1633.[40] By the turn of the twentieth century, with Derry's Catholic cathedral standing tall and proud, it was obvious that more than the city's landscape had changed. Once marginal and beleaguered residents of a Protestant bastion, Derry's Catholic community had become visible and vocal.

The beginning of the twentieth century found Derry a growing city, bustling with industry and expanding at its edges to accommodate a growing population. The economic center for surrounding counties in the northwest, including Londonderry, Donegal, and Tyrone, the city was an anomaly in an Ireland marked by poverty and emigration; only Derry and Belfast grew persistently over the course of the nineteenth century as their commercial and industrial sectors blossomed. By 1906 it was the crossroads for four railway lines, each with a central terminal in the city. The twelfth largest town in Ireland in 1800, by 1911 Derry had tripled in size to become fourth largest.[41] The city would see its financial fortunes falter, rise, and then falter again during the years between 1895 and 1922. Even though its economic difficulties were temporarily remedied during World War I, the inability of its most significant industries—shirt- and collar-making and shipping—to compete effectively within their respective markets saw general decline in Derry's financial fortunes after their peak in the 1870s.[42]

At the turn of the century, travelers noted neat and tidy, if weather-worn, streetscapes and a port humming industriously at the base of a steeply sloping city. They came away from Derry with the impression of clean streets, imposing buildings, a sense of a city generally satisfied with itself.[43] Local writer Alice Milligan expressed the signature quality of the city's beauty in 1897: "Derry City appeared like an enchanted island, a pyramid of twinkling lights under a frosty sky, with the wide Foyle flowing around it."[44]

Indeed, it was a peaceful city in many ways. When, in 1874, police constable Francis Murphy was shot in the back by a subofficer, a reporter noted that the crime stirred Derry up considerably, in part because the city hadn't seen a murder in the past fifty years.[45] At first glance, it appeared to have changed little since Thackeray noted in 1842 that Derry "is not splendid, but comfortable; a brisk movement in the streets; good downright shops . . . an honest air of prosperity."[46]

The city appeared to be tranquil, even staid, on the surface, but the fact was that Derry had undergone significant transformations in the second half of the nineteenth century. In particular, it had become a majority Catholic city, a process that was clear by 1850. It had become home to increasing numbers of Irish Catholics from the early 1800s on, and its Catholic population mushroomed during and after the Famine. Fleeing the poverty of hardscrabble rural Inishowen in County Donegal and the city's eastern and southern hinterlands after the collapse of the linen industry, the new residents joined the city's growing working classes, finding employment at the port, in construction, and in the nascent textile industry. In 1901, approximately 22,000 Catholics lived alongside 18,000 Protestants of Anglican (Church of Ireland), Presbyterian, and Methodist denominations. In contrast, in the same year, Belfast's population was less than one-quarter Catholic.[47] This was due in large part to geography; Derry was a border city and rubbed shoulders with County Donegal, one of the hardest-hit areas of the north of Ireland during the Famine.

A largely working-class city by the early 1900s, three-quarters of its employed residents engaged in skilled, semiskilled, or unskilled wage labor.[48] Class distinctions that emerged in the nineteenth century had hardened by the dawn of the twentieth. Derry was already a segregated city by 1900 by both class and religion. If the outlines of residential segregation had been enforced by law in the eighteenth century with Catholics prohibited from dwelling within the city's walls, in the nineteenth century these patterns were largely enforced by custom.[49] By 1834, segregation patterns based on religious affiliation had already emerged beyond the walls.[50] Between 1870 and 1911, city streets that had once been home to those of all class backgrounds became fully working-class streets; those who could afford to, overwhelmingly Protestants, moved out of the urban core to the newly built suburbs.[51] As members of the working classes moved to the dwellings vacated by the middle class, they did so according to strictly observed religious patterns. Segregated neighborhoods took shape all over the city and working-class districts took on an increasingly sectarian cast.[52]

Faced with low pay and underemployment, Catholics were nearly three times more likely than Protestants to live in the city's least desirable dwellings, many of these situated close to the Foyle River in wet, poorly drained areas that sat at or below sea level and flooded when the river rose.[53] Since the eighteenth century, the area was known as Bogside for obvious reasons and was also referred to as "the Romish district" in the nineteenth century.[54] (In the twentieth century, "Bogside" referred to one street, but by 1969, it again came to represent the nationalist area.) The land itself was owned by The Honourable The Irish Society, which leased it to builders, who in turn rented to tenants. The streets they lived on commemorated heroes of the British Empire with names like Nelson and Wellington, but living conditions were hardly stately. One writer referred to the homes of the Bogside as "the dwellings of the disinherited."[55] The Derry Town Tenants' Association formed in 1902 to protest "rack rents," to lobby for landlords to repair dilapidated houses, and to push for a "rent-to-own" scheme wherein workers could pay rent and build equity at the same time.[56] Dr. Bigger, the medical inspector of the Local Government Board, described typical working-class housing in a 1901 report:

> Mostly of one story, they are built with stone or brick, nearly all are self-contained, only a few being tenement houses. In the older parts of town, the homes are old, dilapidated, damp, deficient in light and ventilation, some situated in narrow lanes and back passages; many are overcrowded and kept in a dirty state. The yards in many instances are unpaved or only partly paved, and defectively designed; some have no back yards and no back doors or back windows, others have a common yard and a common privy, which serves for several houses.[57]

In *Gailey's Guide to Derry and Its Suburbs*, William Gailey remarked on the difference between the Catholic working-class area and the better-off Protestant district inside the walls of the city: "A greater contrast there could scarcely be than that afforded by the trim neatness of the part within the walls and the squalid untidiness without. . . . The quarter lying without (the walls) . . . is commonly called by the natives 'the Bog-side'; it is where the Roman Catholic population is most thickly massed together."[58]

Gailey continued by describing a convergence of streets where an abbey had once stood: "No trace of it now remains and the neighborhood has anything but a celibate look from the swarms of children."[59] Arthur Bennett was even more critical of Catholic living conditions, of the wanton lifestyle he believed they suggested, and of nationalist politics more generally. In his memoir of travels through Ireland in 1892, he described a visit to Derry's largest Catholic neighborhood:

> Descending into the hollow which lies on this side of the city . . . we passed through the poorest part of it, the streets crooked and disorderly, and the houses of the lowest class. It was, we found, the Nationalist quarter; and its slovenliness and poverty confirmed the opinion which . . . we had been induced to form, that in Derry, the men who were against an Irish Parliament were those who had a stake in the country, and the men who were *for* it were those who had practically none.[60]

Bennett saw Irish nationalism, Catholic religious faith, and poverty as amicable if not intertwined categories. Certainly, without political power, it was challenging to bring city resources to bear on cleaning refuse and beautifying the Catholic neighborhood. "Old tin pans, broken bottles, discarded crockery ware, the refuse of byres and stables" littered the area. Its uncomely appearance certainly reflected the habits of its inhabitants, but the situation was complicated by its separateness from more affluent areas.[61] Further, without political representatives to advocate for the district, resources for beautifying the Bogside went elsewhere, such as to the affluent Crawford Square area.[62]

Religion mattered deeply to Derry Catholics. Arthur Bennett described a visit to St. Eugene's Cathedral in 1890 and commented on his perceptions of Derry Catholics as unselfconscious in their faith:

> Large as it was, [the cathedral] was crowded in every part; I was much impressed, not only by the size of the congregation but by their devout behavior. Unmistakably, to them, religion was something more than a matter of custom, and church-going something far higher than a conventional habit which it would have been bad form to neglect. Everybody seemed to feel the presence of a sacred influence . . . and to realize that this was "none other than the house of God" and the "very gate of heaven."[63]

If religion was the bedrock of Catholic life, it was also the stage. By the turn of the twentieth century, myriad groups had formed out of these institutions and out of church sodalities and other parish-centered organizations. In 1886, the local Catholic temperance society, founded by Long Tower priest Father Elliott, built a multipurpose hall hugging the city's walls on Orchard Street, just outside the East Wall. It was named St. Columb's Hall. Planned, built, and paid for with local resources, it cost £20,000 and was completed two years later and celebrated as a hall "the Catholics of Derry . . . could call their own."[64] In 1896, William McCormick celebrated the contributions of Derry's working classes to St. Columb's: "Anyone need only look at the hall to see what working men were able to accomplish with their pennies."[65]

Temperance and the sense of shared virtue and community it fostered played an important role in the cohesion of the Catholic community in Derry, as elsewhere in Ireland and its diaspora. At the turn of the century, the local temperance society boasted 4,000 members and was reputed to be "the largest abstinence society in Ireland."[66] At the twenty-fifth anniversary celebration of the founding of the St. Columb's Total Abstinence Society, in November 1898, Father McMenamin exhorted the praises of the group's purpose and work, saying, "The historian who would write the history of this period and who would not reckon the promotion of temperance and the observance by many of its principles as among the disposing causes of the social amelioration of the people and onward march of the city could not be justly regarded as an accurate and unbiased historian." He went on to say that while it would be presumptuous for the temperance movement to "lay claim to more than its share of the credit for the better state of things now existing in Derry but it might, without fear of contradiction or cavil, claim to have had a steadying influence at least on the progressive movement."[67]

The hall was much more than a gathering place for those who abstained from the drink; it served as a community hub for the Catholic population. St. Columb's Hall was the first public space dedicated for Catholic use; prior to its erection, their only gathering space was a rented room in a grain store.[68] With statues of Éire, Temperance, and Industry looking on from its rooftop, St. Columb's Hall hosted lectures, concerts, dances, theatrical performances, sport clubs, charity club meetings, meetings of the Catholic Literary Association, Gaelic-language classes, band practice, and political meetings virtually every night of the week. One could take a shorthand class on a Monday, listen to a concert on a Tuesday, attend sodality meetings on Wednesday nights, watch lamplight lectures on a Thursday, and enjoy variety shows at the weekend in an auditorium that sat 3,000. Bands practiced in the hall in preparation for a major event of the year—every Catholic band in the city participated in the annual excursion of the St. Columb's Total Abstinence Society and some even borrowed fifes and drums from their Protestant neighbors to make a showing.[69]

At the same time, the Catholic Working Man's Institute, building societies, social insurance societies, and other nonreligious groups sprouted up along William Street, the east–west corridor that ran through the Catholic South Ward and was its main thoroughfare. Groups were fluid, forming and disbanding around particular causes; for example, the Brother Shears' '98 Club, the Henry Joy McCracken Club, and the Wolfe Tone Club all met in the Shamrock Hall or 44 Bridge Street to plan for 1798 centenary celebrations, and St. Patrick's Day Demonstration committees came together to plan for the annual commemorations. The Robert Emmet branch of the United Irish League had its headquarters in Bogside Street, where the group also held dances and concerts. The John Mitchel Club of the United Irish League had a hall at Waterloo Place, and in 1883, the League opened a new hall with a reading room and library in William Street above the Working Man's Institute. The Gaelic League met in Magazine Street and put on plays and operas—but they rented the Opera House and St. Columb's Hall to accommodate large crowds. Derry's Irish bands practiced in some of these halls for the processions on St. Patrick's Day; one could hear the St. Columb's Coal Porters' Flute Band, the Brian Boru Band, the Sarsfields Flute Band, or the Young Bloods play Irish national songs.[70]

By the early 1870s, Catholics, inspired by both the Home Rule and Land League movements and increasingly outwardly focused because of community activities and groups, became increasingly determined to assert their stake in urban life. They vigorously claimed their right to congregate publicly within the walled city. Although party processions were made tacitly legal in 1872, the right to assemble was often challenged. In 1877, a bomb was discovered along the parade route for a St. Patrick's Day march; the *Belfast News Letter* reported that "a jar of powder, with a fuse attached was discovered on the Walls, which it is believed was intended to have exploded among the processionists."[71] Protestants and Catholics confronted one another regularly during marches—Catholics marched on St. Patrick's Day and on the Feast of the Assumption, or Our Lady's Day, in August, while Protestants commemorated the Shutting of the Gates in December, King William's victory at the Battle of the Boyne, and the Relief of Derry that ended the protracted siege of 1689–90.[72]

For all this, though, the turn of the twentieth century found Derry relatively tranquil. In fact, like much of the United Kingdom and the United States, the city was experiencing a brief period of peaceful and mostly cooperative relations after a tumultuous period that had lasted from the mid-1860s until the mid-1880s. Catholics abandoned their marches most years during this time until 1896. The *Freeman's Journal,* the oldest newspaper in Ireland, remarked that "a more peaceable population than the Catholics of Derry is not to be found in Ireland."[73] Madam de Bovet, who traveled around Ireland for three months in 1891, found that she had anticipated scenes reminiscent of St. Bartholomew's Day, because "in this troubled land, you must be ready for everything," but the reality of urban life in Derry was much more prosaic. Tumult and noise in the streets excited her, and yet it turned out to be nothing more than "a big flock of geese being taken through the town to the port," or the collision of frightened pigs, cattle, or sheep headed for one of the city's markets.[74]

Derry's history of sectarian turmoil lay, for the most part, just below the surface of urban social life. By the dawn of the twentieth century, the city was defined by its divisions—the banks of the Foyle River, the communities inside and outside the city walls, the socioeconomic classes, the city and its surrounding liberties, the houses of worship. The late nineteenth century was relatively free from public disorder and violence, but there was always the sense, as de Bovet noted, that it might erupt at any moment. Residents, if not tourists and travel writers, were well aware of the tensions that had led a special commission, charged with examining the riots that rocked the city in 1883, to conclude of Derry: "There is no locality in Ireland, where from the existence of special and exciting causes, the public peace is so liable to be interrupted by party displays, or appeals to popular passions, nor where the cause of public order and social good feeling lie so much at the mercy of persons who thoughtlessly or wantonly incur responsibility of disturbing it."[75]

Derry's conflicts shaped the urban landscape and the way people thought about it, utilized it, and invoked it. The past and the way that it was remembered and portrayed became an increasingly divisive feature of Derry's cultural topography. In addition, struggles over the use of the city's streets, squares, and public buildings to commemorate each community's interpretation of their past were an important facet of conflicts between Protestants and Catholics. The cityscape became a crucible for larger battles over identity, belonging, and political power.

Despite its Catholic-majority population, at the turn of the twentieth century Derry was viewed as a Protestant city, and a British one at that. Its image as a Protestant fortress and bastion was nourished by stories of the rebellions of 1641 and 1649 and the famous siege of 1689–90. The city's walls and their emblematic associations were its principal claim to historical renown, and regular commemorations reinforced this. Irish, English, and European travelers noted the descendants of seventeenth-century English and Scots settlers as Derry's celebrated citizens and uniformly told the city's history from their perspective—a story whose beginning could be traced to the Plantation project at the start of the seventeenth century.

Heroism for standing up for Britain and for the Protestant faith were central themes in retellings of the story of Derry's fame, and the Siege had already become the central fixture of the city's history. In a tone representative of travel guides of the time, travel writer Edgar Shrubsole noted in 1908:

> Who that has read description[s] of the siege of Derry, and learned how a mere handful of starved and dying heroes fearlessly held this beloved city against a whole army throughout 105 days of ghastly suffering, can view the walls behind which those men of mettle stood under the red flag of "No Surrender!" without heartfelt sympathy with the patriotic pride of their descendants? And who can wonder that those descendants so jealously preserve the walls held so long against such terrible odds . . . in their proud remembrance of those stirring days, practically proven in the only way possible—the careful preservation of all that "keeps that memory green"—the Derryites have the hand and heart of every true Britisher.[76]

The city's political leaders maneuvered to project this version of Derry history and believed commemoration to be a critical component of the city's identity. Waddington's 1908 guide extolled the city's infamous battles in the name of Protestantism and the Crown, but was most enthusiastic about the well-tended memorials to the Siege to be found in the city: "The place teems with relics of the past . . . and even if her history hadn't been written by a Macaulay or a Witherow, [they] would still keep alive the glorious memories of nigh three centuries ago . . . first and foremost, the old grey walls themselves."[77]

From the cruciform street layout to the walls that surrounded the urban core, Derry's physical design itself was a historic artifact. Along with Coleraine in the northern corner of what became County Londonderry, it was erected as a Plantation settlement; protection of all that lay within the walls was central to its site, design, and construction. Derry was something of a relic even as it was being built, the last walled city constructed in Europe. The most extensive early seventeenth-century fortifications in the British Isles, Derry's walls—with their battlements, parapets, canons, and gates—communicated the fortress quality of the original Plantation settlement.[78] In fact, as late as the 1790s, the local government remained concerned about maintaining the walls for the purposes of defense.[79]

When Sir Alfred Newton, governor of The Irish Society, was honored by being named a freeman of the city in 1909, he spoke of Derry's loyalty as its most enduring legacy, and its Protestantism as its central defining heritage:

> The term "freedom" is inseparable from Derry. Your forefathers wrested their freedom for great odds. . . . The very mention of Derry evokes in every heart a feeling of gratification—nay—reverence. . . . In connection with the glorious and memorable Siege of 1689 there was evoked the most sublime examples of patriotism which this or any other country ever witnessed. . . . It requires no great imagination to portray to oneself the feelings of joy, thankfulness and aye, triumph, with which these poor emaciated people witnessed the arrival of those two ships. The cheers that arose from those emaciated throats still echo from the walls of Derry, and long may that monument endure to the everlasting credit and renown of this city so sweet.[80]

Debates raged during the 1880s about when and why the Catholics of Derry ceased to be quiescent about Orange Order and Apprentice Boys commemorations and the larger narrative of the Maiden City as Protestant sacred space. Protestants pointed to stories that suggested that the Catholic bishops once processed in Siege parades.[81] The "double aspect" of commemorations, though, was difficult to contest: "One being the memorial of a great achievement, the other a revival 'under the guise of reverence for bygone deeds of heroism' of the memory of a great political struggle between parties whose feuds are unfortunately not yet extinct."[82]

The fact remained that the city was changing. Catholic Derry had begun to emerge as a politically, culturally, and socially coherent community by the century's turn. In 1896, Derry got a political makeover that acknowledged changed demographic realities. Until this point, Catholics had rarely found opportunity to define themselves collectively on their own terms. For the first time in centuries, Catholics were elected to political office in the city; this itself was important. Widening the political playing field changed the political climate in the city.

Efforts by the city's Protestant public officials to maintain political dominance and to secure seats at Westminster despite their demographic minority brought Catholics and Irish nationalists increasingly into public opposition with their Protestant and unionist neighbors. Debates over Home Rule and Irish nationalism raised the stakes higher than they had ever been before. In response, Protestant leaders maneuvered to unite formerly fractious denominations and to reassert authority in the city that had served as a beacon for their religious faith and political identity for more than two hundred years.

The 1896 political changes were the first in nearly half a century and the direct result of eased voting restrictions in England and Ireland. The earliest and most direct effort to claim power in the city took place at the ballot box. Local Catholic and nationalist politicians dated their own struggle for political power and representation to the mid-1870s with the creation of the Derry Catholic Registration Association.[83] Protestants mocked Catholic advocacy as unnecessary in the city and blamed voting advocacy itself for exacerbating difference between Derry's communities. However, there was a deeply engrained fear of Irish nationalism. Protestants called any sign of nationalist strength "fictitious" and continued to claim that Catholics of Derry did not and could not represent the "intelligence, industry or respectability of the city."[84]

The *Londonderry Sentinel* reminded readers in 1878 that the Catholic Emancipation Act of 1829, which allowed Catholics in the United Kingdom to sit in the Parliament in Westminster, had occurred fifty years earlier, so there was no need for a religiously identified voting organization. The paper accused the Catholic Registration Association of "playing out its little game of sectarianism," implying that the confessional divide was purely a matter of religious practice and not related to any other fissures between Catholics and Protestants in the city.[85] Restrictions making property ownership a condition for voting were lifted under the Municipal Franchise Bill of 1895. The election brought many who had never previously voted to the polls.

Despite opposition, the Municipal Improvement Bill was passed with its redistricting adjustments in 1896, creating five wards and forty council seats, leaving Catholics with an average of fifteen seats, or just over one-third of local representation. Protestants controlled the Londonderry City Corporation and also held clear majorities in parliamentary ridings. The new political playing field, still not an even one, opened up space for different kinds of cultural and social contestations. As the twentieth century began, Derry's stage was set for unprecedented engagements. The period between 1896 and 1922 saw Derry's physical and political boundaries change as the city itself grew and its position within Ireland was transformed with Irish independence and the consequent formation of Northern Ireland, its border running just three miles from the city's center. These changes stretched the social, political, and cultural fabric of the city in ways previously unthinkable. During this period, Derry's Catholic population defined itself anew, taking on a coherent identity even as it came to terms with its weak political position in the face of local challenges and national upheaval.[86] Remembrance practices and memorial processes reflected and shaped the tumultuous processes at work, as Catholic Derry gained voice through opposition and leveraged its growing size and political presence to make claims to Irish identity and to connect with the national project at work throughout much of the country.

Chapter Two
_____

FROM UNDER THE HEEL
OF THE MINORITY

Challenging Protestant Memory and
Power in Pre-Border Derry, 1896–1922

Between 1896 and 1922, Derry's physical and political boundaries changed as the city grew and its geographic and political position transformed through enfranchisement, the gerrymander, and eventually the establishment of the border. Battles over Home Rule, Irish independence, and the civil war, plus the formation of Northern Ireland, stretched the social, political, and cultural fabric of the city in ways previously unthinkable. During this critical quarter century, Derry's Catholic population defined itself anew, taking on a coherent identity as it came to terms with its weak political position in the face of local challenges and national upheaval. In the meantime, Derry Protestants maneuvered to unite further formerly fractious denominations in the face of political change in Ireland and to assert authority in what some called the "historic chief city of the ascendancy in Ulster" for the previous two centuries.[1]

Derry's surging Catholic population coalesced and discovered its collective voice, developing parallel religious, political, and social institutions while challenging Protestant unionists' power in the city. In the streets and in the halls of municipal government, commemorations of historic events gave way to pitched battles, both literal and symbolic. At the same time,

45

Catholics and nationalists built a political infrastructure and enacted cultural rituals and celebrations as they carved Irish places for themselves physically and politically in their city, which remained in many ways a Protestant bastion. Seemingly small disagreements exploded in the tense climate. Historical memory and consciousness were deeply contested because the stakes were high, particularly in the context of unionist clamors against Home Rule—the movement calling for domestic self-government for Ireland—the fight for national independence, and calls for Partition.

In all of these things, Derry Catholics' memory work had three principal aims: to contend with the realities of Protestant and unionist domination within the city; to define and unite their community internally; and to support Home Rule and Irish independence. Memory work amplified and lent weight to Catholic claims of Irishness. Memory practices established continuity with a long Irish past of which Catholics could be proud, enabled them to invent a set of heroes and myths worthy to compete with Protestants', and fueled assertions of belonging within Catholic, Irish Ireland as opposed to Protestant, British Ulster. The increasingly robust Catholic community in Derry challenged both the traditional interpretation of their city's past and the implications of that interpretation. They pushed against the idea of a homogenous and loyal "Protestant Ulster" and refuted the notion that Derry was an emblem for Protestant religious liberty. In face of the insistence that "the whole city is a monument to the great deliverance" from religious and political intolerance (in the form of Protestantism and Plantation), Catholics challenged the notion that patriotism in Ireland was categorically associated with the same.[2]

As a result, memory wars often took the form of confrontations over the city's "traditional heritage," which tended to broadcast the idea that Derry was a Protestant bastion, claimed, maintained, and celebrated for its "loyalty and love of law and order."[3] Catholics challenged this public memory of the city through politics, journalistic moral persuasion, and through physical demonstrations and even full-blown riots. Indeed, they used the Siege myth against Protestants, protesting that Derry stood as "a monument in the North of Ireland . . . to intolerance, for they were still fighting for equal liberties."[4] Although they didn't succeed in overturning entrenched narratives of Siege City or the policies those stories bolstered and legitimized, these efforts cultivated a politics of dissent, encouraging

Catholics to establish their own history of Derry and to become active stewards of Derry's Irish heritage.[5]

Since readings of the past had so often been prescriptive, the past became an important tool for crafting a different future. Catholic religious and political leaders and the working-class rank and file used the past to assert a different vision for the future. For political and religious leaders, challenging the monolithic version of the city's history and establishing a formal, Irish, Catholic version of history became part of a larger mission to claim rhetorical, political, and physical space. They both protested the city's official history and opposed representations of it that appeared anti-Catholic or anti-Irish. Working-class citizens, Protestant and Catholic, mostly silent in the official archives, also engaged in the memory wars. Using bottles, stones, and songs, Catholics challenged sentiments aroused by Protestant commemorations, particularly when the observances themselves strayed from public or Protestant space and were performed in Catholic neighborhoods. Finally, in step with the larger Gaelic Revival movement throughout Ireland, Catholics in Derry busied themselves with establishing and reinvigorating specifically Irish and Catholic traditions that might define them as members of a unique cultural community in its own right, separate but not necessarily less than its Protestant and unionist counterpart.

The year 1896 was important for Derry. Thanks to the introduction of proportional representation for voting, it was the first year that Catholics were elected to municipal government. This was significant in itself, as the political climate in which they did so was fraught with tensions. In light of the Home Rule movement sweeping Ireland, the city's Protestant public officials sought to maintain political dominance in the city and to hold its seats in Westminster, despite their demographic minority. The idea that Derry might return Home Rule champions to Parliament was, in their eyes, a terrible prospect. This brought Catholics and Irish nationalists increasingly into public opposition with their Protestant and unionist neighbors.

Thanks to the Municipal Franchise Bill of 1895, value-based voting restrictions were reduced substantially.[6] Catholics hailed this as a victory, assuming that more lenient voting requirements would give them an electoral edge as the majority population.[7] They elected Vesey Knox, a

Parnellite and Liberal MP, in a hard-fought electoral battle that saw, according to the *Freeman's Journal*, "every voter literally with life in him" brought to the polls, including an elderly nationalist in a bed and a unionist on the run from the law who turned up "in a false beard and was carried in a chaise as an invalid."[8] Knox was a proponent of Home Rule, and his election was seen as a nationalist victory.

In 1896, Protestants proposed the Londonderry Improvement Bill. The first gerrymander, it reduced the number of electoral wards from six to five, corralled the majority of Catholic votes into one ward, and increased the number of representatives for each ward. The *Freeman's Journal* referred to this as "an insolent assault on the majority in Derry . . . that should appeal to the self-respect not only of Irish nationalists but of every friend of representative government everywhere."[9] Derry Liberal Unionist MP William Ross dismissed objections to the new plan. Derry's Catholic nationalists, he said, were largely poor and not formally educated and would railroad the political system despite the fact that Protestant unionists footed the bulk of tax bills: "The municipalities would be hobbled; every human being, male or female, would be crammed upon the list and the people who really paid the rates would have no voice whatever. To put every occupier on the list was to reduce the whole system in Ireland to a harlequinade."[10]

Knox railed against the gerrymander.[11] He questioned the legitimacy of the adjustment bill that, in a city of 33,000, took in over thirty square miles of additional area, extending "the municipal boundaries to larger than those of Berlin."[12] Knox insisted that history mattered, arguing that the introduction of the Municipal Improvement Bill followed several years of editorials in the *Londonderry Sentinel* that advocated for splitting wards to ensure Catholic majority representation in only one ward, "where there were about 750 Catholics to about 100 Protestants," thereby ensuring a distinct Protestant majority in all other districts.[13]

An unprecedented public meeting was held to protest the gerrymander at St. Columb's Hall in January 1896. Derry's bishop, the Reverend Dr. O'Doherty, broke with his traditional abstention from politics to address the gathered crowd on the link between votes and municipal jobs. He linked the challenges of the past to the prospect for the future for the city's Catholics: "We have laboured and suffered in the past from a most unjust exclusion from every position within this city." The new law would see Catholics "shut out for all time from our due representation."[14]

Solicitor James O'Doherty followed, detailing the history of voting registration in Derry. The Municipal Bill of 1840, he said, effectively excluded all Catholics, as voters had to own property valued at over £10. Historical consciousness fueled current frustrations, and here O'Doherty took a long view of the situation: "Here they were, 100 years since Toleration had been proclaimed, and fifty or sixty years since so-called Catholic Emancipation had been passed, and there they stood after that time in the city of Derry—outlanders in the city whose Prosperity they had the greatest interest and surely they had been patient under long suffering."[15]

Finally, Dr. O'Kane spoke, addressing directly the argument that unionists often made: they paid the lion's share of taxes and therefore should have the lion's share of votes. Dismissing claims that Protestants paid seven times as much in rates as Catholics, O'Kane did concur that many of the city's Catholics were mired in poverty. There were historic reasons for this, though, he explained. Catholics were poor because of the Penal Laws, because they had been "driven from their lands and possessions, because cruel laws prevented them from holding property and deprived them the means of education." Their presence and strength in Derry, their numbers among merchants and professionals in town, and battles like this one proved to him that Derry's Catholic residents were prepared to stand down the repression that had long dogged them.[16]

Despite Catholic protest and support from all over the island, the Londonderry Improvement Bill passed in 1896, creating five wards and forty council seats, leaving Catholics with an average of fifteen seats, or just over one-third of local representation. Protestants also held clear majorities in parliamentary ridings.[17] However, sixteen Catholics were elected to the city council.

In February 1897, they took their seats as Nationalist Council members for the first time in the City Corporation and created the first Nationalist Council caucus. It was a big day, as "a representation of sixteen was a big change from a representation of none at all," and the newly inaugurated councillors professed high hopes for influencing public life. The editors of the *Derry Journal* certainly viewed the inclusion of nationalists on the Corporation as ushering in a new era and were determined to be optimistic. Derry would come first, before partisanship, because it was everyone's city—"a city of which, differ as we may, we are all proud and for whose success we are all wishful."[18]

A sense of arrival after a long history of exclusion suffused observance of the councillors' inauguration. The *Derry Journal* reminded readers how far they had come, using the city walls themselves to discuss the momentousness of this shift:

> It is almost within living memory when no Catholic was supposed, as of right, to dwell within the Walls. Outside, in the bygone time, were the habitations of the old race—the Irishrie. The cathedral bell at six in the morning summoned the poor Papists to labor—they had the privilege of coming in to labor for their bread; nine o'clock heard it tolling again, warning them to quit the city when the day's toil was over. Well, what is the fact now? Here within the very same walls, the old race are back in numbers, in respect, in prosperity, and in power. . . . The cathedral bell indeed still rings every night at nine, but the papists don't now march to its tune. They are inside the Walls, on the Walls, and without the Walls, going and coming with their duties, business, pleasure calls them, "no man daring to make them afraid."[19]

In Derry, battles over the past sometimes emerged out of ostensibly trivial situations. When Catholic legislators took their seats on the city council, for example, they immediately proposed a passage of steps to be built to allow access over the city walls from the West Ward to the urban core at Society Street, between the Mall Wall and Nailor's Row. Stairs would be convenient for factory workers going to and from factories in the eastern and southern parts of the city. A subcommittee was formed to explore the matter. The city's surveyor estimated a flight of stone steps would be inexpensive—£10 15s. Protestant councilmen, however, railed at the idea on the grounds that it was "piercing the walls," amounting to vandalism, and would "disfigure the monument," disrespecting the walls and all they stood for.[20] Even when nationalists pointed out that public approaches had been built in recent years on the north and east sides of the walls, a strong sense prevailed that easy access for Bogsiders through the walls would be disruptive. Foot traffic from the Bogside would be inconvenient for worshippers at the Methodist and Anglican churches inside the walls.[21] Fear that stairs might "cover [the walls] with improper characters" coming out of one of the poorest parts of the city drove the "no" votes, leading Catholics to accuse Protestant legislators of "siege thinking." In the end the request split directly down sectarian lines and the stairs were not approved.

The *Derry Journal* underscored the sectarian nature of the vote. Pointing out the many places where the walls had undergone construction of this sort, it asked, "Why, then, is it to be stigmatized as vandalism, that which for generations has been in operation? . . . [If] it is not bigotry, the resemblance is striking."[22] A Bogside resident penned a screed about the decision to the tune of the Apprentice Boys' song "Derry's Walls":

The voters of the Western Ward—By civic freedom swore
That trotting round by Butcher's Gate—They would not suffer more.
By their civil rights they swore it and straightway made a call
and sent a strong petition forth (signed in East, West, South and
　　North)
for a straightway to the Wall.

"Twill prove a great convenience—to folks going up and down
from the west side of the city—to the centre of the town
for the weary and the feeble, for the factory workers gay
and give the hunted children safe retreat for play."

But in the bigot council—there was no heart so bold.
But sorely ached and fast it beat—when this design was told.
Forthwith up rose their latent ire—With bitterness of gall
And spurred, with Pump Street whipping in—to guard their
　　Derry Wall.

This was their resolution, calm and deliberate: "We want no steps, no progress, no reason, no debate. / We won't need the western ward for we have private note. / If we accede to this request—We lose the Orange vote."

. . . The bigot heart was sad—and the bigot lip was low
And darkly looked they at the wall—and at the streets below.
"Contempt may fall upon us —before the sun goes down
but if we once erect those steps—what hope to save the town?"

. . . Let the great man crush the poor man—And poor man hate the
  great.
And rights unfairly 'portioned—and Nationalists to be told
that they *alone* are bigoted—As in the days of old.[23]

The song tells the story of the aborted stairs in excruciating detail. Simultaneously, it echoes and mocks the historic memory of the Siege as it was performed by Derry's Apprentice Boys, a fraternal organization formed in 1814 to honor and remember the actions of the young apprentices who had the foresight to lock the gates of Derry's walls in 1689 as the Siege of Derry began. The ditty suggests that Derry Catholics were tired of being invisible in the city. As the nineteenth century closed, they began to seek out opportunities to assert their presence in Derry by inventing traditions, harnessing an Irish past, and claiming physical space.

THE CITY OF COLMCILLE: CELEBRATING DERRY'S SAINT

Increased political representation in municipal affairs and the development of Catholic civic and cultural institutions increased the community's visibility and helped it sharpen its collective voice. Cohesion, however, came largely through interest and participation in local heritage, religious festivals, cultural events, sporting competitions, educational opportunities, and clubs that emphasized local identity that hinged on the cultural memory of a distinctively Irish Derry, and of Ireland as a great and proud nation. Religious and political leaders fashioned the history, and local Catholics embraced it. Inventing traditions for Catholic Derry provided another way of "making a stand." By crafting an alternative history, which Henry Glassie has called "the resort of people who feel removed from power, the imagination's parallel to armed resistance," Derry's Catholics not only resisted the status quo, but they also used the past to take confident steps towards the future (Glassie, *Passing the Time*, 639).

The history of St. Columba's Day provides an illustrative example. Fr. Willie Doherty, prelate of the Long Tower, was a busy man. So busy, in fact, that on the evening of April 28, 1893, he confessed in his journal that his mind was in a "ferment over his duties."[24] The following day, after reporting that his mind was settling down, he listed all of his daily and weekly tasks that went above and beyond saying Mass, hearing confessions, and administering church business. He was advisor to the St. Vincent de Paul and the Sacred Heart societies and president of the Derry Commercial and Literary Debate Society. He visited the sick of the community every three days and taught night school. His responsibilities for the children of the parish were extensive: beyond supervising the activities of two Catholic primary schools, he taught catechism at St. Columb's Hall and organized the children's sodality. Not only did he prepare a sermon for Sundays, but on the first Friday of the month, he delivered a lecture at the hall on Irish history.[25] He continued to do this until at least 1910.

Father Willie's talks were usually delivered to a packed hall. He regaled local residents with stories about important Irish saints and Catholic leaders, ranging from St. Patrick to Daniel O'Connell, "the Emancipator." The battle of Limerick, Grattan's Parliament, 1798, the effects of the Penal Codes on Catholic life, and the heroic deeds of local priests from the past were just some of the topics he examined in his informal school of Irish history. He paid close attention to local history also, and educated Derry people about the Irish language through a study of local place names.[26] He also oversaw debate topics, ranging from benefits of the Revolution of 1688 to the people of Ireland and Britain to the morality of capital punishment to the future of trade and prosperity for Derry.[27] It was St. Columba, though, who received the priest's most dedicated efforts.[28]

The celebrations of the 1,300-year anniversary of the death of St. Columba scheduled to be held in Gartan, County Donegal, provided the catalyst for Father Willie to expand his vision of Derry as a city inspired by Columba, and to invite the city's Catholic population to join together in reverence for their religion and in pride for their cultural heritage. The idea was first suggested by Fr. Bernard Tracey in a speech at the annual reunion of Derry residents in Glasgow in 1895. Father Willie provided the stimulus and organization that enabled local Catholics to express publicly a broader Irish community identity in a way that was respectable, even pious. Invented traditions rarely thrive on the strength of one person; they only take root in ground that supports and sustains them. For Derry Catholics, though Father Willie proposed the idea, celebrating Columba was a way to celebrate themselves.[29]

Born in Gartan, and reputedly a descendant of a high king of Ulster, Columba is one of the most important Irish saints. Many believe that he founded a monastery in Derry, the *Dubh Regles*, or "Black Church." He left Derry and Ireland to establish a monastery at Iona, where the famous Book of Kells was produced in 800, possibly for the 200th anniversary of the saint's death.[30] In an effort to contextualize the events of the thirteenth centenary, *Derry Journal* reporter Thomas O'Kane explained Columba's wider significance: "Far and near, wherever the Irish race had a home, and their Celtic eloquence found a platform, in the cities of America, as well as in the hills of old Tyrconnell by his native Gartan, learned tongues spoke of and saintly pastors dwelt on the life and career of Ireland's great saint, patriot and poet."[31]

Columba had great affection for Derry. Poems from the sixth century attributed to the saint have him grieving the place, asking God to protect it, lamenting his distance from his "little oak grove," his "dwelling and little cell."[32] If Columba loved Derry, then Father Willie wanted to prove that Derry loved Columba even more. According to him the saint's dying words at the altar at Iona invoked the city by the Foyle: "Raise my hands that I may bless you all, higher still that I may bless my beloved oak groves and those that dwell therein."[33]

The celebrations of the thirteenth centenary were a complex affair, not extravagant but ample and effusive nonetheless. Father Willie oversaw restorations of a holy well and attributed it to Columba; he had the well opened for the first time since the 1860s (fig. 1), when the City Corporation had it closed "for sanitary reasons and for the convenience of traffic."[34] Most important, the priest established June 9 as a local religious holiday, revitalized Columban traditions, mapped and sacralized places in the city associated with the saint, and introduced the oak leaf as a symbol worn in honor of Columba, just as followers of St. Patrick wore shamrocks.

The *Journal* explained the reasons the project was necessary when it proclaimed, "The race is fast fading, almost gone in Derry, who knew the

Figure 1. St. Columb's Well remained a site of faith, memory, and community and an anchor of the Bogside throughout the twentieth century.

holy places [associated with the saint], or were familiarized with their history as it came down through the generations. The old order changeth and the old system of thoughtful perpetuation is almost gone."[35] As the case with most invented traditions, fears associated with the loss of reflexive performances of memory necessitated a more formal commemoration. Local Catholics responded with enthusiasm to the prospect of celebrating St. Columba. In all the Catholic churches for days beforehand, parishioners prepared for the first observations of the holy day; their decorations of the interior of the churches and the altars looked, to one reporter, "like a gem from the fretwork of heaven."[36]

The first celebration took place the same year that Catholics sat in the Corporation. On the evening of June 9, 1897, Derry's Bogside overflowed with people, faces illuminated by the glow of hundreds of small lamps strung up along the streets. They packed the chapel day and night. Masses were celebrated every hour and reporters noted that more than 5,000 people received Communion at the Long Tower alone. Streets around the church and the holy well were so full of people that traffic came to a halt for hours on end as Catholics waited patiently to receive a cup of holy water from the well and to say a last prayer at the old kneeling stone. Above them, letters illuminated with the help of gas-jets spelled out "Blessed Columba, Pray For Us."

Father Willie was instrumental in securing what was believed to be the only remaining relic of Columba's *Dubh Regles*, a kneeling stone that the Catholics of Derry had long associated with their patron saint. From the late eighteenth century until the middle of the nineteenth, the stone had lain horizontally beside the well. Its two basins, which tradition attributed to the places the saint had knelt in prayer, served as fonts for holy water that emerged from the well.[37] In the 1860s, when the well was closed, the stone was repositioned to stand upright; it lost its practical use but remained symbolically important. However, it jutted out of a path that gradually gave way to a busy thoroughfare as the nineteenth century progressed. Despite its inconvenience, the city left it alone out of respect for "the people's feelings."[38] Father Willie saw the celebration of St. Columba's thirteenth centenary as a good opportunity to transport the kneeling stone to the church grounds, where it became part of an outdoor Calvary scene. There, he believed, "it would prove safe from all possible vandalism and likely to prove more commemorative of its illustrious owner."[39]

Close to midnight on the first June 9 celebrations, neighborhood residents gathered to witness the transfer of the holy relic. Around the stone, residents had hung a canopy decorated with lights, flowers, and evergreens. Tiny crosses surrounded it, and when the canopy was illuminated, "it seemed indeed a votive altar to Catholicism and Saint Columba in the public streets of Derry."[40] For several days beforehand, men of the community had kept vigil, never allowing the tiny lights surrounding the canopy to extinguish.

Thousands knelt in the street and said the Rosary in the Irish language, only drifting towards home as the evening grew late. It was after midnight when workmen carefully extricated the stone and carried it in silent procession, led by Father Willie, to the Long Tower church, itself built on the site of what was thought to be St. Columba's Derry monastery. Gathering everyone into the chapel in the stillness of the night, Father Willie invoked the revered saint: "Now that the midnight hour has sounded, thirteen hundred years ago, at this hour, that night, Columba lay dying on the altar steps of Iona. 'Raise my hand,' he feebly cried, 'that I may bless you all; higher still that I may bless my beloved Oak Grove and those that dwell therein.' Let us now, before we part, turn to the altar and ask Our Lord to let Columba repeat that same blessing tonight. May every anniversary feast of his be kept in this church as today's has been."[41]

Derry Journal reporter Patrick Brennan was struck by the enthusiasm the thirteenth centenary inspired: "Within the last few days there have been many evidences of the vitality of Catholicity and unaffected piety in Derry, and in the religious services which were attended so numerously and participated in so fervently there was an admirable exposition of practical faith."[42]

The *Sentinel* was not impressed by the observations of the thirteenth centennial and was incensed by the kneeling stone's transfer. In an article, the paper said that Catholic Derry had imbued the saint with "character and attributes to which it is doubtful he would have wished to lay claim." The paper depicted the removal of the stone as a "lawless plot," even though it was connected with "ridiculous superstitions and nonsensical survivals," such as believing that blessed water had curative properties. The notion that a piece of public property could be "smuggled away without a whisper of warning" did not augur well for the city. At any rate, the paper took exception to a Catholic public gathering where "audible prayer and physical force were blended" in the wee hours.[43] The protests hinted at anxiety about the combination of Catholicity and strength.

In the years following 1897, the celebrations of Columba grew. Local people took more responsibility for the event, and its religious observance became integrated into the city's Catholic calendar. The following year, local reporter William O'Kane observed that the event was "more earnest and intense than even last year's."[44] Chroniclers of the event were struck by local involvement, and by the seriousness with which Derry people had participated.

The *Journal* made special mention of "the poorer people," calling the events of 1898 a tribute to their devotion.[45] By 1898, quite separate from Father Willie's supervision, local Catholics initiated a tradition of building and erecting tall arches that towered over the small terraced houses of the Bogside to mark their saint's holy day. Echoing the triumphal arches within the walls that commemorated the Siege of Derry, these gateways that spanned roads all over the neighborhood rose out of the streets of Catholic Derry. Made with flowers, paper, cloth, papier-mâché, and cuttings from trees and bushes, the arches' designs centered around shamrocks, quotations, and images of saints and angels. Flags and crosses hung from their corners, imitating the impressive gates into the walled city upon the hill. People painted oak leaves on their windows.

In 1898, these arches added to a scene that inspired the *Journal* to proclaim, "Catholic eyes have looked upon nothing at all approximating it in majestic impressiveness since pre-Reformation days in the Derry of Columbkille."[46] In 1910, the paper reflected that the celebrations of 1897 would forever be a day "written and embellished in letters of gold in the hearts and minds of Derry citizens," for they had done just honor to "the holiest spot in holy Ireland."[47] In the same piece, the paper reflected some of the turmoil of the day, suggesting that constant, irrevocable change seemed to be the order of things. This infatuation with change made people lose their interest in commitments they once held. But when it came to the celebrations of Columba in Derry City, there had been "no flagging, no waning, but an ever growing passion of deep and true devotion."[48]

The invented traditions surrounding Columban celebrations did not replace politics but they did bring religious and cultural identity together in real ways. Other ways of expressing the politics of identity followed. The following spring, Derry hosted a major St. Patrick's Day celebration, complete with banners of Irish heroes, including St. Patrick, Wolfe Tone, Brian Boru, and Robert Emmet.[49] The city's nationalists sent groups to Dublin to take part in the centenary observances of the United Irishmen's Uprising as part of the 1798 United Irishmen's Rebellion. Derry men walked under the banner of Wolfe Tone, who was captured in Buncrana, thirteen miles away in County Donegal, famous for calling the union of Great Britain and Ireland "the scourge of the Irish nation."[50] Although Wolfe Tone had been brought in restraints, or fetters, and imprisoned in Derry gaol, the city had no major procession of its own. Cultural nationalism and memory, however, did have a place in the city. In the early years of the twentieth century, the Éire Og (Young Ireland) movement was formed in Derry by Bishop O'Doherty, P. S. O'Flannagain, Eamon Mac-

Dermott, and others. The organization was a classic Gaelic Revival strong-hold, and its members, 400 strong, played Irish hurling matches, hosted céilís, learned the Irish language, and practiced military drills.[51]

THE RIOTS OF 1899

There were a few Bogside bards who would engage in politics from the sidelines through letters to the editor, but many working-class Derry residents experienced politics as a rumbling background noise to everyday life. Many remained ineligible to vote because they sublet rooms and therefore were not considered official tenants or ratepayers. However, when sectarian conflict arose, it was more like a contact sport—some engaged directly, others stood on as ardent spectators.

In 1897, as Britain geared up to celebrate the Diamond Jubilee of Queen Victoria, debates over use of taxpayer dollars to observe the Jubilee in Derry got heated.[52] Councillor O'Doherty argued that the reign of Her Majesty had brought no benefit, only "periods of famine, coercion, insurrection and agitation."[53] Catholics, in the main, chose to observe the Jubilee by organizing excursions to Donegal. The *Sentinel* was glad to be rid of them for the celebrations: "Instead of their conduct marring the celebration, it only emphasized the insignificance of their influence on anything that has made for the prosperity of this city."[54]

Memory battles on the streets often came to blows. Parades and processions that commemorated events in both Protestant and Catholic memorial calendars saw each community defending its claims to history. Claims to the past were also claims to space, and vice versa, and gaining entry into segregated areas of the city where the "other side" lived became a lightning rod for larger and deeper tensions between Derry's two communities.

The riots of August 1899 highlighted the ways that commemorative events in the city simultaneously invoked the past and brought it squarely into the present, inciting long-held antagonisms by giving them contemporary shape and substance. As in other years, in 1899 thousands of Protestants from Belfast and other areas of Ulster flocked to the city for the August 12 parades to observe the annual commemoration of the Relief of

Derry and the end of the Siege. It fell on a Saturday that year, making for large crowds. Marching bands and Apprentice Boys' clubs snaked through city streets, performing from their repertoire of songs about the pitched battle in seventeenth-century Derry between the mostly Protestant supporters of William of Orange and the supporters of Catholic James II. They lit cannons that stood on the city walls above the Bogside and unfurled crimson flags in memory of Protestants' sacrifice and death that preceded the long-awaited arrival of provisions and aid that enabled them to emerge victorious from the Siege. Even the cathedral bells sounded at midnight; these events dominated the city.

There was no violence reported that day and no reports of attacks from either side. But later that night, one of the Protestant bands marched and played sectarian music outside the Long Tower as Mass was being celebrated.[55] As the Apprentice Boys marched through Catholic streets late that Saturday night with songs commemorating vanquished Catholics, tensions ran high but no arrests were made. The following day, Catholic bands, led by the Ancient Order of Hibernians (AOH) Derry Division, marched through the center of the city in celebration of the Assumption of Mary. August 15 had long been Catholic Derry's response to the 12th, but their neighborhood bonfires, céilís, and street festivals lacked the ceremonial weight of the Apprentice Boys' commemorations. In Derry, the AOH organized their annual march to assert Catholics' presence in the city, occupying the same streets and thoroughfares that only days before had witnessed the tribute to the Siege.[56]

Protestant youth pelted the St. Patrick's Band from Derry's Waterside with stones as they arrived on Orchard Street at the social and political hub of Catholic Derry, St. Columb's Hall. The *Sentinel* noted that members of the bands provoked onlookers by getting up on the walls, wearing green sashes, and flaunting green handkerchiefs.[57] Catholics returned fire, and the melee turned into a full-blown riot before nightfall. Once bottles and hot pokers were mixed in, the state of the city became precarious. That evening, a detachment of the Inniskilling Fusilliers were called in to restore order. Riots continued into the following week, and the city's Catholic community became frustrated with uneven arrests and the police's and army's use of violence against Catholics.[58] The *Journal* castigated local police for their show of partiality: "Why were those aggressively marching bodies [of Protestants] not dispersed by the police, seeing the excited state of the city? The fact remains that they were not dispersed though charges were made . . . in Nationalist localities. Why allow one party to collect together and aggressively parade when quite a different method was adopted in different thoroughfares?"[59]

What was seen as partial conduct continued into the week when acrimony and violence bled into community relations in the streets and squares surrounding the factories and meat-cutting establishments where working-class Catholics and Protestants came into daily contact. The altercations spread further into the city as they continued. On the Monday following the riots, a few Protestant young men mingled in Carlisle Square when the mostly Catholic young women were getting off work for their lunch hour from the Tillie and Henderson shirt factory. The men waved orange and crimson handkerchiefs at the girls, who dismissed them with groans and continued on their way. A group of boys came into the square, hurling stones at the girls.[60] They had to be pushed back by the police three times. The police pulled their batons but did not use them. Two hours later, the gathering had swollen and taken control of the square; many waved orange and crimson flags.[61]

Underplaying the lunchtime altercations as the antics of a few harmless youths, the *Sentinel* reported that when the girls from Tillie and Henderson left work at the end of the day and made their way through Carlisle Square and up towards the Diamond, they were prepared. Waving green and white favors and Tricolours to show off their Irishness, they alternated between singing "God Save Ireland" and "The Boys from Wexford" and shouting for "Home Rule." Referring to the women as "Amazons," the newspaper blamed the Tillie and Henderson workers for instigating the harassment and unrest that had plagued the area along the factories, but also suggested that their silliness and chatter, "like so many magpies on a March morning," were enough to tempt police to beat their "silly" heads.[62] The antipathy between the factory girls and the men working in the meat-cutting establishments along Foyle Street and the residents of the Fountain Street area led to a staggering of factory closing hours so that working people on opposite sides of the sectarian divide would not meet.[63] By the middle of the week, normalcy settled in. However, the riots underscored the fragility of peace in the city. For Catholics, they also brought home the fact that costs of responding to violence or Protestants' incursion into their spaces were high—but they were sometimes willing to pay the cost.

As this story reveals, taking to the streets to confront Protestant power was far from the purview of only drunks and hooligans. For the ordinary Catholic men and women who gathered on street corners, tossed rocks and fought the police, fashioned flags and favors in the colors of Ireland, sang patriotic songs as they moved through streets filled with those who vehemently disagreed with their points of view, and protected their homes from gangs of Protestants who seemed to be above the law, the riots had taught an object lesson. Their Irish identity made them more visible and less protected in Derry as the victory of the Siege continued to play out on the streets, the strength of the law squarely on the side of Protestants. The *Sentinel* challenged women's femininity and respectability because they confronted Protestant men. Not only did passions run high, but the stakes seemed to heighten at the turn of the century. If the middle class and the small cohort of politicians could confront the beliefs and principles that undergirded Protestant hegemony from within the Guildhall, working-class people showed that they could and would fight it out on the streets.

In 1902, challenges to Protestant memory centered around the Guildhall, quite literally. Opened in 1890, it was originally called Victoria Hall to honor the reigning monarch. The Guildhall was the center of municipal life, where the Corporation met, councillors and municipal employees had their offices, and city events were held. Like the Diamond Jubilee, preparations for the coronation of King Edward and Queen Alexandra and for the annual celebrations of August 12 raised the questions of a proprietary unionist and Protestant memory in the city.

Once again, Catholic and nationalist politicians challenged not only the expenditures themselves but also what they broadcast and sanctioned in terms of behavior towards Catholics. In June, eleven of the sixteen nationalist members of the Corporation called a special meeting to protest the expenditure of £400 on decorations for the city for the coronation.[64] They attempted to pass a resolution "that no appropriation of the rates by this Corporation be used towards the celebration of the Coronation of their Majesties Edward and Alexandra."[65] In front of a large audience of interested citizens, the councillors argued that it was unethical to use public money to pay for a celebration that more than half the city's population did not want to take part in. At issue here was specifically the coronation oath, which ensured that the crown would be passed on to a Protestant and included what some felt to be derogatory language about Catholicism. Edward had requested that Parliament excise that part of the oath, but it had not been taken out because Catholic peers in England wanted to excise both the anti-Catholic language and the declaration regarding security of succession.[66] In Derry itself, the Corporation had recently voted to edit out the parts of the oath taken by the Grand Jury at the courthouse that were offensive to the Catholic population.

Arguing that Belfast had avoided using taxes to pay for their decorations, Councillor McCarter asserted that it was unfair for the Corporation to make nationalists and Catholics foot the bill for decorations they didn't support: "Why should they ask poor men earning their daily bread, who largely lived in the South and West wards, to put their hands in their pockets to pay for the decorations, make men pay to rejoice who were stigmatized as idolators. . . . They who were styled superstitious and idolatrous refused to be made common fools of."[67]

Their protest was not against the king but against the British government, which refused to alter the oath, thereby offending all Catholics. Councillor McCarron argued specifically that the expenditure was "frivolous"; he calculated that the funds could bury all the paupers in Derry for the next forty years. Indeed, he failed to understand why improving the quality of life in the city was less important than ceremonial displays of British patriotism: "In the Corporation of Derry every time mention was made of progress in the city, the want of parks, baths, open spaces, the reduction of fees in the city cemetery, the providing of a public library, all the members of this mechanical majority say the rates cannot bear it."[68]

The mayor dismissed the bill and intimated that those who sponsored and supported it were interfering with the prosperity of the city and with the men who advanced it. He considered it ridiculous that "forty business men would be brought there and have their time wasted in such a way." The amendment lost by a vote of 23 to 11; several Catholics did not turn up for the meeting, and one Catholic councillor voted with the Protestants, arguing that the city should be brightened up for the coronation and pointing out that drama over the coronation oath was overplayed, given that it was drawn up in the days when people still believed in witchcraft.[69]

Derry nationalists were in step with the larger Irish nationalist community in their unwillingness to participate in coronation festivities. Their bishop, Charles McHugh, was an ardent constitutional nationalist and supporter of the Irish Parliamentary Party (IPP).[70] John Redmond, head of the IPP, gave a speech outside city hall in Dublin the day of Edward's coronation. In it, he explained that Ireland was the only nation in the empire not present in London for the crowning of the new king. Ireland, said Redmond, refused to take part in the farce of unity; if the English asked why Ireland was not loyal, he would point to England's "oppression and poverty and misgovernment" in Ireland:

> I say to England in our names, "You may proceed with your coronation jubilations and celebrations, you may assemble all the nations of the world . . . but you cannot hide from your guests the skeleton at your feast. . . . One portion of [the] empire—a portion which was the home of a brave and noble race which has spread throughout the world the fame of their talents, their virtues, and their valor—here lies at your very heart oppressed, impoverished, manacled, and disloyal, a reproach to your civilization, and a disgrace to your name."[71]

And yet, the fact remained that Derry was decorated for the coronation at public expense. The city became an homage not simply to the newly crowned king and queen, but to the idea of the Crown, the monarchy, and the empire. The decorations were meant not only to invoke a sense of celebration within the city itself; reports of the event by the Protestant press emphasized how important it was that the city *appear* to others in Ireland, Britain, and abroad as tremendously loyal. The *Sentinel* noted approvingly that "the manner in which [Derry] celebrated sustained in every respect the reputation it has for loyalty and love of law and order."[72]

Maintaining its reputation for loyalty was one of the most important goals and outcomes of events such as these in the Edwardian era.[73] In 1902 and again for Edward VII's visit in 1903, Derry city was wrapped and illuminated in the symbolism of the British Crown (see fig. 2). Decorations included three-foot-wide swaths of bunting that cascaded out of the top-story windows of the Guildhall; crowns and shields were arranged on the walls of the building. The city walls were decorated with flags. Large gilt crowns were fastened above the archways at the gates so that as one entered the center of the city from any direction, one "walked into" the crown. Union Jacks and the crimson flag of the Apprentice Boys were hung at the Victoria Market, the Butter Market, and the Waterside Market. Large signs saying "God Save the King" adorned each of the three entrances to Brooke Park.

The Diamond was adorned with large canvasses of the royal crown and pictures of the new king and queen. A forty-foot-wide triumphal arch hung with a semicircular top and two smaller arches on each side in the square outside the Port and Harbor Commission in line with Shipquay Street. The bridge was decorated in bunting, and all the boats in the harbor were dressed for the occasion. On top of Walker's Pillar—the imposing statue commemorating both Derry's governor and the Relief of Derry that saw the end of the Siege in 1690—glowed four images of Britannia, flanked by the monogram of the new king and queen. For the Catholics who lived below, many of whose houses were valued at 1/80th the cost of the decoration budget, Britannia and Walker together were a reminder that the public history of Derry was British and loyal.

Nationalists responded to the displays of the coronation, which had been postponed until August and coincided with the annual commemorations on August 12, by again taking their sense of injustice inside council chambers in the Guildhall.[74] They also began to challenge historic use of city hall for sectarian purposes. In the late 1800s and early 1900s, the Guildhall was the central gathering place for Protestant Derry. Their temperance meetings took place there, as did meetings of the Grand Orange Lodge committees, missionary addresses, the Presbyterian boys brigade, the St. Columb's Cathedral "Church Lads" brigade, Londonderry Unionists' meetings, and Bible lectures.[75] It was also the civic center of the city and site of the mayoral offices, city council chambers, and offices of the staff of the Corporation. At the turn of the century, Catholics became increasingly opposed to uses of the Guildhall they considered sectarian.

Figure 2. Decorations to mark Edward VII's visit at Shipquay Place.

They began to struggle against its use as a commemorative space soon after they took office as city representatives in 1897.

In preparation for the annual commemorations of the Siege of Derry in 1901, the Guildhall had been decorated inside and out with a variety of unionist and Protestant flags, including the Union Jack and the Red Hand of Ulster. At the end of a council meeting immediately after the Relief commemorations, nationalist Alderman McCarter decried the use of "property of the people" for these sectarian purposes.[76] Despite continuous interruptions from Protestant councillors, he refused to yield the floor. When unionists maintained that the flags were harmless and the 12th was untinged by bigotry, McCarter objected: "The proceedings were a commemoration to reiterate a fact that occurred two hundred and thirteen years ago, the kicking out of [our] Catholic forefathers."[77] The flags, his nationalist colleague councillor Crampsey argued, fueled bitter hatred in the city: "Whether they took it from the very highest authority or go down to the scurrilous words that were used, (he argued that) their purpose was to stir up acrimony in the city."[78] The mayor denied responsibility for any untoward events of the 12th, including jeers and verbal attacks on Catholic clergy; he argued that the flags on the Guildhall were merely flags and could not be held responsible for anti-Catholic comments or attacks.[79]

McCarter and Crampsey were unwilling to let go of the point even though the council chambers became louder with shouts for them to yield and the councillors found themselves defending their right to raise the matter at all.[80] He drew the distinction between personal prerogatives and public positions, beginning to suggest that the city would have to accommodate difference, not ignore it: "No one could have found fault with the mayor or others if they so felt fit marching in their private capacity but when the property of the citizen was decorated on the day of a party parade that was altogether another matter. It (was) purely unconstitutional and purely illegal."[81]

He also made an opaque threat about likely scenarios should public space continue to be utilized this way. Within the threat, the memory of injustice was tempered by an assertion that things had changed: "The mayor would have to promise that this would not occur again, because if it did and was allowed to continue, matters would pass from their (nationalist leaders') influence, and then might assume an aspect that would be regretted by all. Matters were different in Derry than they were 213 years ago, and this should be kept in mind."[82]

That same year, events on the weekend of July 12 were a barometer for the relationship between officially sanctioned celebrations of the Crown and August 12 and street violence against Catholics. The city's Catholic population saw sectarianism get ugly when the Long Tower's priest, Fr. Willie Doherty, was assaulted after venturing into a Protestant working-class enclave at the height of commemorations.

The assault on Father Willie and the Protestant response to it outraged Catholic citizens and further incited them to fight for recognition and protections in the city. Father Willie was in the rectory of the Long Tower, situated on Abercorn Road, when he was summoned to come and deliver last rites to a man who had been crushed by a train on the Great Northern Railway line at the foot of the Carlisle Bridge. He ran out the door and took a right onto Lower Bennett Street, which was both the fastest route to the scene of the accident and a working-class Protestant quarter. According to a statement he gave to the *Journal*, residents of the area were agitated by the parades and bonfires of July 12 and chased the priest, grabbing, kicking, and jeering at him. He described the events as "brutal and callous."[83] The priest was shaken and incurred minor injuries.

The *Journal* expressed outrage at the incident, calling it an "outburst of savagery."[84] The paper declared that Protestant commemorations of the battle of the Boyne and the Relief of Derry themselves were to blame for igniting hatred and violence towards Catholics; that the Sisters of Nazareth were followed by a drunk who repeatedly cursed the pope was only another example of the same: "These displays in Ulster with the wild harangues—ignorantly offensive to Catholic priests and the Catholic religion, and full-charged with vicious, un-Christian incitement—set aflame a sort of hell-fire in the hearts and minds of the baser sort, and a perilous situation is created."[85]

The paper took city leaders to task for minimizing such behavior and demanded they do something to show they recognized that enflamed emotions around the 12th made Catholic priests and nuns feel uncomfortable and unsafe in Derry. A few days later, "A Derry Catholic" sent a letter to the editor, complaining that violence against priests was pushing bigotry too far.[86] Moreover, they weren't pranks carried out by mischievous and unsupervised children, as the *Sentinel* had suggested.[87] Nor was it mere rowdyism of the working classes; the antipathy was much more pervasive: "There is one thing Catholics will not endure any longer, and this is the habitual insult to which priests are subjected to in parts of the city. Children and growing boys and girls who say the most offensive things say them under the very windows and presumably within view of their parents. Sometimes, too, it is grown up men, and even women and not always of the humblest class, be it remembered, who disgrace themselves in this way."[88]

The *Sentinel* fueled antipathy by suggesting that Father Doherty was exaggerating and Catholics had overreacted to "the fine fun of it all." An alternative version of events—that a loose dog and a neighborhood filled with playing children were responsible for the mayhem—was proffered by the *Sentinel*.[89] Finally, the paper suggested that the priest had been rude to non-Catholics assembled in the streets, speaking to them in a tone they were "disposed to resent," resulting in "murmurs of dissent" during the actual disposal of last rites.[90] This criticism at the priest's failure to be appropriately deferential could have easily been seen as an insult to injury.

Catholics had accommodated marginalization in the public sphere in Derry for centuries, but the idea that parades and commemorations led to outright hostility and violence against their respected leaders incensed them. They began to fight back by claiming power within municipal government, enthusiastically supporting the Home Rule movement and creating a visible public culture that centered around a noble, worthy, and very Irish history of which Derry Catholics might be proud. By inventing traditions and reclaiming lost histories, Catholic Derry came into its own.

Local religious leaders and members of the small Catholic middle class were uncomfortable with the politics of outright protest. The establishment of Church-approved memory practices and traditions offered an alternative. The Bishop of Derry, Rev. John Keys O'Doherty, looked down on marches and parades; in a Lenten Pastoral in 1902, he denounced them as useless and unnecessary. As incidents like the attack on Father Willie show, the clergy empathized more with the daily confrontations and difficulties ordinary Catholics came up against in their city than with the larger political contests of the moment. In this way, they were no different than the clergy all over Ireland: "While the clergy were concerned to obtain home rule and redress national grievances, agitation had not the same immediate bearing for them as the political/religious struggle of the Derry Catholics against unionist domination of urban life."[91] By codifying a distinctly Catholic local history and inviting local people to celebrate and commemorate this past with dignity, religious leaders, politicians, and journalists hoped to garner support for Irish independence and civil rights for Catholics in Derry at the same time. Confronting Protestants' and unionists' histories encouraged Catholics to tell their own.

In an introduction to his 1901 book of essays, *Derriana*, Bishop O'Doherty wrote that for too long, official histories of Derry had been left to those authors familiar with only the most recent three hundred years, in effect, erasing the much longer view. O'Doherty was intimate with the history of which he wrote. Born in 1833 just two miles from Derry City, he was the first "home-grown bishop" in at least three hundred years. He had made his First Communion and had been confirmed at the Long Tower during the Famine years and had only left the area long enough to receive his education at Maynooth.[92] O'Doherty was a scholar of Ireland's history; as such, he would have been familiar with Lord Thomas Macaulay, the chronicler of Derry's Siege. He took to heart Macaulay's admonition that "a people that takes no pride in the noble achievements of remote ancestors will never achieve anything to be remembered with pride by remote descendants."[93]

Bishop O'Doherty's book of essays was a response and a challenge to George Douglas's *Derriana: A Collection of Papers Relative to the Siege of Derry, and Illustrative of the Revolution of 1688* (1794). O'Doherty's Celticized *Derriana* told a history of Derry and Inishowen that long predated Plantation. Bishop O'Doherty recounted events hitherto passed on orally, scoured Latin texts for references to Derry, put myths into historical perspective, read the landscape for insights into unwritten histories, and confounded English narratives of Derry and Donegal, circa the Nine Years' War and the advent of Plantation. The book was meant for a local audience, peppered with reminders to his readers how much those who had come before them had contributed to Irish culture and history and encouraging them to dedicate themselves to studies in local history.

In these ways, Bishop O'Doherty's work was an answer to the other *Derriana*, from which so much of the city's Protestant and British history had been derived and its memorial landscape reconstructed. Douglas had collected primary documents that narrated Derry's part in the Glorious Revolution, detailed crucial moments in the subjugation of Ireland by England, and celebrated the munificence of the Plantation. There was little to say of the city before 1612: Derry was an island covered in oaks where monks had once founded a monastery, and "the leaders of the rude and illiterate natives were either agitated by internecine divisions and petty wars, or employed either in secret machinations or in open opposition to the English."[94]

For more than two hundred years, official histories of Derry, such as Douglas's *Derriana*, had marginalized or mocked native Irish and largely ignored the fact that the Plantation was colonization. However, Ulster had largely been left alone by the Normans and English until the seventeenth century. A hilly and illegible landscape, historians assert that it represented some of the most distinctive examples of the ongoing legacies of Gaelic custom and tradition, including religious practices, language, law, land ownership, and distribution. Like other participants in the Gaelic Revival, O'Doherty wanted to do more than retrieve nearly forgotten facts. It was an unusual choice in the world of book publishing, and it was as if O'Doherty wanted those searching for the Siege history to happen upon his chronicle of the people, stories, and places of the northwest instead. If official histories saw Derry, indeed all Ireland, rescued from the ignominy of native culture by the industriousness and orderliness of the Plantation enterprise, his goal was to rescue a history that had "been buried in obscurity" and endow it with some of the pride and valor of which it had been stripped.

O'Doherty highlighted Donegal's most famous ruin, the fort known as the Grianan of Aileach. Three miles from the center of Derry, it was a not only a link to the ancient past, but a connection to home for the thousands of city residents who had migrated from rural Donegal. Referring to it as "the Northern Tara," the bishop sifted through histories from Petrie, O'Donavan, and O'Curry, archaeologists and champions of Celticity from the Young Ireland era.[95] Like O'Doherty, they "cherished the Past of Ireland, they reverenced it, they believed in it. They determined that the Ireland of the Future should be bound to the Ireland of the Past by the strong links of knowledge and love."[96] Threading myth, folklore, and archeological evidence, he told the history of Ireland's northwest through the materiality of the ancient site. He painstakingly explained the potential veracity of the assertions made over the years about the Grianan. He concurred with Petrie's argument that the fort had never been the ancient Druids' "temple of the sun," an idea that gained resonance because of the etymology of its name, which could be literally translated as "sun palace."[97]

Bishop O'Doherty mounted evidence to support claims that the Grianan was the summer palace of the kings of Ulster since long before the Christian era. According to the "Annals of the Four Masters," the Daghda, the king of the Tuatha de Dannan, had the structure built around 1800 BCE, he told readers. He offered the traditional explanation for the site; it was built as a gravesite for the king's son Hugh, who was killed by the chief of Connacht in retaliation for indulging in sexual relations with the chief's wife. From 789 until around 1088, the chieftains of the Cenél nEógain used the Grianan. It was reputedly destroyed in 1101 by Murtagh O'Brien, king of Munster, who ordered his soldiers to carry the stones away from the fort until all were removed. When Derry amateur historians reconstructed it in the 1870s, the tallest point of the structure was only two meters high; the Ordnance Survey listed it as a cairn, a pile of stones used to mark direction, graves, or simply the summit of a hill.

O'Doherty took care to tell of one of the most enduring legends about the fortress. Oral tradition and folklore preserved a story, the bishop explained to his readers, that loyal troops of Ulster's last great chieftain, Hugh O'Neill, still sleep within caves beneath the old fort. They will awaken when the time comes to "strike a blow against the Saxon 'for the freedom of Ireland.'"[98] He told the story, famous in Derry and Donegal, of a peasant who happens upon some of these mythic sleeping soldiers, arms around their horses' necks. It has been foretold that one of the soldiers awoke and mumbled to the peasant in Irish, "Is it time yet?"[99]

In his summation, O'Doherty asserted that "the story of the Grianan is the history of Ireland":

> It has seen the bloody heathen rites of Baal-worship; the rising of pure light of Christianity; the preaching of saintly Patrick . . . the going forth of Columba; the installation of many a chieftain on its

crowning stone . . . the wars of Shane and Hugh and Owen Roe
O'Neill; the Flight of the Earls; the Plantation of Ulster; the sieges of
Derry; the conflicts of William and James; the protracted agony of
Roman Catholic Ireland during the dark Penal days; the agitation for
Catholic Emancipation; and the dawn of a happier, brighter, freer,
day; aye, it has seen too, the sturdy sons of its own land rallying
around its ruined walls to build them up again with loving reverence
and tender care.[100]

Bishop O'Doherty concluded his history of the site with a note about
its restoration, undertaken by amateur antiquarian and Derry resident Dr.
Walter Bernard, beginning in 1872. The site was falling apart when Bernard began his project; he restored the ruin as best he could, using Ordnance Survey memoirs and enlisting the help of local farmers. This return
to form constituted, quite literally, an historical "reconstruction."

People had frequented the site throughout the nineteenth century; in
1904, Bernard wrote a report detailing the damage done to the site and
summarizing his own restoration efforts. His report detailed the ways the
Grianan had been used and abused. Local people had dismantled the
space both by overuse and by taking away the stones for other purposes.
Local archaeology enthusiasts had ignored best practices as they searched
for underground passages in the middle of the nineteenth century. Local
news stories about the Grianan drew even more attention to it, leading to
"the summer invasion of visitors from" Derry by those who were "un-
thinking, careless, and curious."[101] Despite fears that the fort would be reduced to rubble, Derry Catholics returned to the Grianan at the turn of
the twentieth century. If Bernard had reestablished the site as a place de-
serving of reverence in the last quarter of the nineteenth century, it took
the national crisis to bring that home to Derry people. The Grianan became important, not simply as a site for picnics and mischief, but as a
symbol of Ireland's long history and a beacon for the ongoing fight for
Irish independence. They visited and invoked the site and its history in
ways they had never done before.

On the Feast of the Assumption, August 15, 1897, 1,250 National
Foresters, including many from Derry's branch, made the three-mile excursion in formal procession with pipe bands playing and banners flying

from the city to the site of Grianan. The chief ranger of the Foresters in 1902 was Inishowen-born Derry City councillor Patrick Crampsey, who a few years later would protest so vociferously against the use of public money to celebrate the coronation of the king. The Foresters, Ireland's largest friendly society (one that promotes savings), was founded in 1877 to support constitutional nationalism.

Crampsey opened festivities at the Grianan by explaining that their "pilgrimage sought to perpetuate the memory of those that in days gone by dwelt in those regal walls, and also to cement more firmly the unity that should exist among Forresters."[102] The choice of the site was hardly an accident. Just a couple of months earlier, in June 1897, in an open letter "to all Irishmen," four prominent Derry Catholic and nationalist politicians exhorted all who called themselves Irish, but particularly those of Ulster, to come to Derry's aid to fight the gerrymandered political process. The nationalists' successes throughout the 1890s to elect their own representatives only led to stronger battles from their adversaries, who encouraged unionists throughout the North "TO WIN BACK DERRY."

The unionists had called in important figures, such as James Hamilton, the Duke of Abercorn (and the first governor of Northern Ireland after Partition); and Charles Stewart, the Sixth Marquis of Londonderry and one of the most generous contributors to unionist political causes; he was one of the first to sign the Ulster Covenant in 1912. Derry nationalists had to respond to these attempts to take Catholics off the election rolls; this proved a costly endeavor. By 1897, nationalist coffers had dried up and they needed financial support to continue their fight. The authors of an open letter requesting economic support closed their impassioned plea by invoking the Grianan fortress: "In the old days when the signal flashed from our Grianan of Aileach they answered it in hosts from all the borders of Ulster. The signal is up again. What will be the answer of the men of today? Will they answer quickly and generously? We are not fighting for ourselves alone. If success is not worth a small and general contribution by all Irishmen it is not worth the further heroic sacrifice on our part."[103]

The Catholic community in Derry did not simply invoke or allude to the site as a way to articulate their links to the ancient Irish past. They moved beyond merely talking and writing about the Grianan by using, renovating, and repairing it. Even when they wrote its name down, as they called it, the "Greenan Ely," they claimed Irish identity and nourished their roots and links with Donegal.[104] Their dedication was an act of memory and a call to Irish independence. Chapters of organizations dedicated to Irish nationalism and republicanism—the Gaelic League, the Gaelic Athletic Association, and Cumman na Gaedheal/Fine Gael of Derry—"undertook reparation and devoted Sunday afternoons and holidays to it."[105] When Londonderry celebrated the coronation of Edward and Alexandra, Derry folks took an excursion to the Grianan in 1902. In 1915, just as the possibility of a two-state solution for Ireland began to look very real indeed, the Royal Society of Antiquaries in Ireland toured the Grianan, declaring it one of Derry's, and Ireland's, most treasured monuments.[106]

Reclaimed from obscurity and disintegration by the culture-makers of the late nineteenth and early twentieth centuries, the Grianan was more than a Neolithic monument, site of pitched battles or covert celebrations of Mass during the Penal era. It was a link to the rural Irish landscape, to a history that predated Plantation by centuries and to a cultural geography of which to be proud. For many, it represented home in a very literal sense, as the County Donegal hills and vales around Derry City had been home to many Catholics' forbears. Bishop O'Doherty had codified the long folk history of the site in his book of essays. Local people, in turn, engaged in placemaking on several levels and embraced the Grianan both symbolically and physically. When they made the three-mile trek and climbed the steep hillside, Derry's Catholics reclaimed a history that had almost been lost to them and enacted "the restoration of Gaelic standards."[107]

ASSERTING AN IRISH-IDENTIFIED LOCAL POLITICS AMIDST HOME RULE AND THE QUEST FOR IRISH INDEPENDENCE

Many touchpoints of cultural memory around the turn of the twentieth century in Derry involved local issues, even if they were often informed by issues with a much farther reach. By 1910, however, uncertainty surrounding Ireland's political future had become the overarching preoc-cupation in Derry and across Ireland. Derry, however, was unique. Fram-ing contemporary issues through a past-looking lens was such a fixture of battles over politics there that a London correspondent observed in 1913 that "Derry and its people, different from most others, lived entirely in the past."[108] As the movement for Partition grew among Ulster's Protes-tants, the city's relationship to the rest of Ireland changed and so did the purpose and texture of its memory work. Cultural identity, historical ge-ographies, and battles over the memorial landscapes of the city became increasingly imbricated with the ever-present contention over Ireland's political future. Looking backwards was not a priority during this tumul-tuous time, but when Derry's Catholics did invoke the past, it was often in pursuit of nationalist objectives.

Until the onset of World War I, Derry Catholics had not seriously entertained the possibility they might be left out of an independent Ireland—they believed "there would be no concessions for Ulster," as their politicians assured them; as such, they did not think any Ulster county would actually be allowed to "opt out" of participation in an Irish parliament.[109] Their political efforts focused on gaining and harnessing local demographic power in order to assert Catholic and Irish national-ist strength in Derry itself and utilizing Irish history to leverage political power at home. This changed drastically after 1912, when Ulster union-ists made it clear that they would not concede to an independent Ireland and actively proposed alternatives.

Catholic Derry's position on this might be surmised from its choice of plays to bring to Derry and support for a six-night run: Yeats's overtly nationalist *Kathleen Ni Houlihan* and Lady Gregory's examination of Anglo-Irish relations, *Rising of the Moon*, both certainly "explosive matter to put on the stage in Derry or anywhere else, in the year 1912."[110]

The year before, in 1911, even the relatively minor matter of the city's coal fund had become a touchstone for conflicts over the past and the fu-ture. The coal fund for the poor had been started by local merchants and other business owners in 1855 and administered by a small committee, which often included elected officials. The desire to ensure that the poor-est city residents could heat their homes transcended sectarian relations until political rivalries in the city became pronounced. In 1910 there had been a cold winter, and the city sent out a request for donations, pushed back the date for the opening of the fund availability in 1911, and proposed that the City Corporation would take over administration of the "Mayor's Coal Fund," instigating debate over the fund's very existence.

Several Protestants wrote to the *Sentinel* to encourage a boycott of support for the fund. They pronounced that the generous Protestants of the city had been duped long enough by Catholics who were too poor to procure coal but could seemingly burn through money gambling and engaging in other amusements. Catholics had only contributed "a trifle" to the fund, leaving Protestants to subscribe for Catholic benefit. Further, the authors claimed that Bogside residents stoked their chimneys on the annual commemorations of the Shutting of the Gates every December "to choke Loyalists off the walls with the smoke from the very same coal which (they) out of the fullness of their hearts provided."[111] Indeed, this "kept Protestants from celebrating the greatest day in the history of the city." Politics came up directly, with one writer saying that since Catholics were so proud to say they had finally returned a majority to the (voting) register, "the Catholic majority might celebrate by inaugurating their own coal fund."[112] The coal fund operated only intermittently after 1912, with local churches and charitable groups stepping in to provide funds for fuel. In a city known for its public displays of civility, the introduction of sectarianism in the case of the coal fund augured poorly for the state of the city.

Until the War of Independence, Partition, and the establishment of Northern Ireland, Derry nationalists did more than fight local battles on their own or nod to broader nationalist movements elsewhere; they drew on their local history to assert their belonging in Ireland under Home Rule. The quest for voting rights at the parliamentary level became an increasingly important strategy in this effort for Home Rule. Derry nationalists participated in the push for greater numbers at the registration polls and the accompanying power these numbers brought to elections. The clergy was active in the registration movement, which expanded well beyond the administration of their religious and community responsibilities. Voting rights were the AOH's biggest priority during this time and dominated local chapter discussions.[113] Indeed, Derry's branch of the

AOH combined heritage and nationalism when they named their chapter after "the martyred Bishop of Derry," Dr. Redmond O'Gallagher; the chapter honored the memory of his sacrifice, claiming O'Gallagher's "loved name still sheds a halo of glory over our ancient city."[114] Father Willie called meetings and encouraged use of St. Columb's Hall for political strategy sessions, exhorting "all nationalists and that meant all Catholics" in the city to join together in their "sacred duty" to ensure that their voices be heard amidst the clamor of debate over Home Rule and independence: "Registration should be worked so that every possible Nationalist vote would be made available for the day of battle and every Unionist who had no right to a vote should be kept off the register. There was not one use of it fighting one or two wards in the city; the whole city should be fought and it should be fought from one common platform."[115]

In 1910, local Catholic nationalists failed to secure a seat for their preferred candidate for Parliament, Liberal Shane Leslie, a twenty-five-year-old from Monaghan and a cousin of Winston Churchill. Leslie came to Derry for a meeting to address his would-be constituents, disheartened by an election loss of only fifty-five votes.[116] He exhorted to the crowd that packed St. Columb's Hall that the only way to win back the Derry seat was by clearing away "the great fungus growth of the Unionist accumulation on the (registration) lists."[117] James O'Doherty, one of the meeting organizers, made clear that more was at stake for Catholics than a seat in Parliament: "There may be a statutory peace, stereotyping the conditions of municipal life in Derry. Against such a peace, which would leave my race forever under the heel of the minority, I will ever fight. Rather than such a peace, [I] welcome eternal war."[118]

Leslie had come to town to encourage the disheartened nationalists of Derry to remember their place in Irish history, to maintain their faith, and to "stick to fighting and leave the talk to the Cork end of Ireland.[119] He invoked the past, pointing to the 1782 demand for legislative independence at the Dungannon Convention, an event that marked the early stages of the United Irishmen's movement, thus linking his own history as an Ulster Protestant with a long tradition of coalition-building and solidarity loosely centered around the goal of Irish autonomy. Quoting from "Song of the Volunteers of 1782," he declared, "the North began, the North held on the strife for their native land."[120] He reflected:

The Nationalists of our northern province maintain their ground in sunshine or shadow, and in Derry we have had both . . . (and) they hope on and strive still with the determination of their race . . . that spirit is unquenchable in Derry, the citadel of the North . . . Nationalist Derry is true, undividedly true, to the cause and is stirred by the one unqualified impulse to have the old city do its part and take again its once proud place in the frontal line for the battle for the rights of Ireland.[121]

Maintaining a united nationalist front posed a problem for Derry Catholics as the battles over Home Rule, Partition, and eventually Irish independence became more pronounced. Tensions steadily increased in Derry as aspirations for independence became a more complicated enterprise and factions divided nationalist politics, particularly with the emergence of the National Volunteers and the rise of the Irish Volunteers, who entertained the possibility of using physical force to achieve national aspirations. As local issues moved to the political background, confrontations abounded concerning the best and most effective political expressions of support for Home Rule and independence. When the Irish Volunteers split over Redmond's agreement to press pause on Home Rule and support Britain in World War I in 1914, the Irish Volunteers chapter that moved to Orchard Street embraced the Revival even more wholeheartedly; they formed a branch of Cumann na mBan and held Irish-language classes and classes in Irish history; in those classes they portrayed Britain as the enemy and urged young Derry men not to fight for England in World War I.[122]

For the first time, the Catholic clergy in the city found themselves in competition with secular movements. Like all of Ulster, Derry was a tempest, with nationalists and Home Rule advocates splitting allegiance between political and quasi-political institutions based on attitudes about the best ways to pursue Irish independence. Constitutionalists were represented politically by the Irish Parliamentary Party (IPP) and reflected in the membership of the United Irish League, while republicans supported Sinn Féin and tended toward membership in the AOH, the Irish National League, and the Irish Republican Brotherhood's National Volunteers. The city was turbulent, buzzing with the political debates and questions of

the time. The outbreak of the war occupied everyone in Ireland and dif-
fused the question of the future of Ulster, as unionists pledged to support
Britain in the war and the third Home Rule bill was suspended, with Redmond's support, until the end of the conflict. Many men in Derry,
Catholic and Protestant, enlisted in the war effort. The 1916 Easter Rising
and British response to it altered Irish politics for good. The end of World
War I lit the fuse to an explosive political climate. Memory work did not
directly occupy the city's inhabitants; rather the past imbued a wide range
of issues they confronted.

For Derry Catholics and Protestants alike, a reckoning with the city's
history seemed inevitable even as current events and future prospects rose
in immediate importance. As the future began to look different, the past
inevitably came up for review. Amidst the fiery political climate, the
writer and publisher Douglas Goldring penned a guidebook entitled *A
Stranger in Ireland*, referring to himself simply as an anonymous "English-
man" but taking little care to subdue his enthusiasm for Irish nationalism.
In his book, he observed the reasons Derry was understood as "historic":
"No well brought up English child can possibly fail to learn the thrilling
details of its famous siege, when its citizens, firm in their Protestantism
and their devotion to William of Orange and his papal ally, slammed their
doors in the faces of the besieging army and adopted 'No Surrender' as
their motto."[123]

Goldring challenged this interpretation, complaining that the city's
portrayed sense of history was "arid and unappealing," especially when
compared with the stories of "saints and scholars" he had learned in other
parts of Ireland. It was just another example of Protestant expropriation—
cultural hijacking to unionist ends. He claimed Derry's landscape had
been manipulated to train the eye and ear towards the heroic Protestant
past.[124] He derided the "painfully conspicuous notice boards placed at all
historically interesting sites in Derry." He concluded, "No one who makes
the walk around Derry walls is permitted to forget the fact that the town
was an English colony and that its successful resistance to the besieging
Irish natives was a thoroughly English victory."[125]

But Goldring might have spoken for Derry Catholics when he said,
"But really, when it comes to relics of English history in a city of Ireland,
one has to draw the line!"[126] By 1918, with the end of World War I, the

line was indeed drawn in the agitated city, where memory of the past became an important trope in campaigning, recruiting, and bolstering the resolve of the Catholic community. Just as they had harnessed their demographic and cultural strength to force open a visible space for their interpretation of history, so also they drew from history to create a space in the city to amplify their cultural and political aspirations.

With the bulk of Ireland moving ever closer to Home Rule, and the Protestant North holding fast to the union, Derry was caught in the middle. Nationalist opinion on the subject, and on Ireland's relationship with Britain, was best summed up by Alderman James O'Doherty: "Our marriage has been a complete failure. We demand a divorce. There are sufficient grounds in our discordant temperaments. We cannot live in one house but we would make the most excellent neighbors."[127] In a 1916 letter to John Redmond, Bishop McHugh voiced his worries that Derry Catholics would once again be at the mercy of bigots. "Poor Derry. After all it did to secure a parliamentary majority for Ulster in favor of Home Rule, it is to be treated as a castaway."[128]

Derry's different nationalist contingents called upon the past as they plotted their uncertain future. Even though the conservative clergy urged republicans to tow their line and avoid complicity with political violence, arguing that "we cannot forget that we are Catholics," their admonitions didn't carry.[129] Republicans utilized memory in their own ways. Locally, Sinn Féin put up Eóin MacNeill, the father of Irish medievalist study, founder of the Gaelic League, and leading Gaelic Revivalist, as its Derry representative in 1918. An Antrim native, MacNeill had been one of the founders of the Irish League. When MacNeill won, the *Journal* invoked the great nationalist political leader Charles Stewart Parnell, who once declared that "he would rather hold Derry than forty seats."[130] Republican organizing rallied around the past—meetings were often held in the Shamrock Hall, John Mitchel Hall, or the Owen Roe O'Neill Hall. Derry City's Irish Volunteer corps was said to be one of the best in the North.[131] Quick to memorialize the martyrs of the Easter Rising, they formed a Patrick Pearse Sinn Féin Club in 1918 and invited Pearse's mother to Derry. Combined, these events and tactics had the effect of equating, for Ulster's Protestants, all Catholics with Sinn Féin.[132]

By 1919, the political climate in the city reflected the brittle state of sectarian relations in Ulster as a whole and the incendiary state of Irish politics and Anglo-Irish relations. The Dáil Éireann declared Irish independence in January of that year, setting off the Irish War of Independence. The demand for a republic and Ireland's irrevocable split with Britain stymied unionist sensibilities.[133] Not only did it call into question the state of relations between Ireland and England; it also demanded a reckoning with the place of Ireland within the British Empire as a political and economic entity and as an imagined geography. Unionist Derry responded with fervor, working politically to ensure its inclusion in a Northern state. Locally, unionists tried to remind Catholics of the strength of Protestant power in the city. For example, they used physical force to prevent nationalists in Derry from marching on the city's walls during the August 15 Assumption feast day celebrations, leading to sectarian riots that only army intervention could quell.[134]

In January 1920, twenty-one nationalist councillors were elected to the Corporation Council, besting unionists by one, joining much of west Ulster in turning out the nationalist vote for Sinn Féin and ousting unionist politicians. In accordance with local policy, the nationalists on the council were permitted to name the titular city leader; local solicitor and longtime councillor Hugh O'Doherty was appointed the city's first Catholic mayor since Cormac O'Neill had held the position at the bequest of James II in the 1680s. This represented the most resounding political success in the North that year, for the first time in three hundred years granting political power to Catholics. Protestants reacted with dismay that "the casual laborer who drifted in from the wilds of Donegal" now held more political clout than they did. Meanwhile, gleeful Catholics celebrated their victory and rallied around their new mayor.[135] The *Derry Journal* pulled out all the stops, declaring that the "No Surrender" citadel had been "conquered after struggle for centuries," thus "breaking down the barriers of bigotry and ascendancy."[136] At the time, they concurred with the *Irish News* when it proclaimed that the power shift in Derry "signaled the end of partition as an argument."[137] For nationalists, political success heralded more than self-determination for nationalist Derry; they had faith that by leveraging this new power, they were sure to steer Derry City towards inclusion in the Free State. As County Londonderry was majority Protestant and unionist, this appeared to be the best option, even as Derry's nationalist leaders continued to work with Joe Devlin on behalf of the six counties of the North.[138]

Mayor O'Doherty used the opportunity of his inaugural address on January 30, 1920, to declare publicly a Catholic and nationalist historical perspective: "Today a long and painful chapter in the history of Derry is closed and a new one is opened." He explained that he did "not wholly blame the Unionist members" of the Corporation for the painful past:

> They inherited an evil past and considered themselves bound by its traditions. Since the time when England acting on her conception, then as now, that might makes right, confiscated the lands of the Irish people and carried out what is historically known as the Plantation of Ulster with Protestant settlers, the descendants and successors of these settlers have regarded themselves as being in a special manner an English garrison for English government purposes. England fostered, sustained, and subsidized this feeling by gifts of titles, offices and privileges, so as to drive a wedge between them—the people amongst whom they had come, lest a common interest should develop a regard for the lands which they had adopted and make them Irish in feeling and sentiment.[139]

This approach had been only too successful, according to O'Doherty, and "in process of time they came to be regarded by the people and regarded themselves as an ascendancy party. They looked down upon the mere Irishry whom they treated with contempt and contumely."[140] He continued, explaining that through gerrymandering, Protestants had held the Derry Corporation as one of their privileges until this fateful election. The new mayor called on the city's Protestants to acknowledge that they had been duped by opportunist English politicians, that it was time to join their Irish Catholic neighbors and to embrace hybrid identities that found cohesion in putting Ireland first: "It is now time that you reconsider your position in relation to your countrymen, that you come to the conclusion that you owe your allegiance to this land of your birth, and that you should no longer play the part expected of you by English politicians, but go in with your fellow countrymen in demanding that the Government of this country shall be Irishmen in the sole interests of Ireland."[141]

Mayor O'Doherty made claims about the future and the past. Of Partition he said simply that they should "make shaving paper of the bill." He announced that Union Jacks and other flags symbolic of Protestant dominance would no longer be authorized to fly from the Guildhall. He concluded by saying that though tolerance and respect would be the marks of his tenure in office, he wanted to make it clear that the history of Catholic subjugation in Derry, as in Ireland, was now a thing of the past: "The day when England can dispose of Ireland according to her own sweet will is gone forever. . . . The question is not what will England give but what will Ireland take. Ireland's right to determine her own destiny will come about whether the Protestants of Ulster like it or not."[142]

The time for a section of Ireland to determine her destiny had come. However, the reality was that the prospect of two Irelands had become imminent, inaugurating unprecedented violence in Derry by early 1920. Only two months after O'Doherty's inauguration, the city saw intense violence in March. In May, Irish Volunteers killed the first police officer to die in Ulster. The spark was lit when Irish republican prisoners were paraded through the city to the jail, leading to riots. Sporadic violence erupted throughout the next two months, but June saw some of the worst violence in Derry's history. As the *Irish Independent* observed, "The term 'rioting' does not give an adequate idea of the situation. It was war pure and simple."[143]

These events, all associated with the Irish War of Independence, unleashed unprecedented violence on the city. On June 19, 1920, Derry members of the Ulster Volunteer Force (UVF) took over the Diamond and Guildhall Square and launched artillery attacks into the Bogside from the city walls; four Catholics were shot and killed that night. Members of the Irish Republican Army (IRA) retaliated two nights later when Protestants attempted to take over St. Columb's College, the site of a pitched battle in 1690 that saw the loyalists to King William emerge victorious. The IRA burned Protestant homes in the Bogside and shot two Protestants.

On June 23, 1,500 British troops arrived to restore peace to the city and were joined by 150 Royal Irish Constabulary (RIC) officers. Far from displaying impartiality, they worked closely with the UVF, "thereby aligning themselves with one side of a conflict generations old."[144] There were gunfights throughout the city, and the grounds of St. Columb's College became the scene of open battle.[145] By the time peace was restored, forty people had been killed by the British army and paramilitary and vigilante groups. In the fall of 1920, the B Specials were founded, a volunteer police force, attracting members of the Protestant paramilitaries and offering implicit support for their methods. The IRA went temporarily underground, but local Catholic support for it rose substantially. The violence and the army's partiality awakened fears of how Northern Ireland was to be governed. Derry's bishop, Charles McHugh, penned an open letter equating Partition with "permanent enslavement." And he warned, "To become hewers of wood and drawers of water for Sir Edward Carson, Catholic Ulster would never submit."[146]

The following year, O'Doherty traveled to Dublin as part of a nine-member deputation of Northern nationalists to the newly created Dáil, Ireland's governing body. O'Doherty voiced his concerns about the Anglo-Irish Treaty and a looming sense of betrayal, drawing on his own historical consciousness to summarize what so many of his constituents believed: "Our representatives have given away what we have fought for (for) the last 750 years. It is camouflaged. Once the northern parliament is put into operation, there is a breach in the unity (of Ireland). We are no longer a united nation. You have nothing to give us for the sacrifices you call upon the people to make."[147]

Back at home, Catholics faced regular raids during the War of Independence (1919–21) and the Irish Civil War (1922–23) by both the British army—the Liverpool Regiment and the Queen's Regiment—and members of the Special Constabulary, known as the Black and Tans. Shamrock Hall, the AOH halls, the Patrick Pearse clubs, wakes of murdered citizens, and homes of nationalist councillors were all raided regularly between 1920 and 1922. The border was under guard by foot patrol and the Foyle was guarded by boats.

Local politics underwent subtle shifts in the face of national upheaval. Derry's long history of Catholic poverty and the effects of only one political ward for the city's large Catholic population had led to a housing crisis in the city, often referred to as a "famine." Local trade union organizer Peadar O'Donnell observed that "the housing problem is one of the most serious problems exercising the minds of those thinking of community interests." Derry working people were "too easygoing" and the Corporation needed to be pushed to address the housing problem.[148] One of the first initiatives of the Corporation under O'Doherty was to form the Housing Subcommittee to study and ameliorate the housing conditions of the city's poorest residents. The committee didn't last very long.

Official Partition of Ireland came in 1922, which meant the end of proportional representation and a return to local unionist dominance. The chain of office returned once more to unionists. Derry City was one of several border regions that sought inclusion in the Free State under a border adjustment. Catholic Derry lived in hope that, if the nation was to be divided, its future would lie on the other side of the border, but their hopes would come to naught. Remembrance work was crucial throughout the first decades of the twentieth century as Derry leaders invoked the past to bolster local and national pride, claim rights to the public sphere, and stare down unionist power in the city.

Chapter Three

AGAINST THE WISHES
OF THE INHABITANTS

Memory as Mooring in "Castaway"
Derry, 1922–1945

Bishop Charles McHugh of the Diocese of Derry and Raphoe sent a letter to Irish Parliamentary Party leader John Redmond in 1916: "Poor Derry. After all it did to secure a parliamentary majority for Ulster in favor of Home Rule, it is to be treated as a castaway."[1] It turned out to be prophetic. When Northern Ireland was established in 1922, most Catholic residents of Derry greeted the border with incredulity, holding out hope that a boundary readjustment would place the city in the newly formed Irish Free State. By 1925, however, they had to concede that their efforts had failed. What Clare O'Halloran has called "the trauma of partition" hit hard in Derry.[2]

Beyond the symbolism of division that accompanied the border, meandering through the hills and bogs just a few miles from Derry's city center, long-standing patterns that had organized politics, commerce, and transportation ceased to make sense once the national demarcation was established.[3] More than simply reflecting existing boundaries, the border intensified fragmentation. After 1922, Northern Ireland Catholics stood separately from their southern coreligionists in a variety of ways. While the nascent Free State was contending with the complexities of nation-building and the intimate brutalities of civil war, disheartened Northern

Catholics struggled with a sense of dislocation and battled among themselves over how to adjust to new circumstances. Once blithely referred to by Derry Catholics as a "Carsonia" of which they'd never be part, the six counties (of Northern Ireland) had indeed become a unionist stronghold separated from the rest of Ireland.[4] Regular reminders that they had become a minority population underscored the new situation.

Demoralized and disheartened, Derry Catholics abstained from participation in provincial government until 1926 and from local municipal government until 1931. They could be forgiven for thinking it hardly mattered; nationalists' electoral leverage was meager during these years. In 1922, the Derry Corporation abolished proportional representation and replaced it once more with valuation-based voting privileges. Seven years later, the Northern Irish government followed suit. As a result, nationalists could look forward to approximately eleven of fifty-two seats in the Northern Ireland legislature at Stormont and one-third of the City Corporation seats. Outnumbered and isolated, Catholics moved to the margins of public life.

The popular interpretation of Northern nationalists in the post-Partition era as bitter and passive people warrants reconsideration.[5] As the *Derry Journal* put it in 1931, in the new Northern Ireland, "there was disappointment, but not despair, and most assuredly, not apathy" among nationalists.[6] In Derry, Catholics held their ground in the face of disillusionment and political failure. The period from 1896 to 1922 had seen the rise of new traditions of remembrance within an assertive memorial framework formed to compete with powerful Protestant and unionist narratives about the past and to proclaim Ireland as Derry's rightful nation. This changed with Partition. Memory provided critical moorings throughout the period between 1922 and 1945. Faced with the reality of the border and challenged by political estrangement from the Free State and an emerging status as a suspicious minority with little political leverage in Northern Ireland, Derry's Catholic community looked to the past to steady itself and relied on subtle kinds of memory work to maintain an Irish identity through religious, cultural, and folk practices. In turn, the politics of cultural identity became more dependent on those very practices and on local Catholic nationalist voices.

As they built and strengthened Catholic religious, educational, and cultural institutions, Derry's Catholics created alternative spaces for cultural expression that forged strong links with a familiar and stable Irish past. They also continued to fight against unfair political practices in the city; memories of past injustices fueled their resolve. As politicians stepped to the wings of the public stage during the years of nationalist abstention, the *Derry Journal* played an increasingly important political role, honing its distinctive editorial voice and writing extensively about the city's links with an Irish past.[7] Other memory work centered around religious, cultural, and educational institutions and events, including the establishment of the Féis Doire Colmcille, the celebration of the Eucharistic Congress, the consecration of St. Eugene's Cathedral, and the Golden Jubilee of the founding of St. Columb's College. Politics took center stage briefly in 1936, when Catholics fought against a new gerrymander. Catholic Derry's women played a crucial role during this period, drawing on Catholic ritual and on memories embedded in stories, songs, and nursery rhymes to hold fast to threads of identity in the throes of separation from the Free State.

Derry Catholics faced an array of social and economic challenges during this period. The late 1920s and 1930s were difficult years, as prosperous Ulster took hard financial hits. The "Hungry Thirties" were made hungrier by the closing of Derry's shipyard in 1926, which followed the 1921 closure of the Watt's whiskey distillery. Those jobs disappeared, as did ones in the ancillary industries Watt's and the shipyard had generated and supported. At the same time, Derry's political leaders asserted that the city had the highest cost of living in the UK.[8] Compounding these problems, the border shrunk traditional markets on the Inishowen peninsula, which was seen as Derry's hinterland before the border was established. Job options for unskilled men in the city evaporated; unemployment reached 28 percent of the working-age population by 1930. Thousands of people left Derry in search of seasonal or permanent work in Scotland, England, the United States, and elsewhere. The "Scotch Boat" between Derry and Glasgow became symbolic of the era and the lengths to which people went to find work; the passenger ship scheduled at least three sailings a week from Derry's quay during the years between 1922 and 1945.[9]

Beyond the border and financial difficulties, repercussions of the previous decade reverberated throughout the city in subtle ways. Between the Irish War of Independence and the Irish Civil War (1920 to 1922), nearly 600 people had been killed in civil disturbances in what had become Northern Ireland; 303 were Catholic, 172 Protestant, and 82 were members of the security forces.[10] In Derry City, more than forty people had died, casualties of the city's miniature "civil war." Young men were imprisoned for their involvement in the War of Independence and subsequent border war. In addition, families still grieved the 1,209 young Derry men who had not come home from World War I, several hundred of these Catholic nationalists. As a result of all of these ruptures, a generation of young Catholic men who may otherwise have become leaders in their community were effectively eliminated from public life. Unemployment, emigration, imprisonment, and premature death through violence shrunk the male population, and thus Derry's female population surged during these years; in 1926, the adult female population exceeded the male by 3,600.[11] Meanwhile, the city's women were often the primary breadwinners; they juggled heavy work in shirt factories and other local businesses with family and community commitments.

World War II brought dramatic changes to the city, which became a central operating base for Allied naval forces and a strategic site for naval repair work for the Battle of the Atlantic. Ireland's neutrality in the war invited increasing scrutiny of Northern nationalists. Meanwhile, Derry buzzed with activity and jobs were plentiful. Derry men did return home to work, but the military personnel who swarmed the city outnumbered them. British, French, Dutch, Norwegian, Canadian, Belgian, and Russian servicemen all had a presence in the city, but it was the thousands of Americans, the "swanky Yankees," who had the most effect. As one resident put it, "It was like Hollywood coming to Derry!"[12] The war years brought an implicit truce between Derry's nationalists and unionists as the city became embroiled in the larger issues of war.

The years between 1922 and 1925 found Derry in a state of agitation, as Catholic residents and leaders continued to hold out hope that the Boundary Commission might adjust the border to place Derry in the Free

State. At the same time, unionists sought to add several border townlands from Donegal to Northern Ireland. Both claims were based on the Commission's declaration that that the border would be established "in accordance with the wishes of the inhabitants."[13] When Eóin MacNeill called on Northern nationalists to practice nonrecognition vis-à-vis the newly established government of Northern Ireland in anticipation of a boundary readjustment, essentially acting as if they were part of the Free State, Derry became embroiled in a new set of political problems.[14] MPs from Fermanagh, South Down, and South Armagh followed MacNeill's recommendation; they made statements giving allegiance to the Dáil; their local legislative bodies refused to recognize the authority of the Northern government. The Free State's inability to recognize formally the Northern Ireland government or accord it any status only exacerbated problems and tensions.[15]

Bitter controversy ensued. Those with republican leanings urged O'Doherty, the mayor of Derry, to practice nonrecognition and declare allegiance to the Free State. The Catholic religious leadership, on the other hand, preferred a less provocative approach. Bishop Charles McHugh encouraged Mayor O'Doherty to continue with business as usual. McHugh had faith that the Boundary Commission would transfer Derry City, at least west of the River Foyle, to the Free State. He was afraid that if the Corporation disbanded in a grand political gesture, the mayor would no longer have the authority to present the city's position to the Boundary Commission.[16] Following the bishop's instructions, the mayor bypassed Sinn Féin representatives' motion on the recognition issue in council chambers, so Derry never officially decided whether or not to recognize the government of Northern Ireland. Mayor O'Doherty had to stand up to his own members, who accused him of kowtowing to the religious hierarchy. He stood pragmatically firm:

> Does any man tell me that (anyone in) Derry city, speaking by a heterogeneous mass, going 'round with hat in hand to raise subscriptions to pay counsel, without records and without maps, can present the case of Derry better than the Mayor of Derry, standing and speaking in the name of Derry, can do? I was not born yesterday. I claim when placed here to fight the interests of my country according to

that intelligence God has given me, and I bow with respect to other men's opinions, but having weighed them and come to the conclusion . . . that the Catholics and Nationalists of Derry will have committed a fatuous act, an act that which would be entitled to be sent to Gransha, if they gave up control of Derry and the Council.[17]

O'Doherty's position was tactical. The mayor made his view of the newly established state clear in 1922, when he declared he would rather be "reduced to the gutter" than to take his ex officio seat in a Northern Ireland senate.[18] Having compromised political principles to improve their chances of being taken seriously by the Boundary Commission, Derry Catholics set their sights on shifting the border in their favor. Between 1922 and 1925, the Boundary Commission made three extensive trips to Derry to hear evidence. Representatives presented strong cases for and against the inclusion of the city and its northwestern liberties as a part of the Free State.[19] Derry was one of forty areas of contention, where representatives had appealed to not be transferred to Northern Ireland. Other border communities, including Newry, Warrenpoint, and Strabane, also made appeals, as did the entire counties of Armagh and Fermanagh. All of these areas, like Derry, had formidable Catholic populations; in Derry City, about 65 percent of the adult population was Catholic, but the county itself had a Protestant unionist majority.[20] At the same time, sixteen towns and townlands along the border with Protestant demographic majorities had petitioned to be transferred from the Free State into Northern Ireland.

Catholics saw the Boundary Commission as their last shot—as one local said, the Anglo-Irish Treaty ending the Irish War of Independence had given Catholics in the six counties only one right, "the right to have their claims determined by an impartial Boundary Commission."[21] Nationalists' basic claim was that the majority of inhabitants were Catholics and wanted to be in an Irish nation; since the Treaty had stated that their wishes mattered, they were calling upon the commission to right a wrong.[22] Their position was rooted in historical consciousness; they claimed they had "always desired to be associated with an autonomous Government in Dublin."[23] They also pointed to the economic ties between Donegal and Derry, but the city's Irish identity and its efforts on behalf of Irish independence were reasons enough for readjustment.

The nationalists' case pivoted around their sense of history. In November 1922, when the Boundary Commission made its first visit to Derry, O'Doherty took the members across the new border to the Grianan fort. He highlighted the historic relationship between Derry and Inishowen and invoked the relationship between Derry City and the ancient Irish storied site. For his part, Boundary Commissioner Eóin MacNeill, who had stood for election in Derry in 1918, was so intrigued with the Grianan that he moved the border to leave the monument itself entirely in the Free State.[24]

Unionists marshaled more concrete arguments for Derry's inclusion in Northern Ireland. They also made modest claims for small areas slated for the Free State to be reappointed in their favor. Legally, their position was simple—the 1920 Government of Northern Ireland Act clearly named the city as a part of the new state. No part of the city touched the border, so there was no legal rationale for reconsidering the city's status. Economic arguments for continued inclusion in Northern Ireland centered around the importance of shirt-making to the city's well-being. Representatives from the Shirt and Collar Manufacturers' Federation contended that the industry imported raw materials and exported finished products primarily to Britain; Derry's ability to compete with English factories depended on the city's British status. Since approximately 50 percent of the city's working population depended on the industry, they argued that a change in border status could see economic collapse for the city.[25]

In the end, the Boundary Commission opted to leave the border virtually as it was. Initially, some minor adjustments were proposed, but when this news was leaked to the press in November 1925, the Commission lost credibility and dissolved forthwith, leaving the border as initially drawn. Had the Commission continued, Derry's prospects would have remained the same, however. The commissioners had already stated that Derry City's Catholic population was very modest when considered in relation to the city's liberties. Further, making such a large and controversial adjustment on the basis of "desire" alone was untenable as far as the Commission was concerned. This was well in keeping with its general position; in all of the border disputes, those seeking readjustments carried the onus of proof. As far as the economic and geographic connections between the city and Donegal were concerned, the Commission stated that the inclusion of Fermanagh and Tyrone in Northern Ireland made the separation from Donegal workable since both Northern counties were prominent trading partners with Derry City. From an economic standpoint, it was more important to consider the risks to the shirt industry if Derry was excluded from the British customs jurisdiction.

Nationalists made one last-ditch effort, calling for the boundary line to be drawn at the Foyle River, leaving the Waterside, or east bank of the city, in Northern Ireland, but including the west bank in the Free State. Their proposal was rejected as "wholly impractical."[26] The city remained a part of the UK. Hopes dashed, Catholics in the city began to choreograph an intricate dance of abstention, defiance, and alterity. Far from a mere exercise in nostalgia or an excuse to wallow in self-pity, the subtle cultural and memorial expressions they developed enabled city residents to animate an Irish Catholic identity within the new Northern state, holding the space until an unknown future date when they could once again articulate and act on it publicly and politically.

Caution, rather than defeatism, became a watchword for Catholics and infused memorial practices. Status as a suspicious minority carried new consequences in Northern Ireland. The city's unionists were warier than ever. Over the previous sixty years, they had successfully fought three Home Rule bills, but the battles had left their mark and set the stage for policy choices that would shield the unionist North. The chief of these was the development of "an exclusive politics in which there was no room for diversity."[27] Having secured the six northeastern counties of Ulster, unionists continued to be ill at ease with their neighbors across the border and nervous about the Catholics who made up one-third of Northern Ireland's population. Amateur unionist historian Ernest Hamilton hinted at Protestants' fears when he declared that nationalism in the North had "a deeper and far more sinister meaning—the expulsion from Ireland of the Protestant colonists."[28] Unionists endeavored to protect themselves against that which challenged their sense of security, belonging, and rights to the six counties they held.

Thus, the garrison mentality that had long characterized Protestant Derry's political position persisted despite political victories. The city was policed heavily and infractions of the newly established Special Powers Acts met swift justice. Created in 1922 by the Northern parliament to re-establish order in the wake of civil violence in the new state, the legislation governing the Acts was renewed annually until 1928, when the Special Powers gained a five-year extension. At the end of that period, they were made permanent through legislation.

The Special Powers Acts stifled overt nationalist and republican political and cultural expressions. Irish nationalism in the North was seen as a threat to Partition and a challenge to the new state. As such, displays of Irishness were considered disruptive to stability and fell under Special Powers policing. Between the 1920s and the 1950s, Derry, like the rest of Northern Ireland, saw the gradual increase in regulations that prohibited meetings, assemblies, and processions, and the display of Irish symbols such as the Tricolour or the Easter lily or the singing of nationalist or republican songs. Nominally inclusive across the population, the fact remained that many of the Acts were enforced almost solely against nationalists.[29] The Special Powers Acts gave the state wide berth, granting it the power to impose curfews, close pubs, ban protests, processions, and public meetings, prohibit any kind of military drill and military uniforms, and to police heavily any possession of firearms, explosives, or petrol.[30] Each year between 1926 and 1935, Derry's Easter commemorations were banned under the Special Powers Acts. In an effort to subvert the orders, city nationalists called for an "Easter meeting" to be held at St. Columb's Hall in 1933, but it too was banned.

During the 1920s and early 1930s, authorities often looked the other way when Catholics expressed less overt forms of Irish cultural affinity. This was in keeping with the early purpose of the Acts—to restrain violence. However, as the Acts came to be understood as a means of safeguarding the constitutional structure in Northern Ireland, any expression that might suggest support for Irish nationalism became suspect.[31]

After 1936, the government placed a blanket order banning Easter commemorations throughout the province. Otherwise, events tended to be banned on an ad hoc basis, often the day before or the day of. By the 1940s, other prohibited events included commemorations of the 1798 Irish Rebellion, St. Patrick's Day parades and celebrations, Gaelic sports events, anti-Partition meetings, celebrations at the release of republican prisoners, AOH functions, and gatherings of unemployed workers. In addition, police could arrest anyone for putting up materials that announced Easter commemorations or for wearing Easter lilies or other symbols of the 1916 Easter Rising. Monuments reflecting Irish nationalist or republican sentiments were similarly outlawed for fear that the sites might become gathering spaces for large numbers of nationalists. This unease, coupled with a deep suspicion of the Catholic and nationalist minority in the North, led to overzealous policing of nationalist life. In places such as Derry, where Catholics held strong demographic majorities, it makes sense that the Special Powers Acts were enforced with a strictness that was out of proportion with individual offences. The Special Powers Acts didn't stop all anti-British behavior, though. In 1932, for example, effigies of J. H. Thomas, the British Dominion secretary, were hung in several streets; in one street, he had a bottle of castor oil in one hand and the effigy held a sign that read, "You must take your oil; we won't have your bluff."[32]

Given this, Derry Catholics developed subtler and more localized expressions of religious and cultural identities, many of which invoked history, tradition, and ritual. Overt articulations of Irish patriotism brought negative attention, and the fear of being criminalized for singing, marching, or flag-waving was real. Hence, Catholics retreated to their own institutions, bolstering their own cultural, religious, and social spaces to regroup and reframe what it meant to be Irish-identified in the new Northern Ireland. Outside of the home and neighborhood, "wee huts" (where people gathered for local news, stories, and do-it-yourself entertainment), church-based activities and entertainments, the Catholic school system, and other cultural outlets became some of the most trusted places for community residents to articulate, explore, pass on, and reinforce their links to their Irish cultural inheritances. In light of the taboo on politics and political references, culture and faith meant more than ever.

TURNING GUNS INTO TUNING FORKS:
THE FÉIS DOIRE COLMCILLE

The founding of the Féis Doire Colmcille in 1922 was one of the first and most important efforts by local Catholics to connect with Irish tradition in the aftermath of Partition. The féis provided opportunities to turn informal cultural rituals into touchstones that linked Derry to the Free

State. Derry had a reputation as a city of song, and its residents were re-
nowned for excellent singing voices. Given the high levels of deprivation
in the city, this was understandable; locally, they would tell you that the
voice was the instrument that cost the least to buy and maintain.[33] Street
performers were common, and most streets in the city boasted at least one
remarkable talent. Most famous perhaps, was tenor Josef Locke, born Joe
McLaughlin in 1917 on Creggan Terrace in the Bogside. In the 1940s and
'50s, he became famous in England for his "lachrymose ballads about the
problems of love and life in Ireland."[34]

The fame of most Derry balladeers, however, extended only as far as
the next block; the exceptionally talented might be asked to sing at parties or church functions. Besides céilís and church choirs, opportunities
to come together in the early twentieth century to play music and dance
were communal, informal affairs. Music pervaded family and neighborhood life; neighbors might gather at the Oaks Hall, or Emmet's Hall at
the back of the walls, or at other small structures, tin huts, that were used
as community gathering places to sing and listen to "come all ye" ballads.
More often, the sounds of singing from the street corner or a neighbor's
front step could be heard, particularly as the pubs closed for the night.
Many Derry residents later recalled impromptu sessions in the kitchen;
favorites from the era included "I Love Old Ireland Still," "Oft in the
Stilly Night," and "Love's Old Sweet Song," made famous by James Joyce
in *Ulysses*.[35]

The first Derry féis—the Féis Doire Colmcille—got underway
during the last week of June 1922. It harnessed Catholic Derry's artistic
energies and was a welcome diversion in the city during a particularly
bloody period in modern Irish history; the civil war between pro-Treaty
and anti-Treaty forces raged, and the IRA stepped up its campaign in the
North. So challenging a year was 1922 that Bishop McHugh characterized
it in his annual pastoral as "the year (that) will ever be remembered as one
stained by deeds of blood so cruel and in some cases so revolting that it
would be difficult to find a parallel to them in any Christian country."[36]

The féis began on a Tuesday; by Friday, as competitions ended, Dub-
lin's O'Connell Street "was a mass of smoking ruins" as the battle of
Dublin raged between the Irish Provisional Government and the anti-
Treaty wing of the IRA.[37] In Belfast, seventy-five people had been killed

in violent attacks that spring. Things were so bad that one Belfast priest sent a telegram to Winston Churchill, declaring that local Catholics "were being gradually but certainly exterminated by murder, assault and starvation."[38] At their annual meeting in Maynooth, the Irish bishops declared that the events were unfathomable to anyone with Christian values: "Every kind of persecution—arson, destruction of property, systematic terrorism, deliberate assassination, and indiscriminate murder reign supreme."[39] In March, five members of the McMahon family were murdered in Belfast for being Catholic. To retaliate, in Buncrana, just over the border from Derry, all Orangemen had reportedly been "ordered to leave the town."[40]

Féis Doire Colmcille was also a distraction from local upheaval and the struggle to come to terms with life in a border city. Organizers and observers commented on the "terrible odds" against which the new féis contended and marveled that such an event could be organized amidst current conditions.[41] Just one month before the féis got underway, the bishop himself had learned firsthand about the new realities of Northern Ireland. While driving across the border to administer to parish business— the diocese did (and still does) encompass Derry and parts of Donegal, he was stopped by B Specials. Although the officers recognized the highest Catholic authority in that part of Ulster, he was ordered out of his car and subjected to a roadside search.[42]

The féis took place in Derry's Guildhall, where for one week the space filled with Irish music, the Irish language, and the buzz and excitement of Derry's Catholic community. Its Gaelicized name had two purposes—to announce its emphasis on Irish culture and to make a clear distinction between the new Féis Doire Colmcille and the "Derry Féis," later renamed the Londonderry Féis.[43] Unthreatening and enjoyable, it gave local people a feeling of uplift while impressing the city's Irish identity on spectators near and far. As John Maultsaid, who had been involved with the Féis Doire Colmcille since its inception, observed, "The original intention was to promote Irish culture, so the language section, the dancing section and the singing section, they all had a predominantly Irish feel to them."[44] Embroiled as they were in an ongoing effort to express "their right and determination to become embodied in the Free State," dancing and singing bodies had to stand in for the time being, performing Catholic

Derry's Irish cultural and national aspirations in an effort to claim a place in the Free State.[45] At the beginning of the week, the *Derry Journal* celebrated the new cultural event in Catholic Derry and praised the impetus behind it. "Impediments of disturbed and restricted social conditions" notwithstanding, Derry was making a sound effort to "join in the interest that had seized the rest of Ireland for all things Gaelic."[46]

The first Féis Doire Colmcille included more than 600 entries in more than twenty categories, including solo and group singing and dancing, bands, choirs, storytelling and historical knowledge, violin and piano, Irish recitations, and a "national" costume competition. In its inaugural year, the event was already as large as the long-standing Londonderry Féis. Adjudicators who had traveled from all parts of Ireland generally remarked on the competitors' talent and enthusiasm. Dr. Larchet from Dublin congratulated Derry, saying that "Dublin would have to wake up or come to Derry to be awakened."[47] Belfast man Sean MacMaoilain, who adjudicated the Irish language events, said that Derry's féis was as good as any in Belfast, emphasizing the weight of his compliment in that "Belfast people had no ordinary opinion of themselves."[48] He reminded his audience that there remained pockets of Belfast where one heard only Irish spoken.

Dr. Annie Patterson did note that many of the young competitors seemed to be faking their knowledge of Irish after she judged the singing competitions. They did not know where to place the emphasis in the songs they sang and recitations they read, as their knowledge of the language was strictly phonetic; they had memorized the sounds without knowing what the words meant. She declared, though, that Derry was off to a good start and expressed a hope that future féiseanna would see young people more familiar with the Irish language.[49]

Féis Doire Colmcille ended on June 28 in high spirits with a rousing band competition, performed in front of a packed house. The Hibernians, the Young Bloods, the Oaks, Friar Hegarty's Band, the Martyrs' Band, and the St. Patrick's Band were just some of Derry's performers, all composed of local boys and men. Plans were made to add new categories—including written Gaelic and Gaelic drama, as organizer Father McGettigan reminded the audience that the most important objective of the original committee had been "the revival of our national language."[50] As

Dr. Larchet returned to Dublin, he reflected that the experience of the féis, and the kindness of all those he had met, had been soothing. He trusted that "the time was not distant when peace would come, and that guns would not be turned into ploughshares, but tuning forks."[51]

The conclusion of the féis involved the conferral of medals to winners in each of the categories. The medal itself, though appearing to be merely decorative, encapsulated Catholic Derry's cultural and national identities (see fig. 3). Its shape was a Celtic cross, "a symbol of our country's suffering."[52] At the center of the medal was a "typical Irish landscape" with a river, mountain, and field backgrounded by a round tower and a rising sun bursting forth as a symbol of hope. The Irish harp symbolically foregrounded all of these images as a symbol of both music and Ireland. Oak leaves festooned each corner of the cross. The flip side depicted a cross, on which a dove, a book, and a bunch of shamrocks were engraved; at its center stood a chapel.[53] The medal was designed "to stand at once for music and learning—Doire and Erin—Colmcille and God."[54]

Figure 3. Féis Doire Colmcille medal.

The first Féis Doire Colmcille provided important opportunities for Catholics in the city. It showcased local talent and created a sense of excitement and enthusiasm for Irish language and culture. It also enabled organizers to invite some of the most talented adjudicators from Dublin and the rest of Ireland to Derry, thereby cementing Derry's place within Irish cultural tradition. One of the Gaelic adjudicators summed up the celebratory spirit of the event. "The world has gone a bit mad these days, but thanks be to God during the past week we've been living on top of the world here in Derry," he said. "In all sincerity I believe there is not in Ireland today a more Gaelic place than Derry."[55] The event was just as important from a local perspective. Sister Kathleen, who prepared students for poetry and choral competitions in later years, described the early féiseanna as "a great coming together," "a community effort," and a place and time for bonding through all things Irish.[56]

In the 1980s, John Maultsaid remembered fondly his experiences preparing for féis competitions in the 1920s: "We trained in Magazine Street, in Mrs. O'Doherty's house . . . this was a fantastic house. From early morning until twelve, one o'clock in the night, there was music going on in that house."[57] Even those who didn't perform got involved. The women of Derry, many of them expert seamstresses, spent hours designing and embroidering costumes with shamrocks, harps, and other symbols of Irish heritage. Even the audiences got swept up in the excitement of the féis. Gallagher recounted how weekly passes for the event were cardboard badges purchased for 3s 6p for children, and 5s for adults, a formidable sum for those struggling to make ends meet. This, however, didn't stop people from attending. Pass holders would enter the Guildhall, then put their badges in matchboxes and toss them out of the lavatory window to friends waiting below. They, in turn, would don the badge and saunter into the building to join in the fun.[58] Like many things in Derry, the féis became a family affair, the daughters and sons of one generation's teachers and organizers following in their parents' footsteps. For the Sharkeys, O'Dohertys, Burkes, Huttons, and others, involvement and leadership in the féis was a legacy passed on generation after generation.[59] Indeed, musical families even developed their own quartets and small choirs, or a set of families would come together to perform.

Lillian O'More, who taught Irish dancing for more than thirty years in Derry and "produced five world champions," reflected in the late 1980s about her early experiences with the Derry féis. It was generally a non-competitive atmosphere in that era, but it was especially important for children to have an annual event, a performance to work towards.[60] The féis was much more than a weeklong event because students and teachers prepared for months in advance. Derry's Catholic schoolteachers drove youth involvement in the féiseanna. Like all Catholic schools after Partition, the primary schools in the city were experiencing a period of insecurity and uncertainty amidst fears that the Northern Irish government would not take seriously Catholic educational interests. Many Catholic schools in the North had followed Éamon de Valera's calls for nonrecognition of the Northern state. They had refused to accept their salaries from the fledgling provincial government. Instead, the teachers had been reimbursed by the Irish Provisional Government. The Catholic hierarchy declined to appoint representatives to the Lynn Committee, which oversaw policy recommendations for the new Northern Ireland educational system, precluding opportunities to address their concerns through policymaking. By the autumn of 1922, the Free State was no longer willing to cover the salaries of dissident teachers, and the educational plans set forth by the Lynn Committee reflected Protestants' proclivities and priorities.

Even for those teachers who had committed to the nonrecognition plan, by the time of the 1922 féis, the consequences of Catholic nonparticipation had become obvious, though it still remained a question if their involvement in the planning process would have made a significant difference. Schools affiliated with the Catholic churches and dioceses were designated as either "voluntary" or "four and two" institutions, because they did not submit to the authority of the state on budget, curriculum, and policy decisions. They initially received no funding and ultimately only 50 to 65 percent of their operating costs. In contrast, "state schools," which were Protestant-run, were fully funded. The fact remained, however, that British history was mandatory in all primary schools; only one school in Derry in 1922 was allowed to teach Irish history as a compulsory subject, St. Columb's College. Thus, the Féis Doire created an alternative space to teach about the Irish past and to engage students in the stories, events, and characters that animated Irish history. The féis did more than dedicate one week in the year to the expression of Irish culture. It helped to harness disparate energies and focused Catholic Derry on its Irish cultural inheritances. In 1926, James McGlinchey, former IRA commander of the Bogside, founded the Comhaltas Uladh, or the Ulster Gaelic League, to continue to promote the Irish language in the North, but it was the féis that inscribed Irish cultural traditions on the city after Partition.

DUELING HISTORICAL CONSCIOUSNESS: *THE STORY OF DERRY*

Despite coming together as a community for the féis, Derry's Catholic community was certainly no monolith. In the 1920s, memory wars came to the city as Catholics debated how to remember the past in order to face the future. Should historical consciousness gesture towards a hybrid Derry identity, one that embraced the city's Protestant unionist heritage alongside the Catholic nationalist past? In 1927, a small piece entitled *The Story of Derry* appeared in a souvenir booklet of the Catholic Christian Brothers Brow of the Hill School that answered that question in the affirmative. Compiled by an editor who never tipped his cap by presenting his identity, *The Story of Derry* tried to bring together Protestant and Catholic—settler and native—perspectives on the city's past. An attempt to create a shared narrative for the pupils at the Christian Brothers' school, its stated objective was "to not offend any class, creed or political party."[61] *The Story of Derry* told the history of Plantation and the Siege, detailed the city's industrial history, offered biographies of prominent local businessmen, and focused on Columba as a shared figure that both Protestants and Catholics revered. The history was likely the first place ever to hyphenate the name of the city: "London-Derry."

The *Derry Journal*'s editorial writer, who called himself "Onlooker," lashed out immediately at the history when it was published on the grounds that it catered "for the young son of the Planter and the youthful scion of Ascendancy [and] holds little or no appeal for the boy who is Catholic in religion and Irish in sentiment."[62] Onlooker expressed

particular disappointment because there were so few written histories of
Catholic Derry. He contended that this contribution fell flat. The problems with the book, he explained, were to be found as much in what it
omitted as in what it said. Focusing on Siege heroes, it downplayed the
Irish Catholic past. Celebrating the construction of the city and its walls,
it didn't sufficiently address the destruction of the churches and monasteries that characterized the vibrant settlement that predated Plantation.
Worst of all, *The Story of Derry* did not include the events of 1920 and
glossed over the large number of Catholics killed during the riots that
engulfed the city during the violence that accompanied the Irish War of
Independence. It was a sanitized history, deliberately devoid of conflict.
Onlooker claimed that the book represented a "nauseating sycophancy"
characteristic of Irish Catholics: "Our idea of impartiality is to practice
a gross partiality for the other side. Our conception of fair play is being
unfair and unjust to our own . . . when we sit down to write a 'history' of
our country or any part of it which will not 'offend any class, any creed
or political party,' we invariably produce an abortion that ignores our
rights, hides our glories and magnifies a hundredfold our mistakes and
our weaknesses."[63]

The *Journal*'s editorial board backed Onlooker, claiming that *The
Story of Derry* was not a fair, authentic, or even impartial look at Derry's
past, but rather "a mongrel, a bowdlerised thing."[64] Nine former students
of the Brow of the Hill defended *The Story of Derry* and lambasted "Onlooker" in a letter to the editor. The paper then accused the men of not
having anything to do with writing it—their former teacher and *Story of
Derry* author had them sign their names.[65] The nine took pains to remind
readers of the *Journal* that they were all businessmen and had little time
to dedicate to petty debates in the newspaper because they were being
productive citizens, but they demonstrated some semblance of backtrack-
ing when they insisted that *The Story of Derry* was never intended to be
"a history, or even a story of Derry," but rather a series of answers to oft-
asked questions about the town's past. Objecting to Onlooker's cheap
sneer at the "Planter's history of Derry," they made their case plainly when
they said that the *Journal* should not "confuse Catholicism with sectarian
politics."[66] In a final swing, they accused the *Journal* of publishing critiques of *The Story of Derry* because it was published in Belfast and not
under the local paper's imprint.

With that, the *Journal* was not about to let the matter rest. A few days later, a parody, "Tours with Our Tame Historian," ran in the paper. It imagined a historic walking tour for Catholic young men around the walls of the city and told the tale of Governor Walker's death at the battle of the Boyne and King William's reaction to the news of Walker's demise: "His Dutch phlegm completely failed him. He quivered, he shivered, he sniveled, he driveled. And, finally, through his sobs, those who were nearest and dearest to him, those to whom he had given countless broad acres that did not belong to him, and which were not his to give, could hear him say in broken accents, 'Serves him jolly well right! What in the name of Van Houten brought him here?'"[67]

The article included both a Gilbert and Sullivan skit and a Shakespearean read on the death of Walker. In addition to the parody, the paper directly called out the editor of *The Story of Derry*, making the point that he had to have known that the book's handling of the famous siege and defense of Derry and the events commemorated every August and December in the city "was bound to be regarded as an affront to Catholics" and "to give satisfaction to non-Catholics." Defending itself for the way it covered the debate over the historical interpretation of Derry, the *Journal* argued that the paper had no other choice because *The Story of Derry* had been written under Catholic auspices. "In pointing out the blemishes in 'the Story of Derry' and deploring the tone permeating it," the paper claimed it was merely doing its job as an organ of the nationalist community.[68]

ST. COLUMB'S JUBILEE

In 1929, the fiftieth anniversary of St. Columb's College, a secondary school, offered an occasion for middle-class, educated city residents and religious leaders to reflect on Catholic Derry's successes, to recognize the growth of Catholic public life, and to hold at bay the worries and uncertainties attendant to their status in Northern Ireland. Situated close to the site where St. Columb's monastic community had reputedly stood, the college had opened its doors in 1879. It catered to boys preparing for seminary, but it became the first educational institution in Derry to welcome young Catholic men who did not intend to join the priesthood.

The school's goal was to "fashion young men capable of shaping the culture of their time."[69] In the first year, St. Columb's accepted eighteen students; by its fiftieth anniversary, there were more than three hundred students enrolled. A few scholarships were available, but the majority of students came from middle-class families. Some were day students, but those who hailed from County Donegal and rural areas in the counties of Londonderry and Tyrone boarded.

The golden anniversary provided the first occasion for current and former students, teachers, and school leaders to reflect on five decades of St. Columb's efforts to fill a vacuum in the intellectual life of Derry and its environs. For Catholic Derry, St. Columb's had forged a crucial link between the city's storied past of "scholars and poets" and an aspirational future that would see Catholics rise above their old status as the uneducated, untrained working classes. The school had struggled to stay afloat, gradually building a reputation through the successes of its early students that helped it to grow. Even amidst the gloom of the Great Depression, a celebration was in order.

Given the more bourgeois nature of the commemoration, as compared to the féis, the events were attended by a relatively small number of alumni, diocesan priests, and the city's Catholic leaders; the best-attended event was a banquet for three hundred in the Guildhall. However, St. Columb's both shaped and reflected the intellectual climate of Catholic Derry. Moreover, amidst sectarian tensions in Northern Ireland, the celebration of the school's history was an opportunity to defend Catholicism and the Catholic clergy from criticisms popular among Protestants, such as those published by the *Derry Standard* in 1925. In a series called "A Glimpse of Old Derry," the paper insulted the memory of the Columban monastery, of which Catholics were very proud: "The Derry monastery did not escape the general corruption of doctrine and morals so prevalent in the Dark and Middle Ages. It was just like the vast majority of those in other places, being a centre of dishonesty and immorality, the abbot and monks keeping concubines in the monastery and embezzling its funds and stores for the purposes of their gross sensual satisfaction."[70]

It was no surprise, then, that city residents would consider the anniversary celebrations an important local news item. A three-day affair, the jubilee was assiduously covered by the *Journal.*[71] In many ways, it was solemn, even officious. At the high Mass celebrated at St. Eugene's, the celebrant, altar boys, assistants, and choir all came from the ranks of the college. Bishop Bernard O'Kane, who had served as the president of St. Columb's from 1909 to 1915, presided. His sermon reflected on the original mission of the school, contextualizing its opening by offering a bleak description of the options available to young Catholics from the northwest on the eve of its founding in 1879: "Our Catholic youth . . . had no place to turn when their primary education was completed, except the Protestant High School or the poor substitute for a school conducted by a single teacher in a common farmhouse . . . bearing the obvious mark of inferiority, recalling the hedge school from which condition it had only just emerged."[72]

O'Kane's address was a history lesson, describing the significance of peripatetic Irish monks, whose knowledge of Greek and Latin safeguarded Europe's "ancient remnants of culture and learning" during the Middle Ages. He derided accusations all too common to the men of his generation, who had been taught by "those wretched handbooks of history through which we had to derive our earliest knowledge of our country" that the monks were ignorant automatons, laboriously copying manuscripts that they did not understand. "This disparagement of our culture arose partly from prejudice, partly from bigotry, mostly from ignorance."[73]

O'Kane drew on the past to demonstrate the importance of maintaining education, undoubtedly speaking from the position of one embroiled in contemporary political challenges of securing funding and autonomy for the Catholic school system. Invoking Derry's patron saint, he drew a direct line between the college and the monastic community Columba had led 1,300 years earlier. St. Columb's College had a responsibility to carry on a legacy of faith and learning: "We celebrate the Jubilee of a school which can claim with much justice to be the lawful successor in faith, in management, even in site and surroundings of the glorious ancient seat of learning under the guidance of the same patron."

At the banquet in the Guildhall, current college president and future bishop of Derry Fr. Neil Farren called the anniversary a triumph for more than Catholic education; it was a chance to show "all, ourselves particularly, what the Catholic community of Derry can do."[74] He had previously remarked that the college authorities had a right to judge the college "by the mark it had made in the Catholic public life."[75] Father Farren was particularly complimentary of the "old boys," St. Columb's alumni, who could be found "in honoured positions in the medical profession, in the army, in education, in trade, in commerce, in all departments of the civil service, in the diplomatic service and even amongst statesmen and politicians." His frustration became obvious, though, when he raised the issue of discrimination that kept qualified Catholics out of good jobs in the new Northern Irish state: "In this part of the country . . . the very fact that a man is branded with the name of St. Columb's is enough to discount his marks . . . to nearly nil."[76] St. Columb's students also had trouble securing scholarships for universities; the only ones available were for Queen's in Belfast, which in that era was "a university to which Catholic students will not go."[77] Farren heralded the newly created alumni association as an opportunity to build networks that might mitigate the worst effects of discrimination.

When it came time to raise their glasses to their country, alumnus and toastmaster District Justice L. J. Walsh considered Northern Catholics' contemporary dilemma regarding national identity. First, he proposed, rhetorically, that there was no nation to drink to, that the suggestion was a joke because "there is no Ireland. The Ireland that we knew was rent in twain."[78] In that case, to which Ireland were they supposed to toast? Was it to "the portion in which the children of the ancient Irish race and Irish nation are trampled under by an Ascendancy?" Or was it the other part, "which at times seems so callously indifferent to the fate of its Lost Province?"[79]

In keeping with the Catholic orthodoxy of his day, he intimated that independence had diluted traditional religious and cultural values on the other side of the border, where a floating ballroom in the Liffey and jazz clubs represented civic ideals and where the middle class was set on imitating "the extravagances and vulgarities of the idle rich in other countries." Here, he had to wait for the applause to die down, for he had clearly struck a chord with his audience. Walsh, however, went on to wax nostalgic, painting his image of Ireland: rural, bucolic, good-hearted, and Catholic. This was the place to which they owed their allegiance. Walsh ended his toast: "What God has joined let no man put asunder. It will take more than an Act of Parliament to sever the Irish nation, and what Cromwell failed to do, Craigavon will not accomplish. We will yet win through to freedom and political unity! I give you the toast of 'Our Country, Our Ireland!'"[80]

The jubilee reflected the hopes and worries of Derry's educated Catholics. They had achieved much and were proud of the caliber of students the college had produced and would indeed continue to produce. At the same time, the Depression, coupled with Partition, obscured the road ahead. There were funding concerns and fears that alumni would not get ahead—discrimination in university scholarships and jobs might hold them back. Through it all, there was a pervasive worry that the "bad old days" of marginalized Irish and Catholic education were back. The jubilee offered opportunities to reach into the past, providing reassurance, motivation, and balance. More than that, it allowed Catholic Derry to draw on a broad Irish memory to claim cultural space in a city and a province that did not reflect or represent them and to insist on the legitimacy of its own cultural and historical inheritances.

THE EUCHARISTIC CONGRESS AND THE CONSECRATION OF ST. EUGENE'S, 1932–1936

Events like the jubilee of St. Columb's went virtually unnoticed by the city's Protestant population and the Corporation government. Taking place as they did in private spaces, they operated as a twentieth-century version of Corkery's "hidden Ireland."[81] Central to Catholic Derry's ongoing efforts to articulate its successes while acknowledging obstacles to economic strength, political power, and cultural parity, gatherings within the community often took place in settings that were barely visible to the city's Protestants. Occasionally, however, the city's Catholic population became very visible. It was difficult to ignore the celebrations and religious observances that captivated Catholic Derry during the Eucharistic Congress of 1932. Local celebrations associated with the Congress, which took place in June of that year, provided Catholics a rare opportunity to showcase their faith and Irish identity in the city. The largest public event to date in twentieth-century Ireland, the Congress commemorated the death of St. Patrick. "A high-profile expression of self-confident Catholicism," it provided Ireland an opportunity to present itself as a confident, optimistic Catholic nation.[82] Just as important, it enabled the country to lay to rest some of the pain of civil war, coming together through celebrations and religious observance.

An estimated one million people, approximately one-quarter of the country's population, thronged Dublin's Phoenix Park to attend high Mass and receive the papal message. Hundreds of thousands lined the streets to greet the papal legate, Cardinal Lorenzo Lauri. Millions more participated by listening to Radio Athlone, a station created for just this purpose, which eventually became the country's first national radio station, Radio Éireann.

One hundred thousand Northern Catholics journeyed to Dublin for the Congress. It was not a particularly safe choice for them. The Congress was viewed by Protestants as threatening, and extremists attacked parties of Catholics traveling south for the Congress in a number of Northern towns.[83] However, even those who stayed at home participated enthusiastically. Catholics all over Ireland responded to encouragement from Dublin to decorate their homes, neighborhoods, and churches as a way to take part in the festivities. For Catholics in the North, whose independence had not been won in 1921, the Congress enabled them to assert their Irishness, press for their sense of belonging within the Free State, and claim obliquely that the struggle for independence had not been forgotten or abandoned. Even though the event had no sense of triumphalism in the North, it tapped into and nourished a long memory of religious faith and national aspiration.

Catholic Derry embraced Congress week. The year before, savings clubs were founded to help people put away money to go to Dublin.[84] For those staying home, the churches helped to establish street committees, which collected funds, pooled resources, and bought materials to decorate the streets of the West Ward. Men, women, and children built large street arches, made their own flags, and painted bunting, all prominently displaying blue and gold to echo the Congress emblem, and yellow and white in papal tribute (see fig. 4). Committee members designed and built street altars throughout Catholic neighborhoods, and volunteers assured that fresh flowers were replenished daily. They enjoyed their handiwork, gathering every night in the streets of Catholic Derry. Even those less pious were moved by the events. People clustered around radios to hear John McCormack sing the Panis Angelicus and wandered through

Figure 4. Eucharistic Congress arch.

the streets looking at decorations. For many, the event was spiritually grounded; they knelt in the streets by the altars, saying the Rosary together. People also socialized and chatted, took pride in their community, and gathered in faith:

> By evening, thousands of people swarmed through the Catholic quarter, viewing and comparing the decorative schemes. As dusk deepened, thousands of colored lights strung from houses and arches, sprang into life. . . . Windows and doors were kept open to catch a small breeze and the occupants of the little houses sat on window sills or kerbs, in shirt sleeves or light dresses, taking a simple pride in their efforts to beautify their homes and streets, not for a mundane celebration, but for the greater Glory of God.[85]

In Derry, Eucharistic Congress celebrations gave Catholics in the city the rare chance to exhibit their Irish Catholicism publicly.[86] When one person came up with the idea to make a stencil of the Congress emblem, and painted it, people clamored to have their own Congress badge. Thus, on nearly every house in the West Ward the badges stayed affixed long after Congress week and "for years, even for decades, the badge could be descried above hundreds of doors."[87] Religious identity was more innocent when divorced from traditional political issues, but the fact remained that for the Catholics of Derry, to display their faith was akin to demonstrating Irish heritage and allegiance and often considered a criminal offense. When they gathered night after night during Congress Week in the streets of the West Ward, they came together as Irish men and women, honoring an enormously significant and distinctly Irish event without running afoul of authorities.

Celebrations of community spirit were central to observances of the Eucharistic Congress throughout the Free State and the North. Fostering a strong sense of community, in fact, was integral to the vision of Catholicism expressed through the events. It accentuated a core principle of the Church, that happiness could be best achieved by belonging within a community of the faithful, by serving God and the Catholic Church. An *Irish Times* reporter summed up this perspective: "It was at that moment of the Elevation of the Host, the supreme point in Catholic ritual, that one fully realized the common mind that swallowed up all individuality in the immense throng. Flung together in their hundreds of thousands, like the sands on the seashore, these people were merely parts of a great organism which was performing a great act of faith, with no more ego in them than the sands themselves."[88]

Protestants in the North found this exaltation of community disturbing and the showy demonstrations of Catholicism unnerving. Congress week highlighted the difference between the two states, and the two faiths, and thus strengthened unionist resolve: "When looked at through the lens of the northeastern Protestant, June 1932 was evidence, if any was needed, why a border was needed in the first place."[89] Members of the Orange Order protested Northern politicians wearing their official robes to the Congress: "The presence of the alderman and councilors robed in their official attire will be taken as an indication that Protestant Belfast is weakening in its attitude to the idolatrous practices and beliefs of Rome."[90]

Protestant fears found fuel in the grandiosity of the Congress. Only a month later, Lord Craigavon, the province's prime minister, declared, "Ours is a Protestant Government and I am an Orangeman."[91] Distrust of Catholics and a defensive posture in community relations increased after the Eucharistic Congress. In 1933, Sir Basil Brooke, who later became prime minister, was even more adamant about the need to maintain strict divisions:

> There are a great number of Protestants and Orangemen who employ Roman Catholics. I feel I can speak freely on this subject as I have not had a Roman Catholic about my own place. . . . I would appeal to Loyalists, therefore, wherever possible, to employ good Protestant lads and lassies. . . . I want you to remember one point in regard to the employment of people who are disloyal . . . Catholics had got too many appointments for men who were really out to cut their throats if the opportunity arose.[92]

Expressions of Irish nationalism became increasingly troubling to the Northern government in the following years. In 1933, the year after the Congress, the Irish Tricolour was banned completely. Easter processions, because of the holiday's nationalist echoes of the Easter Rising, had been outlawed in Derry, Belfast, Armagh, Carrickmore, Donaghmore, Dungannon, and Newry as of 1930, but in 1936, the ban spread to all of Northern Ireland for the whole of Easter week.[93] In 1935, the government banned all renditions of the Irish national anthem. Unionist leaders feared the incendiary lyrics of "A Soldier's Song" would evoke strong emotions in Northern Catholics that might lead to unrest.

Given the crackdowns on public displays of Irishness, it is not surprising that Northern Catholics relied heavily on religious ceremonies as legitimate ways to gather publicly. In 1936, Catholic Derry observed the consecration of St. Eugene's Cathedral and hosted Cardinal Joseph MacRory, a County Tyrone native and archbishop of Armagh.[94] The cathedral's consecration was the seventh in Ireland; it signaled that the church building had been cleared of all debt and could be sanctified by God and the Catholic Church. More than a century had passed since the first conversation was held to propose a Catholic cathedral in Derry in 1828.

Catholics in the city, led by the clergy, took advantage of the consecration to reflect on the struggles and sacrifices of their community over the previous century and to celebrate its resilience. The Eucharistic Congress had certainly enabled them to forge a connection with Catholic Ireland, but the consecration occasioned a distinctly local celebration. The memory work that took place in the context of the consecration was held in conversation with contemporary Northern preoccupations and concerns.

The event was grand despite Depression economics making resources "slender to the point of distress and beyond it." Volunteers once again joined together to erect arches and to make flags and other decorations with which to adorn Catholic streets; the scene was described as one of the most elaborate and lovely efforts anyone had ever seen in Derry.[95] From the AOH's building along Foyle Street, the entire route of the cardinal's procession through the city to the cathedral was bedecked with arches, signs, and flags. Towering arches with handmade signs welcoming the cardinal in Gaelic were erected over the gates leading to the grounds of St. Eugene's. Even the streets, such as Fahan Street and those abutting Lecky Road off the course of the procession, were fully decorated for the event.

The event was viewed widely as an achievement for all Catholics in the city, who, just as the generations who had come before, funded the construction of St. Eugene's through subscriptions and collections. Beyond the pride that their sacrifices had yielded an imposing edifice, they honored a place that they had made themselves, a gathering for worship, a site of community, and a symbol of fortitude: "St Eugene's is inextricably woven with the whole fabric of our existence. It has seen us in our joys, and perhaps much more often in our sorrows. . . . It dominates our existence, not merely our physical existence but our thoughts, our hopes, our aspirations . . . it is in a word, in everything our own, our very own."[96]

Irish Derry came out in full force to welcome Cardinal MacRory, the leader of the Catholic Church in Ireland, to their city (see fig. 5).[97] The crowd swelled and cheered when his car arrived. Schoolchildren gathered at the William Street entrance to the cathedral, singing songs in Irish, as the cardinal made his way through thronged thoroughfares from St. Columb's Hall to St. Eugene's.[98] The participation was grassroots. Cardinal O'Kane reflected that the demonstrations, decorations, and songs

Figure 5. Cardinal MacRory greeted by children at St. Eugene's.

were "entirely spontaneous," and his primary role had been to "try to moderate it and keep it within bounds."[99]

Some Protestants watched the cardinal's arrival with interest; others were affronted by boisterous displays of Irish Catholicism and offended by his presence in the city. They taunted members of the procession, but the police quickly quelled disturbances.[100] The insults were a reminder that the cardinal had not been received officially by the City of Londonderry, nor greeted by its civic representatives, because several months earlier he had critiqued the Protestant faith publicly, saying that the Protestant Church was "not only not the rightful representative of the early Irish Church, but not even a part of the Church of Christ."[101] The Ulster Protestant League staged a formal protest to the cardinal's presence in the city. They accused the cardinal and other Catholic leaders in Northern Ireland of teaching and modeling bad citizenship: "Their whole outlook is vitiated by hostility to the system of government established in Northern Ireland and the ideals for which the Legislature and the Loyalist majority stand."[102] Derry had been saved "from the power of the Papacy" in 1689, and the cardinal's presence in the Maiden City was galling to the memory of the Apprentice Boys.

The *Londonderry Sentinel* printed articles objecting to the celebrations and calling the consecration nothing more than Catholic propaganda, but the city's Catholics were undeterred. Welcoming the cardinal, the chair of the reception committee declared the consecration to be "an occasion which crowns the memories of a great struggle and marks a glorious triumph in the life of our city and the Diocese."[103] Cardinal Mac-Rory professed pride and pleasure at the prospect of being in the city. He reminded the hundreds of people who crammed into St. Columb's Hall to welcome him that 800 years earlier, in 1136, the abbot of the Columban monastery at Doire Colmcille had traveled to Armagh to become primate and to advance the Catholic Church in Ireland.[104] Stressing the antiquity of both the Church and Derry's Catholic community, he declared that just as Derry sent Columba out to live a Christian message in the world, "today Armagh sends you the Primate to share in your rejoicing at the progress of Derry in that same work."[105] He urged his audience to continue to fight for its rights in Derry. Ending his address with a call for peace, the cardinal decried the "evil heritage" of partisanship in the North. "This violent sectarian feeling," he declared, "is not only shameful; it is perfectly absurd and ridiculous in people who all profess to be followers of the Prince of Peace."[106]

The consecration itself was solemn. The bishop and diocesan priests began before 7 a.m., blessing the church and its grounds, protecting it from evil. The ceremony lasted five hours; the final two were open to the congregation. In his sermon at the high Mass, Rev. Dr. James MacNamee, bishop of Ardagh and Clonmacnoise, celebrated the consecration as the culmination that extended beyond the ninety-seven years of the cathedral's life, beginning as a proposal in 1838, to its moment of consecration. His homily was a history lesson on the sacrifices and struggles of Ireland's Catholics. The bishop heralded the event as an iconic moment that saw its inception in the erection St. Columba's Dubh Regles (Black Abbey) in the eighth century, and continued through the Middle Ages, when O'Brolochain oversaw a cathedral at the See of Derry, the Tempul Mor. From the time of the Elizabethan conquest that saw the burning of the cathedral, the bishop noted, the people of Derry had persevered through years of persecution: "The faith lived on, enthroned in the people's hearts, enshrined in the inner temple of the soul, though there was not a shred of roof to cover them, as they gathered around their rude altars for the supreme act of Catholic worship."[107] The Church *was* the people; in consecrating St. Eugene's, Derry's Catholic community members heralded the physical embodiment of their long-standing faith.[108]

The *Journal* portrayed the consecration as nothing short of a victory for Catholic Derry, blending religion and politics with feisty and unambiguous rhetoric. Acutely aware of Catholics' position of weakness in local and provincial politics, the paper reminded readers that their community had seen worse, telling the story of the parish in terms of the death and resurrection of Catholic Derry. Beginning with Plantation and the murder of Derry's Catholic bishop, Redmond O'Gallagher, in 1601, one article described how the destruction of the cathedral was followed with an even more grievous insult to injury: the use of its stones to build the fortress walls of the city.[109] For 180 years, it continued, there was no bishop in Derry, but the English settlers did not break Catholics: "They were excluded from the city of the Planters by a decree of 1615. They were hunted, oppressed, persecuted, starved—but they refused to leave Derry. They clung to the land outside the walls, and though reduced in numbers and enduring unspeakable hardships and tortures, held their ground."[110]

The *Journal*'s tale had an uplifting ending. The story of how the small Catholic community had stayed on at Derry, in the area that now made up the West Ward, and finally in 1786 was able to build the city's first Catholic church since Plantation, the Long Tower. There "was no turning back" for Catholic Derry: "Its sufferings were not over, but no sufferings could stay its progress. It had won back the first of its possessions, and with that as a starting point, it marched on, growing in strength and numbers, to the glorious triumph now achieved."[111]

THE 1936 GERRYMANDER AND INQUIRY

It was no coincidence that *Journal* framed the narrative of Derry's Catholic community as one that had survived oppression and persisted. In fact, the cardinal himself introduced politics into consecration observances, something the *Londonderry Sentinel* found offensive and said was "adding fuel to the flames of contention."[112] Nationalists had taken up their seats again in the local Corporation in 1931 after a period of abstention from local politics. They had returned "to defend Catholic rights, to fight for fair play for the Catholic people and to repudiate and expose Unionist intolerance."[113] They wanted to "let an Ascendancy minority know that the Catholic Nationalists can no longer be treated as an inferior race in a city in which they form an overwhelming majority of the population."[114] Having returned, they were now facing a new redistricting proposal that would see their representation shrink in the Corporation.[115] At the consecration, Cardinal MacRory called the gerrymander an insult to democracy. He urged Catholics to stand firm for their rights, asserting that "sooner or later, the numbers tell."[116]

The redistricting proposal attempted to secure the city's unionist representation despite a growing Catholic nationalist population. The 1931 elections saw diminishing unionist votes in the city's North Ward. The Limited Companies Act, offering businesses a vote for each £10 valuation (up to six votes), shored up the numbers, but unionists in the Corporation had become concerned that the swelling Catholic population would outnumber Protestants at the polls. In 1934, Minister of Home Affairs Richard Dawson Bates had communicated his concerns over the Derry Corporation to James Craig, Northern Ireland's prime minister: "Unless something is done now, it is only a matter of time until Derry passes into the hands of the Nationalists and Sinn Fein parties for all time. On the other hand, if proper steps are taken now, I believe Derry can be saved for years to come."[117]

The 1936 redistricting plan achieved Dawson's goals. It reduced the number of representatives from forty to twenty-four, returning to the representation scheme of 1840 that had been replaced in 1896 but with differently drawn wards. The Corporation redrew the voting districts to ensure sixteen unionist and eight nationalist members. The sixteen unionist members would come from 7,536 unionist voters, and the eight nationalist members would come from 9,409 Nationalist voters.[118] Denying that this was a gerrymander, the Corporation voted to send the proposal to the Ministry for Home Affairs, which had to approve the measure either way. No Catholics voted for the proposal, but the unionists did unanimously, arguing that they were the ones who had a greater stake in the community, valuations in unionist areas were higher, and the vast majority of residential construction was happening in unionist areas and would eventually even out the numbers. Derry Catholics were used to losing political battles and assumed the plan would be upheld. They were as surprised as anyone when word came in April that an inquiry would be held to investigate the proposal.

This news was cause for hope. Nationalists hurried to prepare their case, mapping the ward changes that had taken place since the first significant gerrymander in 1896. In preparation for the investigation, members of the Derry Catholic Registration Association wanted to highlight the historic struggle for Catholic voters to obtain a political voice. They decided to make a Protest Covenant similar to the Ulster Covenant (see fig. 6).[119] They designed a scroll that documented the voting numbers in every major local and parliamentary election between 1918 and 1939 and showed the discrepancies between Catholic representation in parliamentary elections as compared to local ones. The numbers reflected a gap that was swiftly closing by 1936, when the redistricting plan was proposed.

Frank McAuley recalled the propaganda value of the Ulster Covenant: "The signing of that covenant was surrounded by all the solemnity it was possible to display." The Catholics of Derry needed something similar to rally public opinion and build momentum to halt the gerrymander. He proposed that St. Columb's Hall be booked for some Sunday "for the purpose of enabling voters to call in and sign the Protest." Some members of the Registration Association believed that if a long queue extended down Shipquay Street, "it would be so much more publicity." Others argued that the registration committee should go door to door, getting as many signatures as possible. Another plan was put forth to set up booths all over the city where people could sign the Covenant. The proposed Protest Covenant made it clear that the history of political gerrymander was Catholic Derry's equivalent to the Ulster Covenant—a rallying cry, a pledge, and a marker of identity. However, since the committee could not agree on how to move forward, they voted to not roll out the Covenant.[120]

Derry Catholic Registration Association.
Revision reports, years 1918-38.

Years	Number of Catholic Parliamentary Voters	Catholic changes	Number of Catholic Local Government Voters	Catholic Local Government Voters disqualified
1918-19	8961	183	6366	11
1919-20	9177	984	6868	528
1920-21	8652	699	6869	491
1921-22	9413	1551	7442	954
1922-23	9746	1879	7707	1219
1923-24	9390	1479	7421	931
1924-25	9745	1769	7578	1093
1925-26	9951	1996	7681	1195
1926-27	10166	2341	7855	1413
1927-28	10202	2442	7924	1523
1928-29	10477	2640	8066	1601
1929-30	15185	4855	8806	1580
1930-31	15104	4529	8987	1466
1931-32	15162	4516	9049	1689
1932-33	15344	4502	9116	1643
1933-34	15681	4728	9265	1742
1934-35	15896	4878	9326	1802
1935-36	15962	4923	9409	1873
1936-37	16082	4931	9543	1925
1937-38	15922	5001	9527	2021
1938-39	15953	5194	9691	2247

Figure 6. Image of the Protest Covenant prototype created by the committee.

Ultimately, symbolism was downsized in exchange for detail, and the Covenant was never unveiled to the public in that form. Instead, the *Journal* ran an article, "The Reason for Gerrymanders," using the data that the Catholic Registration Association had compiled since 1918 and narrating the efforts made since 1885 to keep nationalist and Catholic representation in check. These included a three-year residency requirement in 1932, later changed to a seven-year residency requirement for people from Ireland but only six months for people from England, Scotland, or Wales. It also included the 1928 Limited Company Franchise Act, or "the company vote." This legislation increased unionist votes by providing business owners with a separate vote from their civic one.[121]

When the inquiry set up in Derry, the inspector presented and picked up several salient points of information. All twelve of the Corporation members who had refused to pass the resolution were Catholics. The North Ward, which had been obliterated, had previously been a unionist stronghold, but in recent years had seen its Protestant majority reduced to fewer than 500 people. The North Ward was combined with the overwhelmingly Protestant East Ward; parts of the West Ward also went into the East Ward. The rest of the West Ward became subsumed by the overwhelmingly Catholic South Ward. Questions regarding the logic for the new districts were apt; one of the many bizarre changes put the Long Tower School grounds into two separate wards. It seemed impossible that the plan would go through, as the inquiry team itself had difficulty finding anything other than a political justification for the plan. Councillor Kerr had even admitted to a Ballymena audience that the objective was to keep the unionist majority intact.[122] In a letter to the Corporation, the inquiry team concluded:

> Very considerable opposition was offered to the scheme at the Inquiry, while the evidence put forward in support of it was of a most unsatisfactory character. The new line proposed as a boundary line between the two wards was not separated by a river, followed in some courses very difficult to define and no evidence was given in justification of this complication, and none of the witnesses examined on behalf of the scheme had ascertained or were aware of how this boundary would actually run.[123]

However, the Ministry for Home Affairs ultimately approved the redistricting, agreeing that the Corporation was too unwieldy with forty councilors and needed to be a smaller legislative body for the sake of efficiency. As a result, twenty-four members sat in the new Corporation, eight nationalists and sixteen unionists, despite the substantial Catholic majority in the city. Once more, opportunities narrowed for nationalists to influence local politics.

After the elections of 1938, nationalist councilor Maxwell spoke for the Catholics of Derry when he expressed a sense of injustice:

> The eight members of my side of the House represent the majority of the people—the majority of Corporation electors, because we have 9,000, or 2,000 more than all the others put together; [we have] the majority of Parliamentary electors because we have 16,000, a majority of 5,000 more than all the other put together; and [we have] a majority of the citizens, because we have 29,000 or 11,000 more than the others put together. Each man on this side of the House represents almost 1,200 Corporation electors, but only approximately one half of that number is sufficient to return any person on the Unionist side of the House.[124]

Gerrymander was old news. For Catholics, the 1936 gerrymander was simultaneously incomprehensible and all too familiar. A political defeat for the community, it also carried material consequences. More aware than ever that unionists were willing to go to extremes to hold electoral advantage, Catholics grappled with the most significant outcome of those maneuvers: poor housing. Currently crowded into one electoral ward, it became increasingly difficult for Derry's Catholic population to leave that area, because to do so would upset the electoral balance in other wards. Plans and proposals for new construction contended with the political imperative to build only in the already overcrowded South Ward. Unionists would not risk scattering the Catholic population into the other wards, and Catholics had neither the financial collateral to fund construction nor the political clout to gain approval to build anywhere outside the South Ward. As a result, the housing conditions for Catholics in the city continued to deteriorate.

Housing in Derry had been on the political and social agenda since 1920, when the short-lived Nationalist Corporation set up a housing subcommittee to try to address the problem. In 1927, a tragedy underscored the fact that the problem had not disappeared. In September of that year, a tenement went up in flames, taking the lives of two families. The *Journal* blamed the fire on Corporation neglect, decrying the "famine" of houses in the city:

If the Derry Corporation was doing its duty, tenements and flats, that in a fire would mean almost certain death for its occupants, would not be passed for human habitation. They are tolerated here for the reason that they serve as some sort of screen for the Corporation's own neglect to provide sufficient housing accommodation for the people. In no city in Ireland is there the same famine of houses as in Derry and in no city has the Municipal Council done so little to solve this vital problem.[125]

In the 1930s, the Bogside's John McGilligan and others established a Tenants' Defense League to fight unfair rents and to push owners of substandard housing to make improvements on their properties. Most Catholics, though, took what they could get, probably concluding that "a half a loaf was better than no bread."[126] Most of the homes in the South Ward had only cold water. There were no indoor toilets, and sometimes several houses shared a single outdoor privy. Looking back in the 1980s, local community developer and activist Paddy "Bogside" Doherty described typical housing at the time, suggesting the concerns were probably justified. At the same time, the community had become adept at "making do" and considered these crowded and rudimentary spaces home:

At school, I was drawing one time and I was asked to draw my own house where I lived—your home—and I drew this house in the Bogside. And remember, it was a house that you nearly jump up and touch the eaves-spout, it had one door and one window and to me it was home, it was a fantastic place and there were a lot of us living in it, so I drew this. I did the door, I put a "20" on the door, I put the knocker and I put the handle on it. I put the window in it and I also put the shutter on because away back in the times of the troubles in the Twenties you weren't allowed to show your light, so all the places had shutters that locked up at night, we used to put a bar through and there was a bit of a nut on the inside you know and our house had one even in those days retained and I did this and I put the curtains on the windows and the slates on the roof. . . . And the teacher comes along and he says, "My god, where did you ever see a house like that?" and he very quickly sketched another story with two more windows and said, "that's a house."[127]

The Corporation established a housing and planning committee again in 1937, but it reviewed few building permits and authorized virtually no new construction. According to the census taken that year, there were nearly three times as many tenements in the South Ward as there were in any other district in the city. In 1939, Bishop Farren asked the priests in the Derry churches to conduct a housing census. However, the war interrupted this work and focus moved away from housing. In 1943, as unionist councillors clamored for a plan to bring tourists to the city to explore its architecture, Councillor Paddy Maxwell reminded them that housing, not tourism, remained the highest priority for Catholics. He said he knew a house in which seventeen families resided—ninety-seven people in all—and "they had that all over the city."[128] For Catholics and nationalists, however, little faith was left in the will of Corporation to ameliorate the squalor. For them, politics and housing had long been an intertwined problem; new housing was needed but there was no room in the South Ward, the area of the city where Catholics—and their votes—resided.

The flip side of housing shortage was the cultural life it bolstered and anchored in the streets and lanes of the Catholic area. In 1945, when Paddy Maxwell, Corporation member and chairman of the Nationalist Registration Society, declared that "Derry is an Irish city," he spoke largely of the tightly knit communities that housed the nationalist population. Behind the scenes, they maintained traditions through stories and rituals, tying them to a past that was equal parts invention, creation, myth, and faith. During the interwar period, the majority of Catholics in Derry, as in all of Northern Ireland, experienced Irish nationalism as a primarily cultural, rather than a political, identity. In 1977, poet Seamus Heaney, a native of County Londonderry who had been a boarder at St. Columb's College, described his memories of this phenomenon from his own 1940s childhood and explained the ways it contrasted with an overtly political Irish identity: "There's a Popish house, definitely nationalistic in their approach. They thought of themselves as Irish. They were against the Unionist majority and against the British connection but had no active political Sinn Féin ideology."[129]

In Heaney's depiction of Irish Catholic homes in the North, being Irish and Catholic was less an ideological position than an embodied and experienced one. It was felt more than thought, lived more than articulated. Identity was expressed, experienced, and shared in small acts that rarely went remarked upon explicitly. Festivals, events, and processions established memorial traditions and celebrated Irish Catholic life in Derry, but memory flourished in daily performances of habit, ritual, and tradition. Through heritage, people often explicitly and intentionally (and selectively) draw on elements of the past to assert or redefine desires, worries, or principles in the present. Here, subtler, less consciously staged performances and expressions of memory transmitted and preserved "collectively remembered values" through tradition, ritual, and very specific and particular ways of talking, doing, and being.[130]

Quotidian rhythms of family and community life connected city residents to their Irish and rural roots. Observing and maintaining rituals tied Derry's Catholics to older, often rural, folk and religious cultural patterns. Stories, whether they were religious, superstitious, or tales meant primarily to entertain, embodied and encapsulated people's long-standing and deeply felt values, concerns, and hopes. If oral storytelling was believed to be a dying art in the 1930s in Ireland—demonstrated by the extensive oral history collection projects underway in the Free State—many stories still circulated. On the streets and in the alleys, children's street rhymes maintained oral tradition and kept alive a rendering of events and expression of community attitudes that were in keeping with a long Irish oral tradition. Diana Taylor calls these "acts of transfer," an engaged and fluid process of transmission that centers around participation.[131] Particularly for Derry's working classes, the stories people told and the rituals in which they engaged helped to express and maintain a consistent and coherent cultural life in the wake of economic depression and political defeat.[132] These were significant in their ordinariness, important in their apparent innocuousness. More than art, or entertainment, or even moral education, the rites, rituals, rhymes, and tales enabled Catholics in Derry to animate and share core values far from the unwanted attentions of the police, the state, even the Catholic middle classes, whose eyes were fixed on propriety and modernity. In that they made it possible for Derry's Catholics to package and transfer important cultural information from generation to generation and to instill core values and principles that the community upheld, they were crucial components of remembrance.[133]

Women, in particular, were responsible for cultural transfer and for holding the line between Protestant Derry and Irish cultural heritages without allowing differences to calcify into animosity at the personal level. When Shane Conway looked back on his childhood in the Bogside as an adult in the 1950s, he remembered that for children, "the *mater* was particularly well versed in such subjects."[134]

Within these cultural expressions lay the roots of Irish cultural identity and foundations for Catholic cultural and nationalist political resistance. De Certeau described these sorts of tactics: "They are like waves slipping in among the cracks on the rocks by the shore, defiling the established order . . . the only way you know they are there is because they erode the established order."[135]

Religious rituals, many of which had been adapted from older pagan rites and not acknowledged by formal Catholic leaders, reminded members of the community of their spiritual, familial, and neighborly responsibilities. Before television became commonplace in the 1960s, there remained snippets and shadows of an older folk culture replete with fairies, curses, and banshees; its traditions and beliefs occasionally surfaced in Derry. In the 1920s and 30s, traditions marking the change of seasons and celebrating Ireland's patron saints were still maintained by many of Derry's Catholics, particularly those with strong Donegal ties. These rituals carried both religious and folk importance and had been observed for hundreds of years. Passed down from generation to generation, they were recast to lend meaning to present contexts when necessary. The potency of stories and rituals lay precisely in their familiarity and the assurances they brought through allusions to faith, family, and community.

"Old Derry" traditions embodied and represented cultural ties that could not be severed by politics or geography—they could not be partitioned like political connections. On St. Patrick's Day, St. Brigid's Eve, May Day (or Lá Bealtaine), the Feast of the Assumption, and All Souls' Day, Derry's Catholics engaged in rituals that enabled them to perform and embody important aspects of cultural identity. Whereas St. Brigid's Eve and All Souls' Day were family-centered, St. Patrick's Day and August 15 focused more on linking the community through acts of faith and expressions of Irish heritage.

St. Brigid's Day was celebrated in the beginning of February, usually on February 2, a date that fell exactly midway between the winter solstice and spring equinox. It marked the beginning of spring and was celebrated partly to pray for the good health of one's household. A Donegal Gaelic saying had it that "February kills the sheep; March kills the people."[136] The rituals around the feast day were believed to ward off ill-health during the crucial late winter months, when both food stores and incomes were typically low. A festival originally called "Imbolc" and dedicated to the Irish goddess of healing, it was later adapted as a Christian celebration. On St. Brigid's Eve, many Derry children and their parents gathered new rushes of long green grass along streams and fashioned them into sheaths. These were blessed and braided into crosses around the family fireplace to commemorate the miracle of St. Brigid's transformation of food into rushes when challenged by her father, who disapproved of Brigid's acts of charity. The crosses were sprinkled with holy water and hung in every room in the house to protect inhabitants from evil and illness.

St. Patrick's Day arrived next in the calendar year. It was a solemn religious celebration throughout all of Ireland during this period. Unlike in the Free State/Éire, it was not recognized as a religious holiday in Northern Ireland; however, Catholic schools were closed and many working adults took the day off, suggesting tacit approval by Protestant employers.[137]

The holiday provided Derry Catholics one of their few opportunities to identify outwardly as Irish during the interwar years, by wearing a cluster of shamrocks on one's jacket or coat. Collecting one's own shamrocks remained a Derry tradition until the 1950s. Those from the Bogside would go up the hill to the countryside (where the Creggan Estate was eventually built) for their shamrocks, and residents of the Brandywell would collect theirs as they walked along the Great Northern Railway tracks along the Letterkenney Road. In addition, entrepreneurs such as Sean Reddin and Paddy McGilloway grew shamrocks along a small stream in Pennyburn to sell to local shops. Attending Mass and "wearing the green" as a symbol of Irish identity were much of the day's cultural expression, but one Derry storyteller recounted that after Mass, many local men went to the pubs to "drown their shamrocks," contemporary parlance for serious inebriation.[138]

Drinking was not the only pastime on St. Patrick's Day, however. Derry Catholics celebrated the day as both a religious and national festival, and an opportunity to commit anew to their faith and to Ireland. Traditional observances included Mass in the morning, a procession in the afternoon, and a concert or dance in the evening. Districts vied to erect the most ornate arches, the designs of which were taken as seriously as "a state secret."[139] Shane Conway remembered that the keenest rivals for best arch were from Bogside and Bishop Street; on the evening before St. Patrick's Day, each street would send scouts into the other to spy on their arch design.

Even in their estrangement from the Free State, or perhaps because of it, for the people of Derry the week surrounding the feast day became a platform for the celebration of all things Irish. Masses were said in Gaelic and collections were taken up for the Irish Language Fund. Stores stocked up on and displayed Irish goods. In addition, in the years before the Special Powers Acts banned them, there were Gaelic sports matches, Irish and Gaelic music concerts, reunions, and gatherings, in short, expressions of "everything that being Irish implies."[140] Even though processions and demonstrations were banned, Derry Catholics crossed the border and took part in celebrations in Donegal. A green flag was hoisted on the Slaughter House. They remembered the days before Partition when those from surrounding areas would all gather in Derry, following the same route every year for the St. Patrick's Day procession that gathered at the foot of Brae Head, went to the top of Creggan Street, and wound through Derry's Catholic neighborhoods.[141]

August 15 was another community-wide festival. It was widely celebrated in Derry with bonfires and céilís that lasted through the night. The 15th observed the Feast of the Assumption, when Mary ascended into heaven. Originally celebrated early in August as the harvest festival of Lughnasa, it was incorporated into the Irish Catholic calendar. Lady Day gave Derry Catholics the opportunity to come together for music, socializing, and dancing around the bonfire, thereby cementing community identity without overt confrontation during the height of the marching season. Effigies of "anti-Irish or anti-Catholic" figures were burned, echoing the Protestant tradition of burning effigies of Lundy on the anniversary of the shutting of the Gates every December.[142]

Lady Day, especially, was a response to the Protestant celebrations on August 12 in Derry. In Seamus Deane's description of the summer of 1949, he referred to the Feast of the Assumption bonfires that ignited the Catholic quarter of the city: "It was a church festival but we made it into a political one as well, to answer the fires of the twelfth. The police would sometimes make us put out the fires or try to stop us collecting old car tires or chopping down trees in preparation. . . . When the bonfires were lit at the foot of the sloping, parallel streets against the stone wall above the park, the night sky reddened around the rising furls of black tire smoke."[143]

Halloween and All Souls' Day were family-centered holidays. In the 1920s and '30s, most Derry Catholics engaged in traditions associated with All Souls' Day, which followed the feast of Samhain (Halloween). Halloween itself retained vestiges of the days when Derry Catholics believed more firmly in folk and fairy lore. Shane Conway remembered, in the 1950s, a song heard frequently in Derry when he was young at Halloween:

> Down by the holly bush
> On the edge of the mireland
> The wee folk will gather for their rites of enchantment;
> Round and round the bush they'll go,
> Wearing sparkling silver shoon,
> All in sweet contentment
> Underneath the golden moon.
>
> Down by the hollybush
> they'll bring me to fairyland
> On prancing steeds as white as the stars,
> Over many a brae and moorland.
> On and on I'll ride with them
> 'til the grey dawn breaking
> When Halloween has come and gone
> and from my dream I'm waking.[144]

Like the Feast of the Assumption, All Souls' originated in a pagan ritual that had been incorporated within the folds of Catholicism. People believed that on this night, souls of their loved ones who had died would come to visit their homes. Houses were cleaned fastidiously. In addition, people cleared fires and placed bowls of fresh water out for souls who might visit the home. Many would go visit their loved ones' gravesites before attending Mass, and then return home, going to bed very early.[145] Embodied in these practices was the belief in a strong connection between the living and dead and in the permeability of the veil between the two. The practices that continued throughout the 1930s in Derry reached back hundreds of years, connecting contemporary residents with traditions and values that had been passed down for many generations.

Other holidays had their associated rituals. On New Year's Eve, families opened wide their front doors, to allow the old year to depart and the new to enter. In the days before Palm Sunday, one would see many Catholics at the Derry City Cemetery searching for palms to have blessed. On Good Friday, many women from the working-class neighborhoods of Derry washed their hair as a way of identifying with Mary Magdalene, one of the women who cleansed Jesus's body after it had been taken down from the cross.[146]

Most celebrations with pagan roots had been Christianized, but celebrations of May Day were still noted during the years before World

Figure 7. Neighbors gather around St. Columb's Well.

War II. Called "Bealtaine" in Gaelic, May Day derived from Celtic tradition and had been observed since before the arrival of Christianity in Ireland. Many Derry residents remembered one devotee of the ancient rite of spring—Nailor's Row resident Paddy Dean. Every year on May 1, Dean would hang a bunch of "whinbush" (gorse) on his front door and on the doors of all of his neighbors. At the end of the day, he took them down and used them to light a big bonfire at the bottom of the street; it was a long-standing tradition to light the fires with gorse. Bealtaine, in traditional lore, was when Druids traditionally lit bonfires for the purposes of healing and purification. People would greet one another with "Good fire!"

Dean thus engaged in a centuries' old ritual of the beginning of the spring. The gorse was used to ward off evil spirits from animals and inhabitants, to spur fertility, and to express hope for a prosperous planting season and harvest.[147] By the 1920s, it was also still possible to find women in Derry gathering yarrow and primroses for Bealtaine. Yarrow had traditional associations as a protective and healing herb and was used in charms to protect people from the fairies. It was also popular in love charms of all kinds and would be strewn outside homes, along with primroses, to attract love and ensure protection. In 1928, "Onlooker" observed he had only seen a few houses with yarrow branches above their doors for Bealtaine and was saddened: "To me it seems like a breaking of tradition that marked us a distinct race, reaching back in our traits, our characteristics and our usages into the dimness of the ages past."[148] Even though perhaps only a few residents of Catholic Derry engaged in the practice by the 1920s and 30s, their engagements in the ritual kept it alive in the city and fresh in the minds of their neighbors and friends.

May Day celebrations were not the only vestiges of alternative beliefs and explanations for events still in practice. One former Derryman recounted a fairy thorn (that is, a hawthorn bush) that stood on the grounds of the old Foyle College.[149] As A. R. Foster explained in a 1972 reminiscence, a local gardener, "Hughey the Scalper" from Inishowen, warned him not to cut the fairy thorn that grew near his home. Many local people believed that hawthorn bushes were gathering places for spirits, fairies, or "little people," and Hughey commanded him to leave it alone. "You won't touch it," he said. "Man, that thorn has been there since before the siege of Derry."[150] Foster explained that his uncle, a pragmatic man not given to belief in fairies, ignored Hughey's warning and sawed off the hawthorn's branches. Retribution was fast and furious, according to lore. "Next day, cycling in Clarendon Street, he fell and broke his skull." Then, the family and even Hughey himself believed that the fairy spell was lifted. Foster's father and Hughey each trimmed the thorn. As he explained, they both suffered. "My father's hair fell out in round patches, and Hughey fell over the half-door of his pig house and broke two ribs."[151]

Foster went on to explain how he finally got involved in the drama by sawing off a bough from the hawthorn. As he explained it, "That was on Thursday; on Saturday I was carried home from Dublin with a displaced cartilage, knocked out in a football match and had to spend weeks in bed." The hawthorn was extremely powerful in the eyes of local men. To interfere with it was to interfere with a long-standing belief in and respect for stories about fairies, if not for the fairies themselves. In Foster's Derry, every man who cut the hawthorn tree "suffered and suffered quickly."[152] Information that might offer pertinent clues to the physical and cultural landscape habited by the tree has been lost in time; all that remained by the 1920s was the warning not to interfere with it. However, if we understand fairy stories as "pre-modern culture's way of storing information," there was probably good reason to leave the tree alone. As Angela Bourke has explained in her excavation of fairy stories, "Fairies belong to the margins, and so can serve as reference points and metaphors for all that is marginal in human life. This mostly underground existence allows them to stand for the unconscious, the secret, for everything that is unspeakable in human life."[153]

There may have been myriad reasonable explanations for avoiding the tree and the space surrounding it. Perhaps the college grounds were an unsafe space for Catholics. Perhaps chopping off boughs of any trees had been an offence that met harsh justice. Perhaps the college itself was widely seen as a place to avoid. It is hard to say what may have led people to view that particular hawthorn as something untouchable. Harder still to explain are the tales of strict and swift retribution that followed interference with the fairy thorn. Perhaps, in an inverse of Bourke's analysis, the wider social universe did not explain the significance of the hawthorn, but vice versa. Accidents, injuries, and bad luck were the lot of the many, not the few, in Depression-era Derry. The enchanted tree could offer meaning and reason for the countless misfortunes that befell local people.[154] Stories like Foster's tale of the fairy thorn abounded throughout Derry, indeed all over Ireland, for a variety of reasons. They encapsulated within them lessons, warnings, or longer histories that were not written down. And so the stories told above tie Catholic Derry to a much older, longer community narrative, but other local tales served as entertaining parables, replete with the values and concerns of the city's residents. Many Derry ghost stories that originated before or during this era held within them the same kinds of preoccupations, concerns, and lessons as the story above.

GHOST STORIES

In "A Derry Ghost," originally told and written in Gaelic, there were two Catholic families living on the Waterside of Derry, the Meehans and Dohertys. In each house lived a boy of the same age; they were best friends throughout childhood.[155] They left together to study for the priesthood at Maynooth; after ordination, Father Doherty went to Scotland; Father Meehan was assigned to a parish in Moville, County Donegal. The two aunts who had raised the priests lived alone in the Waterside house. Sometime between 1900 and the early 1920s, there began to appear "a dead light," accompanied by loud noises every night from 11 p.m. to 1 a.m.[156] Neighbors began to write to Father Doherty asking him to come home from Scotland to sort out the trouble. Father Doherty wrote to his friend in Moville, who went to the Waterside as soon as he could. When he arrived at the house, heard the noises, and saw the light, he knew he needed support and called for the priest from the Long Tower.

The two priests prepared a plan for banishing the spirit present in the house into a shed up the street. When they entered, they saw a figure standing in a corner of one room. It looked like an upright goat. The priests ordered it to leave, and it went directly into the shed. There were no further problems until the aunts died and the house was sold to an English couple. In 1926, the lights and noises returned. The couple, having heard of Father Meehan and the parish priest's work in banishing the spirit, wrote to him.

This time, the bishop came with him to the Waterside house. They discovered that the roof of the shed had blown off, allowing the spirit to escape. The spirit was in the exact same spot in the house as he had been the previous time. The new residents said that they had built a small coalhouse at the back of the house, and it had not been used yet. The bishop entered the room where the spirit dwelled and ordered it into the coalhouse; after it went, the door was locked. The bishop asked if the couple had seen anything unusual. The woman replied that she'd seen something that "looked like a goat walking on its hind legs."

"Well, you certainly saw it," said Father Meehan. He imposed a penance on the couple to abstain from meat on Fridays. Soon after the event, they converted to Catholicism "and remained Catholics ever afterwards."[157] The story effectively tied together the pull of the supernatural, the power of God, faith and the Catholic Church, the fears attendant with leaving Derry, and the importance of friends. If Father Doherty felt helpless in Scotland as his aunts were tormented by a dramatic spirit, he could fall back on his childhood friend to try to address the problem of the haunting. Father Meehan, too, required backup; he turned to the priest of the Long Tower and then the bishop to exorcise the spirit. The English couple was integrated into the story, and by extension into the community, by their belief in the power of the priests and their choice to convert to Catholicism. Not only did the story entertain those who told it and those who listened eagerly, but it also reminded members of the community what mattered most—family, friends, church, and faith. Mysterious evils could easily present themselves in Derry, but could successfully be held at bay, though never obliterated altogether.

Another popular ghost story, which originated slightly earlier and was told in several versions, was even more explicit about the presence of evil. In "The Devil and the Long Tower Gamblers," there used to be a farm at the top of Howard Street, just outside the city walls, owned by a man named Milligan. It burned down in the early 1900s, but some of the outbuildings remained on the site. One was used as a blacksmith's forge. Men who lived in Bishop Street and other lanes in the Long Tower area used to meet there to play cards at night. As the tale went, the men were conscious of financial scarcity and bet only nominal amounts.

One night, one of the regular card players met a stranger at a local pub. The man professed an interest in cards, so the Derry man extended an invitation to their regular game at the forge. No one was happy that a strange man had been invited to play. However, he started to bet and lose large sums of money, mollifying the group. After a long losing streak, though, the stranger began to win. As the story went, the stakes kept getting higher and higher. The gambling men got desperate and began "backing beyond their means, most of them betting their wages and going home without any money."[158]

One man commented that he would "sell his soul" to best the stranger, who, in turn, laughed and banged hard on the card table. At that moment, the man who was dealing the deck dropped cards when the table had been jostled. When the dealer glanced down, he saw that instead of feet, the stranger in their midst had cloven hooves. He jumped from the table and ran, yelling to his mates to run.

But the man who had joked about selling his soul was frozen to the spot; he seemed to be completely stuck. Two others went back, and they tried to yank him away, but the stranger held onto him tightly. All the men returned and together they pulled their friend free. They all ran down into The Wells, only stopping when they arrived at St. Columb's Well. They were terrified and spent. So the story goes, in the glow from the gaslight, they could make out fingers, burnt like a brand into the arm of the man who had been pulled away. "They blessed themselves and at that moment they saw the flames lick into the night sky."[159] The next day, only ashes remained of the old forge; it had gone up in flames that fateful night.

The story was a powerful one for many reasons. It reflected the tenuous financial realities of Derry men and suggested that gambling might begin as an inconsequential diversion but could become something much more unsettling very quickly. The tale underscored that strangers should not be trusted even as it highlighted the necessity of friends to protect and rescue one another. Community was paramount; after all, it took the strength of all the men to rescue the one whose soul was on the line; in a pinch, the members of one's community could be relied on to do the right thing, even if individuals could not. The devil might present himself in

many guises, but the story illustrated the steadfast and assured presence
of God and the ringing power of faith. The Long Tower men ran without
stopping until they reached St. Columb's Well. Here under the protection
of their patron saint they blessed themselves, thus destroying the devil's
hold over them.

Not all Derry ghosts were malicious. In fact, in two ghost stories
that originated around the 1920s, the spirits of the departed came to protect and safeguard members of their families. "The Great-Grandmother's
Warning" depicted a typical family from the Glen, where the husband
was working in England and the women of the family worked in Rosemount shirt factory.[160] In the home central to the story, four generations
all dwelled in the same small terraced house—the great-grandmother,
grandmother and her husband, and their daughter, her husband, and a
new baby.

The great-grandmother had always taken care of the children in the
house; she would often rock them to sleep in her rocking chair in the
corner of the kitchen. When she passed away, her daughter and granddaughter were heartbroken. With their husbands away, they also needed
a childminder. Since both women worked in the factory, a neighbor
agreed to look after the baby.

One day while she was working, the story goes, the baby's mother
thought she could hear a rocking chair, even above the din of the factory
floor. Try as she did to ignore it, it just got louder. Next, she was sure she
heard the sound of her grandmother singing a lullaby. The woman ran
from the collar-room to find her mother, who was on a different floor of
the factory. Her mother believed her daughter's story and thought that it
was a warning of some kind. So, the mother took her daughter and together they ran home. When they entered the kitchen, the neighbor
wasn't there. But the old rocking chair was going at full pace in the corner. No one was in the room. In fact, it was filled with gas, which was
leaking out of an old gas pipe that was used for the gas iron. Upstairs, they
found the baby lying quite still; it wasn't until his mother ran with him
outside that he began to come to. Meanwhile, the neighbor was trying
to recover from gas inhalation in the backyard. She explained that she
thought she had passed out, and then immediately began to become hys-
terical with worry and guilt over the baby.

When they told her how they knew to return to the house, she admitted that just before she had become overcome by the gas, she saw the chair rocking but had discounted it, thinking it must have been pushed by the wind coming in through a window. When the women and baby went back inside the house, the rocking chair stood still and silently in the corner.

The worries and preoccupations of the poor and working women of Derry surface in this ghost story. The plight of overcrowded spaces, men living away from home and the necessity of women in the workplace, frustration at appliances that don't work properly and insufficient funds to replace them, and the concerns working women had about their children all herald the crisis in the story—a baby entrusted to the care of someone outside the family unit.

The importance of elders comes through strongly. The protection of the grandmother was paramount to the baby's well-being, but the mother's belief that a message was being delivered through the strange sounds the granddaughter heard spurred the women to action. This was not only the tale of a protective and present spirit, but also of the importance of faith, maintaining belief in things beyond one's conscious understanding. The young mother and her baby benefited from her mother's trust in something that was clearly "superstitious"; the story and its popularity suggest that the people of Derry did not want to lose altogether their belief in spirits of the dead. It also suggests that folk customs, such as believing in the presence of the dead, passed down from mothers to daughters.

"The Haunting on Wellington Street" proffers a very similar message with a different moral; it is still told regularly in Derry and exists in many permutations. The story centers around a family with many children that saw the unexpected death of their mother. The family's eldest daughter, Mary, had to take responsibility for caring for the younger children; her father was little help as he had begun to drink heavily and was rarely home. As the story goes, Mary tried her best. With little money for coal to keep the house warm, winter was difficult. On one very cold night, she put the children to bed early; it was the warmest place for them. The baby, though, was coughing and could not settle. Mary didn't know what to do—when her mother was alive, she would put a big army greatcoat on top of the other blankets to add extra warmth. But when she tried to get up from the bed to get the coat, the baby stirred and cried. As Mary lay there fretting about what to do, "the bedroom door opened and the figure of her mother came in with the coat and laid it gently over the other bed. She shushed the children and they fell asleep again."[161]

Mary had no fear; she felt that her mother was still watching over them. When the baby fell asleep, she went downstairs. The fire had been lit and the house had been tidied. Mary waited for her father to come home and told him what had happened. At first, he did not believe her. But it happened again, and then he too believed that the spirit of his dead wife was present in the home. The man told the tale to his priest, who suggested that the wife could not rest in peace since she worried that her children were not being looked after properly. The father took the pledge, swearing not to drink again. The mother's ghost never returned.

In this tale, the familiar troubles of poverty and illness are secondary to the distraught father's reliance on alcohol. The ghost of Mary's mother was a protective and benevolent spirit, but it remained that her soul was agitated. Allowing her to rest in peace was the most important goal for the family; the priest's push for abstinence solved two problems at the same time. Derry women's role in telling these stories and keeping them alive was an easy way for them to draw on folk traditions to transmit values that led directly to healthier and more stable families.

Similarly, Derry street rhymes transmitted stories, opinions, and cultural identities. Their context lent them innocence; they also passed on important information and taught young children the correct opinions to adopt. Just like learning language, learning street rhymes inculcated young Derry Catholics in the norms of their community. Some rhymes simply reflected on the harsh realities of Bogside life in the 1930s. At the same time, though, they insisted on the importance of self-respect and dignity:

Oh, it's tough, mighty tough, in Walker's Square
But they always wash their face and comb their hair.
They all go to Mass on Sundays and to Arthur's Pawn on Mondays.
Yes, it's tough, mighty tough, in Walker's Square.[162]

Figure 8. Children looking down William Street in the 1930s.

Occasionally, street rhymes reflected and articulated contemporary political stances and attitudes towards people in authority. There were many derogatory rhymes about King Billy and various members of the British royal family, but some of the rhymes talked about those closer to home and to their own historical moment. In one Derry rhyme, Éamon de Valera is castigated for standing aside and doing nothing as the North was partitioned. In another rhyme, the ubiquitous policeman on his beat was simultaneously mocked and portrayed as a despotic character who had the power to punish you severely for the slightest of crimes:

> De Valera
> One, two, three aleera
> I spy De Valera
> Sitting on his bumbleera
> Eating chocolate biscuits.[163]

A Bobby
There's a bobby 'round the corner
With buttons on his coat.
If he sees you playing football
He will grab you by the throat.
He will land you up in Derry jail
And swear your life away.[164]

Some street-corner chants articulated Derry Catholics' religious and folk beliefs. Below, "I Met a Man" recounts a familiar story of a haunted staircase in a Bogside house; "St. Columba" humanizes and personalizes the saints. Here, Ireland's patron saint, Patrick, stands out as heroic for not snitching and highlights a key survival tactic for children and adults in the days of oppressive oversight from the police and B Specials:

I Met a Man
As I was going up the stairs
I met a man who wasn't there.
He wasn't there again today.
I wish that man would go away.[165]

St. Columba
St. Columba broke a winda
And he blamed it on St. John.
St. John blamed it on St. Patrick
And St. Patrick never let on.[166]

If history paints an image of an unbending and often inhumane Irish Catholicism during this period, Derry's women remember their mothers having a much more instrumental relationship with their faith and with Church authority figures during the interwar period. Madeleine McCully described the evening ritual of gathering around after her prayers as her mother read from *The Book of Saints*:

Well, I thought she would read from it. But it would be, "St. Teresa was born and she was this lovely little girl. And she was very good to her mammy and all of this." So, she just told us stories and I thought they were in this book. When my mother died, I got this book, *The Lives of the Saints.* Teresa, born, such and such a date. Died. Venerated at Lisieux. I mean. So. She just told us stories and I thought they were all in this book. And I was dying to get this book.[167]

Church doctrine might have dictated some of the rituals that formed the architecture of family life, but it did not penetrate as deeply as one might assume. Improvisation was an integral part of Catholic cultural life. It is important to note that for McCully, storytelling was just as much a part of her inheritance and her identity as the Church and its teachings and rites were. In explaining her mother's penchant for making up her own "stories of the saints," Madeleine McCully referred to Donegal, to the family homestead where she spent summers as a child in the 1940s: "It was known as a 'céili' house. 'Céili' means together. So people would come and tell stories and yarns and all that. We of course were sent off to bed. But, my great aunt always left a mattress on the floor and that kept the door open. So we would lie down and listen to these stories. So, I mean, becoming, late in life, a storyteller, it was just natural. I could see where my mother got that from."[168]

The stories and rhymes described above were not only texts; they were performances. During the interwar period, they functioned in important ways as both. Echoing long traditions of Irish oral culture, they were versatile and subtle communication tools that defined, reinforced, and supported the community's understanding of itself. As Glassie explained in his exploration of the meanings of stories in Ballymenone, County Fermanagh, the stories operated as texts, coordinating "multiple responsibilities to time, to the past event, the present situation and the future of the community."[169] Entertaining as they were and were meant to be, the stories and rhymes were no less important. The places where stories were shared, the way they were told, the words that were chosen—all of these mattered in relation to the cultural experiences of Catholic working-class Derry: "As entertainment, stories intend functions, they feed their listeners, nurturing their future life together. As entertainment, stories are art. Their discourse is more than the transparent veil through which plot is read."[170]

In all of these ways, identity and experience infused everyday life with a set of values and sensibilities that made Catholic Derry different from both Protestant Derry and from the "Free State." Woven through city life were the memories of a range of experiences that were indeed exceptional—ties to rural cultural inheritances, the ways poverty led to mutuality and a culture of sharing, the fragility of public life, and the dislocations that resulted from Partition. Expression of these memories, though fluid, also offered structure and order to daily life. The truth was that for Catholics and nationalists in the North, maintaining traditions and one kind of order upset a different order. With unionism flexing its cultural muscles and nationalism fallen into beleaguered status, Catholic community life remained robust, vibrant, and coherent. Through stories and rituals, Derry's Catholic community maintained its Irish identity. As World War II came to an end, a new era commenced in Northern Irish politics. It saw Derry's Catholics and nationalists fired up once more to take on some of the larger questions of local and provincial/national political life. Without their traditions and the spaces that gave them voice from the creation of the border through the war, it would have been difficult indeed to emerge in the postwar period with a cohesive and vibrant community.

Chapter Four

___

TICKLING THE LION'S TALE, 1945–1962

Eighty-nine-year-old John Doherty watched the procession of Thanks-giving in early September 1945 from a chair that had been carried onto the street so he could observe expressions of gratitude for Derry's survival of World War II. "I've never seen anything like it, not even in America," said Doherty as he watched Derry Catholics walk quietly through the Bogside in a procession of the Eucharist.[1] More than 20,000 men, women, and children had gathered to engage in a public act of thanks.

They had prepared for weeks, building grottoes and making flags and banners. Volunteers such as Eddie Coolie and Dickie Connor built the Brandywell grotto in the Lecky Road, for example, with donated materi-als, in this spirit of thanks in the spring of 1945.[2] Air raid shelters were recast as symbols of glory when Bogside residents painted them in papal colors and adorned them with flowers. On the evening before the proces-sion, families, "armed with buckets and brushes, washed clean the two miles of roadway along which the Eucharistic procession was to pass."[3] Gathering at St. Eugene's, the procession made its way to the murmur of Rosary beads and the music of hymns until it arrived at St. Columb's Col-lege for the benediction. From a purpose-built outdoor altar, Bishop Farren invoked St. Columba and Catholic Derry's storied past as he her-alded the city's survival: "I am as proud of you and as proud of our city as ever Colmcille was proud of this, his first monastery, his first school."[4]

Clergy, journalists, and the police took pains both to underscore and to secure the peaceful nature of the gathering. One reporter celebrated the lack of overt sectarian tension, observing that "no drums beat challenge. No bonfires licked in savage celebration."[5] Even Bishop Farren urged for unity, calling on his flock to pray for all of their fellow countrymen and expressing his hopes "that bitterness may end."[6]

In Derry, inclusive expressions of relief and dancing celebrations in the Guildhall Square had met news that Germany surrendered in the spring of 1945. Celebrations took place under floodlights, and Guildhall Square was illuminated for the first time since the war broke out. As Robbie Crockett remembered, "Thousands of people [were] out, and the boats in the Foyle colored all their search lights, green and blue and crimson, shading them all about . . . everybody was there; they were all there."[7] Echoing Derry's long Lundy tradition, effigies of Hitler and other Nazi leaders were burned in the streets. The mayor himself lit a ceremonial bonfire in the tennis courts at Crawford Square.[8]

As the Americans packed up and went home and the German U-boats were sunk off the docks at Lisahally, observances became both more sectarian and, for Catholics, more muted.[9] By August, the *Londonderry Sentinel* noted that victory celebrations coincided with Lady Day and that Catholics abstained from participating. As the war officially came to a close, impassioned renditions of "God Save the King" in Guildhall Square were matched by young women and men singing "A Soldier's Song" nearby in Waterloo Place.[10] Around the corner in Shipquay Place, one woman was arrested and fined for shouting "Up the Rebels!" on Victory over Japan (V-J) Day.[11] The war brought national identities into sharp relief. Catholic Derry insisted on giving thanks for the end of the war without casting its lot with Great Britain or with unionists. Many had adopted the position of their neighbors in Éire, for whom "the equation of neutrality with independence, and independence with uprightness, had become widely accepted wisdom."[12]

By September 1945, processes of remembrance and thanksgiving had become segregated in the city. Indeed, their purposes differed. Catholic Derry focused on religion with a special Mass and procession on September 9, but official municipal observations portended civic and political goals. On September 22, the new governor of Northern Ireland, Vice-Admiral Earl Granville, officiated at a formal municipal ceremony to mark the conclusion of a massive war savings campaign. On the weekend between these two events, Derry conferred the Freedom of the City to Field Marshal Sir Bernard Law Montgomery; the famously black-beret-wearing Monty had seen action in both world wars. Montgomery was known as "Ulster's greatest soldier son," since his mother had inherited an estate in Moville, County Donegal, where the family spent summer holidays when Montgomery was a boy.[13] In his acceptance, Montgomery referred to Derry's strong connection to London and proclaimed to loud applause, "We of Londonderry thus have a link with the Empire that can never be broken; a link that binds us strongly to the very heart of the Empire."[14]

BBC Northern Ireland broadcast the event from the city's walls themselves. The mayor, who himself had served under Montgomery in the war, explained that so many who served under Montgomery were in attendance that the Guildhall was too small for the event. However, there was more to the choice: City Corporation members marched formally as a body in their robes along the city walls and stopped along "the famous battlements" so Montgomery could pay respects to his grandfather, buried within the walls.[15] Claiming the walls officially and publicly as a space associated directly with the Protestant unionist tradition and the British Empire was just one of the ways Derry's unionist leaders tried to harness the war's victory to cement the city's place within the UK.

Divided observances of victory were one sign that the implicit truce between Derry's nationalists and unionists had ended. Catholics had stewed over the 1936 gerrymander, wartime censorship of the *Derry Journal,* and ongoing Special Powers legislation, but they had largely avoided public contestations during the war.[16] Unionists, for their part, had felt Northern Ireland's fragile status.[17] Although Northern Ireland was a crucial coordinate in the Battle of the Atlantic and a staging ground for the Allies, Northern conscription had not been enforced so as to avoid offending the Free State. Moreover, few could forgive Britain's 1940 offer to dismantle Partition if de Valera would guarantee Irish support for the Allies. Despite the brittle relations that ensued between the province and England, Northern service to the war efforts paid dividends and ultimately strengthened Northern Ireland's ties with Great Britain even as it widened the gulf between the governments north and south of the Irish border.

Tensions had been exacerbated by Churchill's victory speech in May 1945, which included an extolment of Northern Ireland and a castigation of Éire:

> If it had not been for the loyalty and friendship of Northern Ireland we should have been forced to come to close quarters with Mr. de Valera or perish forever from the earth. However, with a restraint and poise to which, I say, history will find few parallels, His Majesty's Government never laid a violent hand upon them though at times it would have been quite easy and quite natural, and we left the Dublin Government to frolic with the Germans and later with the Japanese representatives to their hearts' content.[18]

Ireland's neutrality remained a raw issue even amidst celebrations of the Allied victory. There were some who could not forgive "that powerless little cabbage garden" for refusing to side with the Allies.[19] In Dublin, Protestant students had commemorated Victory over Europe (V-E) Day by hurling a burning Tricolour into the streets outside Trinity College.

Official celebrations across the North highlighted the province's close relationship with Britain. As one report observed, "All the spirit of the Twelfth was there, doubled and redoubled . . . it was an opportunity not only for rejoicing but to stage demonstrations of loyalty to crown and constitution."[20] Through songs, images of king and queen, and decorative bunting and air raid shelters painted in shades of the Union Jack, unionist Northern Ireland communicated that its bond with Britain had been tested and rendered inviolate.

The conflict also opened a chasm between Northern nationalists and their southern neighbors. Like the differing time zones—Éire had opted out of "summer" daylight saving time when the war began and was thus an hour behind Northern Ireland for half the year—Catholics on either side of the border were out of step. Before the war, Northern Catholics believed a significant percentage of the Irish population considered the border a significant political issue, even after 1937 when de Valera wrote a new constitution for Éire and appeared to accept a twenty-six county future. World War II changed this; southerners became less interested and concerned with the fate of Northern Ireland: "Despite verbal flag-waving over partition, the focus shifted from the goal of national reunification to the survival of the partitioned Irish state."[21] As the British prime minister Clement Atlee and his Labour Party worked to assuage unionist fears regarding the security of Northern Ireland's constitution under Labour, political leaders in Éire became increasingly occupied with their own concerns.

Partly because the Northern state was embraced by Britain and left well alone by Éire, and partly because the period was largely free of political violence and civil disturbances, the prevailing consensus among historians is that the postwar era constituted the "province's most harmonious and most promising years . . . broadly characterized by economic growth, steady social improvement and a unique degree of peace and stability." Viewed through the refracted lens of memory work, a study of the period suggests a more complicated history. Sectarian divisions hardened as nationalists across Northern Ireland publicly raised the issue of Partition and insisted they be treated as something other than the "disloyal minority."[22] As they came out of the shadows of public life, they claimed the role as "dissident minority" instead.[23]

The purpose of memory work changed in Derry as the nationalist community abandoned defensive postures and took a more direct—if often unsuccessful—approach after 1945. Urged by political leaders to equate Irishness with both cultural and political inclinations, local people engaged more directly in discussions and battles over national politics. They animated anti-Partitionist impulses by challenging laws that prohibited displays of Irish symbols and by embracing aspects of local history and heritage that connected current struggles to a long tradition of Irish experience.[24] Catholics utilized memory work to assert themselves as Irish, to catalyze renewed efforts to contest partition, and to protest provincial policies that appeared to overlook Derry in major development schemes.

For those born during or after Irish independence, the Troubles of the 1920s and the establishment of the Northern state, invoking the past provided opportunities to claim Irish identity in public and to debate what Northern nationalism could and should be a generation after Partition. At the same time, older people instructed younger ones about their cultural inheritances and used the past to wrest Catholics out of political defeatism. Local leaders penned pamphlets that highlighted

Catholic Derry's history and instructed residents on why and how to
protest Partition. They took to the streets and made bold moves to defy
bans against the display of Irish national symbols. Derry countered the
Festival of Britain with its own Gaelic Week and brought Irish Taoiseach
(prime minister) Éamon de Valera to the city. Memory evoked and animated the depiction of Derry as a quintessentially Irish city deeply involved and implicated in the historic nationalist struggle. The *Journal*
facilitated extensive conversations about the past as it sought to contextualize contemporary debates about urban and regional development as
well as disagreements over physical force republicanism and the IRA's
border war of 1956–57.

NATIONALISM, MEMORY, AND THE NEW
PROPAGANDA WAR, 1945–1948

The Derry City Registration Association began the postwar era with a
strong statement about history and the future. In the 1945 annual report
of the organization, the executive council pointed to the long history of
gerrymander and the equally long history of Catholic struggle:

> It is fifty years since the first gerrymander was carried out in Derry
> City. It was found necessary by those in power here. . . . We have suc-
> ceeded in time in overcoming [the] obstacles which they have placed
> in our path and now . . . we feel confident that, once more, we will be
> able, with assistance of our people, in time, to nullify its effects and
> show that in spite of this flagrant abuse of their powers and deliberate
> disenfranchising of thousands of voters, that Derry is still ours.[25]

For nationalists, it was necessary to enter the new era with a new program; in this, the Registration Association was not alone. Propaganda had
infused most Northern Irish civilians' lives during World War II, as radio
broadcasts and film reels communicated the British Ministry of Information's messages to the populace. After the war ended, Derry politician
Eddie McAteer and journalist Frank Curran set out on separate propaganda campaigns on behalf of nationalists of the city and the province.

Hopeful that sharing their message might instigate a reaction and usher in an era of change, Curran and McAteer drew from the past to try to encourage a different future. McAteer was the older of the two, born in 1914 and old enough to remember the turmoil of the 1920s; Curran was born in 1921 to their echoes. Both men were members of the newly formed Irish Anti-Partition League (IAPL), founded in November 1945 at the Dungannon Convention when 480 delegates created the nationalist political organization.[26] With its mission to "appeal to the people of the Irish race at home and abroad for moral and material support in the solution of the partition problem," the IAPL urged nationalists to publicize their perspective on politics and history and to call for a united Ireland.[27] Fully abandoning abstentionist tactics, which had seen their representatives enter and leave provincial politics in a piecemeal fashion since 1922, Northern nationalist politicians harnessed the IAPL to bridge political differences among nationalists in favor of unity and common purpose. Hopeful that the newly elected Atlee and the Labour Party in power at Westminster would be more sympathetic to their position and to their cause, IAPL members believed information was power, and the first step towards dismantling the Northern state was to tell outsiders about the injustices it had perpetuated. As McAteer explained in his foreword to Curran's short treatise, *Ireland's Fascist City*, "Nothing is so fatal to the reign of the bigoted quislings of this part of an Irish Province as exposure before the glare of world opinion . . . [so] I regard this book a most valuable addition to our armoury."[28]

Curran's booklet (see fig. 9) was the first overtly nationalist version of Derry's history published since Bishop O'Doherty's *Derriana* at the turn of the century. It was an altogether different sort of publication, written in the catchy and accessible prose of a journalist who had cut his teeth covering sports. Twenty-five years old and poised to enter the political fray, Curran was a middle-class Derryman and a graduate of St. Columb's College. He described himself as lucky, as his family "had a bit of money."[29] An ardent nationalist, he took great pains to make clear that he had no beef with the average unionist, only with unionism.

Ireland's Fascist City drew explicit links between the battle against fascism waged in Europe and the situation at home in Derry. Curran called 1945 a year of "total victory and absolute defeat; of unsurpassed valor and

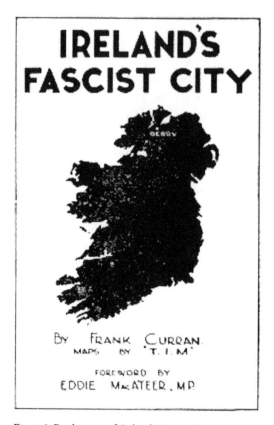

Figure 9. Book cover of *Ireland's Fascist City.*

unparalleled betrayal; of liberation and enslavement, of ebullient hope and despairing fear." Though Harry Truman had declared fascism dead and democracy triumphant, Curran explained that "even while he spoke, his own troops were billeted throughout the British-made first puppet 'State.'"[30] Likening the Northern gerrymander to Gestapo tactics, Curran declared it would take too long to detail unionist political malfeasance in all of Northern Ireland. He focused on the history of gerrymander in Derry, as it constituted the most egregious case of unionist efforts to maintain political control despite Catholic population majorities.[31]

It was a commemorative publication, in observance of the fiftieth anniversary of the 1896 Derry gerrymander. Curran's small book aimed to expose unionist thinking by detailing how unionists had maintained political hegemony through "a succession of unashamed juggling acts each time their position was threatened."[32] Through an exploration of past injustices, Curran wanted to encourage his peers, a generation that had only known Partition, to take up the mantle of nationalism. All men entering public service, Curran argued, needed to be armed with the facts of the gerrymander: "We want spokesmen and representatives capable of authoritatively debating questions of public interest, men who take the trouble to know . . . Derry's municipal history."[33] That history, of course, began not in 1896, but in the tenth century, when Doire Colmcille became "a city of monasteries and schools, a haven of rest and comfort for the weak, the weary, the poor, the unhappy, a stronghold of Faith, a place the fame of which shone brightly throughout all of western Europe (as) . . . a beacon of learning and civilization."[34]

By beginning his history lesson with monastic Derry, Curran reframed the city's political struggle in the way Bishop O'Doherty had reframed its cultural history. Whereas official narratives continued to equate Derry's development and ascent with Plantation and the 1613 design of the walls, Curran's Derry long predated the colonial era. His native Irish were not the savages, mongrels, or nomads often portrayed in other histories of pre-Plantation Ireland.[35] Indeed, Curran took pains to cast the city as an oasis.

In contrast, he made light of the famous siege that dominated traditional histories of the city and served as an origin story of Ulster Protestantism. Reframing the historical narrative on which Ulster unionism relied, Curran called the Siege "a squabble between two foreign kings" and claimed that most native Irish around the city did not take sides.[36] He pushed against the popular image of a trapped and embattled Protestant people, arguing that those within the walls were better armed and more prepared than the besiegers. He even intimated that the thousands who perished within the walls because of hunger and disease could have been spared if only the settlers had been a little less willing to believe siege leader Governor Walker's fears that "Catholics were going to massacre the Protestants."[37] Paranoia, he implied, had laid siege to sensibility. At any rate, Curran claimed that the Siege commemorated by Protestants as a victory for liberalism and religious freedom brought Catholics struggle and persecution. Further, it meant little as a historical event; it was only through the commemorations that Catholics were drawn into engagement with the Siege.

Yet, Curran argued that within the tale of 1689 lay the potential to defeat unionism itself. Mythological aspects of the narrative drove Protestant intransigence. Destroy the myth of Derry, he argued, and the whole enterprise might come tumbling down. Long before scholars noted the power of Siege mythology, Curran identified its central importance to the Protestant sense "of an endless repetition of repelled assaults, without hope of absolute finality or of fundamental change in their relationship to their surrounding and surrounded neighbors."[38] As Curran put it in 1946: "Around Derry, the Walls of Derry, the Apprentice Boys of Derry, the spirit of Governor Walker, the magic catch-cry of 'No Surrender!' has been built the mythology of modern Orangeism. . . . By the loss of Derry, this unhappy statelet would receive a most serious blow."[39]

Like late nineteenth-century nationalist leaders, Curran reclaimed unionist mythologies for his own purposes and declared that "the political siege of Derry" actually started in 1840, when the Catholic population began to grow. "Since then, the Unionists, in their position of privilege, have been ceaselessly besieged by more determined opponents than those against whom their ancestors held the city in 1688."[40]

Derry's history of gerrymander formed the core of the book. Curran outlined the changes made to ward boundaries in 1896, 1919, 1922, and 1936, detailing the scramble to maintain unionist political majorities in light of demographic realities. Curran was quick to point out that unionists had received extensive support from the Northern state in their bid to hold political sway in Derry, but he had as much to say about dissension within the nationalist ranks as he did about the calumny of unionist ward manipulations. He also intimated that Irish nationalists in Dublin had sold Derry out, needlessly using the city as a pawn in their own petty squabbles. Going into great detail about the "Knox-Dillon-Healy episode" that followed the proposal of the Londonderry Improvement Bill of 1896, Curran argued that Irish Parliamentary Party (IPP) leader John Dillon had allowed mistrust for Cork Redmonite Tim Healy to get in the way of standing up for Derry.[41] Since he didn't want Healy on the parliamentary committee, Dillon himself filled in. Knowing little of the situation, he asked no questions and did not engage in cross-examination. Even worse, according to Curran, he didn't use his influence to ensure that the Liberal members would turn up on the day of the vote. The

Tories showed, outvoted the three Liberals present, and "Ascendancy achieved their aims" to institute the gerrymander.[42]

Curran wanted his readers to learn from this parable of personal enmity. Arguing that Dillon's and Healy's mutual antipathy resulted in "the loss of Derry," he urged his fellow nationalists to remain "united, not only in the front presented to our opponents publicly, but behind the scenes too, that unity will be unconditional and free from personal reservations."[43] This was particularly apt at the time of his writing, when republicans and constitutionalists were struggling to come to terms with political differences in favor of their common goals. Tying contemporary politics in Derry to a long history of Irish nationalism, Curran declared that "the struggle for Derry must never be released no matter what difficulties decaying Unionism strews in the path of the irresistible onward march of the Irish people for territorial unity and national independence."[44]

A reframing of history, the booklet argued that momentum towards Catholic and nationalist political power in the city had been building since the middle of the nineteenth century, but it was impeded by a combination of unionist machinations and nationalist infighting. Curran took pains to take current political initiatives out of isolation, claiming that they were intricately linked to Catholic and nationalist Derry's long political history. Instead of focusing on the downward spiral since Plantation, Curran highlighted the "pertinacious policy of political patience against grave obstacles."[45] *Ireland's Fascist City* operated simultaneously as an invective, a cautionary tale, and a call to action.

Curran was not the only Derryman to encourage readers to connect politically urgent issues with the past. Nationalist leader and MP for mid-Ulster Eddie McAteer was born in Scotland but had lived in Derry since he was a child. After a brief stint in the Northern Ireland Civil Service, he had returned to Derry and opened up an accounting practice. The McAteer family reflected both Northern Catholic political cleavages and a familiar ability to transcend them. Eddie was adamant that social change be nonviolent, but his brother Hugh was an ardent republican. Hugh had gone to prison in 1932 after the police searched the family's Bogside home and found weapons; he took the blame and insisted no one else in the house was aware of the guns. He later won fame for a dramatic escape from the Crumlin Road jail. While on the run, he was well known for showing up sporadically in Derry and enjoyed the local nickname, "the Scarlet Pimpernel." The McAteer brothers, Eddie, a hard-boiled constitutionalist, and Hugh, an advocate of physical force republicanism and one-time chief of staff of the IRA, represented the two faces of Northern nationalism.

Eddie McAteer penned two treatises between 1945 and 1948. Neither one was a direct invocation of the past, but both drew heavily on memory in order to face the future. The first, *100 Hours of Nationalism or Irish Made Too Easy: Written for Those Who Are Too Lazy, Too Old, Only Mildly Interested, Too Busy,* stressed the importance of learning Irish as a part of the nationalist agenda even as it jabbed good-naturedly at those who found reasons not to. It encouraged everyone to take an interest in the language and called for a civic campaign to promote Irish in schools. It also suggested that teachers and civil servants needed to learn the "nationally essential" Irish language.[46] Mirroring similar efforts in Éire to expand the teaching and utilization of Gaelic, McAteer's pamphlet encouraged his Northern nationalist neighbors to not get left behind as their cousins south of the border embraced their patrinomie. The Irish language should not be an artifact of Ireland before colonization, but instead, a living, breathing link to centuries of Irish heritage. This encouragement to learn Irish ran directly counter to unionists' growing hostility towards the Irish language on account of its role as "part of the political weaponry of Irish nationalism."[47]

The second book, 1948's *Irish Action,* outlined a series of everyday strategies for nationalists who aimed "to rid themselves of the foolish Border."[48] McAteer invoked Mahatma Gandhi's legacy in advocating a "third way" of anti-Partitionist tactics that moved beyond both physical force republicanism and traditional constitutional efforts. Here, McAteer was in conversation with Northern republicans. The 1948 Republic of Ireland Act spelled trouble for Northern nationalists by increasing distance between Ireland and the six counties; it declared Ireland a republic and signaled withdrawal from the British Commonwealth. The act included guarantees to unionists that consent to end Partition would be required for any change of status for Northern Ireland.[49]

As a founding member of the IAPL, McAteer and other constitutional nationalists were criticized by republicans as "false leaders" who would "make statements and then slither off and do nothing."[50] Republicans were soon to splinter and form Fianna Uladh (Soldiers of Ulster) in the early 1950s, but in 1948, McAteer tried to persuade them to embrace nonviolence. Even as he was claiming respect for Irish revolutionaries of the past, McAteer saw civil disobedience as a more prudent approach in the postwar era. Reminding his readers of the sacrifices of Irish republicans in the past, he stated: "I do not want to see a handful of our best men die so that the majority may be shocked back on the road to national freedom. No more unsuccessful insurrections, please. And no unnecessary risks either. Ridicule can be every bit as effective as rifles. Laughs are not banned yet even under the Special Powers Acts. Chuckle your way to freedom. It is still a little risky to twist the British Lion's tale. Just tickle it."[51]

Irish Action seemed to build directly out of the community-based relationships and institutions that developed in the wake of Partition. In an echo of Chicago-based community organizer Saul Alinsky, who published his own primer on grassroots social and political change in 1946, McAteer celebrated political organizing as a bottom-up process that took hold within community institutions and built upon local strengths.[52] *Irish Action* highlighted tactics such as the use of humor and ridicule, nonparticipation in events that reified Partition, and unity around bread-and-butter issues, such as housing. *Irish Action* was forward-looking even as it drew on the past. Filled with concrete suggestions aimed specifically at Irish nationalists in Northern Ireland, it drew heavily on a nationalist historical consciousness and invited readers to see themselves as part of a long lineage of Irish patriots. Invoking the Parnellite notion of the boycott, McAteer instructed readers to avoid any public events at which the British national anthem, "God Save the Queen," was played, to stay away from parades and military processions, and to make clear to British soldiers in any way they could that their presence was unwelcome.[53] In terms of the Northern government, he advocated avoidance of paying taxes and various obstructive tactics that would make the work of governance more onerous, "anything at all that will clog the Departmental machinery."[54] In favor of anything that might make it more difficult, time-consuming, and costly to maintain the province, McAteer highlighted the new medical insurance program as a target: "I don't need to tell you anything about the Medical Scheme. You are assured that the scheme is 'comprehensive.' Make sure they look after you as 'comprehensively' as possible."[55]

McAteer urged Derry people to turn up "in the thousands" to City Corporation meetings, to cheer the nationalist members, and to make clear their displeasure at the machinations of their political adversaries. McAteer also advocated turning to commemorative street names as a place for practical redress: "Nelson Street? Wellington Street? Blucher Street? Waterloo Street? Are these proper names for Irish streets, peopled exclusively by nationalist Irish? Certainly not. Organize a petition and get your street name changed to something more in keeping with your ideals."

Clearly influenced by Gandhi's work, *Irish Action* suggested an alternative to formal nationalist processions, which had been banned to a far greater extent than they had for unionists: "Forbidden to march in procession, it is still possible for a few thousand of us to appear on the streets. Surely we can walk (not march) on our own streets and if we all walk in one direction and in perfect silence, what law do we break? Anyone who has ever seen a vast silent crowd knows the uncanny effect it produces."[56]

Finally, McAteer asserted that "a movement based on hatred of English rule rather than a love for Ireland is a barren thing."[57] He suggested that each and every Northern nationalist find some small way to engage in the anti-Partition movement, arguing that by simply being active in Irish cultural organizations—through dance, Gaelic sports, the Irish language—they could further the nationalist cause.[58] Wise to frame popular cultural activities within Northern nationalism, McAteer could easily point to legions of active anti-Partitionists. Most Northern Catholics participated in Irish dance, music, and sporting activities without giving much thought to the larger issue of the border, but in stressing that these pastimes were in fact reflective of a broader Irishness, he reminded his audience that their Irish cultural and British political identities continued to clash.

He also may have been reminding any readers in Éire. In the same year *Irish Action* was published, a major case was heard concerning the status of salmon fishing in Lough Foyle. Concerned about Donegal fishermen "poaching" salmon from the Foyle, The Honourable The Irish Society wanted to claim the river as theirs. The case raised myriad historical questions regarding common law, the ownership of the river waters by the Crown, and the ways water behaved in relation to national borders.[59] Some of the most important historians of the era, including Theo Moody and Robin Dudley Edwards, were brought in as experts on the case, tried by George Gavin Duffy. Duffy ultimately ruled that The Irish Society had not proven private ownership and awarded damages to the defendants, who had been caught fishing in the Foyle. As a result of this case, the governments in Dublin and Belfast purchased the rights to fish the Foyle from The Irish Society, and the Foyle Fisheries Commission was established as a cross-border body with executive powers. For McAteer, legislative teamwork on the part of the two governments augured poorly; it meant that Partition had become status quo, even acceptable, and managing it a part of good governance.

The *Londonderry Sentinel* responded to the "pin-pricking" campaign advocated by McAteer by insinuating that within it lay opaque threats of violence. The paper chose two sentences from McAteer's text to print in boldface: "I know another answer to the ban (on civil processions) but it can wait until we are more practiced in the art of civil disobedience. I have quite deliberately left out a lot of good material—you know why."[60]

McAteer used the past to assert a long and unbroken lineage of Irish resistance, but Protestants asserted a different memorial framework, one that had threatened the community's existence since the days of the Siege. Framing McAteer as a paranoid troublemaker for his opaque reference to Special Powers legislation while leaving Protestant and unionist readers of the *Sentinel* with a lingering sense that nationalist organizing always included the threat of violence was ingenious. It simultaneously trivialized Catholic nationalist concerns and legitimized the policies that would keep nationalists in check. For Protestant unionists in postwar Northern Ireland, the only sensible road ahead was the one that embraced Ulster's claim to belonging within the British Empire.

POLITICS IN PUBLIC, 1948–1952

Postwar Derry was sharply divided along sectarian lines, a town populated by two groups that interacted about as well, in the words of Eddie

McAteer, as "oil and water."[61] When Victor Griffin arrived in the city in 1947 to serve as deacon at the Church of Ireland's St. Columb's Cathedral, he discovered "two separate communities, never meeting except perhaps for some professional and business people who found themselves fellow golf club or Rotary members."[62] Griffin inhabited a world populated mostly by parishioners close to his own age, playing field hockey, tennis, and going on hikes and rambling tours: "I joined the City of Derry Rugby Club but Northern Roman Catholics did not play rugby. The Protestants for their part knew nothing about Gaelic games or the Irish language. The segregated schools went their separate ways with no contact whatever. . . . Protestants were suspicious about Irish and had no idea of the origin of place names which they used every day, Belfast, Coleraine, Ballymena, etc."[63]

Catholics observed that even in innocent social interactions, sectarian divides remained prominent in their minds. Knowledge of a person's religious faith and politics was considered a prerequisite for engagement. Eddie McAteer described this phenomenon: "You have to know what a person is. If the door opens and a stranger comes into a crowded room, you must know what that man is. There is a moment of silence always. And the question that springs into everyone's mind . . . 'What is he?'"[64]

If social interactions were largely segregated, provincial leaders hoped to project the image of a politically and culturally unified place. The late 1940s saw the Northern state trying to bury troublesome ghosts from a less secure past.[65] Northern Ireland was undergoing a process of consensus-building as old class antagonisms gave way under the pressure of the welfare state and emergent political and cultural solidarities.

As such, Catholic nationalist memorial practices in Derry were framed by broader unionist efforts to establish a dominant narrative of a harmonious, productive, British-identified Northern Ireland. The resurgence of nationalism in political circles had increased the bellicosity of debate as each faction grappled with its own minority status: Catholics in Northern Ireland and Protestants on the island of Ireland. In a 1947 speech, Northern Ireland prime minister Sir Basil Brooke lashed out at nationalist legislators who reminded unionist colleagues of demographic realities and who suggested that they live elsewhere if they couldn't abide Catholics or Catholicism, bringing unionists' worries into sharp relief: "In view of the fact the Protestant population in Eire [*sic*] has fallen by 41% and in view of the threats of the Honourable Members opposite, that any person who does not believe in a united Ireland should get out, I think the Protestant population are entitled to take whatever action they think fit, provided it is legal and legitimate . . . to protect their own interests."[66]

Debates over postwar education reform, for example, took on sectarian tones and engaged historical consciousness. New policies promised to open up opportunities for secondary education to a much wider segment of the Northern Irish population. Catholic leaders argued that their parishioners were essentially taxed twice for education, once through the rates and again at the offertory.[67] They had refused to join the state system because "state schools were, in effect, Protestant schools," and the bishops lobbied hard for increased funding for the Catholic school system.[68] Unionists launched a massive protest campaign. Lt. Col. Samuel Hall-Thompson, Northern Ireland's minister for education overseeing the reforms, was heckled off the stage at a meeting of the Ulster Women's Unionist Council in November 1946 after claiming he wanted to remain impartial. "We want another Cromwell," jeered the audience.[69] The meeting disintegrated amidst accusations that Hall-Thompson was betraying his religion and letting his side down.[70] As the crowd broke into song, the hall rang with a celebratory rendition of the Siege commemoration song "Derry's Walls." These kinds of outbursts disturbed the broader unionist strategy to build common cause and establish harmony among various Protestant constituencies.

Nationalists made efforts to express Irish identity in public without being shut down for troublemaking and disloyalty. Since Ireland had withdrawn from the Commonwealth and the anti-Partition movement had become politically organized, Derry Catholics found themselves facing a paradoxical situation. Their struggle was not recognized enough to legitimize it; instead they were portrayed as whiners. At the same time, though, the anti-Partition movement continued to be seen as a real threat to the province. In 1948, when nationalist councillor Thomas Doherty drew attention to sectarian unevenness in Derry's employment opportunities, the *Sentinel* published a letter stating that "the vast majority of Roman Catholic unemployed would probably prefer to draw the 'Dole' and exercise greyhounds round the streets and roundways leading into the city rather than take a job where punctuality and a measure of discipline are required."[71] Arguing that the "best men" got the jobs in the city, the author suggested that a visit to any bookie's shop would provide a clear sense of how Catholic men in Derry preferred to spend their time.[72]

At the same time, efforts to quiet and marginalize nationalist agitations increasingly shaped political, cultural, and social life in the city. The Catholic population had been consistently growing in Derry and this was anxiety-provoking in its own right.[73] Derry nationalists' clamors over the gerrymander were widely seen as obsessive and divisive. Hugh Delargy, Labour MP from Manchester and the child of Irish parents, for example, saw Derry's Catholic leaders as men with the talent to be leaders of industry, medicine, education, and economics. Instead, he noted that they were weighed down by the past and obsessed with the border largely because they were the only ones involved and invested in challenging the border. Writing in the *Irish Press*, he concluded, "They talk too much about the Border only because so many of us talk too little about it."[74]

Stormont's decision to ban Derry's St. Patrick's Day parade sponsored by the Anti-Partition League in March 1948 reflected unionist concerns over nationalist attention-seeking. Fears that the feast day of Ireland's patron saint would bring disorder were historically rooted in nineteenth-century altercations. The idea that Irish nationalist symbols would be on display within the city incensed Londonderry Protestants, especially when they learned that other St. Patrick's Day observances were being canceled so nationalists from around the province and across the border could convene in Derry. The prospect of the Tricolour waving in Derry was particularly irksome. One letter to Edmond Warnock, the minister of home affairs, from the Mitchelburne Club, representing a segment of the Apprentice Boys Club in Derry, exhorted that nationalists intended "to desecrate the walls of the maiden city by their filthy flags and their disloyal music": "We demand that necessary steps and precautions should be taken to make sure that the Republican Tricolour is not carried or displayed. We are of opinion that the display of this flag in the heart of our country would be an insult to our loyal people and the sign of a threat to attack our northern government."[75]

They found sympathetic ears at Stormont. Warnock railed against the proposed St. Patrick's Day parade as he made a motion to ban it, saying that the parade was not a "demonstration of the people of Londonderry or of Northern Ireland."[76] He saw the event as a deliberate provocation and accused nationalists of "trailing the coat."[77] "So long as this government lasts and so long as I am Minister of Home Affairs, I shall not permit the Republican flag to be carried through London-Derry City . . . No Surrender."[78] The IAPL replied that the ban would strengthen the nationalist movement. Invoking the historic notion of Irish subjection as a stimulating force in liberation struggle, the group reframed political loss as a win: "[The] History of Irish Nationalism shows that the more attempts are made to repress it the more does it gather momentum. The Government has really rendered us a service in banning this meeting because the anti-partition movement will grow all the stronger."[79]

Drawing on this historical consciousness, Eddie McAteer invoked Derry as he predicted that ultimately obstructionist tactics would backfire on the unionists: "The banning of this meeting will have served its purpose and will have done far more good to our cause if in the various parts of Britain and the world where Irishmen assemble on St. Patrick's Day . . . remember that in the historic city of Derry . . . Nationalists were denied the elementary rights of public speech and public meeting."[80]

On March 17, 1948, the city was heavily policed. One reporter observed black bags hanging from the police officers' shoulders, rumored to carry "service rations and tear gas bombs."[81] Local people tried to see the humor in the situation. As the 17th dawned rainy, one man commented, "Mr. Warnock was right after all. He just didn't want us to get our feet wet."[82] However, few Derry Catholics were pleased when BBC Northern Ireland chose as its St. Patrick's Day program "Lillibulero," an account of the Siege of Derry that was intended to appeal to unionist pride and British identity.[83] The *Sentinel* called the choice "a fitting climax to all the anti-Ulster" propaganda of nationalists, who threatened to rob Northern Ireland "of that heritage for which the men of Ulster fought and bled, suffered and died, on Derry's historic Walls."[84]

THE BATTLE FOR THE FLAG

In 1951, Derry's Catholic leaders decided to test the new Public Order Act ban against displaying the Irish national flag within the city on St. Patrick's Day. In their insistence to display the Tricolour, the nationalists were invoking a long tradition in Catholic Derry and drawing on a much older republican tradition. The Irish Tricolour, like almost all republican flags, was based on the French *Tricolore* and was originally presented as a gift to Thomas Francis Meagher, leader of the Young Ireland movement in 1848. Its colors reflected inclusion of Catholic and Protestant traditions in the Irish state. The *Journal* reported on the use of the flag as an Irish national symbol since 1916. Since 1922, flying it had been an offense inciting political unrest and was punishable by law in Northern Ireland. After 1945, the flag appeared sporadically in Derry, including on the *Journal*'s flagpole in 1950.

Political leaders, including Eddie McAteer; Alderman Frank McCarroll; city councillors James Doherty, James Hegarty, Jack Harvey, Joe Canning, and Michael Coyle; Anti-Partition League member James Lynch; and four other men gathered at the Diamond on St. Patrick's Day in 1951. They slowly walked down Shipquay Street towards Guildhall Square. Lynch led the small entourage, holding the Tricolour high.[85] They had walked approximately twelve yards when the contingent was stopped by two uniformed police officers and one in plain clothes, who tried to take the flag out of Lynch's hands. Lynch was not about to let go without a fight, however, and as his fellow marchers marshaled around him "there was a sharp, exciting struggle."[86] In the midst of the melee, the flag separated from the flagpole, and as one of the marchers stooped low to get it, a police officer landed on top of him.

By now, more than a dozen officers had arrived on the scene, and the spectacle of officers wrestling the Irish flag away from marchers animated a gathering crowd of Catholic bystanders. The *Journal* reported the play-by-play, describing the police's determination to stop the group and the flag from entering the public square: "Amid a deafening burst of cheering, and in what resembled a gigantic rugby scrum, the Anti-Partitionists swept through the gate and into Guildhall Square."[87] Their flag now tattered, the men fought off the police reinforcements who had been waiting in the square. Jack Harvey's arm was dislocated in the scrap.[88] James Doherty found himself flanked by two constables who forcibly led him to their van by hooking each of his arms.[89] James Lynch had not fared well either; photos show his face covered in blood as he was physically carried away into police custody.[90] As the van pulled away, Derry Catholics filled the square. Heeding their leaders' calls for calm, the crowd remained peaceful. Taking off their hats, they sang the Irish national anthem.

The crowd headed towards Victoria Barracks on the Strand Road, lodging a protest outside the jail and waiting for the men to be released. When the instigators emerged, they told the crowd of several hundred that they had been charged with assaulting police officers. As the men made their way back towards the Catholic quarter, the crowd fell in behind them; someone pulled out an Irish flag. Gathering at the Little Diamond at Abbey Street, the protesters told the gathered crowd that they had acted as representatives of nationalists in the city in their attempt to process with the Tricolour, but the police's response had widened the scope of the action. As Hegarty, Doherty, and Lynch were arrested, James Doherty announced that "the citizen majority had endorsed their action in no uncertain manner."[91] The *Journal* was quick to draw the historical connection, refuting the notion of an apathetic populace: "All, those in the procession, the flag bearers, the men who were injured and maltreated, and the large numbers, young and old, men, women, boys and girls, who demanded the release of the prisoners and held their ground until they were released, proved that the spirit of their fathers and mothers still lives strong in Derry Columcille."[92]

The flag took on increased significance after it had been fought over physically on St. Patrick's Day. The Irish Anti-Partition Association in Dublin addressed the City Corporation, taking the event personally:

It is with feelings of sadness and dismay that we learn that in the ancient city of Derry, our National Flag was insulted on our National Festival. In America, land of the free, our flag and nation are honoured. France, Holland, Germany, Belgium, Italy and all countries of the civilized world join in honoring our traditions, our flag and our country. Even in London, our flag flies proudly, unmolested. Is it your wish that your city . . . be recognized as a citadel of bigotry and intolerance?[93]

The battle to display the Tricolour in Derry continued. Ten days later, the Irish flag made another appearance in the heart of the walled city of

Derry. Late on the Saturday night preceding Easter Sunday, local republican Manus Canning broke into the locked base that led up a ninety-six-
foot-high turret, on which the monument of Governor Walker towered
over the Catholic neighborhoods below the west wall. Climbing the 110
steps to the top of the pillar, Canning hung the Tricolour from the flagpole. The statue was located a stone's throw from the Apprentice Boys
Hall, which hugged the city's walls at the Royal Bastion, overlooking the
South Ward. Canning had managed to do this while a dance was going
on in the hall. The sight of an Irish flag billowing out under a bright moon
over the head of Walker as he peered out over the city reportedly led the
Catholics below to "stare in amazement at the unique spectacle."[94] The
city's unionists removed the flag under police protection, before 1:00 a.m.

Canning's deed led to a conversation in the pages of the *Journal* about
memories of other events in which the memorial landmarks of Derry's
siege had undergone revision. Ample space was dedicated to a cherished
myth among the city's Catholics, "handed down from father to son for
one hundred and fifty years," which according to the paper was the best
evidence of the story's veracity.[95] The statue of Governor Walker had been
constructed in the mid-1820s to memorialize Derry's siege and narrate the
history of the Plantation city. Local opinion had it that the timing was no
accident; the statue of Walker wielding a sword as he towered over the
Catholic neighborhood below the walls was constructed at the same time
Catholics were lobbying for full emancipation. The *Journal* reprinted
the following tale, written by Irish nationalist Thomas D'Arcy McGee:

> A lofty column . . . bore the effigy of Bishop Walker, who fell at the
> Boyne, armed with a sword typical of his martial inclinations rather
> than of his religious calling. Many long years, by day and night had
> his sword turned its steadfast point to the broad estuary of the Foyle.
> Neither wintry storms nor summer rains had loosened it in the grasp
> of the warlike Churchman's effigy until, on the 13th day of April
> 1829, the day the royal signature was given to the Act of Emancipa-
> tion, the sword fell with a prophetic crash upon the ramparts of
> Derry and shattered to pieces.[96]

The *Journal* explained that McGee had most likely received the story
from Bishop Maginn, whose biography he penned, published in 1857.

Maginn, the *Journal* explained, had championed "the right of the Catholics of Derry to march in procession inside the Walls of what was once an English city," and had gone on to take an active part in ecclesiastical debates in the mid-1830s that came to be known as the Derry Discussions. This, according to the *Journal*, was enough to suggest that Maginn had "been there," and Magee had therefore received the story as "the evidence of a witness."[97] As further evidence that the story was true, the *Journal* informed readers that only in the past decade or so had Orangemen denied the tale; however, they could only say it was a lie, offering no alternative explanation for the disappearance of Walker's sword.

The article conveyed another story a reader had sent in about another effort to silence vestiges of local Protestant heritage. In the heat of the 1848 Young Ireland movement, local "repealers" set out to "spike" or plug up the famous Siege cannon, the Roaring Meg.[98] "There was mixed amazement and chagrin in Orange circles in Derry" when Meg was quieted.[99] Coaxed into action at every Orange celebration, on July 12, August 12, and December 18, Meg was a signature feature of commemorative events. Protestants lauded her "metallic lungs" and "iron lips" and welcomed her "thundering voice of approbation," but Derry Catholics saw Meg as an organ that "spat hate over the Nationalist and Catholic districts."[100] Tired of the cannon's roar, a group of Catholics used a St. Patrick's Day snowstorm as cover as they tried to silence Meg: "A small group of men . . . spiked it with a tailor's goose.[101] Short of a bit of stuff to complete the work, one of the spikers, the late John Flanagan, took off his coat and despite the snow, used it to supply the needful. The Roaring Meg never roared again."[102] The story concluded by asserting that the Catholic community had wholeheartedly supported the spikers; even though the men and their deed were well known, police efforts to investigate the vandalism proved fruitless. No one was ever arrested for silencing the cannon.

The day after the article ran, the Easter Commemoration ceremony was held in the Bogside at Meenan Park. Planners of the event harnessed the St. Patrick's Day scuffle over the flag as an opportunity to build on the broadly felt sympathy and outrage that had followed it. Groups converged from different corners of the area, each led by a flag-bearer carrying the Tricolour and by a group of boys carrying hurleys over their shoulders.[103] In one speech, republican Neil Gillespie invoked the events of St. Patrick's Day, declaring that Derry people were getting fed up with the status quo.

In the bellicose rhetoric common to the republican movement of the 1950s, Gillespie declared that Derry's response to St. Patrick's Day had shown that "there are signs of the hardening of the attitude of the people towards their overlords."[104]

Sean Keenan, another local republican, took a different approach as he addressed the gathering. Keenan told those who had come out to re-member the Easter Rising of 1916 that in the ideal of a united Ireland there was "no room for bitterness or hate."[105] Keenan pronounced that the nationalists of the North had to prepare for reunification with Ireland. He extolled the virtues of Gaelic sports, Irish music and dancing, and the national language. "By learning their own language, supporting their own national games, and putting Irish culture in its proper place . . . they would be worthy of freedom and they would have freedom."[106]

In November 1951, nationalist councillors James Hegarty and James Doherty appeared in court over the charges that they had assaulted a po-lice officer on the previous Saint Patrick's Day. Their attorney was in-formed that the charges had been dropped, to which he replied that his clients were disappointed because they believed they had successfully made their case "that they had the right to assemble publically [sic] and they had the right to use the King's highway and the right to carry their flag."[107] There was laughter in the court when the presiding magistrate commented, "This is the first time anyone has protested against cases being withdrawn."[108]

Disturbances were even more pronounced in 1952. On St. Patrick's Day that year, an anti-Partition meeting was held in the Diamond at noon. Nationalist politicians urged those gathered to disperse, and to the tune of "A Soldier's Song" most participants began to leave. Several young men hoisted a Tricolour and carried it through the streets past the Victo-ria police barracks. The police charged with batons in hand, and approxi-mately thirty demonstrators and passersby were injured. Six arrests were made and several people required hospitalization. Later, the *Journal* com-plained that the "Public Order Act makes the police the judges, juries and executioners in the case of public processions" in Derry.[109] The police did not face consequences for batoning bystanders; indeed, they were consid-ered the aggrieved party by city and provincial officials. Many Catholics were fined, however, and John Lafferty was sentenced to two months' imprisonment with hard labor for assaulting District-Inspector John Shea during the incident.[110] The incident proved that police force could be provoked by the sight of an Irish flag.[111] Derry became known hereafter as "they city of the ban," with Stormont prohibiting St. Patrick's Day processions because provincial leaders believed heavy police presence was needed to enforce a ban on nationalist activity.[112] The *Journal* made no bones about their reading of Stormont's decision: "The political successors and heirs of Carson allege . . . that the unarmed Nationalists of Derry were lying in wait to launch a civil war."[113]

DUELING FESTIVALS: FESTIVAL OF BRITAIN MEETS GAELIC WEEK 1951

The battle over flying the Tricolour was overtly political, but cultural events inflamed tensions in more subtle ways. Events such as the Festival of Britain in 1951 brought Protestant citizens together and promoted the idea that "in temperament and culture the people of Northern Ireland are British."[114] The Northern government took pains to project an image of "a Protestant, industrial, homogenous community free of disharmony."[115] Organized by the British Labour Party to commemorate the Great Exhibition of 1851, most Festival activities centered around London. However, local committees were established all over Britain, and their organizers were charged with the task of creating spectacles that captured both local identity and a sense of Britishness.

Festivities were organized around joint themes of commercial enterprise, history, and arts and letters. Some of the cultural legacies highlighted at the Festival included the Plantation, the Siege of Derry, Georgian architecture in Belfast, the development of Belfast as an industrial hub, and the establishment and growth of Queen's University.[116] These examples provided ample opportunities to illustrate the province's personality and to showcase its strengths. Dinah McNabb, unionist MP for North Armagh, described Northern Irish participation in the Festival of Britain as an opportunity for Northerners "to demonstrate to the world the undaunted courage and patriotism of the British people."[117]

In Derry, a new history of the siege was commissioned, curbs were painted in the colors of the Union Jack, Walker's pillar was floodlit, and trees were planted on the Mall Wall on the city walls.[118] For their part, nationalists engaged in a long tradition of fighting the expenditures on celebrations of Brittania when they claimed that the festival was something "they had no part of and which they resented." They railed at having to use taxpayer dollars to enable unionists to "flaunt [their] shoneenism."[119] Nationalists in the City Corporation voted against granting £500 for festival activities, though they were outvoted by unionists.

As the Festival of Britain celebrated one version of Northern life, Gaelic week in Derry offered an alternative picture. Catholic Derry scheduled a parallel festival to commemorate the fiftieth anniversary of Comhaltas Uladh, the organization dedicated to fostering Irish language and arts in Ulster. Taoiseach de Valera accepted an invitation to come to the city in July 1951 for the festival launch. This was momentous. He had just returned to the Taoiseach's seat on June 13, 1951, after he and Fianna Fáil won the May 30 election. It was to be de Valera's first visit to Derry since he sneaked over the border in October 1924 to address an audience in St. Columb's Hall in support of Sinn Féin candidate Charles MacWhinney, a Protestant republican. He had been arrested as he tried to enter the building and was detained for one month for defying an order prohibiting him from entering Northern Ireland. He had last spoken in the city during the War of Independence. Organizers wanted to make certain that he would be welcomed in Derry.[120]

Gaelic Week was scheduled during a tense era. In early June 1951, Stormont had responded to ongoing efforts to display the Tricolour by introducing a Public Order Bill to clamp down on demonstrations of Irish nationalism without invoking the Special Orders Act. As the act had been intended to keep the peace during times of chaos and uncertainty, Stormont found itself under scrutiny for using it under "normal" circumstances. Eddie McAteer had dubbed the Public Order Bill "the Derry Democracy Bill," saying that it stood for the city's singular expression of democratic rule, where "the minority have free rein whilst the majority are to be muzzled and driven off the streets."[121] The bill gave the minister for home affairs the right to prohibit all meetings or processions deemed likely to threaten public order for up to three months. As nationalists were quick to point out, the bill left leeway to grant the rights of unionists to process and congregate as usual because their gatherings were considered "customary," but it sanctioned the silencing of nationalists, whose gatherings were viewed as threats to the Northern state and therefore inherently disruptive to public order.

De Valera was not granted an audience with the mayor, and no unionist politicians were on hand to welcome him to the city. Unionist attitude about the visit likely matched the *Ballymena Observer*'s position that de Valera personified "the bomb-throwing rabble opposed to them"; as such, the visit to Ulster was a "barefaced provocation" reflecting "bad manners."[122] Republicans upset with the Taoiseach also refused to be part of the event because de Valera had become less than resolute about a united Ireland.

The visit, therefore, sidelined "official" Londonderry and highlighted the city's Irish population and Irish history. The choreography of even the smallest details evoked a proud Irish citizenry even as it marginalized official, Protestant unionist Derry. De Valera crossed the border and entered Derry at the city boundary on the Letterkenny Road. There the Owen Roe O'Neill Fife and Drum Band greeted him with a drum roll as he emerged from the car. Along both sides of the road, fifty members of the Derry City Battalion of the Old IRA stood at attention, wearing their medals. They had been organized symbolically as a "personal bodyguard."[123] As the music started up, James Lynch, who had been carrying the Tricolour on the previous St. Patrick's Day when the battle for the flag ensued between police and nationalists, led the procession into Derry with the Irish flag waving proudly. He was joined by Paddy Lafferty and Michael O'Donnell, the two surviving men who had helped de Valera sneak across the border and into Derry City in 1924 (see fig. 10).

His motorcade's route transported "Dev" through Catholic and nationalist Derry, highlighting its landmarks and public spaces; the procession bypassed the city center completely, coming from the Lone Moor Road, down Creggan Street to William Street at the heart of the Catholic quarter: "The Taoiseach entered city streets that were alive with the colour of spectacular and lavish decorations. Great numbers of Tricolours, continuous lines of streamers and inscriptions of greeting marked the route."[124] The main events of the day took place in Brandywell's Celtic

Figure 10. The Irish Taoiseach Éamon de Valera arrives in Derry City to open Gaelic Week festivities in 1951, with Eddie McAteer (walking in light sports coat) directly behind him, and MP Paddy Maxwell (at side of car to de Valera's right).

Park. By staying in the South Ward, avoiding sites of official city events like Guildhall Square or Brooke Park and steering clear of the ceremonial center of the city within the walls, Derry Catholics endeavored to give de Valera a welcome uninterrupted and uncomplicated by sectarian tensions. At the same time, the Catholic and nationalist community constructed an alternate political geography of an Irish Derry from the border to the heart of the South Ward, with all the pomp and circumstance they could muster.

When "Dev" emerged from lunch at Roddy's Hotel, the waiting crowd broke into the Irish national anthem. Effusiveness continued throughout the day; more than twelve bands and rows of Irish dancers preceded de Valera en route to Celtic Park for the official opening of Gaelic Week. The *Journal* described the welcome, declaring that Catholic Derry was pleased to have "their national leader in their midst": "It was a welcome possibly unsurpassed in the history of Nationalist Derry—a welcome warm and deeply sincere, springing from the hearts of a people to whom, as to so many others all over the world, the Taoiseach is, in the words of Most Reverend Dr. Farren, the personification of resurgent Ireland."[125]

Nationalist leaders gave a welcome in both English and Irish to the Taoiseach. Apologizing for the fact that they could not welcome him to Derry "in full official form," they hastened to point out that "our greeting to you, from the citizens of Derry, carries much more real weight than those official receptions which have not the approval of the citizen majority."[126]

In a bilingual address, de Valera acknowledged the work of the Comhaltas in encouraging Irish language acquisition in the North, noting that the group had expanded greatly since partition. In 1921, it had 28 chapters; by 1951, it had 154. De Valera heralded Gaelic Week as an opportunity for Irish people to celebrate "what they had received from the past," the cultural and linguistic legacies handed down from their ancestors that had ultimately saved them from becoming "absorbed in the powerful nation that was beside them."[127] Derry residents filled the week following de Valera's visit with Irish football matches, "battle of the bands" contests, dancing exhibitions, performances of Irish plays, arts and crafts exhibitions, and tutorials, in addition to the focal Irish language competitions that encompassed poetry, history, and conversation.

The following week, the *Journal* ran a story reminiscing about the events of 1924 and regaled readers with the tale of how local men struggled to get Dev through gauntlets of police, B Specials, and military and across the border to speak at St. Columb's Hall. "The True Story of How the Armed Cordons Were Outwitted" detailed how, through an intimate knowledge of the landscape between the border and the Catholic area that now was known as the South Ward, local men successfully avoided "the panoply of rifles and guns" and the "thoroughfare hiving with plainclothes" officers to get de Valera to the door of "Minor Hall," known later as the Little Theater.[128] He was arrested there by the police commissioner. Amidst battles over the flag and increased confrontations with the police, the story about Dev's arrest and the wily and brave Derry men who steered him through the city reminded Derry readers that conflict had long been a steady companion of Northern nationalism.

MEMORY WORK AND THE BORDER WAR

The IRA's border campaign began with isolated raids against army installations in the early 1950s and developed into a guerilla onslaught by 1956, after some of those raids resulted in the procurement of weapons.[129] The campaign could be seen as the result of Northern nationalists' failure to gain political ground through participation in governance or public demonstrations. The IRA, in attacking British military installations, intended to set up "liberated zones" as the first step towards "an independent, united, democratic Irish republic."[130]

Historians have used the campaign's reception north and south of the border to highlight the weakened position of the republican movement and the diminishing popularity of the nationalist cause. Its failure has been regarded as a powerful example of Northern Catholics' dimming interest in a united Irish state and the Irish Republic's waning concern for the North. IRA historian Richard English described the fatal flaw of the campaign: "Irish nationalists North and South failed to rally at all significantly."[131] This view was corroborated by Ulster historian Jonathan Bardon, who conceded that although the Catholic minority in Northern Ireland "remained faithful to political aspirations expressed in previous decades," they rejected outright the IRA and its methods of violence.[132]

At the start of the campaign, the *New York Times* reiterated unionists' wishful predictions that the current effort and, indeed, the republican project as a whole was destined to fail. An article paraphrased the Stormont position, implicitly concurring with it:

> In 10 years . . . full employment on Britain's scale will have made partition cast-iron and foolproof. By then, neither parties nor gunmen will be able to make a United Ireland an urgent political proposition. As living standards march ahead of those in the republic, the Nationalists in the North slowly lose their fervor, it is asserted here. The difference between the shadow and the substance is too plain to be obscured by the heroics of border raids.[133]

A generation later, the leaders of the Northern Ireland Civil Rights Association (NICRA) would write about the border campaign as a failure that led to a transformation in goals and tactics. In a public statement in 1978 narrating the history of its own movement, NICRA railed against the "five-year guerilla campaign of violence [that] had produced a handful of dead bodies on both sides, a marked increase in the number of people in prison and a strengthening of the Unionist political system. It was a campaign which had been fought and lost . . . far removed from the mainstream of Northern politics."[134]

There was some support for the campaign, but more pervasive was a deep ambivalence.[135] In a letter to the editor published in the *Journal* in April 1957, Charles Early, one of many Derrymen who had left the city seeking employment, wrote from Fife, Scotland, to criticize the IRA:

> I am a Derryman and . . . a good Irishman. The freedom of my country as is dear to my heart as it is to any Irishman anywhere in the world. I have met Irishmen in South Africa, New Zealand and South America, aye, even in China, and all share the same hope that one day our country will attain its freedom. But youths who endanger the lives of poor people . . . by their senseless attacks are first and foremost, Not Irishmen [*sic*]. The unnatural division of Ireland is self-evident . . . I don't want an Ireland filled with B men with rifles and bayonets, as the 6 Counties are at the moment, but I don't want an Ireland so called "free" if the men who will be its architects are limited in their ability to tossing petrol bombs.[136]

Early's letter, like much of the discussion in the *Journal* during the mid-1950s, provides an opening into deeper and more complex understandings of Catholic nationalism as it was expressed and debated in the city. His statement belies the conflation of antiviolence with an etiolated nationalist impulse; it is unambiguously and simultaneously critical of the IRA *and* aspires to a unified Ireland. Seamus Deane amplified Early's comments when he explained that the border campaign made young Catholics hate the police more than ever, but the IRA seemed laughable. He explained that during the campaign, which brought with it intensified police intrusion in the lives of ordinary Derry Catholics, "they almost demanded the hate we had in such abundance to give. But the IRA campaign was a farce. . . . We sympathised in a general way with the aims of the IRA but knew its means were stupid, its timing wrong and its inefficiency an embarrassment. And yet through it all, we felt the reckoning had to come. The police had to be driven off the streets someday. At any given point, people would want to start breathing again."[137]

As they played out within the pages of the *Derry Journal*, public discourses of memory in Derry illustrated both the complexity of the current moment and myriad uses to which the past could be put. Whereas the editorial impulse during the 1950s was to educate readers and to bequeath upon them a usable past, the traces of personal, highly localized memories found in letters to the editor offered Catholics the opportunity to explore, define, and debate their own sense of Irish identity. At times, *Journal* editors implicitly sanctioned the ideals behind the border campaign. The paper invoked the IRA heroes of the 1920s and celebrated the city's history during the pre-border era. However, citizens' contributions through letters to the editor reflected a much more ambivalent position. Derry was their home, and a place for which they felt deep loyalty. Any attacks on it were inexcusable, even in the name of Irish reunification.

DERRY'S PART IN THE IRISH WAR FOR INDEPENDENCE

In 1953, the *Journal* published a series by former IRA volunteer Liam Brady about his experiences between 1915 and 1921 and during the Irish War of Independence. Brady expressed hope that others would come forward with "any authentic material or historical facts" about the time the IRA "forced the greatest Empire the world has ever seen to seek a truce."[138] The series was designed to rouse memories of Derry's older generation and to educate young people about the tradition of republicanism they had inherited. In Brady's local history of the republican movement, he aimed to bring home, quite literally, Derry's role in fighting for Irish independence at a moment when the city, like the six counties as a whole, was being excised from modern histories of Ireland while simultaneously not figuring in newly produced Ulster unionist histories. In an era of conflict and failure, Brady reminded his readers that the days following the 1916 Easter Rising also "were days without hope." He went on to say, "It looked like the end but instead it was only the beginning."[139] Brady used the past to suggest that adversity was just a prelude.

Brady's story began with his own failed effort to join Na Fianna Éireann because he was too young. He continued with a reminiscence of the night The O'Rahilly came to town the following year, in 1915. Michael Joseph O'Rahilly was the founder of the Irish Volunteers who would go on to take part in the Easter Rising and become a republican martyr when he was shot in April 1916.[140] The O'Rahilly gave the Derry outfit some ammunition and put Brady himself in charge of the Derry Fianna unit. It was only a short time later, Brady remembered, that a Derryman stationed with the British army smuggled 6,000 rounds of ammunition to the Volunteers. Hidden in Derry, the stash "eventually went to Dublin for the Rising."[141] It was as if Brady was demanding the city belonged in the histories of Irish independence, "We were there! Derry was there."

Brady recounted how Derry men assembled and readied for rebellion and how they were disappointed at Eóin MacNeill's countermanding orders ostensibly calling off the Easter Rising of 1916. He detailed all of the local sites slated for destruction if the Rising had made it north and named all of the Volunteers and their female supporters by name. Most, he noted, were dead at the time of his recollections in 1953.[142] The *Journal* ran a photo of three of the "survivors" of 1916 along with one of Brady's posts. The narrative continued with harrowing tales of how the Derry spaces and places associated with republicanism were torn to shreds in raids following the Rising. He recounted Edward Duffy's arrest for carrying a copy of St. John's first aid book out of the Volunteer's hall, so certain the police were that it held important documents. It was the first of at least seven arrests in Derry that week; Brady detailed Derry IRA men's travels from prison to prison and of their jubilant return to the city in time for Christmas 1916. In Derry, the IRA grew and changed, adopting guerilla tactics. Brady took great pleasure recounting how, when IRA members of the Active Service Unit (ASU) heard that Craig's factory on Strand Road was making hand grenades for the British army, they acquired keys to the building and made several visits "until 5,000 of those hand grenades were safe in the hands of the IRA." Surely a few readers scratched their heads at that turn of phrase.[143]

Contrary to general assessments of republicanism in Derry on the eve of independence, Brady called Sinn Féin in Derry City "a real live organization with plenty of pep."[144] The arrival of the Black and Tans and

"Britain's Reign of Terror" soon followed, however, in Brady's recounting of the turbulent history. His story became broader, not centered on Derry, but rather asserting Derry's belonging in the center of the story of republican struggle. He told of Patrick Pearse's mother's visit to the city in 1918 and recounted her assurance "that the lessons of her son's life were enthroned in the hearts of the men of Derry."[145] Continuing to include the city in broader histories of Irish independence, Brady shared the story of de Valera's 1918 visit to Derry when Dev spoke to an overflowing crowd at St. Columb's Hall.

Eventually, Brady's story made it back to nuts and bolts, or rather, bullets and hand grenades. The former Irish Volunteer told tales of risky exploits to procure ammunition, including trying but failing to relieve a trawler of its gun, breaking into Ebrington Barracks and Protestant residences in the rural hinterland where weapons were stored, and raiding Derry's General Post Office (GPO). He told of "good Presbyterians" who signed on for the cause of Irish freedom and of "paid agitators" enlisted by Orange lodges to attack Catholics in the early summer of 1920, the most violent period in the city's modern history.[146] According to Brady, they were armed with British service rifles, suggesting a direct connection between the army and local loyalists.[147]

Brady's accounts of the events of the summer of 1920 were heartrending. He explained that the IRA could not believe members of the Dorset regiment were arming Orangemen, but Brady had come to believe that the soldiers proffered weapons specifically "to create trouble, and if possible, a civil and religious war."[148] After a drunken squabble at Bishop's Gate on the night of June 20, men armed with service rifles started firing from the Protestant quarter at Fountain and Albert Streets into Long Tower Street and Bishop Street. John O'Neill, Fr. Walter O'Neill, John McVeigh, and Thomas McLaughlin all died that night from bullet wounds. A woman was shot while waving a white apron as she left her home to come to the aid of the fallen, Brady remembered.[149] The fact that four policemen vacated the area, leaving it to the Orangemen, was a sinister affront.

The attacks began at 8:00 p.m. on June 20, 1920, according to Brady; by 11:00 p.m., five Catholics were dead and twenty-four were wounded. Two days later, they started up again. This time the IRA in the city mobilized. They were poorly armed, he remembered, with three rifles and thirteen revolvers between them. Under orders to "take stern measures against the armed Orangemen, they were to protect the lives and property of all citizens, even the Unionists."[150] The IRA, he said, even protected unionist shops in the Catholic quarter from being looted by their angry coreligionists.

Brady explained that the IRA took weapons from their arms dumps that night and the battle began in earnest. One British soldier said that "it reminded him of Hill Sixty," a Canadian and British attempt to take a hill occupied by Germans during the first battle at Ypres in World War I. Brady suggested that the city magistrates were complicit with the violence, saying that soldiers were supposed to arrive from Dublin, "but as long as the Orangemen had the upper hand, no troops arrived."[151] Having clarified the uneven nature of the battle, Brady went on to detail how the IRA procured its weapons, illustrating the danger and emphasizing that everyone involved knew the risks involved and took them "with determination."[152] More than one hundred Derry men were "on the run," sleeping in a different bed every night as they tried to escape interrogation and arrest.[153]

Brady explained that young boys in Derry, frustrated by the army presence and the curfew, took matters into their own hands and booby-trapped area streets with black wire and shards of glass designed to do as much damage to soldiers' bicycles as possible. They also painted a Tricolour on a gable wall, which so irritated the soldiers that they bought a tub of tar to paint over it. This led the boys to sing the following ditty:

This is the flag the Dorsets hate,
It drives them all insane.
But every time they wiped it out,
It blossomed forth again.
The English failed to tame us with their guns and armoured car
So of course they sent the Dorsets,
With their little tin of tar.[154]

Clearly a favorite story of Brady's was of the night the IRA rescued Sligo republican and political leader Frank Carty from the Derry Jail. He went into careful detail, explaining how the wounded prisoner cut his bars, the oak rungs and rope that constructed the ladder, and the IRA men who went from unionist yard to unionist yard, knowing that police officers lived on the street and that one dog's bark would sink the operation and land them all in jail, or worse. Carty, who weighed fifteen stone, also took grave risks, but he made it out of the window of the jail's hospital wing safely. "When he landed, they embraced each other while tears of joy streamed down their faces."[155] Carty was kept hidden for several days and then smuggled on the coal boat, the *Carricklee*, which set off for England with the fugitive safely aboard.

Brady wanted his story to be inclusive. He did not want to leave women out and therefore detailed the fate of all six Derry teachers who were fired for refusing to take the Oath of Allegiance. Lizzie McLaughlin, Mary O'Doherty, Nellie McDaid, Delia McVeigh, Julia Flanagan, and Cassie Bradley all had to figure out a different path for themselves. Brady reminded readers that Father Doherty didn't approve of the aims of the IRA or their female counterparts, but he believed in their general cause and found four of the six women new jobs. He also expressed gratitude to five unnamed members of the Royal Irish Constabulary (RIC) who on occasion passed information on to the IRA. He was particularly grateful to the RIC officers on duty when a British soldier and five companions called into Victoria barracks in 1920 and asked for the names of republicans who should be shot in Derry City. The officers told them "their services were not required."[156]

Brady's reminiscences of the days and weeks following the Anglo-Irish Treaty of 1921 amounted to a narrative of loss. B Specials paraded through streets made quiet by curfew. Hundreds of local men were rounded up for their involvement in the Irish Civil War; in prison they were "subjected to every possible hardship and privation." He told of inmates being nearly gassed in their cells and recounted hunger strikes, solitary confinement, and a news blackout for months on end. He clearly spoke from experience, though he never mentioned his own imprisonment specifically.[157] Liam Brady's reminiscences took readers on a journey both intimate and very public. His memories were also the memories of his community and his city. The attention he paid both to "naming names" of those Derry men and women involved in the republican movement and those who died in the Troubles of 1920–22 was only matched by his insistence that

Derry was an integral part of the drama of the fight for Irish independence and the Irish Civil War. The city was not on the sidelines then, he implied, and should not be on the sidelines now.

OBITUARIES

Obituaries of public figures in Derry and the northwest of Ireland in the late 1950s invoked and reflected on the past with sentimentality and poignancy. They were important declarations of values espoused by the last generation to have reached adulthood before Partition. Two models of nationalism appeared in the articles honoring Derry and Donegal's dead: the "freedom fighter" and the "nationalist community man." Some men were revered for both their participation in fighting for independence and their community leadership. The men who fought for an independent Ireland and those who toiled to create a place worthy of such a fight received recognition and praise.

The death of John Fox in 1952 and those of Eamon MacDermott and Paddy Shiels in the spring of 1957 were commemorated with front-page newspaper stories with photographs and elaborate descriptions of the funerals. MacDermott, from Donegal, and Derrymen Fox and Shiels were well known "freedom fighters" who had been active during the Easter Rising, the War of Independence, and the Irish Civil War. All three were IRA men, revered not only for what they did and what they stood for, but for their close connections to powerful republicans all over Ireland.

Johnny Fox was lauded as one who "to the cause of an Irish republic had given the greater part of his life and for it he suffered much."[158] Fox had gotten his start as a member of the Irish Republican Brotherhood (IRB) and was reputedly one of the first in Derry to join the Irish Volunteers, out of which the IRA formed after the Redmonite split.[159] He was ready in 1916, only to be stopped at Carrickmore when the countermanding order was given, then only to be arrested weeks later in Derry. In other accounts, the stories of continuous raids on the Fox home during the War of Independence and the Irish Civil War helped to paint a portrait of a family whose sacrifice helped birth the Free State but did not change the fate of those in Derry or the North.[160]

According to the *Journal*, Eamon MacDermott's life story was "the story of Gaelicism and Nationalism in Derry, Donegal and Tyrone."[161] MacDermott himself had joined the Irish Volunteers at its founding in 1913 in response to Carson's creation of the unionist Ulster Volunteer Force and had been jailed for more than a year for his participation in the Easter Rising of 1916, but he was lauded primarily in the newspaper for his exhaustive efforts to revive the Gaelic language and Irish Gaelic customs and folk arts in Derry. MacDermott helped found the branch of Cumann na Gaelige in Derry, an organization dedicated to animating Patrick Pearse's romantic nationalist vision of "an Ireland not merely free but Gaelic as well, not merely Gaelic but free as well."[162] The lectures, debates, classes, and events at the center made it the hub of "national life" in Derry.[163]

MacDermott did more than fight for Irish independence. He prepared, counseled, and urged young men in Derry to join the IRA; the paper noted that this "great and gallant Irish soul" was quite proud of the exemplary service young men under his tutelage provided the movement. MacDermott, according to the *Journal*, understood what he was fighting for; he fought the "good fight" himself, and trained a younger generation to carry on. "Unchanging in his national faith and uncompromising in his ideals, he remained an unrepentant republican until his last break."[164]

Derry's Paddy Shiels, who died a month later, in April, was remembered as a hero to both Derry city and the Irish nation. Whereas MacDermott's passions were primarily cultural and his desire to fight for Ireland emerged, it seems, from his dedication to preserving and strengthening the Gaelic aspects of Irish life, Shiels was a political figure whose interest in Irish culture was born out of nationalist fervor. A friend to the political greats of his time, such as de Valera and Patrick Pearse, Shiels had traveled to the United States as a young man in 1898 to collect money for the Fenians.

He was "one of the few surviving members of the number who mustered in Derry in 1916," and was commanding officer for the Derry battalion of the IRA during the years between the Rising and the War of Independence. He was arrested for his involvement in the Irish Volunteers in 1916, and the *Journal* noted in his obituary that he was such a trustworthy prisoner that he was allowed to leave jail daily to go to court to oversee voter registration appeals from the South Ward for the election of Sinn Féin candidate Eóin MacNeill. Shiels was not a stranger to the inside of a prison cell; he was arrested on arms possession after a raid on his house in 1919. The article also referred to Shiels's ability to put the broader Catholic community of Derry before himself; it highlighted his heroism in response to "the pogrom in June 1920."[165] Shiels was depicted in his obituary as a republican hero for his role in protecting the city, with "an outstanding and proud" record. "While the city mourns his death it can at the same time feel pride in having produced such men as he."[166]

Republican fighters were lauded at time of their deaths, but another type of Derry nationalist also was honored, men who, such as Richard Doherty, were quiet, devout Catholics, community leaders whose nationalism took the form of institution-building and example-setting.[167] In his obituary, in April 1957, Doherty was venerated for his "lifetime of service" to the AOH; the paper noted that Doherty had been in Banba Hall in Dublin's Parnell Square at the 1904 founding of the first Irish chapter of the AOH and had led the Derry chapter and also the district board. Doherty was also an active member of St. Eugene's parish and a fifty-year member of its temperance society. If his political work as an alderman and an organizer of voter drives in the South Ward was "carried out quietly and behind the scenes," the significance of what he had accomplished accorded him a reputation as "a sterling and outstanding Nationalist."[168]

Doherty and Frank Deeny and Richard Gallagher, two other Bogside residents who passed away in May 1957, were remembered in the newspaper at the time of their passing as "three splendid Derrymen." None of them earned their status in the fight for independence but rather for being athletic, hardworking, sober men, staunch Catholics, upstanding pillars of the city who lived according to "principles that were the old Derryman's rule of life."[169] Acclaimed and appreciated for their long years of daily participation in the institutions that gave Catholic Derry stability and pride, they were important in a very public sense and "worthy of Derry's finest traditions."[170] Their deaths were met with both personal sadness and collective melancholy. "Their passing severs more of the remaining links with the old Derry . . . and the city is all the poorer for their deaths."[171]

MacDermott, Shiels, Doherty, Feeny, and Gallagher were memorialized as public figures, though only one of them ever held public office; two, in fact, had done jail time. They were regarded as heroes at the time of their deaths and as exemplary Derry and Irish citizens. In narrating the stories of their accomplishments, the *Journal* reporters continually returned to particular themes—their faith in both Irishness and Irish independence, their links to the larger-than-life heroes of the Irish independence movement, and their role(s) as the social cement that held Catholic Derry together and made it strong. They were remembered not simply as nationalists, but as leaders of the nationalist community. Most important, they represented "old Derry," a place the reporters who penned these men's obituaries feared was being lost. Further, at a time when the Northern Irish, Irish, British, and American press were vilifying the IRA's 1957 border campaign, the *Journal* not only continued to highlight the city's nationalist histories but to cast the men who had fought in earlier eras for the republican cause, who at the time of their own IRA campaigns had certainly been castigated and criminalized, as Irish heroes.

"OLD DERRY"

Between 1954 and 1957, correspondents and local editors at the *Derry Journal* wandered through turn-of-the-century Derry, through the streets and into the businesses that lined them, an ambling reminiscence of the people and places that brought old Derry alive for readers who had never known that city. The guide for some of the journey was Shane Conway, a well-loved Derry expatriate who had moved to New York during the period of violence that surrounded the Irish War of Independence and Partition. A journalist and orator, Conway had started the Derry Association in New York and ushered in a celebration of St. Columba that was observed by both Catholic and Protestant Derry expats.

Conway's memories fell into several themes—the economic and social vitality of pre-Partition Derry, the histories of nationalist activities that made Derry a quintessentially Irish city, and the people, organizations, and traditions that gave Catholic Derry its character and identity. The stories were highly specific and detailed. Additionally, readers sent in photographs of "old Derry" that were published weekly, giving the column a sense of living history, as opposed to an archival romp designed to highlight "the way things used to be." Conway certainly intended to illustrate the changes to Derry wrought by partition with the twenty-six counties of Ireland and discussed rupture perhaps more than continuity. As readers' engagement with the column shows, however, this wasn't simply the work of a lone journalist with a penchant for the past. He often mentions in a tone of surprise that the columns captivated *Journal* readers, striking a deep chord in members of the Catholic community.

The "Onlooker" column of the *Journal* took up the story where Conway left off and continued the theme of Old Derry until 1957. According to the *Journal*, the streets of Derry at the turn of the twentieth century were lined with well-loved shops and locally owned businesses—the Old Curiosity Shop, John Brown's bakery, Doherty's bakery, Campbell's dye works, McElroy's Toffee Co., Stilley's bakery, McCarron's Pipemakers, Watt's distillery, Roddy's Hotel, John Casey's pub, and Mulholland's Drapers. These were just a few of the establishments Conway named as he mapped Derry's city center, circa 1900. The journalist invited his readers to remake the old city in their minds, and in so doing to remember the Derry that was no longer:

> Half a century ago, there were businesses so large, so strongly established and with such a large clientele that no one, least of all their owners, imagined they would so soon disappear and many of them be forgotten. . . . Where great shops flourished, there are now branches of English chain stores. Only one or two of the old establishments—and they are mostly under different proprietorship, remain to remind us of the glory that was.[172]

Locals, both Protestants and Catholics, often owned these shops; they employed local people. They situated Derry as the economic center of a wide territory that included parts of counties Derry and Tyrone and Donegal's Inishowen peninsula.

The establishments mentioned in the column were run by people who, according to the "Onlooker," had given Derry its character—people such as Powers, the Dublin Quaker who was such an ardent scholar of

Gaelic he donated a slide lamp to the Gaelic League so they could view Irish historical slides, or Stilley, whose wife gave away all the unsold bread left in the shop every Saturday evening. McElroy didn't mind if young people hung around the toffee shop all day watching him create his confections. Bernard "Barney" Hannigan donated £9,000 to help renovate the Long Tower church in 1907.

Joseph Shaw Mulholland left his job at his draper's shop, Mulholland & Co., each day and pursued an evening career as a gifted orator whose stirring speeches on nationalist topics could still be recalled fifty years after his death in 1915. A barrister, he served on the Port and Harbor Commission. One of his employees, James McLaughlin, went on to be "a teacher amongst teachers" at St. Columb's College. McLaughlin studied the Irish language for the pure love of it, according to Conway, learning Old and Middle Irish in addition to the spoken Irish language. It was also noted that he authored a persuasive and stirring booklet, "The Facts and Principles of Irish Nationality," "as fine and as logical a case for an independent Ireland as have ever been written."[173] McLaughlin had chosen to remain anonymous, but signing his 1907 pamphlet "Eireannaigh Eigin" (Some Irishmen), Onlooker wanted to point out that a Derryman had written the treatise geared to "every Irishman anxious 'to know his own mind and comprehend the rights of a Nation.'"[174]

Some Derry personalities were remembered for the effect they had on the area's physical and social landscape. Dr. Bernard was singled out for his work preserving the Grianan and other "memorials."[175] These memorials weren't expensive statues or sculptured works created by artists; they were landscape features such as rock formations and wells reputed to have healing powers: "It was he who saved St. Mura's Well at Fahan from obliteration. It was neglected and weed choked. He had it cleaned up, cleared the surrounding area and at his own expense erected over it a beautiful cross." Conway took pains to describe what was considered the doctor's greatest contribution—the 1870s restoration of the Grianan. Dr. Bernard's intervention and restoration protected one of Ireland's national treasures, something Conway believed all Derry people should remember and honor.

Certain places in the city had more than economic importance or meaning as a heritage site. Roddy's Hotel, for instance, was a center for nationalist political activity, evidenced, of course, by de Valera's 1951 appearance. When reminded by a reader of Roddy's, Conway responded enthusiastically with memories of his own:

> I don't know how I forgot about Roddy's Hotel. Headquarters for every nationalist M.P. and speaker in the days of the Land League, it was, in fact, a landmark in the northwest. Land War prisoners on their release from Derry Jail were escorted there by cheering processions and many a rousing speech I heard delivered from its windows. I'll never forget the enthusiasm that marked the release of Father (later Canon) McFadden of Gweedore and Father Daniel Stephens of Falcarragh. The only parallel I can remember was the crowds that welcomed the Easter Week prisoners returning from English prisons.[176]

These recollections in the *Journal* placed Derry and its establishments at the epicenter of some of the most tumultuous political events of Ireland in the late nineteenth and early twentieth centuries. By placing Roddy's Hotel in Derry, for instance, into a dramatic scene of anti-landlordism, of the priests' fight against what they considered an oppressive and unjust legal system, "Onlooker" located Derry and its people squarely within a history of Irish nationalist struggle. Home to important sites of that struggle, Roddy's was more than a building, or even a business establishment; the *Journal* was asserting that Roddy's had been a nationalist treasure.

"Onlooker" dedicated several columns to Derry traditions with religious, community, and nationalist implications, claiming that the traditions had faded and diminished in importance to the cultural life of Catholic Derry over the course of his lifetime. He singled out St. Patrick's Day festivals and the feast days of Columba as the "two big Catholic outdoor events of the year," and detailed the ways that Derry Catholics marked them by elaborate decorations, festive processions, music, and nationalist politics.[177] Expressing nostalgia for the pride taken in the decorations, "Onlooker" said that "exterior decorating was a tradition in Catholic and nationalist Derry. It seemed to have been born in the people. Certainly no other part of the country . . . could equal them."[178] His articles conveyed the solemnity and sense of community spirit that arose out of Derry's Catholic neighborhoods around the feast day when they prepared, prayed, and lit "the illuminations": "In every pane of every window of every home was a lighted candle, and there was a feeling of intimacy about its flickering and its winking that electricity never can generate. There was something personal in those candles, they were outward manifestations of the joy of the welcome and the wishes that burned in every heart."[179]

Just as "Onlooker" attributed piety and religious participation to every member of Derry's Catholic community during the patron saint's feast, he went to great lengths to characterize St. Patrick's Day as a day of nationalist strength in which all Catholics came together dating far back in time. Not only that, but "Derry was the place to which the entire Northwest turned its eyes and every district, with its bands and processions, was preparing for the big day."[180] These events, at least in memory, reflected communal accord in Derry's shared religious and political expressions and in Derry's place as an Irish city in pre-Partition Ireland. It seemed important to tie Derry's traditions surrounding Ireland's festival day to colonization and the struggle for independence. Describing an arch from 1898, "Onlooker" said that "it represent[ed] one span of the famous Walls of Limerick . . . there was in it a wonderful sense of the artistic, a re-creation of one of the focal points of a siege that . . . was for Irish participants another glorious episode in the centuries' long fight against the invader."[181]

Sensitive to the contemporary politics of St. Patrick's Day, "Onlooker" explained how Derry had once been the northwest hub for celebrations honoring the national saint. People would gather from Counties Derry, Donegal, and Tyrone "to demonstrate Catholic and Nationalist strength, and to assert their right to march through the streets." He went on to tell of memorable St. Patrick's Day processions—the year Catholics were denied entry into the center of the city by mounted police, or when the city's most vocal nationalist leader was shot after a St. Patrick's Day procession, or when angry Protestants hurled bombs at Catholic marchers or tore the green flag at Lindsay's Corner.[182] Despite the violence and fear, "those were great days in Derry," for Catholics stood up to the "ascendancy" and asserted their rights and their history.[183]

Implicit in all of these memories of old Derry is both a sense that the past remains present in the life and landscape of the city and a parallel or balancing sense that the people, places, rituals, and traditions of Catholic

Derry were somewhat stronger in the past than they were in 1957. The journalists and editors responsible for preparing the news wanted to highlight the way things used to be, to bring people's attention to a time and a way of life that was on the wane. The purpose was also to educate the young and remind the not so young of their city's history from a Catholic and nationalist perspective. This should come as no surprise; as cultural producers in nationalist, Catholic Derry, the newsmen of the late 1950s saw themselves performing a vital social role.

No one has ever accused the *Derry Journal* of being objective. "You've got to love the *Journal*," historian and Derryman Dermot Quinn once observed. "It never fails to do a good impersonation of itself. The subheading, 'Corporate Unionist majority opposes progress?' It was probably typeset fifty years before and used three times a week in every edition thereafter."[184] More striking than exhortations from the *Journal* is the response from local people—their impassioned memories, which "Onlooker" published regularly, conveyed a shared memory process that rose from the people as much as it descended from their newspaper.

The *Journal* was nationalism's organ in the northwest, but evidence that local residents embraced Irish identity can be found in the letters to the editor that followed Conway's "Memories of Old Derry" series. The proof that Derry Catholics loved their city and were proud of their Irish heritage comes across clearly, if more subtly; Conway's narratives were unambiguous efforts to recall a "purer" past, but those who wrote into the paper traversed the private and public terrains of memory more seamlessly. Memories of quotidian beauties and life's simple pleasures were interspersed with stories about sectarianism, violence, and ardent nationalism—the "big" issues in Catholic Derry. For those who wrote from England, Scotland, the Irish Republic, and the United States, Derry itself was a part of their past; their stories were geographic and temporal bridges linking the place that had shaped them to the people they had become. Although the occasionally sanctimonious and preachy articles in the *Journal* and bits of story from Conway sometimes read as prescriptively as they did descriptively, the letters to the editor suggest a vibrant, multivalent, and complex set of community memories.

People wrote in with memories of their favorite places in and around Derry. Many of the sites they remembered were in the center of town, like dance halls such as the League, up the Bog, up to "Heaven." They usually went on to depict the rambles they had taken to areas in Donegal, close to Derry City, across the Irish border. Hughie Nicholl wrote from Aberdeen about his favorite rambles, "around the Belt, up Maggie's Lane, Bligh's Lane and around the town."[185] He continued with stories of jaunts he took with friends: "We'd all walk to Fahan to the Sally Bush, running the course . . . for the old dog racing on Irish Street."[186] Jack Doherty wrote in from the Bronx, New York, to recall hiding under the seats of an excursion band headed to Buncrana or jumping on the back of the "Lady Clare" to spend a summer day in Moville.[187] Busty Canning wrote chiefly about his fondness for the streets of Derry: "Abbey Street, at the foot of the Bogside, Cinderfield on summer evenings until 10 o'clock; I will always remember my young days in Derry City. No place like it."[188]

When "Onlooker" responded to these letters and others like them with the prediction that "the present generation" had become so seduced by dance halls and cinemas that they would never be able to understand that for people like Nicholl and Canning "the greatest joys were to be had in rambles round the picturesque spots in which a lovely former Derry is set," a man in his twenties wrote in: "I write [to take] you to task for your comment on today's Derry youth . . . the first fine Sunday will find our roads filled with teenagers cycling to Fahan, Buncrana or Carrigans, and you'll find dozens of Derry youth heading countrywise toward Holywell Hill, Grianan or even Burnfoot or Inch . . . my fondest days were spent clamoring around the wonderful hills that are adjacent to our city."[189]

It is interesting to note that "Onlooker" responded to this letter, saying he had meant that young people no longer go "out the road" by foot.[190] The difference between walking over the countryside and traveling by bicycle may seem minimal, but one of the differences is the necessity of engaging the fact of the border. Walking through the hills and valleys outside Derry towards Donegal, there is no physical manifestation of the split created by the national boundary. Cyclists traveled by road, though, and the roads between Derry and Donegal in the 1950s had at least nominal checkpoints and guards. For "Onlooker," memories of an unbordered landscape allowed for the sense that Derry and Donegal were fully linked areas.

Journal readers, many of whom had left the city in search of work, wrote with their memories of places that invoked a happy past filled with innocence, friendship, and fun. Places they remembered were old stomping grounds where they played sock ball or hiked the hills, cavorted in the fort at Grianan, or cycled out to the sea at Buncrana or Inch Island, all in County Donegal. There was certainly nostalgia at work in their recollections; the good times became amplified to such an extent that "Derry" had become synonymous with all that was authentic and happy.[191] Nostalgia, of course, was much more than an innocent and childish pursuit. It was also restorative and redemptory. The practice and performance of reworking the past lent coherence and value to unsung histories, claiming and proclaiming the value of a worldview, indeed a world, that had too often been evaluated by outsiders inclined to identify its problems.[192] By reiterating the strengths in what it conferred, those who had experienced "Old Derry" insisted on the significance of their experiences and their community. And yet this was far from all they remembered. For those who responded to the "Old Derry" stories, the past was also filled with conflict and tension.

Memory of urban space was cast more darkly in stories people sent in about Derry Catholics' struggle for equal access and equal rights in a city that had become dominated by Protestant unionists. One reader wrote in about Bishop Kelly's residence in Shipquay Street, right outside the city walls, in the 1880s. "Onlooker" paraphrased his comments:

> An interesting fact is that it was in the Bishop's House that the St. Columb's Temperance Abstinence Society was founded. At that time the Orangemen claimed the city inside the walls as their own and Catholics, especially on Saturday nights, walked through Ferryquay Street at risk to life or a limb. The Catholics were not organized to withstand these attacks, and one of the hopes of those who cooperated in the establishment of the Society was that, in addition to the discipline that would follow from a total abstinence body, there would be an organization that would make the attackers afraid to continue their policy of assaults on individuals and individual groups.[193]

"Onlooker" continued: "They were right. From that time onwards the Catholics could walk the streets at night without molestation. Another of the tyrannies of the Ascendancy was broken. The Catholics won their free exercise of another of their civil rights."[194] Memory of the bishop organizing a religiously based civic institution to protect the Catholic public is powerful. It speaks to the ways Derry people wove together their experiences of urban space, Irish Catholicism, and sectarian discrimination into narratives in which their strengths—faith, community, discipline—prevailed over their political, economic, and even personal human weaknesses to enable them to negotiate public space with more dignity and clout.

The omnipresent tensions between Orangemen and Catholics, often alluded to in the "Old Derry" series, arose in people's memories of Derry. Shane Conway followed carefully from New York and wrote in to ask if others remembered the days when the city was balanced politically between Protestant unionists and Catholic nationalists, and the Protestant tradition of burning an effigy of Lundy, an infamous traitor to their cause, was outlawed in the center of the walled city:

> Who was the leader of the Apprentice Boys' organization that denounced the authorities and had the alleged traitor's effigy burned elsewhere? And who was the man from the Bogside reputed to have walked off with Lundy on his back early of an 18th December morning before daylight after removing the effigy from the Town Hall pole? I heard of the man from a cousin of his in Brooklyn when I was a tenderfoot in America.[195]

At the time of his letter, the Orange Order in Derry was free to march where it liked and to burn Lundy at any site it chose.[196] As "Onlooker" noted, "The present generation will find it hard to believe that there was a time when the burning of Lundy had been such a nuisance and such a disturbance of the peace that it was banned by the law."[197] Memories like Conway's suggest that Derry Catholics paid close attention to the shifting dynamics between Protestants and Catholics. Just as they understood that they needed to unite to counter sectarian discrimination, they also knew the political tides had turned in the past in Derry and, by extension, that they might do so again.

Memories of small indignities suffered by Catholics lingered in the community's psyche. One reader wrote in to ask Derry readers, "What do they know about the young woman that wrote a splendid volume about the city and whose garden was planted with orange lilies at the Waterside [a mixed but majority-Protestant area of Derry] by the children of a minister who was notorious for his anti-Catholic sentiments?"[198] This memorial shard points to people's sense of historic legitimacy for their distrust of Protestants. Not only was the Protestant clergy capable of such an absurd cruelty as setting a Catholic's garden abloom with lilies, the symbol of Irish independence, in the colors of Protestant loyalism, but, in this narrative, even children were suspect, complicit in a culture of ill will and trickery.

William Toner wrote in about his memories of one historic challenge to Protestant authority in the Waterside. He wrote about Waterside chemist "'Dr.' Sheppard . . . the central figure in the most amazing election ever fought in the Waterside. He was a bit eccentric and had a grievance against the Corporation on account of a loose flagstone outside his shop which when trodden on squirted dirty water in the wet weather and despite his complaints, was never remedied to his satisfaction."[199]

Urged by other local Catholics, he agreed to stand as a candidate to represent the Waterside in the next municipal election. Toner went on to tell the story of the election results. Hundreds gathered in Duke Street, "led by a band in which the musicians had corned beef tins as drums, tin whistles and a host of other 'musical instruments.'" Doc Sheppard and his entourage went to Corporation Hall in the Diamond to discover the "results of the poll, which gave him only eight votes."[200]

Dr. Sheppard's ill-fated run for office resonates with exuberant failure and celebrates trying over winning. This, of course, has long been a trope of Irish memory and identity: life is in the struggle on the side of right, and strength lies in solidarity with others who have been wronged. In Toner's narrative, an ordinary businessman who had played by the rules as they had been established by the Protestants who held sway in his part of the city decided to do something about the injustices he suffered. He was encouraged by other upstanding Catholics, including George Scott (whose claim to fame was car ownership!). Despite the enthusiasm and support Sheppard garnered from Waterside Catholics, his was a lost battle from the start. Too few Catholics had the right to vote, and even though hundreds may have processed through the streets for him, only eight people could actually use their political voice.[201] In spite of the loss, which in the end was utterly predictable, there is in Toner's memory a sense of the value Derry Catholics put on not only fighting the good fight, but on doing it to music.

The men and women who wrote into the *Journal* sent photographs and stories of the city as it had been before Ireland was partitioned and the Northern Irish state was formed. They told stories of places they loved, sites of protest and contest, and memories of standing up to assert their rights. Very few stories from readers were solely of nationalist or religious sentiments, but these aspects of Derry Catholic identity appeared over and over in the pages of the 1957 *Journal.*

One reader, who didn't want his name mentioned, wrote to "Onlooker" with a story of a "famous Twelfth" in the 1860s, when Irishmen from Donegal's Inishowen peninsula challenged the Orangemen. They "tramped for over 25 miles and crowded all approaches to the Walls. The inside was held by mounted police and troops. The 'Wallycoats' [the name of the Catholic band] managed to get some barrels filled with stones. The barrels scattered the mounted police, the Inishoweners effected an entrance and held Derry for two whole days, which was then a Unionist Holy of Holies."

As "Onlooker" contemplated this story, he mused that the Wallycoats' occupation of the city was an event long talked about around Derry firesides. Their resolute action called the bluff of the Orangemen, even backed as they were by the police. They made history because they destroyed the legend of invincibility of Orangeism and its vaunted "'prerogative' to the mastership of the city."[202] On his part, the writer who shared the story reminded readers, "Really, Derry is populated from Inishowen, a hard fighting race."[203]

Toner also remembered a rebel song that was no longer sung but still remembered in Derry. The song memorialized the rapparees—men who took to the hills from the era of the English Civil Wars and especially after the Jacobite losses in Ireland, living as outlaws and enemies of the new English order. They were called "rapparees" after their weapons: short pikes that in Irish were called *rápaire.* Toner wrote, "A well-known baritone in the Waterside about sixty-five years ago, named Eddie Boyce, the 'Foreigner,' taught me the words of the enclosed song, which he sang at many Irish gatherings. This song is now out of print and, as I believe no one else has a copy."[204]

Toner's memory of learning the rebel song penned by Monaghan man Charles Duffy was couched as a local interest piece, an artifact from an earlier time. However, the song portrayed the struggle for independence as a tradition that spanned three hundred years even as it conveyed melancholy at the Jacobite loss and the marginalization of those who had fought for a different future for Ireland. Not only did Toner not want to see the song lost in the folds of time, he wanted to provide it with a public airing; the "Onlooker" column provided an optimal venue. "Historic interest" couched the publication of a fierce anthem, long sung in Derry. Toner clearly believed that the song was at risk of being forgotten, and he wanted it to have a bit more life.

Other writers often began or ended their letters by alluding to their nationalist passions, making it clear that though it did not define their existence, the partition that cut Derry off from the Republic of Ireland weighed on them and shaped their sense of the city. Hugh Nicholl wrote, "Please God when Ireland's free, I'll be back for good to the sweetest place this side of heaven."[205] Another wrote that "Onlooker's" memories of old Derry made him feel closer to "*Ireland's* greatest city," emphasis his own.[206] Charles Early, who'd written to condemn the IRA border campaign, suggested with Catholic fervor that "the freedom of Ireland has a simple solution—pray for it and it will come."[207]

The political issues troubling Northern Ireland had become increasingly obvious after World War II and throughout the 1950s. In Derry, the separate cultural spheres occupied by Protestants and Catholics in the era immediately following Partition gave way to a more contentious set of political and cultural engagements. For Catholics and nationalists during this period, remembrance practices accompanied and shaped broader efforts to make space for themselves in the city and to contest both the border and the idea of a Protestant and unionist Northern Ireland. If the lion was unionist hegemony, then Catholic memory work in Derry after 1945 challenged it in word, deed, and spirit.

Between 1945 and 1966, politicians, journalists, and community leaders continued to press for social and political change, using the written word, public protest, and cultural performances of all kinds to tickle the tail. They pushed the issue of Irish reunification and continuously sought to illustrate that their national identity was an Irish one. They did so in an unfriendly environment; unionists in Derry and in Stormont attempted to keep in check nationalists' efforts to raise issues related to Partition and sectarian discrimination. Battles over St. Patrick's Day and the right to carry the Tricolour, in particular, refracted the long history of identity politics as a contact sport in the city, but the Northern state's power to crack down on anything likely to challenge public order underscored the uneven terrain of politics in public.

In the meantime, Derry Catholics connected past and present in a variety of ways. They maintained older traditions of religious festivals and spiritual processions, but the *Journal*'s emphasis on the vitality of those events in previous years suggest that by the late 1950s they were on the wane. They embraced "Dev" when he visited Derry and continued to engage actively in Irish arts and language. Derry Catholics articulated a complex and rich community memory focused on the Derry cityscape as Irish, Catholic, and much loved. They drew connections between their local identity and a sense of themselves as Irish even as they challenged republican clamors for physical force. As the city mourned the generation that had been born and raised before Ireland was partitioned, a new generation looked to the future. The past did not compel them nearly as much as what lay ahead. The 1960s would see the past become a lightning rod for more pointed conflicts over space, politics, and the future. By the mid-1960s, change had become the watchword in Derry.

Chapter Five

SULPHUR IN THE AIR, 1963–1968

At a community development conference held at Derry's Magee College in May 1975, Paddy "Bogside" Doherty outlined the history of grassroots civil rights and community development in the city. He flouted the busloads of academics and journalists who had flocked to Derry since the onset of the Troubles, implying they offered few practical solutions for a city desperately in need of them. For Doherty, Derry's troubles had begun long before the first stone was thrown in 1969. Furthermore, the violence that engulfed the city could not be separated from the fight to allow Derry to grow and prosper: "Everybody comes here to talk to Derry people, to look inside their heads, to analyze the situation and then to go away and write books on it. I've got fed up listening to these people for it's a pity they didn't come in 1966 when there was nothing here."[1]

The assertion that 1968 saw "five decades of frozen politics" finished has forestalled serious consideration of the ways a localized historical consciousness spurred Derry Catholics to take part in the civil rights movement by the end of 1968 and into 1969.[2] Contextualizing this period more deeply invites exploration of the very early days of the civil rights movement in Derry through some of the memories that captivated people during that tumultuous time. Paying particular attention to a web of connected issues—housing, economic development, and political representation in the city—I argue here that a historical consciousness of unfairness did not motivate the leaders of the movement as much as other factors did, but ordinary Catholics in Derry framed their experiences during the push for civil rights through a long historical lens.

Particularly in the battle to obtain decent housing, Catholic Derry's story of itself returned again and again to the wrongness of gerrymander, the absurdity of a population choked by its inability to grow physically so as to secure unionist power, and the increasingly high costs of political impotence. I argue that Derry's "old guard" nationalist political and cultural leaders were not dinosaurs, even though a *New York Times* reporter called them as much in 1968 for their outdated beliefs and traditions.[3] To outsiders, they may have been dredging up ancient history, but contemporary debates over houses, jobs, and votes could not be untangled from the history of gerrymander and the longer histories of Catholic disenfranchisement.

The frustrations and hopes that inspired the civil rights movement were encapsulated within this historic sensibility. Ultimately, historical consciousness of injustice would motivate thousands of local Catholics who ordinarily might have steered clear of anything resembling trouble to support and eventually to participate in the early civil rights movement. However, this perspective alone sells short the deep roots of community organizing and self-help of Catholic Derry. Actively engaged in progressive causes and projects with an eye to the future as they were, members of the nationalist community performed memory work through their approach to solutions just as much as they looked at the problems of the 1960s through a long historical lens. Their struggles for a better future were built on foundations from the past: the intimate geographies, extended families, long-held associations, self-help prowess, customs and values of Catholic Derry.

Derry was a grab bag of social and economic problems by the mid-1960s. Unemployment levels hovered at one-quarter of the working-age population, the highest for a city of its size in Western Europe, and emigration rates soared as people fled the city.[4] Every major industry in Northern Ireland saw significant decreases in those it employed.[5] Nearly one in eight of Northern Ireland's unemployed people were from the city on the Foyle.[6] As investments in both opportunity and infrastructure bypassed the city, some wondered if its problems might be part of broader political calculations. The 1965 decision to overlook Derry in favor of small Coleraine as the site of the second campus of the University of Ulster and the closure of the Great Northern Railway line, which ran the daily direct train link to Dublin and was one of two direct rail links to Belfast, seemed designed to isolate Northern Ireland's second city.[7] So too did the decision to eliminate cross-channel shipping services from Derry's port. Bishop Farren's 1967 Easter sermon urged Catholics to pray for jobs, and he implored his parishioners that faith might enable them to "bear up against those difficulties that were not of their making but which were with them every day."[8]

Contraction of opportunities and outlets for growth in the northwest ran counter to overall strategies and proposals taking shape in the rest of the province, particularly in towns and cities east of the River Bann.[9] There, a concerted effort to help the province catch up with the European postwar economic boom was underway. In his opening speech as prime minister of Northern Ireland in 1967, Terence O'Neill articulated a grand vision for Northern Ireland's future, setting into motion a series of initiatives that had the effect, if not the intention, of restructuring space. The plans represented the most comprehensive redesign of Northern Ireland's landscape since the seventeenth-century Ulster Plantation. O'Neill envisioned progress in these terms: "It is a new motorway driving deeper into the province. It is a new airport that will match our position as the busiest air centre in Britain outside London. It is a new hospital in Londonderry—the most modern in the British Isles. It is new laboratories and research facilities at Queens to carry us to the frontiers of existing knowledge and beyond. It is a replacement of derelict slums by modern housing estates."[10]

With the exception of the new Altnagelvin hospital on the Protestant-dominated Waterside area of Derry, redevelopment plans earmarked modernization and predicted population growth in Belfast and eastern parts of the province, even creating and investing heavily in the "new city," Craigavon. The 1962 Matthew Plan, the most comprehensive provincial planning document of the era, indicated that population would expand significantly in the east but decrease gradually in counties Londonderry, Fermanagh, and Tyrone, all of which had significant Catholic and nationalist populations.[11] The Registrar General predicted an increase in the population by 197,000 east of the Bann by 1981 but total population growth in Northern Ireland of only 196,000.[12] Population would thus have to grow significantly in the eastern counties and decline even more significantly in Tyrone, Fermanagh, and Derry City. The demographic consequence would be the dilution of nationalism where it was strongest. When O'Neill declared that the effect of the plan would be to "transform the face of Ulster," nationalists worried about the effects on Derry.[13] The city's population was two-thirds Catholic by this point. Nationalist councillor T. J. McCabe summarized their concerns: "Already there was a drain of people from Derry City, due to the development of Ballymena, Larne, Antrim, Craigavon and the Coleraine triangle, because there were jobs and houses in those areas."[14]

In this, nationalists were not alone. The cramped development outlook initially brought many liberal unionists into early civil rights discussions and campaigns.[15] The failed University for Derry campaign led them to predict that the northwest of Ulster would be left to wither because of its extensive border and its nationalist majorities. Outspoken Church of Ireland minister and liberal unionist Victor Griffin gave a Christmas sermon in Derry's Christ Church at the height of the controversies over development, saying, "We are the forgotten people. The star in Ulster is always drawing nigh to the north east."[16] He later explained that he was motivated to speak from the pulpit because he was appalled by the position some of his neighbors had taken: "I actually heard a prominent Derry Unionist declare, 'We don't want any more industry here because if we upset the apple cart, the RCs (Roman Catholics) will come and swamp us.'"[17] Siege mentality persisted, despite the economic consequences.

RADHARC FILMS: BROADCASTING A "RANGE OF VISION" FROM DERRY

In 1964, Derry nationalists welcomed broadcast journalists from Dublin who came to examine the politics of economic development, housing, and broader issues of sectarian relations in the Maiden City. Eddie McAteer and several other prominent nationalist leaders were eager to share their story with audiences in the Irish Republic and hoped that an informed Irish populace would press for change; they welcomed Radharc Films to Derry.[18]

Radharc was a division of Telefís Éireann, established in 1961 as Ireland's national television station. De Valera inaugurated the station, acknowledging the power of television "to influence the thoughts and actions of the multitude" and expressing hope that beyond mere entertainment, Raidió Teilifís Éireann (RTÉ) would bring "information, instruction and knowledge" to the people of Ireland.[19]

That same year, John Charles McQuaid, archbishop of Dublin, sent two priests to New York to learn tools to shape the nascent Irish television broadcasting industry. As the first independent Irish broadcasting unit, the Radharc team endeavored to do what its name implied—seek a "range of vision" about contemporary social, religious, and cultural issues. In practice, Radharc tended to follow a format emphasizing a "problem-solution discursive narrative in which the solution was inevitably some recourse to faith or Catholic social teaching."[20]

Journalist Patrick Cunningham and his crew came to Derry to do an exposé on sectarian relations, but unionist politicians purportedly refused requests for interviews. The presence of the past provided the framework for the film. Opening shots depicted an Orange Order commemoration of the Relief of Derry, interspersing sights and sounds of lambeg drums and orange sashes with visuals of Bogside poverty and crumbling homes. Cunningham did a series of face-to-face interviews with Eddie McAteer, Councillor James Doherty, voting registration organizer Frank McAuley, and teacher Paddy Friel.[21] Those involved in the film undoubtedly walked away from the experience confident that the long history of gerrymander in the city and the challenges facing Derry Catholics and nationalists would receive ample airing.

However, the film, *Radharc in Derry*, got shelved for twenty-five years. After it had been edited, RTÉ management decided it was too inflammatory and abrogated section 31 of the Broadcasting Authority Act of 1960, which "required the RTÉ to refrain from broadcasting 'any matter that could be calculated to promote the aims or activities of any organisation which engages in, promotes, encourages or advocates the attaining of any particular objective by violent means.'"[22] Particularly in light of thawed relations between the new Taoiseach Seán Lemass and Prime Minister O'Neill, *Radharc* leadership found it prudent to keep the film under wraps for fear of igniting republican sympathies. In 1989, it made its premiere as part of a Radharc anniversary program on RTÉ.[23]

Radharc in Derry reflected the chasm between North and South that had deepened in Ireland in the postwar era. McAteer even pointed this out, telling Cunningham that it was difficult to explain things to, "forgive me, but an uninformed stranger."[24] Indeed, the film assumed its viewers knew little or nothing of Derry's history. As he perched along the walls near the Walker memorial, Cunningham emphasized the official historical narrative of the city as it had long been projected by unionists: "The walls and guns stand here today, symbols of a city that lives on the memory of [the Siege] and prides itself on the watchword 'no surrender.'"[25] Cunningham conveyed sectarian relations as sharply inscribed communal divisions between Protestants and Catholics. However, he was quick to point out that the politics of Northern nationalism were, in fact, political—Derry's "nationalist majority are truly nationalist in that they want to see a thirty-two county republic."[26]

Taking a long view of the contemporary conflicts over jobs, housing, and votes, James Doherty described Derry as "the backwash of Britain's first colonial effort." He went on to observe that "by and large the plantation mentality still prevails." Doherty conflated politics and economics: "There is the dividing line between haves and have-nots and there is difficulty persuading the haves to surrender their position of privilege in the interests of fair play." McAteer also referred to the longer history of sectarian relations of the city when he commented on the "glowering colonial attitude [and] atmosphere of watchfulness" that prevailed in Derry. The weight of marginalization weighed heavily on schoolmaster Paddy Friel when he said, "We are not regarded as equals of the others in this city. They try to make us feel and do everything in their power to ensure that we feel that we are second-rate citizens."[27]

The film strived to be balanced journalism. Cunningham detailed the famous story of the Siege and the twelve Apprentice Boys who bravely shut the gates of the city as representatives of King James were en route to discuss Londonderry's submission. He recounted the privation, malnourishment, and illness that caused many to die within the walls before the boom was broken by the *Mountjoy* on August 20, 1689. The film delved into the symbolic significance of Siege history and linked its material implications from a nationalist perspective: "Catholics feel [the annual parade] is meant to be an annual reminder of who won and who lost in 1689 and who intend to stay winning."[28] Stating that "we live continually in the atmosphere of the siege," longtime Derry registration agent Frank McAuley chuckled, "We get it at our breakfast and our tea, as the saying goes." McAuley equated the commemorations of the Siege with elements of religious observance. Such "intense, almost pathological concentration on an event of so long ago [that] it is out of all historical perspective and proportion," McAuley stressed, came down to resonance of the Siege narrative to unionists' identity: "All this Williamite war business, it serves as the mythology for the whole Orange movement . . . it seems to me it is a substitute for religion . . . all these regalia and banners and all, it is equivalent of a liturgy."[29]

Eddie McAteer found that "the mad month" that began with parades commemorating the battle of the Boyne on July 12 and ended with the Relief of Derry on August 12 dug up and exacerbated old anxieties and was "a drum-drugged ecstasy . . . in which . . . the pope of Rome, the Belfast Celtics and Mr. de Valera and all the vague fears all get rolled together and they become very real."[30] For McAuley, McAteer, and others interviewed, the Siege mentality was more than simply an expression of a historical victory or salve for contemporary anxieties; it had material consequences that affected nationalists' access to employment, housing, and political representation. McAuley expressed the fatal optimism of Catholic Derry when he observed that the community had a "grin and bear it" approach to the "unpleasant facts of life of this place." It did not stop them from enjoying life, he said, as "we try nevertheless to knock out as pleasant an existence as we can in spite of all these drawbacks."[31]

The film exposed the fact that no Catholics currently held jobs inside the Guildhall building itself, "not even a cleaner," and explained that all the heads of City Corporation departments were Protestants, and that 80 percent of the Corporation jobs were held by the same. What did this mean for Catholics in 1964 Derry? Teacher Paddy Friel was asked where were the thousands of pupils he had taught over the years: "The majority might be in England, the remainder, I suppose, are scattered," said Friel. When Cunningham asked him, "Has it been your experience—do they get a fair shake?" Friel responded quickly, "Ahh, they never do." He continued, "I rather felt heartbreak talking to boys who have no other opportunity of earning a livelihood except by leaving Derry and going to

England." Asked what a young Derry Catholic might find locally in terms of opportunities, Friel explained, "He finds on leaving school that the opportunities are very limited. He knocks around in dead-end jobs until he is tired of looking at himself. He is tired of everybody, everyone is tired with him . . . until he goes."[32]

Lack of adequate housing accommodation for Derry's Catholic citizens was explained in conjunction with the voting ward policies that kept Catholics, two-thirds of the city's population, within one ward, the South Ward, thus reducing their political representation. McAuley also explained that business owners were entitled to additional ballots. James Doherty reflected, "I think they honestly think that those who pay the rates should have more voting rights." Ultimately this didn't wash, he argued, since most businesses in the city relied on custom, and the custom on which they relied to function was Catholic and nationalist.

Asked to predict the future, nationalist leaders responded with a mix of ambivalence, frustration, and hope. Frank McAuley detected "a considerable breeze of change" in recent years.[33] He believed that Protestants and Catholics in the city "seem to be getting along ever so much happier now than we did some years back," but it seemed to Paddy Friel that in order to maintain harmony, "all the concessions to make it worthwhile would have to come from us . . . and we get nothing in return."

McAteer held out hope that the Irish people might press the government in Dublin to intervene, saying that "it will take a blast of informed public opinion in order to sweep away this rotten system."[34] Frank McAuley reflected on the importance of outside influences in shifting the stalemate in Derry:

> It has been said that Ireland is the country where the unexpected always happens and the expected never. And we can only hope and pray that will be true in this case. I have a feeling that personally that if and when the question is solved, it will not be solved in the sense of a victory of any one side over the other, but rather by a fusion of the interests through the pressure of world events, the tendencies, and the other influences that I have referred to.[35]

Radharc's Cunningham reflected that "an imaginative break with the past is needed if there is to be any future for the young people of Northern Ireland today."[36] McAteer acknowledged that this would necessarily entail a simultaneous process of chipping away at suspicion: "The two elements of the community are mixed together but they are not really mixed, they are not part of the same community . . . we want to see more mixing but we want to see rather a lessening of mistrust."

McAteer faced the issue of Protestant fear directly: "There is a fear in their minds which is real to them and which will have to be overcome if there is to be any living together of the two sections of the community.[37] He went on to say, "[Protestants] may have their privileged wings clipped a little bit, but I can assure them that there will be no Night of the Long Knives following the day Catholics receive their proper place in this community or the day there is a united Ireland."[38]

Cunningham concluded his reporting with the observation that "the Siege of Derry ended on the 12th of August 1698 [*sic*], but in fact the siege of Derry is still in progress."[39] Even though the old walls of the city no longer excluded Catholics, as they had during the famous Siege, barricades remained, "no longer walls of bricks and mortar but real walls nonetheless. They are walls of prejudice and discrimination and mutual suspicion."[40] Reflecting on future prospects for Derry, he faced the camera and asked prophetically, "Will the growing numerical superiority and economic strength and educational opportunities of the Catholic community soon make a vital breach? It seems to be only a matter of time."[41]

McAuley reflected on the same question, drawing on a historical consciousness shaped by his life in Derry and in the partitioned North: "It may not be in my time. But the Irish people had to wait 700 years for what measure of freedom they got in the other part of the country. They're good waiters, they can well afford to wait."[42]

MEMORY AND DERRY'S HOUSING CRISIS

The fact remained that without political power, Derry Catholics had little opportunity to ameliorate problems facing their city. Most pressing was the city's housing crisis. Derry was continuously ranked the city with the most overcrowding and slowest efforts to reduce it in Northern Ireland.[43] With the highest birthrate in the UK, Derry's problem promised to get worse.

Politics stood squarely in the way of improved housing conditions. The city's electoral geography demanded that the Catholic vote be crowded into the South Ward if Protestants were to retain their slim majorities. Likewise, extending the city boundary for the purpose of building homes for Catholics would upset the already delicate electoral balance. As long as the Corporation was led by Protestant unionists, the prospects for building new housing in Derry were slim. The issue of housing scarcity had been troubling the city since 1920, but little had been done during the interwar period to address Derry's housing problems.[44] The Planning and Housing Act of 1931 had made redevelopment the sole discretion of local authorities.[45] Since it was also incumbent on local authorities to foot the bill for local housing, there was no way to force local councils to improve housing.

The creation of Northern Ireland's Planning Advisory Board and Commission in 1943 and a series of postwar policies brought changes.[46] The Commission's initial audit and report suggested that two-thirds of all residential structures in the province demanded renovations and 200,000 new structures would be necessary to address Northern Ireland's long-term housing needs.[47] The Housing Act of 1945 created generous subsidies and set up the Northern Ireland Housing Trust as a public authority that could bypass local councils and corporations. Local officials had to approve plans, but this opened up unprecedented opportunities for housing development.

Derry's Creggan Estate was one of the first public housing developments under the direction of the Housing Trust. However, Creggan's 1,750 units could not solve the city's staggering housing problems, even though it housed 5,000 residents and was overwhelmingly Catholic. Michael McGuinness, Derry local historian and longtime resident of the Creggan, related this story to sum up the social geography of the estate:

> There is a story, very possibly apocryphal, about a young boy playing ball in the fledgling Creggan estate when it was only a couple of dozen houses standing on a green mountain top. The lad is bouncing the ball against a gable wall to the rhythm: *The Protestants have all the houses, the Protestants have all the houses.* With that, a priest comes up and . . . tells the youngster: "That's not true, son, sure wasn't our Lord

himself born in a stable?" Duly chastened, the wee lad recommences his bouncing to the time of: *Our Lord was born in a stable, because the Protestants have all the houses.*[48]

Political stalemate prohibited accommodations that would require building out of the South Ward. There, population density levels for private households, which tracked how many adults lived in a situation with more than two persons dwelling in one room, was more than twice as high in Derry than in Belfast in both 1951 and 1961.[49] This led commentators to suggest that the Corporation "had minimal reduction in actual numbers of overcrowding" during that period.[50] Bureaucrats noted the politics of housing production in the city, identifying Derry as "the most striking example of highly localized provision . . . where public housing for Catholics was provided only in the South ward."[51] In 1965, the Campaign for Social Justice, a precursor to the Northern Ireland Civil Rights Association (NICRA), highlighted the skewed geopolitics of Derry's housing allocations; the data they collected showed that Catholics received less than 10 percent of available housing units outside the South Ward, but they received 95 percent of units within the Catholic area.[52]

The 1956 Housing and Rent Restriction Act of Northern Ireland called for each authority to assess local housing and to determine the number of unfit dwellings. The results, published in 1959, stated that one-quarter of Northern Ireland's housing stock was unfit. In Derry, figures hovered around 40 percent.[53] Housing, what there was of it, was in bad condition. By the mid-1950s, one hundred Derry families were being interviewed every week for public housing, and the waiting list for subsidized accommodation in Derry had stretched to six years. Most people on the list were Catholic. In 1953, D. A. S. Murphy, the city's housing manager, took pains to explain that impatience borne of desperation was common: "I should point out here that I endeavor to prevent undue weight from being given to cases who constantly call at this Office or contact members of the Council."[54] That constant phone calls did little to shift one's place in the queue did not deter people from calling. In 1955, Murphy requested that he be allowed to unplug his phone extension because fielding inquiries had begun to take up virtually all of his time.[55]

Derry's Catholics saw the housing shortage as purely political, tied inextricably to the gerrymandered history of the city. Derry had the distinction of being the city whose electoral boundaries were most frequently manipulated in Northern Ireland, and the fact remained that as far as unionists were concerned, Catholics needed to live and vote in the South Ward. It was the only way to return sufficient Protestant unionists at the polls in the other wards. By 1966, more than 30,000 people—more than half of the city's population, lived in the ward, the highest population density in Ireland. Quarters were cramped, with more than two people per room more common—three times more than on the Waterside and four times more prevalent than in the prosperous North Ward.[56] Extended families shared houses, and residents were incensed when they learned that between 1946 and 1967, only 70 new dwellings per 1,000 inhabitants had been built in Derry.[57] The numbers paled when compared to much higher rates of construction in much smaller towns—144 in Newry, 140 in Larne, 109 in Coleraine.[58] Between 1958 and 1966, the Derry Corporation had built only 252 houses, despite the fact that by 1960 the waiting list for accommodation had risen to more than 1,500 families.[59] In the same year, the unionists on the Corporation voted in a bloc against Councillor Doherty's proposal to extend the city's boundaries because this would upset the fragile Protestant majority in the North Ward. Decisions to block the boundary extension prevailed despite the recommendation from consultants from the London-based planning firm the Muncie Partnership and the strong endorsement from the unionist-led Junior Chamber of Commerce.

One solution was found in urban renewal. By 1966, hundreds of old dwellings in the South Ward were condemned and slated for demolition. In an effort to address the housing shortages, an initial plan for a fourteen-story-high building of flats at the Lone Moor Road was proposed by the Corporation. The new developments were incongruous within the context of the old South Ward. In the mid-1960s, the Housing Trust complained that it could not move forward with the demolition of condemned houses to make room for new housing in the Fahan Street area because a piggery was still in use. Thomas Keys, its proprietor, protested that he had fourteen fattening cows and two sows that he still needed to dispose of, and no other place to put the pigs.[60]

Nationalist councillors weren't comfortable substituting pig pens with pens for people, but felt hamstrung nonetheless. They disapproved of the plan for high-rises, but supported it as the only opportunity for building additional housing in the crowded South Ward. Despite the desperate need, many were hesitant to support the proposal. Paddy Doherty, who had built a house for himself and his family in the area after having been told that it would take nine years to get Corporation housing, remembered his wife Eileen's skepticism of the towers and the community's shock that the long-familiar footprint of their district was slated to be destroyed: "She says to me, 'It'll be crazy, hundreds of people living in that small place and fourteen stories high,' she says. 'Incredible.' So she got meself and Jackie Boyce out onto the street with this model of the high flats with all the houses around it and we went round the streets and the reaction we were getting was, 'Well where's my house, where's Elmwood Road?'"[61]

With support from neighbors, Paddy Doherty raised £80 to hold a public inquiry into the efficacy of the high-rise flats. He remembered James Doherty pleaded with him to call off the public hearings: "'Our people are in such a dreadful state,' he says, 'and we can't build outside of the Bogside, we have to build up,' he said. 'I'd build flats in your backyard if I had to, to house our people.' I says, 'James, that's not the battle, the battle's to extend the boundary,' I says. 'You're fightin' the wrong battle, putting your energies into flats. . . .' [I was] pleading with them at the end of the day not to carry out this awful experiment on my front door."[62]

Confronting urban renewal was an exercise in ambivalence for Catholics. By 1966, the Rossville Street/Lecky Road redevelopment plan called for three multistory buildings of flats to be built on Rossville Street, on the grounds of the cattle market, which had ceased operations in 1960; 179 units were planned for the first two of three high-rise buildings, which put a dent in the larger housing problem. As I have argued elsewhere, Derry's Catholics initially cheered the bulldozers and wrecking balls. Tearing down the damp, decrepit houses of the South Ward was tantamount to smashing the physical remnants of a political universe they believed had curtailed political and economic opportunities and threatened well-being. As plans for new housing got underway, relief outweighed regret. Yet, even as it was welcomed and valued, people like

Eileen Doherty predicted correctly that redevelopment would weaken community vitality, decimate the physical footprint of old Derry, and ultimately augur emotional and physical dislocations.[63]

ACHIEVEMENTS AND LIMITS OF THE "BOOTSTRAPS BRIGADE"

Despite unionist harangues that Catholics were whingers and grifters, Derry had a long history of self-help.[64] Some residents followed the sentiment quite literally. For them, building their own accommodations, inhabiting caravans, squatting in condemned houses, refusing to pay rent for substandard accommodations, or moving into the Nissen huts at the Springtown Camp recently vacated by U.S. soldiers were ways of looking after themselves. Others, however, looked to the past and found models and inspiration in the community's long history of meeting its needs through networks of support.

In 1947, for example, under Bishop Neil Farren's instructions, volunteers formed the Derry Catholic Social Service Centre to help local people navigate complicated bureaucratic hurdles and access public benefits. As a completely free service, the Centre's volunteers helped residents fill out paperwork and apply for old-age pensions, unemployment assistance, and family allowances. In 1949, the group helped more than 4,000 people seek government assistance.[65] In 1945, twelve men also founded the Oak Leaf Building Society. "The directors had encouraged their friends to save and invest in the society," offering low-interest mortgages at a time when Catholics had difficulty negotiating with banks.[66] Oak Leaf intended to offer mortgages and thus increase Catholic home ownership, but it also encouraged savings for any reason, "for holidays, old age or just the rainy day." Those who deposited their funds into Oak Leaf enjoyed a good rate of return, easy access to their money, and the knowledge that they were helping members of their community to purchase a home.[67] It was a subtle act of political resistance; by abstaining from participation in the British banking system, they kept their money local and could be confident that it would be recycled within Derry's Catholic community. By 1966, the society was holding 226 mortgages and had more than 500 shareholders.

Building on this tradition, a new generation of middle-class leaders and clergy in Derry's Catholic community sought creative solutions to local financial and housing problems in the 1960s. In 1965, Fr. Anthony Mulvey founded the Derry Housing Aid Society, a voluntary organization dedicated to improving housing options for poor people. The Housing Aid Society followed on the heels of the development of the Derry Credit Union; both organizations were led by local men whom Paddy "Bog-side" Doherty would later refer to as the "up by your bootstraps brigade," or more simply, the Bootstraps Brigade. The housing group provided free advice three nights a week to members of the public seeking better accommodation.

With no statutory support for setup or seed money, most initiatives began with a small amount of funding from a few individuals and were run by volunteers. Doherty recalled the inaugural meeting of the Derry Credit Union: "I put in a few pounds into it and John (Hume) put a pound and Seamus Bonner put a pound, Paddy Joe Doherty put a pound and I think Eileen put a pound into it so there was about seven pounds fifteen shillings that night and that was the start of the credit union."[68]

The credit union was founded to help local people gain more access to and more control over financial resources. Others tried to tackle the housing problem through self-help. In 1966, members of the Housing Aid Society founded the Derry Housing Association (DHA). Group members interviewed 400 families and visited 100 homes in an effort to gain a better understanding of local housing needs. They called local conditions Dickensian. John Hume, one of the founding members of the DHA, stated that "the conditions in which many young families are forced to live through lack of housing can only be described as a blot on the conscience of the community."[69] More than simply invigorating community development, the DHA and the Credit Union brought Derry's Catholic community closer together. As Michael Canavan, a founding member of the Credit Union, explained, it became more difficult to pretend that the problems facing others did not affect them. It was impossible to visit homes and hear people's stories and not notice the domino effects of poverty, poor housing, and unemployment. What's more, a historical consciousness of injustice developed, bolstered by a growing awareness that so many crises "had their roots in political problems."[70] Canavan explained:

A lot of people's economic condition was due to the fact that they had no housing, they were paying high rents, they would never own a house, their economic difficulties were due to the fact there was discrimination against them in jobs, that industry would be prevented from coming here, and it wasn't enough to be simply interested in things that would change people's lives, within their own experience, but that the effort needed to be on a much wider basis.[71]

As they became more conscious of the ripple effects of Derry's political history, the Housing Action Council made practical advances to solve terrible housing conditions. The housing situation in Derry was encapsulated by one young woman's plea to her doctor, asking for his help in obtaining better housing for her family. The doctor turned the letter over to the *Derry Journal*, noting that he believed "she expressed the feelings of hundreds of young mothers in this city."[72] As the young mother explained, her apartment, located on the fourth floor of a walk-up, was damp and the bannisters rotten; broken windows and a nonworking fireplace made it drafty, and an unresponsive landlord collected a high rent (over £3) but never fulfilled promises to make repairs. Her family shared one bathroom with two other large families. The women explained that her husband, who had "a steady job and works shifts," couldn't get enough sleep because the children were playing in house. "They cannot even go out to play in the street, as we live in the city centre and the street is very busy."[73]

The woman's situation was hardly unusual. An assessment of amenities in the city, conducted in 1961, concluded that a large number of residents lacked uninterrupted access to water. Close to half of the city's households did not have sole use of a hot water supply, while more than 54 percent of households shared a fixed bath/toilet; 16 percent of families shared a kitchen sink.[74]

In an effort to rectify situations like the ones described above, the DHA purchased two and a half acres of land off the Buncrana Road in Pennyburn, and undertook to build thirty-two semidetached housing units. The group, working through the Derry Credit Union and the Oak Leaf Building Society, offered three options for families in need: It helped those in the position to pay a mortgage to obtain a loan in order to buy their own homes; it offered a "lease-to-own" option whereby a percentage of the monthly rent went towards a down payment on one's dwelling; and it helped some to become property managers and then they could let accommodation to the majority of Derry families who were in no financial position to become homeowners.

Although the development appeared modest, the DHA had accomplished as much on its own as the city government had within the same time frame. In the 1966 fiscal year, the Derry Corporation had built only fifty-two dwelling units.[75] The DHA set its sights on a larger project and in 1967 proposed to build 700 units of housing in Pennyburn. As the land in question lay in the politically precarious North Ward, it came as little surprise when the Corporation refused planning permission.[76]

Lack of surprise did not ease the blow, however. Catholics were increasingly frustrated that even their own "bootstraps" strategies were repeatedly rejected by unionist leaders. Frank Curran remembered the aftermath meeting at which unionist councillors voted down the Pennyburn proposal:

> The atmosphere of members of the two sides of the Chamber was frigid as they left the building after the meeting. Councillor Paddy Friel, the calmest and most unaggressive of men, still accompanied his friend, Unionist Alderman Alex "Sandy" McGowan, up Shipquay Street on their way home. Their mutual respect had so far survived all the political clashes, but that day there was a strained and unusual silence. I had left the meeting with the pair and as we headed up the steep hill, Friel could contain himself no longer. "Alex," he said, "how do you, the decent man I know you to be, sit there and listen to the arguments for the building of those badly needed houses, and vote against what you know to be right? How do you feel about it?" McGowan looked at us as he replied . . . "Ah, Paddy, how do you think I feel, with my hand up and my head down?"[77]

Sandy McGowan's response is telling. His comment to Friel suggests that some Protestant unionists felt compelled to vote against their conscience and with their party. Meanwhile, nationalists' efforts to solve the housing problem on their own continued to meet stiff opposition. In

February 1968, the DHA came back to the Corporation with a proposal to build its own houses at Shantallow, which lay just on the other side of the city boundary. The housing subcommittee agreed to seek legal opinion on the matter, but it came back stating that the Corporation "could not acquire land outside the urban limits."[78] In the meantime, a Northern Ireland Housing Trust proposal to develop a 250-acre site in Shantallow was rejected when the Derry Rural Council refused to provide essential services for the area.[79]

A report released in the first week of March 1968 made clear the enormity of the housing problems facing the city, further incensing those who had been calling for change and those who were trying to effect it.[80] Planners from Muncie Partnership stated in their assessment of the city and surrounding liberties that 5,000 houses were substandard and that 9,600 dwellings would be needed in Derry over the next thirteen years in order to meet the requirements stipulated in the 1956 Housing Act, for one, that all substandard housing units in Northern Ireland be replaced or preserved by 1981.

The notion that Derry could build 800 houses per year over the next thirteen years seemed inconceivable given the stalemate in the city over the boundary extension and the intractability of the political situation that caused it. This is where memory and historical consciousness came into play. The Bootstraps Brigade and the other informal sources of Derry's self-help model of solving problems consumed the time, energy, and resources of residents trying to address their community's needs. However, the sheer scale of the problem dwarfed their efforts. What's more, the solutions seemed as simple as they were unattainable. Given the political and social history of gerrymandered Derry and a very real sense that Catholics' strategies had failed continually and would be bound to continue to fail, frustrations ran high. Housing became a rallying issue in Derry precisely because it was the concrete by-product of an entire set of social, political, and economic relations that had always been tacitly understood but not articulated or externalized in Northern Irish life. The issue held both tangible and symbolic meaning and therefore attracted local residents' support.

"I CAN SMELL SULFUR IN THE AIR."

By 1968, a growing number of Derry Catholics were increasingly unwilling to stand by and watch politics block progress. Like others in Northern Ireland, they were inspired by protest and civil rights movements in other parts of the world and began to seek more direct means of influencing politics. The vital concerns over housing in Derry exposed indefensible and unsound aspects of life in Northern Ireland and helped to catalyze a series of events that irrevocably changed the city and the province.

The early months of 1968 saw youthful agitators heading up protests, but the movement was growing and the rank-and-file Catholic population of Derry became increasingly invested and involved in the civil rights movement. Current events struck a nerve that linked the news headlines about housing and jobs to a long history of struggle against uneven politics and disadvantage. They had become tired, in the words of James Doherty, of "trying to force, cajole or argue the Unionist party of Derry out of the nineteenth century mentality in which they are sunk."[81]

Eddie McAteer clearly sensed this when he addressed the minister of home affairs at Stormont on March 7, 1968. McAteer specifically raised the issue of the prohibitions placed on nationalist marches and protests, but his concerns were relevant to mobilization around the broader issues of voting, employment, and access to housing. He later said that he chose his words very cautiously, wanting to appear moderate as opposed to alarmist; yet, his short speech would soon be seen as a premonition. In it, he expressed concern that the people involved in protests and getting arrested were "not the teenage, out-for-excitement type; they are mature people who feel they are being denied their basic rights." He warned government officials that they were "pressing the spring to a dangerous point." He continued, "It is only because I can smell sulfur in the air that I think the government and the House as a whole should be alerted. There is a problem here . . . we are rushing into a very dangerous situation and it behooves us as a people of common sense to do our best to avert what might very well be a permanent catastrophe to community relations."[82]

McAteer's instincts were well founded. Northern Ireland's earliest civil rights demonstrations took place in Dungannon in the mid-1960s, but sustained direct action originated in Derry. The Derry Housing Action Committee (DHAC) was formed in March 1968 to demand solutions to the city's housing problems publicly and dramatically. Mostly composed of young people, the DHAC was tired of accommodationist politicians who leaned towards propriety at the expense of change. On March 7, 1968, the small band of activists crowded into the monthly meeting of the Corporation with banners and placards for their first action.

The group disrupted proceedings and read a prepared statement demanding that the local government immediately extend the city boundary and speed up housing construction. Undeterred by the political leaders' derisive admonitions that "the Communists" be removed or by the presence of the police, the DHAC continued to attend meetings. In May they requested that a deputation from their group be allowed to present the Corporation with a dossier on housing problems. At the meeting, committee member Bridget Bond handed over a list of demands and said, "This is our last attempt through normal channels to have our demands met."[83] Mayor Anderson promised he would look into their requests, among which were an improved, transparent system of allocating houses and a rapid mobilization to step up construction.

DHAC members made every attempt to unbalance normal proceedings of all city meetings dealing with housing, despite their concerns being repeatedly dismissed. Politicians and bureaucrats brushed aside efforts to link the housing situation with broader political issues. When Eamon Melaugh challenged Housing Trust architect D. Craig on the "battery-hen conditions" in the Rossville flats and suggested that a particular area was not developed so as to protect fragile unionist voting majorities, Craig replied, "I am afraid you are beyond me."[84]

Having had little success with the politicians and planning experts, the DHAC resorted to bolder tactics. The group took up the case of John Wilson, who had been living for three years with his wife and two children in an eighteen-foot caravan parked up a mucky lane in the Brandywell district. After Wilson was told by the Corporation Housing Department that he had "no chance" of a house, he approached the mayor, who promised to look into the matter.[85] Both his own and his wife's health had suffered; they had lost an infant, and many believed that the death was a direct result of living in the trailer with no plumbing.[86]

On June 22, 1968, ten people, including Wilson, picked up the caravan and hauled it into the middle of the busy intersection of Anne and Hamilton Streets, blocking Lecky Road, the main artery and bus line from the city center into the South Ward, for close to three hours. The DHAC distributed leaflets in the surrounding streets explaining that they intended to keep the caravan there for twenty-four hours as a protest against the Wilson family's living conditions; they asked for the community's support. They phoned the police, mayor, and newspapers, inviting each to come and see. The caravan was moved only when Councillor James Doherty promised that Wilson's case would receive special attention.

The activists returned the caravan to the intersection on June 29 and 30 after waiting a week for follow-up on Doherty's promise without a response.[87] This time, police were quick to respond; however, they had not counted on residents of the area supporting the disruptors. Witnesses at the scene relayed that when Sargent F. Flynn asked the crowd who had pulled the caravan out, they replied, "We all brought it out."[88] Community support notwithstanding, police arrested DHAC organizers, who were fined between £3 and £5 for their participation in the protest. They also had to produce £50 bail and agree to be bound to the peace for two years. Alternatively, they were required to do three months of prison time, which two members of the group opted to serve; they ultimately spent one month in Belfast's Crumlin Road Jail.

Despite the high levels of unemployment and deprivation in Derry, when those who had been arrested and fined for moving the caravan into the street went door-to-door collecting funds to pay their fines, they managed to raise £20. Telling police on the scene that they "all" had moved the caravan into the street was one thing; contributing to the material cost of protest took community further. Growing local support for the activists was evident in the sacrifice people made to help them pay the fines.

During the summer of 1968, a core group of activists began to come together for regular meetings: "Johnnie White, Liam Cummins and Finbar Doherty from the Republican Club; Charlie Morrison, Dermie Mc-Clenaghan and [Eamonn McCann] from the Labour Party; Matt O'Leary of the Housing Action Committee; Eamon Melaugh, a free-wheeling radical who had ten children and a bizarre vocabulary; and a few others."[89] The group saw itself as the stirrer of Derry's political pot; those involved—and their politics—differed in myriad ways; however, all shared a commitment to direct action and civil protest. Most self-identified as activists and agitators.

Ordinary people became increasingly involved in protests over housing in Derry as the summer of 1968 wore on. Irish cultural nationalism also played a role rallying people. Residents of the high-rise flats followed through with the formal complaint they had lodged against the Housing Trust for forbidding reception of Irish television and radio stations, part of a policy allowing only "home" stations on shared aerials in public housing. The condition of the licensing agreement for communal aerials that served the flats was that they only could receive BBC and British commercial programs. Tenants were particularly frustrated when they learned that their TV sets would not be able to receive "foreign" Irish stations. A representative from the General Post Office exacerbated the problem when he gave a statement on the issue, likening residents of Housing Trust properties in Derry who wanted to watch Irish television to residents of England who might wish to watch French channels.[90]

By July, DHAC had become a large umbrella group. Committee members stepped up activities by staging a sit-down protest during the opening ceremonies for the lower deck of the Craigavon Bridge. The action coincided with court hearings for those who had been arrested for moving the Wilsons' caravan. During the protest on the bridge, six DHAC members were arrested for disorderly conduct and obstruction. Fionbarra O'Doherty protested later that the group had been respectful: "'disorderly conduct' consisted of breaking into 'We Shall Overcome.'"[91]

In the aftermath of the protest, the housing activists contacted NICRA and suggested they sponsor a peaceful civil rights march in Derry; it was scheduled for October 5, 1968.[92] The purpose of the march was to call attention to the grievances of the Catholic majority: unemployment, the housing situation, discrimination in jobs, and the gerrymandered political reality. As Catholics and nationalists had faced episodic prohibitions against gathering and processing in public since the 1930s, the declaration that they would take to the streets and march to the symbolic center of Derry at the Diamond was significant.

Activists hoped to harness strong feelings around housing to broaden the struggle for civil rights and anticipated at first that as many as 5,000 people would congregate.[93] They were lukewarm about the participation of mainstream politicians and community leaders, however. Members of "the bootstraps brigade" such as John Hume and many of Derry's nationalist politicians ultimately agreed to participate in the event, though they refused to sponsor it when NICRA asked them to.[94] Undoubtedly led by activists, it was the first event that saw unity among the city's disparate change agents.[95] As Paddy Doherty described it, "the direct action group" and the "up by your bootstraps brigade" joined forces at Duke Street.[96]

Through the actions of the DHAC, Catholic leaders understood that housing had become the lightning rod for a long list of charges and complaints Catholics in Derry leveled against leaders in the city and the province. For many, the battle over housing opened up a space in which old frustrations blossomed into public indignation.[97] The housing crisis was a bread-and-butter issue, certainly, but more importantly it was a symptom of a deeper problem: "Housing, they felt, was being denied them because of blatant religious discrimination, political blocking tactics against proposed developments by various housing associations, and the refusal by Unionist-controlled councils to undertake crash house building programs."[98]

In 1973, McCann acknowledged this in his assessment of the work and purpose of the Housing Action Committee. He explained that attacking housing was a way of launching an assault on the political and economic structure as a whole. For McCann and other socialists in the housing action group, the emphasis on sectarian politics elided pressing economic issues and impeded working-class solidarities, but most Catholics in the city did not separate the long history of sectarian divisions that shaped Derry and Northern Ireland from the day-to-day problems they faced. The activists took on the unionist Corporation confident they had the entire Catholic community's support: "The gerrymandered Corporation was the living symbol in Derry of the anti-democratic exclusion of Catholics from power. The stated reason for our activities . . . was to highlight the housing situation, but they were generally regarded by Catholics as an attack on the whole political set-up; which, of course, they were."[99]

Most Derry Catholics quietly condoned the larger purpose of direct action, but it was those who were poor and with little to lose who rose to the occasion financially. Seeking funds for the march, the DHAC went back to their base. The march's organizers considered their goals to transcend the sectarian divide and did everything they could to disassociate themselves with the nationalist party, but it was Derry's working-class Catholic community that offered them the most material support. Fionnbarra Ó Dochartaigh, the organization's secretary, recounted, "The bulk of the finances required were collected on a door-to-door basis in the working class Creggan estate. The collection books were later to reveal that those who contributed most generously came from the poorer area of the estate known as 'The Heights.'"[100]

Minister for Home Affairs William Craig banned the scheduled march. He argued that an Apprentice Boys of Liverpool march would take place on the same day at the same time, along precisely the same route—from the Waterside railway station to the Diamond; that no one was aware of the Liverpudlians' scheduled visit to the city mattered little.[101] As a *Derry Journal* editorial rightly noted, "The ban has long since been a conventional weapon in the armory reserved by Stormont for use against its political opponents."[102]

Catholics were used to forfeiting their right to public demonstrations, just as they were resigned to the reality that Protestants could march. Organizers had always planned to walk whether the march was allowed or not.[103] Ultimately, somewhere between 500 and 2,000 people defied the ban and congregated for the march on the afternoon of October 5, 1968. As people congregated, tensions were evident: 130 police officers and members of the B Special reserves formed two lines from the starting point of the march across the Craigavon Bridge, one in front of the marchers and one behind them. Ominously, two water cannons stood at the ready.

When the inevitable call came to dispel the marchers, police and reserves used indiscriminate force. NICRA leader Gerry Fitt and Eddie McAteer were batoned by the police, when no order to draw batons had been given.[104] According to the Cameron Report on the disturbances in Derry, "the use of batons on these gentlemen was wholly without justification or excuse."[105] By the end of the day, approximately 100 people had to seek medical attention for injuries they sustained. Twenty-nine people were arrested.

When scenes of the violence were broadcast, "an elemental howl of rage was unleashed across Northern Ireland and it was clear that things were never going to be the same again."[106] Duke Street quickly came to be understood as a lightning rod in the outbreak of the Troubles. The *Journal* suggested that the response by police and B Specials "had shaken the hinges of decency clear off the door of Northern politics." Stormont, the paper said, "has been caught in such a backlash of world opinion that nothing will ever be quite the same in this little corner of the world."[107] Everyone understood that Duke Street was a watershed. Thanks to the presence of television reporters, the world had watched as the police used force to stop the marchers. Derry people all over the world sent in clippings and transcriptions of radio recordings from Thailand, New Zealand, Zambia, and all over the United States and Europe. Outrage rippled far beyond those who participated in the march.

THE HURRICANE OF CHANGE

For years, Derry's Catholics had hoped that Protestant leaders in their city would see the common sense of electoral and economic fair play and the moral sense. Politics in the city thus had the air of a waiting game—for the entire twentieth century, leaders had insisted that "sooner or later, the numbers tell." Local Catholic leaders assumed that as their community's population steadily grew, Derry's Protestant elected officials would eventually concede some local power and embark on a politics of fair play. Duke Street confirmed their suspicions that this was not going to happen without a fight.

Gerard McMenamin likely spoke for many when he explained, "When the Inspector drove his baton into that protest, he burst an abscess that had been festering for generations. It was an abscess whose pus came from the very heart of our society, from the very heart of each of us."[108] Duke Street also drove home the connections between a set of seemingly disparate experiences that had constrained Catholic life—the hiring fairs, the 1951 St. Patrick's Day riots, and Duke Street. For Seamus Deane, memory work conflated the events of Duke Street with other wrongs:

My parents remembered the hiring fairs of the 1920s. They took place in the Diamond and were apparently a sight to make anyone with a conscience wince. Children who spoke no English were hired out to farmers and householders who spoke no Irish for £6 a year, payable upon completion of the work. I remember the '50s and one St. Patrick's Day in the Diamond when Eddie McAteer and the Nationalist Councilors turned down Shipquay Street, tricolour aloft, to face a brutal baton charge which sent us all catapulting through the streets. Then came October 5. What had these events in common? People bartered, people battered.[109]

Catholics no longer believed that a stronger moral compass could yield a new politics. Their demands for civil rights were shaped by memories of unfairness and tinged with distrust that arose from those memories, but they were hopeful that change could come. The events of Duke Street dashed those hopes even as they sharpened historical consciousness of the intransigence of their adversaries and catapulted Derry into the most tumultuous period it had seen for sixty years.[110]

Just a few nights after the march, at meeting in the City Hotel, representatives from several different groups joined ranks to form the Derry Citizens' Action Committee (DCAC). Staunch activists derided the new group as "middle-aged, middle-class and middle of the road," but others found that the new organization represented and clearly articulated their position, which previously had been a set of inchoate but deeply felt murmurs:

> The Citizens' Action Committee's strength was that it struck an attitude which perfectly matched the mood of the Catholic masses in the aftermath of 5th October. John Hume was its personification: reasonable, respectable, righteous, solid, non-violent and determined. The average Bogsider wanted to do something about 5th October; he could go out and march behind Hume, confident that he would not be led into violence, in no way nervous about the political ideas of the men at the front of the procession and certain that he was, by his presence, making a contribution to the struggle. The [D]CAC did not challenge the consciousness of the Catholic masses. It updated

the expression of it, injected new life into it and made it relevant to a changed situation.[111]

On October 19, hundreds of people turned up for a sit-in demonstration in Guildhall Square. As Frank Curran explained, no one knew quite what to do. Most of those who had come were unused to activism and wary of doing things that ran afoul of the authorities. Yet, unionist leaders viewed their presence alone in Guildhall Square as provocative. Entrance to the city walls had been blocked off and armed police were gathered at all the points of departure from the square. It was seventy-year-old veteran nationalist councillor Joe Canning who sat down first: "Joe settled down as if he was at the seaside on a sunny summer day, lit his pipe and puffed away contentedly. Everyone else followed his example and soon the whole crowd were reclining in the square."[112] Bishop Edward Daly remembered that a few people began quietly and unsteadily to sing "We Shall Overcome," "and soon the entire square was enveloped in song."[113] Paddy "Bogside" Doherty remembered the good behavior of those who attended: "It was a wet day and most people sat down on newspapers and then everybody got up and picked up all the newspapers and took them away, wrapped them up and took them away so that whenever I went up to the wall afterwards and looked down there wasn't any presence of hundreds of people having gathered in that place, we were so respectable. I thought they'd been at a prayer meeting, you know."[114]

Although Free Presbyterian minister and ultra-unionist Ian Paisley had been busy organizing in Derry, the small counterprotest at the Guildhall did little to dampen the protestors' resolve. The demonstration ended peacefully, and although Craig reserved his congratulations for those who did not condone the sit-in, saying that they had maintained the peace, there was a sense that a small victory had been won. Momentum began to grow for another mass event.

On November 2, about 4,000 people watched as fifteen members of the DCAC marched along the route that had been banned less than a month earlier. The DCAC organized more than 200 stewards, led by Vinny Coyle, who created distance between the thousands who lined the route and the police, and from the small band of loyalists who had come to wage a counter demonstration. Again, things came off peacefully, though Michael Canavan's comment to the press before the men began to march suggested that the organizers themselves had had their doubts: "No matter what happens to any of us, we go on. If there is one man left standing, he walks on."[115]

Derry people remained calm in the face of provocation. Major Ronald Bunting, leader of a group called the Loyal Citizens of Ulster and organizer of the counterprotest, for example, advised his followers through a bull horn: "When the rebels move off, walk behind them, but keep out of their way if you want to avoid the stench."[116] By day's end, the DCAC could affirm that Derry people were capable of marching peacefully in the city center. November 2 proved wrong Craig's argument that nationalists and civil rights adherents could not be trusted to behave with civility.

Frustrations were high and the city was buzzing. At a meeting of the City Corporation, the gallery packed with demonstrators, nationalist politicians castigated the unionists, who, like Alex McGowan, with "heads down, hands up" had for so long governed the city. Historical consciousness of the long years of gerrymander and overt discrimination worked their way into the discourse surrounding Duke Street and the police brutality towards the marchers. Councillor Doherty declared, "This didn't bring us back forty years—it brought us right back to the days when the curfew bell tolled the knell of parting day for the Catholics of this city, when they had to be out of the city Walls after the bell rang."[117]

Councillor James Hegarty was even more explicit as he exhorted that the time for change had finally arrived. His frustration was shaped by two decades as a political representative of the city's Catholics and nationalists:

This Unionist clique, with their powerful backroom boys, must no longer be allowed to keep Derry in ferment. They must be disowned by all right-thinking people and be swept from the power which is wrongfully theirs. I do not expect they have the guts to go gracefully, but go they must—and go they will. . . . I speak perhaps in parts bitterly but remember I have endured twenty years of the heart-breaking task of trying to force, cajole or argue the Unionist party of Derry out of the nineteenth century mentality in which they are sunk.[118]

Church leaders and politicians attempted to temper hot emotions even as they tried to steer the tide of change that now seemed inevitable.

As plans were made for a mass protest and demonstration on November 16, Derry's Churches Industrial Council, the group that represented all the main churches in the city, asked that an inquiry be held to examine allegations of discrimination in housing, electoral policy, and employment. When Craig placed a ban on all marches through the city center, "except for those customarily held," a cross-denominational team attempted to get him to change his mind. They hoped to show him that allowing the Apprentice Boys' traditional Lundy Day parade to go on as scheduled while denying the civil rights' demonstrators the right to march would instigate a strong reaction. Craig defended his decision, saying that the scheduled march within the city's walls was deliberately provocative. His comments reflected a growing sense of frustration among many unionists with the frequency of public protests and an accompanying sense that those marching did not reflect general public attitudes: "Demonstrations may be a safety valve when used sensibly and in moderation, but when they become a weekly or daily occurrence then they become an instrument of provocation . . . all decent people must call a halt to the politics of revolution."[119]

Church leaders were not alone in their efforts to set the parameters for peaceful social change. Veteran nationalist politicians such as Eddie McAteer tried to promote a vision commensurate with the new era and proposed an inclusive future with a different kind of political calculus. In his speech at the November meeting of the Derry Nationalist Party, McAteer challenged some time-honored shibboleths of Northern nationalism. His dream of ending Partition and reuniting the two parts of Ireland shaped his response to the political turbulence:

> If indeed the ugly discrimination era is nearing its end, what are our reactions, what are our new attitudes then? When Protestants and Catholics both stand upright as free and equal, must we not then strive to welcome back to the Nationalist fold our too long estranged brethren? Yes, there will be startling amendments to Nationalist thinking. What of it? Nationalism has already changed greatly in fifty years—further accelerated change is natural and to be expected. If Belfast is in Ireland, would it be treasonable to work towards rule from Belfast rather than Dublin? Could a two-piece Ireland not be fitted into a sort of little United Nations grouping of these islands? I

have no cut and dried answers. But we must think, think and open our minds to the hurricane of change which beats upon us all.[120]

Still, unionist political leaders were unmoved. Catholics were affronted when informed that demonstrations would be disrespectful to the memories of city representatives who had fought in the two world wars, since the city's official war memorial stood in the center of the contested Diamond within the city's walls. As one resident put it, it seemed an odd time to begin to think about the patriot dead and to classify the space as sanctified: "Is it not a fact that rabbles were held there and was it not a centre for farmers exchanging hired hands?"[121]

Banning the November 16 march from entering the city walls had the opposite effect than Craig intended. People who considered themselves decent and law-abiding became more intent on showing Craig that their concerns could not be easily cast aside. The intentions of the civil rights organizers reflected the general will of the city's people.

Emboldened by their successes, Derry Catholics set their sights on the November 16 march, and determined to participate despite the ban. Paddy Doherty was named chief steward of the march, in charge of keeping the peace. He asked his best friend, Donal McCafferty, to be his deputy. Doherty turned up at McCafferty's on the evening before the march, as 2,000 people were making their way to St. Eugene's to pray that the city would remain quiet and peaceful the following day. Doherty remembered dissonance between what he and many others hoped would transpire and what they feared. Particularly for the men and women of his generation, the scenes of 1951 and 1952 resonated as they prepared for the march:

Whenever I went in [McCafferty] was on his knees and he had a lid belonging to a pot which he was flattening down and he had on one of those hunting hats that you would get from America, you know with the peaks, and there he was fitting this inside a cap and I was watching him, and he said, "what do you think of this?" and he put an inch of foam on it and he put it on his head, he says, "that'll stand the weight of a baton, you know," and then he got up and he showed me, he tied on his shin guards and he put on a big coat in which he'd sewn various leather things, amulets kind of, and he put the big coat on and he marched up and down showing he was rigged for battle the following day and then he picked out of his pocket a blackjack and from the other a knuckle duster . . . and I thought, "my good God, here, I know this Civil Rights thing where there's going to be no violence and I am supposed to make sure there's no violence, that's my job, and here McCafferty, this man who wouldn't hurt a flea, and he's rigged for battle."[122]

Doherty also recalled that everyone who planned to participate in the march made certain that everything they wore was clean. Everyone was terrified, not that they would be killed, but that they would end up in the hospital, "and be found with dirty underwear on them, that would be the worst possible thing that could happen. As a result, it was a very clean march."[123] The sense of propriety, reflective of long-held Derry values, would prove useful on November 16.

Nearly 15,000 people gathered at the Waterside Railway station in advance of the 3:00 p.m. start time on November 16, 1968. Father Daly described the scene: "The spirit was good humored. The sheer numbers of people walking across Craigavon Bridge reassured everyone. The crowd encompassed all ages and classes and there was a substantial sprinkling of Protestant people there as well. Nobody was in any doubt about the justice or the reason for the march or the injustice of banning the march."[124]

Since the ban was not imposed on the march itself, but on the route, the epicenter of tension lay at the intersection of the Craigavon Bridge and Carlisle Road, about thirty yards from the place where police had erected barricades to block the marchers. Organizers were concerned that Craig had deliberately deployed a small and poorly armed police force so that in the event that violence broke out, blame would fall on the demonstrators themselves. Doherty asked people to sit and remain calm, telling the crowd, "The Minister in a moment of madness banned our parade and we stand now in open defiance of the Minister. He banned our march in order to get the people of Derry at each other's throats. Was he right or wrong?"[125]

Doherty remembered that it was difficult to hold back the throng of agitated marchers at the site of the barricades. It was two old men and their decision to create a place of pause amidst the scene that temporarily calmed the crowd. As the crowd jostled the march stewards, something unexpected took place: "What do you think happened, but Eugene O'Hare and the old republican Frank, remember, they were great draft players or chess players. In the middle of the bridge, these people got out their board and began to sit on the pavement and when everyone else was worried about the march, they had their own match together playing chess on the bridge. However, the thing got so hot I knew there was no way they could hold the crowd."[126]

Michael Canavan and three other members of the DCAC were finally called to cross the barricades ceremonially. As they did so, John Hume announced that the ban had been broken. At the same moment, a lone stone from a small group of Loyalist counterdemonstrators landed close to marchers. The police did not react, leaving many in front of the march to wonder whose rights the police would protect. The stewards had a difficult job directing increasingly angry marchers away from the loyalists and onto John Street, towards the Guildhall. As the Protestant group sang "No Surrender," a group of marchers responded with "We Shall Overcome," but others, just behind the front lines, lobbed stones, coins, and pepper bombs at the police. Stewards had to keep the peace and direct the crowd towards John Street.

Thousands of marchers fell out of rank and veered up the hill, heading towards Ferryquay Street and "the forbidden territory" of the walled city.[127] As Frank Curran explained later, the police seemed uncertain about whether or not to stop the crowd: "They were unwilling to face another October 5 style encounter and they withdrew into Shipquay Street leaving the Diamond in the possession of the ban breakers."[128] At 4:45 p.m., the officer in charge ordered his officers to withdraw.

The march organizers encouraged the elated crowd to sit down at the Diamond. John Hume took the megaphone to laud the peaceful demonstration:

We are within the Walls and we will stay here. We have the force of the like of which has never been seen in the city before, and had we wished to use it, we could not have been stopped. But we chose instead to pursue our aims in a non-violent manner and there is now an assembly within the walls. Mr. Craig told us this could not be done without violence. We have thrown that lie back in his teeth. I am not a law-breaker by nature, but I am proud to stand here with 15,000 Derry people who have broken the law which is in disrepute. I invite Mr. Craig to arrest the lot of us.[129]

In an editorial on November 19, 1968, the *Journal* heralded "the end of apathy" in Derry and celebrated the congregation that was "representative of all walks of life among the citizen majority and so single-minded of purpose and determination." The time had finally arrived; Derry Catholics would now "attain their full civil rights of which they have so long been deprived, a state of affairs they are no longer prepared to take, nor will they settle for any less than an end to such conditions."[130]

The magnitude of the November 16 march impressed itself on virtually everyone who was paying attention. By walking through Ferryquay gate, Derry Catholics did more than assert a right that had been denied to them since the establishment of the Northern state: "They demonstrated to themselves, to the rest of the people in Ireland, that they were first class citizens, not in any way second class."[131] Within a week, their assertion received affirmation from O'Neill. Proposing a set of reforms for the city, O'Neill exclaimed, "Let us lift Derry out of the turbulence of politics for a time; let us concentrate all our energies upon houses for its people, jobs for its people, a decent, fulfilled honourable life for its people—and for all its people."[132]

The *Journal* ran letters to the editor that offered different perspectives. Some smacked of bitterness, suggesting that accommodations were "too little, too late." For example, W. R. O'Connell from Westland Avenue wrote: "Thank you, thank you, Captain O'Neill for your 12,000 jobs and 10,000 houses by 1981. But of course we must be good little boys and not annoy papa or we won't get any sweets. Be your age, Captain. Those days are over. Give us our civil rights first and then other things will follow."[133]

However, others suggested that this was the beginning of a positive new era in Northern Ireland's history. They entreated others to be careful. Harry McCourt from Creggan drew on imagery dating to the 1798 Rebellion when he wrote, "No good will come of violence. Listen to your

Civil Rights Committee's directives, stop all acts of violence, do not allow yourselves to be dictated to by the bad element. The 'West' is indeed awake. The eyes of the world are on us. By following our '15' we shall indeed achieve and truly 'we shall overcome.'"[134]

By the end of November 1969, a host of things had changed in Derry. On November 22, the prime minister invited the councillors from the Corporation to Stormont, where he read them a prepared statement suspending the Londonderry Corporation and the Londonderry Derry Rural Council, effective immediately. The gerrymander was dead.

He announced the appointment of the Londonderry Development Commission (LDC), which would be responsible for implementing the city's new development plan. One of three "new town" development commissions in Northern Ireland, the LDC was led by a group of credentialed and impartial outsiders appointed by the prime minister. It was charged first and foremost with implementing Housing Trust proposals for new residential housing construction in the city. The city's boundary had been extended and a massive hyperspeed development initiative promised to build thousands of units of housing north of the city, two miles from the urban core. Many in Derry considered O'Neill's response to the housing crisis and the replacement of the Corporation with a Development Commission due reward for a peaceful march and an affirmation that their concerns had been well justified.[135]

For his part, unionist councillor Leonard Hutchinson grappled with the news that the Corporation was to be disbanded and "put in cold storage for an unknown number of years whether we liked it or not."[136] Expressing dismay that none of the elected representatives had received so much as a thank-you for their many years of service, he likened the arrival of the proposed development commission to a heart transplant. Hutchinson called for calm during this process, but said that "when recovery does take place, the new heart will never beat as loyally as the old heart."[137]

For the Catholic residents of Derry, that was good news. At the final meeting of the Londonderry Corporation, onlookers in the public galleries serenaded the unionists with "Auld Lang Syne." Change had arrived in the city. As O'Neill declared, Ulster was "standing at the crossroads."

At the end of 1968, it appeared as if significant social and political transformations were in the offing. The city faced an unprecedented political era. Derry Catholics celebrated the visible signs that their voices had been heard and continued to press for social and political change. Citizens had reason to be hopeful their requests would be favorably met. It seemed that two months of agitation had accomplished more than years of patient politics on behalf of Derry. Many residents, giddy from the gains, seemed unaware of the rising tide of tensions unleashed by the mass protests. But 1969 would open with violence; that violence would grow exponentially as the Troubles developed.

Looking back on the civil rights movement in the mid-1980s, Eamon Melaugh said "housing was the major victory."[138] Likewise, when the Cameron Commission drew its conclusions on the causes of early incidents of civil unrest in Northern Ireland, it identified issues related to housing as the first general cause. Housing, however, was simply the most obvious by-product of the longer and more endemic issues of political discrimination. The web of social and political concerns that had constrained housing development in Derry was one of the major catalysts for the movement. Paradoxically, housing continued to play a role in both memory work and continued violence during the height of the Troubles in Derry.

The urban redevelopment schemes that built much-needed homes in the city also destroyed neighborhoods, broke up communities, and exploded the coordinates of "old Derry." The physical landscapes of Catholic Derry destroyed, local people experienced the violence of the Troubles through the lens of multiplied loss. Troubles-era Derry was indeed a ruptured city; its new physical design was directly related to civil unrest. Linking the housing issue to the Troubles, Melaugh reflected on the victory as a Pyrrhic one: "We paid a substantial price for that (the housing victory) in terms of human blood, which has been lost since in the pursuing of these things. Would I do it over again, the answer is no."[139]

Chapter Six

_____

OLD DERRY'S LAST STAND, 1969

On July 19, 1969, more than 15,000 people crowded into St. Eugene's Cathedral and surrounding grounds, spilling onto sidewalks to attend Samuel Devenny's funeral. They came to pay respects to a man who had died as a result of violence that had recently engulfed Derry.[1] The outpouring of public grief reflected both Devenny's stature in the community and the sense of shock and injustice that accompanied his death. It was a foreboding sign of the violence and turmoil that would leave few in Northern Ireland unaffected in the ensuing decades.

Devenny was forty-three years old and the father of nine children. The first fatality of the Troubles in Derry, he had been beaten severely by police officers who had entered his home on the evening of April 19 in pursuit of street rioters. Hospitalized that day, he suffered his first heart attack four days later. After a second heart attack in July, he died (see fig. 11).[2]

Devenny had been standing at his front door at 69 William Street, watching the riot with his son Harry while talking with family friends. Clashes between the Royal Ulster Constabulary (RUC) and young people were commonplace after January 1969; watching the riots had also become customary. They were hard to miss. The Devenny house stood at the east end of William Street, close to the intersection called "Aggro Corner" for its reputation as a flashpoint between Bogside youth and the police they delighted in aggravating.

231

As the police moved down William Street in a pincer formation and tensions heightened, Devenny and the others retreated into his home; they were about to shut the door when eight young rioters barreled into the house. Some ran straight out the back door. Others headed upstairs. Devenny shut the door behind the rioters. A moment later, police kicked it down and entered. They beat him and several members of his family. The Devennys were not known to be especially political and had not been involved in recent standoffs. The primary evidence against them was their open door.

Pausing outside one's open door on William Street in 1969 was not necessarily an affirmation of support for the civil rights movement or the grassroots rebellion being waged by members of the Catholic and nationalist community. The Derry in which Devenny lived, especially in the small streets of the Bogside area, was a city of open doors. Leaving one's door ajar was a tradition with a long history. With cramped quarters within and friends and relatives without, little divided street and home. Devenny and the others may have been witnessing a novel phenomenon in the rioting before them, but their behavior was anything but new. When the Troubles began, rioters utilized an intimate knowledge of backyards and alleyways to escape police. Access was through Catholic Derry's open doors; young rioters found that they could count on this geography of neighborliness, entering through a front door, exiting out the back yard, and disappearing into the meandering back alleys of the community.

The death of Samuel Devenny was a shock for the whole Catholic community. Madeleine McCully's wedding veil still bears witness to that shock. It was her wedding day, and her father was smoking a cigarette in the cab on the way to the chapel when the taxi driver told them the news: "Burned a hole clear through my veil."[3] The violence, unpredictability, and sense of rupture encapsulated in that burn were a material reminder of what was to come.

The quietly understood and politely enforced divides in Northern Irish culture became public, actualized, and animated in the streets as Catholics and nationalists began to challenge them openly and met vociferous reactions from both the police and loyalists. Less than one month after Devenny's funeral, the annual Apprentice Boys' Relief of Derry parade on August 12, 1969, erupted into a pitched battle between Bogside youth, loyalist agitators, police officers, and the local Catholic commu-

Figure 11. Devenny memorial.

nity. What became known as the Battle of the Bogside drew the British army onto the streets of Northern Ireland on August 14; they would remain for more than thirty years. The Troubles are considered to have begun during this tumultuous weekend: "The genie [had] come out of the bottle."[4]

In the years that followed, Derry experienced both directly and obliquely the effects of civil war. During an era of violence perpetuated by the security forces, the police, paramilitary organizations on both sides of the sectarian divide, and citizens themselves, much of the physical, economic, and social fabric of the city was shredded. Amidst this, community life changed dramatically.[5] Familiar ways of understanding the present, past, and future were refigured. The Troubles constituted a deep rupture and inaugurated an era of unprecedented violence, the effects of which were experienced in virtually all aspects of life in Northern Ireland.

More than 3,700 people were killed, as many as 50,000 were injured, close to 40,000 imprisoned, and damages to property and expenses associated with security cost hundreds of millions of pounds. In retrospect, the figures are staggering. In the midst of the Troubles, these levels of violence, the disruption they caused, and the price they exacted were experienced as simultaneously catastrophic and quotidian.

As the heady days of the civil rights movement bled into heated altercations with members of the police force and then the British army, Derry Catholics continued to form a coherent community with a long "history of holding together."[6] Instead of mobilizing *against* history, civil disturbances in the early years of the Troubles saw many Catholics drawing on their shared history in order to mobilize. They spoke, acted, and thought within a culture that had been shaped and maintained through the lived experiences of generations of Derry Catholics.

The early civil rights movement led to civil disturbances and the establishment of the no-go zones. The Bogside briefly existed as a "free-standing" entity to which the army had no access and in which the police could not exert control. The events of 1968, particularly Duke Street and the massive civil rights march on November 16, stirred people up. Just as surely, the "pure nationalism" and "puritanical Catholicism" Seamus Deane identified as the balustrades supporting "old Derry" culture had lost resonance for many people in the community by this time.[7]

These events were not the rupture they initially may appear to be.[8] At least, they were not simply rupture. Rather, people's choices and behavior during those tumultuous early weeks and months of the civil rights movement and into the early Troubles reflected a strong connection to the shape and tenor of their community life, which itself was inseparable from the area's local history and its physical form. From raising funds to offset the fines young activists incurred challenging the system, to playing chess on the Craigavon Bridge in the midst of a standoff between citizens and the police, to singing "We Shall Overcome" during a rain-soaked sit-in demonstration in the Guildhall Square, many Derry Catholics acted more in accordance with their established cultural patterns than against them. The Battle of the Bogside and the weeks that followed saw both the apex and the twilight of that community spirit.

The solidarities that fueled the civil rights movement grew out of "old Derry" and its culture. Its foundations were a product of the physical spaces and the relationships they sustained, both among the city's Catholics and between the two communities. The tradition of segregation had possessed a geography. Even as it proscribed full Catholic visibility in the public spaces of the city, it also afforded a veil of privacy and a place of cultural independence in the South Ward. This cultural dynamic was expressed particularly clearly during the Battle of the Bogside and the ensuing six weeks, which saw Free Derry keep out the police, the British army, and anyone else who residents and their allies felt did not belong.

CONTEXTUALIZING THE BATTLE OF THE BOGSIDE

In November 1968, Stormont released a report stating that "the Government considers it essential that there should be no more disturbances in Londonderry and appeals for a period of calm in which rational discussions on positive steps may take place."[9] Many had reason to hope that calm would prevail and believed change could come peacefully. This notion was challenged almost immediately.

The established power brokers in Protestant and unionist Derry had little patience with the civil rights movement or its participants and adherents. The level of anger and frustration was embedded in public discourse during the period and offers a glimpse at the source of rising tensions. For example, the discussions surrounding the disbandment of the Londonderry Corporation in November 1968 pointed to historical fault lines within Derry. Some unionists acknowledged changes were inevitable, but Alderman McCartney disagreed. Not only did he accuse nationalist leaders and civil rights demonstrators of being complainers with no constructive agenda, but he argued they had been content to do nothing but complain for many years. In McCartney's castigation of nationalists, one of the most pervasive attitudes towards the Catholic community emerged: the notion that there was nothing beyond the nationalist tradition of protest other than a culture of grievance. In other words, there was no substance, only poor form:

> The Nationalist Party for years had contributed nothing to the progress of this city or the State. They had no constructive policy. They appeared as if they had injected themselves with vitriol before each

Corporation meeting and came to soup out their invectives and half-truths. They had tried to vilify the city and the State and give the worst possible interpretation of every action. They had done nothing to assist the prosperity of the people at large and had held back industry from coming to the area, thus causing more hardship to their own people than anyone else.[10]

Within this climate of mutual frustration and growing agitation, the Burntollet march introduced an unprecedented level of violence and volatility. The weekend of January 5, 1969, brought the worst violence to the Bogside since similar outbreaks had taken place between B Specials and residents in 1920. The People's Democracy, a province-wide civil rights group, had staged a march from Belfast to Derry in an effort to maintain momentum for their agenda for social and political change. Though they had been discouraged by moderates within the civil rights movement from marching, the young activists wanted to keep the pressure on.

Five miles outside Derry at Burntollet, marchers were attacked by a group of loyalists in full view of police officers.[11] As marchers straggled into Derry, telling stories about the attack and telling those they met that the police had protected the attackers instead of those being attacked, residents became enraged. Riots erupted in the city center and the Bogside area. In the midst of the heightened tensions, particularly after B Special police officers came into the area singing sectarian songs and wreaking havoc, residents constructed barricades out of found materials in an attempt to keep the reserve police officers and other outsiders from entering. Lord Cameron's report on the events of January 4 and January 5, 1969, issued in September of that year, corroborated local experiences:

> We have to record with regret that our investigations have led us to the unhesitating conclusion that the night of the 4th/5th January a number of policemen were guilty of misconduct which involved assault and battery, malicious damage to property in streets of the predominantly Catholic Bogside area giving reasonable cause for apprehension of personal injury among other innocent inhabitants, and the use of provocative and sectarian and political slogans.[12]

In the midst of this scene of heightened tension and apprehension, a local resident (long believed to be John "Caker" Casey, but was actually Liam Hillen) scrawled, "You Are Now Entering Free Derry" on a gable wall at the corner of Lecky Road and Fahan Street, marking the area as a site of struggle against the police and drawing a boundary line (see fig. 12).[13] Over the next several months, Free Derry corner became a gathering place for news and conversation about the ongoing tensions associated with the civil rights movement and the changes afoot in Northern Ireland. This made sense; it was adjacent to Fox's Corner, which had long been a gathering point in the Bogside area. The "Battle of Fox's Corner" was a popular song, with people adding verses to it over the course of the 1940s and 50s. It was never recorded or written down, but Derry historian Phil Cunningham remembers that it went something like this:

There was a battle as big as a fight,
it lasted all day and it went on all night.
They were allowed to kick and to fight, at the Battle of Fox's Corner.

Holy Moses, what a crew, some of them black and some of them
blue.
Over the 'banken, they all flew, at the Battle of Fox's Corner.

Over the 'banken, they all ran, some of them Black and some of them
Tan.
Betty Coyle was choking a man, at the Battle of Fox's Corner. . . .

Paddy Dean hit Paddy Long over the head with a treacle scone.
They were hairing each other all day long, at the Battle of Fox's
Corner.
Bernie Doherty, he was there, and was split on the head with the leg
of a chair.

When the battle was over and everything done,
they all shook hands with everyone.
And all agreed they had great fun, at the Battle of Fox's Corner.[14]

Figure 12. Free Derry drawing.

It was a spatial point of convergence, accessible to people coming from all ends of the South Ward—Bishop Street and the Long Tower area, the Brandywell, and Creggan—and also the central core of the Bogside. The site did not become significant because "You Are Now Entering Free Derry" was scrawled on the wall of 33 Lecky Road. Rather, the site was marked because it was already significant.

THE BATTLE AND THE NO-GO AREA: OLD DERRY'S LAST STAND

In the wake of Devenny's death in July 1969, many Catholic leaders sought strategies to bring a measure of quiet to the city, but they knew that a measure of accommodation by unionists would be required. Bishop Neil Farren stated in May 1969, "I know that the Catholic people here long for peace, but in their present attitude they will not settle for less than justice. This ought not be too much to ask."[15]

Nationalist leaders had pressed for a ban on the Relief of Derry commemorative parade since it was certain to exacerbate tensions. At the very least, they pushed to reroute the procession in order to create fewer opportunities for rowdiness and rioting. They were disappointed when the parade and its customary routes were approved and concerned that there might be violence in Derry. Tensions ran high as virtually every group involved felt that the presence of others aimed to intimidate or taunt them.

When the march got underway, police officers appeared to protect the Apprentice Boys, most of whom came from outside the city to Derry for the day in a show of Orange strength.

Waterloo Place, where two Bogside streets intersected with the city center, was the "center of tension" on August 12, as it had been sporadically in January, April, and July 1969. Russell Stetler described the geography of the conflict on the 12th:

> The police had placed crush barriers across William Street and Waterloo Street to prevent anyone from entering or leaving Bogside. Five Reserve Force Land Rovers were parked around the public toilets at the centre of the intersection, to form a sort of screen between Bogside and the procession, which entered the area at the far side of the intersection, in front of the large Wellworth's store, before turning sharply down the Foyle Road, away from Bogside and out of sight of any observers behind the crush barriers. Although these barriers are light constructions of tubular steel (designed mainly for royal processions and football matches), they were very seriously maintained by the police that afternoon. It was assumed on both sides that this would be the major potential trouble spot.[16]

Young people behind the barricades began hurling stones at the police in the middle of the afternoon. Civil rights stewards tried to keep them in check, but were unsuccessful. Rioters hit John Hume, Ivan Cooper, and Councillor James Hegarty with stones when they attempted to get between them and police officers. As Paddy "Bogside" Doherty recalled, the police "took the full rattle of stones for about two hours before they moved."[17]

The RUC and B Specials moved into the Bogside in the early evening, apparently convinced that the stone-throwers and rioters were going to burst out of the area and loot the stores and businesses in the city center. They also claimed to be there to discourage loyalists from wreaking havoc on the Bogsiders. As the standoff between the two communities yielded to more direct confrontation, boys and young men built barricades at the perimeter of the area to keep out the police and loyalists. Their self-defined area encompassed 880 acres and included the Bogside, Brandywell, Creggan, and Rosemount areas—effectively, the South Ward.

Even the most temperate neighborhood residents saw reason to distrust police objectives to maintain peace and order as rocks whizzed back and forth through the air in early evening. The rubble left behind in the way of urban redevelopment provided ample ammunition for both sides. Bricks, stones, and cement used for building or remnants of demolition projects littered the streets, and area residents remembered the ways the civil unrest and urban redevelopment collided; for example, the booming voice of civil rights steward Vinnie Coyle could be heard for blocks shouting through his megaphone in a tongue-and-cheek reference to building materials at large, "Dispose! Dispose! Don't Corrugate Here!" as a play on words of the all-too-familiar police refrain, "Disperse! Disperse! Don't Congregate Here!"[18]

As young people hurled stones at the police, the police officers began to throw them back, purportedly to try to maintain the distance between themselves and the rioters. Tempers flared and anxiety amplified as the stone-throwing became more heated as youths and the police broke the windows of area homes with the stones. Dr. Raymond McClean remembered that people became increasingly tense once they began to believe that the police officers were there to protect loyalist mobs. When rumors spread that loyalists were attacking St. Eugene's Cathedral, even the most law-abiding citizens of the area came out of their doors and entered the fray.[19] Nell McCafferty recalled that as the news of St. Eugene's spread through the crowd, she became aware of the presence of "respectable citizenry with anger on their faces."[20]

Later that evening, the RUC commenced to shoot CS gas (tear gas) into the crowd of rioters after bearing the brunt of the fusillade of stones and in response to increasing numbers of people in the streets. CS gas travels, and soon many area residents were overcome. At some point in early evening, members of the Citizens' Defense Association—a group of local men— took the organization's funds and sent boys out to buy petrol. The petrol bombing campaign commenced after dark.

As young men and women perched over the ledge of the high flats in Rossville Street and sent petrol bombs flying down onto the police, the community below became more involved in the drama. In an interview held during the height of the melee, an RTÉ reporter observed to civil rights activist Ivan Cooper that Bogside residents were "highly organized" and asked him what he thought of "the systematic way they conducted petrol bomb warfare."[21] Cooper stated that he had tried to preach non-violence, but as he walked through the streets he witnessed "total involvement in the defense of the area." Although Cooper, a liberal unionist and civil rights leader, had called on people to stop the violence, "every man, woman and child was committed to keeping out the police force."[22] Cooper remarked that people were motivated by fear that the entire community was going to be wrecked by police and "Paisleyites."

Eamonn McCann remembered Father Anthony Mulvey interrupting a looting mission to Marcus Harrison's petrol station on William Street and chastising the young people to "only take as much petrol" as they needed. Nell McCafferty recalled women, experienced in assembly line work, organizing the bomb-making: "When I watched those women make petrol bombs, I knew that the revolution had come."[23] Frank Doran, a member of the Derry Citizens Action Committee, noted the sense of teamwork and camaraderie that came into play: "It was really a community in action, strange as it might seem, it was like one of those 'lads' battalions in the First World War, everyone knew one another."[24]

Hopes were raised at one point during the melee, when rumors flew that Taoiseach Jack Lynch was going to send Irish troops to Derry. Lynch had made a speech on Irish television condemning the actions of the RUC and declaring that the Irish Republic was considering setting up field hospitals at the border for injured Derry residents. Yet, for the most part, residents of the area believed that they had to rely on one another. For better or worse, this was their fight. There were disagreements, particularly between those who had been active in the civil rights movement and in the unrest of the previous months and those who had only just joined. Overall, however, people stood together.

In the 1980s, James Coyle Wray looked back at the Battle of the Bogside as a high point in community life. Far from the chaos and upheaval that accompanied a failure of civility, he saw it as a demonstration of solidarity:

> When we started we had a great body of people. I saw young children gathering stones, I saw young men with vans and lorries making petrol bombs. I saw old women coming to the doors and placing

bowls of water and a facecloth for people who'd been overcome by CS gas so they could bathe their face. You had from the very young to the teenager to the middle aged, who would just stand at the barricade shouting encouragement, to the old people who placed those bowls, we'd every age group involved in our struggle.[25]

The scene became more out of control as the hours ticked by. Civil rights leaders and nationalist politicians called on Westminster to intervene. Eddie McAteer spoke for many in the area when he said, "As an Irishman, I am reluctant to accept any degree of British rule, but when the house is burning, I suppose you don't ask if the fireman is a Protestant or a Catholic."[26]

The Battle of the Bogside ended after two days on August 14, 1969. Police and B Specials withdrew from the area. Three hundred soldiers from the Prince of Wales's Own Regiment entered the city center on orders from Westminster. Their military leaders followed Bogsiders' demand that they remain outside the no-go area beyond the barricades community residents had erected. From August 14 until the second week of October, the barricades remained up, effectively cutting off "Free Derry" from the rest of the city.

FREE DERRY

The checkpoints and barricades were tedious and the disruption to everyday life required constant negotiation, but many local people saw the no-go area as a respite and sanctuary. Kevin McCallion remembered a feeling of relief: "Now you're safe, now is a time to reflect, there is no one coming into your area . . . the streets were ours for a while."[27] It also confirmed the separate nature of the Catholic area; what had been an invisible boundary was now made tangible in the barricades and signs.

The Derry Liberation Fleadh, held in late August, captured some of the community feeling of Free Derry. Realizing that the people would likely soon tire of the problems associated with the no-go area, local activists took advantage of the community's high profile and invited musicians and performers from all over Ireland to the city to celebrate "Derry Merry, Derry Free."

The atmosphere was a paradoxical one, musician Tommy Makem remembered: "My god. [There were] thousands of people there, the place crowded and jammed but the excitement was absolutely fantastic. There was electricity in the air. But there was a terrible tension. But this whole fleadh thing was to ease that tension."[28] There were activities for children, food, games and music; even The Dubliners came up and played a marathon set. It was this attention from outsiders local people responded to most keenly. Free Derry had become a hub for activists and journalists; now the artists had arrived. Kevin McCallion noted, "This was the victory dance, if you like, this was the recognition of what we had done. And stars came from all over Ireland . . . we felt all of the sudden Derry was the center of the universe, we had claimed it, we had won it, this was our area . . . and now people were coming to celebrate it with us."[29]

Tommy Makem felt as if he was taking part in something radical: "It was like being asked to go and sing for people behind the Berlin Wall." The sense that people had stood up to injustice captivated him most, but Makem reflected on strands of Irish nationalism palpable at the event; a cultural, if not political, Irish identity came across clearly. As he broke into his most famous composition, an argument against Partition, "Four Green Fields," he felt the crowds in Derry respond: "When I sang that song it was like a huge electrical storm, the whole, it seemed like the whole city was electrified and lit up and turned on . . . seared by it. That evening I got some sort of an impression that this was more than a song, that it was touching a lot of people in their souls and in their hearts, you know, 'my fourth green field will bloom again, said she.'"[30]

Community spirit was in evidence during the three-day standoff and the weeks that followed, but there was also chaos as Derry Catholics struggled to grapple with the effects of the battle in which they had taken part. There was abject horror in the community when Willie King, a Protestant father from the Fountain, was killed after he joined in an altercation at a flashpoint for conflict near Bishop Street, purportedly to pull his sons out of the fighting. John Hume insisted on going up to the Fountain to offer condolences, but he was not allowed to come in for fear angry residents might take their fury out on the rising star of nationalist and Catholic Derry. Rosemount protestors' willingness to trade a new bus they had "liberated" from the Ulsterbus service for an old bus that did not run for use as their "operations base" showed a degree of lawfulness and cooperation with authorities. The outpouring of support during the visit by James Callahan, British home secretary, reflected desire for both recognition and a return to normalcy.

Framed as a riot and a burst of incivility, the Battle of the Bogside was indeed chaotic and cataclysmic. Violent and in clear contradiction to the rule of law, it caused ordinary business to halt in the South Ward. At the same time, "riot" does not capture the essence of the battle. Thousands of area residents participated; many of those involved were not in the habit of breaking the law. In fact, residents' behavior was anything but antisocial. It was as much an affirmation of the long-standing code of Catholic Derry's community life as it was a dramatic rejection of the RUC, the B Specials, the Northern state, and British involvement in Northern Ireland. Far from being led by the radical wing of the civil rights movement or republican paramilitary leaders, people joined in the rioting because they felt that their district and their neighbors were threatened, that their community was in danger.

The Battle of the Bogside is cited as an important first, the initial incident of widespread civil unrest that brought British soldiers onto Northern Ireland's streets and introduced the era known as the Troubles. It was also a last—old Derry's last stand. The battle took place specifically within the context of a parochial and tightly bound Catholic Derry, which itself was a product of larger historical, political, social, religious, and economic forces. The long strands of mutual support, woven through shared living in cramped quarters, working, worshipping, and celebrating life's gifts and heartbreaks together, came into play during those critical weeks in 1969. There were certainly moments at which behavior became profoundly uncivil, but the events reflected the same kinds of coordination and cooperation evidenced in the district during the 1897 processions in honor of St. Columba, the ritual cleaning of the streets for the Thanksgiving procession at the end of World War II, the surreptitious spiking of a Siege cannon to stop it from firing, or the unfurling of a Tricolour from Governor Walker's statue in 1951. Free Derry didn't augur a new pattern of behavior. Rather, it revitalized a much older one.

Residents pulled together in ways they had established over several generations. When Sean Quinn and Barney Ferris remembered day-to-day life at their Lecky Road pharmacy, they portrayed a scene of deep community engagement: "Mrs McCloskey called in every day with tea for us, Ria Gallagher from Foster's Terrace brought us tripe soup every week and every Friday, Annie McCloskey brought us a fry."[31] They made connections with broader notions of politics and even nationalism sporadically throughout the tenure of the no-go area, but residents' sense of cultural and political identity was deeply intertwined with their attachments to the physical spaces of their community, to what those spaces represented, and to their neighbors and friends.[32]

A long history of deprivation and disenfranchisement had helped to create and sustain a mutually dependent, close-knit way of life in Catholic Derry. To live in the Catholic neighborhoods of old Derry in the half century before the Troubles meant that one belonged to a community that functioned according to a clear, even rigid, set of codes. Designed for survival, those codes established a shared identity and nurtured, even policed it. Communal life, life lived according to a communal ethos, had its foundations in the physical spaces of Derry's Catholic neighborhoods and the relationships they sustained. The poet and writer Seamus Deane summed this up eloquently:

> The respect for the idea of the autonomous individual is tempered by my experience growing up in Derry, of being from the North of Ireland. My experience reveals something that neither Rawls nor the Western tradition either advocates or sufficiently takes into account: community, a reality characterized by the intermeshing and interconnecting mutual support which is soldered and held together as a result of people working in concert with each other for a purpose that transcends their individual selves. . . . When people are in a position of weakness, one of the ways they try to overcome their weakness is by "bonding," by finding ways to connect with each other, by embracing what we might call their "identity," whether national or cultural.[33]

The physical spaces, material conditions, and collective experiences of the denizens of old Derry facilitated convergences and fostered intimacies. Eamon Melaugh summed up the effect of this community life when it was in its eclipse during the decade that followed the Battle of the Bogside. In response to a question about lessons from his childhood and young adulthood in the city, he noted that the people of Derry did not always like one another, but they always had reverence for each other: "When I was a young boy in Bridge Street, the community in Bridge Street was a community, a very tight knit community. There was a great deal of poverty and deprivation and if people didn't love each other, they certainly had respect and duty for each other. When you have to have a substitute for love, it's got to be duty."[34]

Respect, duty, and responsibility wove Derry Catholics together in a web of interdependency. These same values and experiences were still in place as Derry Catholics catapulted towards social and political change in the late 1960s. The community that mobilized in 1968 and 1969 was grounded in place and forged in dialogue with its past. Its identity was made and shaped every day through the accreted interactions and engagements that constituted it. The events of 1969 indeed wrought a hurricane of change, but remnants of much older attitudes, practices, and ways of holding together helped members of the community hold their ground.

When seventeen-year-old Arthur McVeigh penned an ode to the civil disturbances, he captured a pivotal moment at which "old" Derry and "new" Derry briefly coalesced. He did not write of broken glass, CS gas, fear, fire, or fury. Rather, he trained his eye on one of the community's eccentrics. In "Thoughts on the Derry Riots," he reflected:

> As I was walking round the streets of Derry
> I saw Hobbit looking very pleased.
> He was wearing a policeman's hat
> And about six watches on his arm.
> On his bicycle was half a Land Rover
> And in his hand a bottle of wine
> I got to thinking there was a riot
> And it looked like old Hobbit had won.[35]

Here is none of the fiery determination civil rights leaders identified, the mad-eyed frenzy reported by some of the unionist papers in the North, or the devastation usually accompanying retrospective analysis of the Troubles. A local teenager, a member of the demographic most likely to be caught in the riots, had taken note of the Hobbit as an integral part of the Bogside scene. This speaks volumes to the simultaneous ordinariness and extraordinariness of the violence and to the familiarity amidst turbulence.

Seamus Deane noted that "Bogside used to be a street. Now it is a condition."[36] In fact, conditions in the area had changed little over the course of the twentieth century. However, the *condition*—the lived social, political, cultural, and economic experience—of the people living in the area that became known as the Bogside underwent radical change over a relatively short period of time between 1968 and 1969. The daily and symbolic meanings of neighborhood life in Derry shifted dramatically with the onset of the Troubles, the arrival of British troops, and the resultant dénouement between residents and soldiers and the police. Particularly after Bloody Sunday in 1972, collective trauma, distrust of the state, and emergent fault lines within Catholic Derry shook the community to its core. At the same time, changes within the Catholic Church, urban renewal, and emerging class divisions opened up new schisms. Arguably, Catholics in Derry had not experienced that much change since the Famine era.

As with any cataclysmic event, the Battle of the Bogside has been framed and understood in terms of what followed it. Viewed within the context of what came before, it offers a different perspective. Catholic working-class Derry experienced the events of August 1969 from within its shared community spaces and from the perspective of a long historical pattern of communal solidarity in the face of sectarian conflict. Poverty, poor housing, tightly bound social rituals, and limited opportunities constrained the community in myriad ways, but the spaces of Catholic Derry also accommodated trust, mutual regard, responsibility, and a sense of belonging. The battle didn't just create community solidarities; it was also fueled by them.

CONCLUSION

As armored cars and soldiers in riot gear entered city streets in 1969, the gerrymandered city of Derry/Londonderry ceased to exist as a political entity. Its governing body, the Londonderry Corporation, was put in cold storage and replaced under New Town legislation with appointed commissioners to a Londonderry Development Commission by order of Northern Ireland prime minister Terence O'Neill.[1] British soldiers became a fixed presence across Northern Ireland, and men and women joined paramilitary organizations by the hundreds and then the thousands. Through urban renewal, the rise of the surveillance state, attacks on the physical landscape by the IRA, and a constant air of watchfulness, Derry was a changed place.

The Troubles inaugurated an era of unprecedented violence that reached deep into virtually all aspects of life in Northern Ireland, from which, particularly in Belfast and Derry, few people could fully insulate themselves. However, to consider the Northern Ireland Troubles only in terms of surprise and rupture is to ignore significant aspects of the history of places such as Derry. In 1896, representatives from the Catholic Workingman's Club announced to the *Derry Journal* that someone raised the nationalist green flag of Ireland on Walker's Wall.[2] Unionists were in an uproar, out to punish the culprits who challenged unionist loyalty in the city so flagrantly. Local Catholic leaders brushed off their threats: "It was only when struggling under adversity that [Derry Catholics] showed their best qualities."[3]

Traditional historiography of Northern Ireland asserts that Northern Catholics' sense of Irish nationalism was etiolated—if not defunct—by the late 1950s. Historians argue that the IRA Border War of 1956–62

249

failed largely from lack of support; they further suggest that the idea of a united Ireland simply failed to incite Northern Catholics or to ignite their imaginations. Largely because this perspective gained traction, the beginning of the Troubles at the end of 1968 is often described in cataclysmic, incendiary terms. Violence "erupted," the result of a "highly explosive mix" of circumstances. Historian Roy Foster refers simply to the late 1960s as the time "the whirlwind struck."

Historians have done valuable work examining the cocktail of contributing factors in an effort to discern why, after fifty years of stalemate, things exploded in 1968. These include the influence of mass media and exposure to global fights for human rights, civil rights and democracy, the passionate and contagious exhortations of the '68 generation, the emergence of the welfare state and increased educational opportunities that bolstered Northern Irish Catholics' economic expectations in postwar society, and the failure of the Catholic Church to exert the authority it had long held over its flock.

As with any consideration of rupture, historians have tended to emphasize the ways the events that began in the late 1960s broke with the past. The very language of civil rights bolsters this tendency. Deeply embedded in and structured by legal and political discourse, it highlights the need for freedom from discrimination, equal protection under the law, and equal opportunity for each individual. Indeed, the civil rights leaders in Derry and across Northern Ireland focused on precisely these issues and demands. At the same time, many others supported and participated in the movement because it sought redress for the broken social contract. Paradoxically, the language of individualism was the best way to express the collective and collected experience of being Catholic and nationalist in Northern Ireland.

As I argued in chapter 6, though, it was not simply rupture. A sense of history dominated the events and the way people framed and made sense of them within a larger framework.[4] Memories wove their way through the key events of the period and added significance to each protest and pitched battle over housing and local governance. Particularly in the battle to obtain decent housing, Catholic Derry's story of itself returned again and again to moral themes and to the wrongness of gerrymander, the absurdity of a city choked by its inability to grow physically so as to maintain unionist power, and the increasingly high costs of political impotence. They were content to watch from the sidelines as the city's young people, political leaders, and longtime activists drove home the need for change through a series of public campaigns and protests, but ordinary Derry Catholics eventually embraced the call for social change as the best hope of claiming their place in a city that had for so long denied them full rights of belonging.

Between the first gerrymander in 1896 and the start of the Troubles in 1968, struggle and adversity were central to the experiences of Catholics in Derry and across the North. Adversity and struggle, too, were at the heart of many narratives they constructed about themselves. Tom Maguire has argued that after 1921, the new Northern Irish state engaged in activities that amounted to "hatred made systemic." He argues that anti-Catholicism and anti-Irishness were institutionalized "in discrimination against the minority population, for example, in the allocation of economic resources, access to political representation, the deployment of state security forces, and control on the representation of Irish identity."[5] The things that happened and the narratives that emerged out of what happened cannot be disentangled from one another. Catholics developed a historical consciousness from their place at the margins, which the heritage practices that emerged in the wake of the Troubles, so astutely detailed by many formidable scholars, took into account.[6]

In this book I have attempted a subtler reckoning of identity and experience than prevailing historical interpretations grant Catholics in the North. Using memory, I have drawn connections between their historical experiences and their own readings of their circumstances—their sensibilities, desires, beliefs, and anxieties. For Catholics in Derry, the past was a safer topic, both in conversations within their tribe and with confrontations with those outside it. It was also a much looser category of analysis and a more expansive, generous, and flexible mode of transmission for a diverse group of people—from the well-educated to the illiterate, the emigrant to the person who had rarely ventured out of the South Ward, the bishop to the Christmas and Easter Catholic. By reading Derry's social, cultural, and political history through the memory work of its citizens we glimpse something more complex and far richer than a seething acquiescence followed by outrage and turmoil.

In Derry's memory work, we witness the myriad tools people mustered in order to claim their cultural and political identities in a place that was often hostile to those very things. Organized politics certainly mattered quite a bit, but it was just one venue for constructing and negotiating identity. Catholics invented traditions. They challenged unionists' use of city expenditures to express a unilaterally British-identified Derry. They used newspapers, books, radio, television, and film to tell their stories. Catholics preserved and transformed landscapes and monuments that served as touchstones in uncertain times. They also celebrated a uniquely Catholic geography of the city that faced Donegal and was marked by Catholic businesses, chapels, and schools. They mourned their dead and took care to pass on to younger generations stories of sacrifice and courage in the name of Derry. They created institutions and then insisted that the histories of these institutions would remain well known and cherished. Derry Catholics celebrated Irish cultural traditions and made the city a center for Irish dance, music, and language. Informally, they told stories, sang songs, played street games, and performed rituals that connected them to one another and to their ancestors.

Catholics also demanded that Derry be a part of the story of Irish independence and the establishment of the Irish nation. They insisted the city not be forgotten by those on the other side of the border. They also negotiated disagreements and conflict through the lens of memory when they debated the utility of creating a history that accommodated plurality and reconciled their minority status in the Northern Ireland of the 1920s. They practiced a "both/and" politics when they took up the memories of old Derry as a means of thrashing out the moral and political implications of the Border War—most disapproved of the IRA's tactics, but they also remained staunch Irish nationalists. At the same time, through obituaries they held up as examples those who represented core community values of hard work, generosity, and mutuality and those who embraced republicanism as role models and heroes.

Derry Catholics married their sense of justice with a long-standing pride and trust in their own community. They battled over the gerrymander and the housing crisis it engendered on historic grounds, but they also built organizations that drew on the community's long history of mutual support, collective trust, and informal grassroots self-help that "got the job done." Those ties were critical in the early days of the civil rights movement. They were in full display on November 16, 1968, and again during the Battle of the Bogside. Derry Catholics as a group responded to the events of 1968–69 perfectly in keeping with who they were and who they had been for generations, even as all that had shaped them was on the brink of transformation. It was definitely a time to remember.

NOTES

Acknowledgments

1. Paul Gillespie, "Can Powersharing Lead to Place of Through-otherness?," *Irish Times*, May 12, 2007.

2. Ibid.

3. Ibid.

Introduction

1. Barney McMonagle, introduction to *No Go: A Photographic Record of Free Derry*, ed. Adrian Kerr (Derry: Guildhall Press, 1997), 1.

2. Ibid.

3. Diana Taylor, *The Archive and the Repertoire: Performing Cultural Memory in the Americas* (Durham, NC: Duke University Press, 2003), 2.

4. Neil Farren, written statement, "Cameron Report, May 1, 1969," Public Records of Northern Ireland (PRONI), File GOV/2/1/116.

5. For more on memory work, see Annette Kuhn, *Family Secrets: Acts of Memory and Imagination* (New York: Verso, 1995), 157–60.

6. For a political history of Northern nationalists, see Enda Staunton, *The Nationalists of Northern Ireland* (Dublin: Columba Press, 2001).

7. Tom Maguire, "Curating Hatred: The Joe McWilliams's Controversy at the Ulster Museum," special issue, "Hate and Heritage," *Journal of Hate Studies* 13, no. 1 (2017): 61.

8. John Lees, "Rioting Reopens Old Wounds in Northern Ireland," *New York Times*, October 8, 1968, 3.

9. Brian Keenan, introduction to *Beyond Hate: Living with Our Deepest Differences*, ed. Eamon Deane and Carol Ritner (Derry: Guildhall Press, 1994), xvi.

10. This argument veers away from the dominant one that the two major ethno-religious communities in Northern Ireland have utilized competing understandings of the past expressed through separate heritages to justify their actions

and beliefs. For this perspective, see Elizabeth Crooke, "The Politics of Community Heritage: Motivations, Authority and Control," *International Journal of Heritage Studies* 16, no. 1-2 (2010): 17

11. Henry Glassie, *Passing the Time in Ballymenone* (Philadelphia: University of Pennsylvania Press, 1982), 161.

12. "St. Patrick's Day in Derry," *Belfast News Letter*, March 6, 1884.

13. For more on this, see Ian McBride, *The Siege of Derry in Ulster Protestant Mythology* (Dublin: Four Courts Press, 1997).

14. "Catholic Registration," *Derry Journal*, February 16, 1876, 2.

15. Lees, "Rioting Reopens Old Wounds in Northern Ireland." Protestants have historically struggled to understand why 400 years of putting down roots, building communities, and working hard with the soil or in industry does not constitute belonging in Ireland. They have refuted the notion that political, economic, and cultural ties to Great Britain diminish or negate one's attachments to Ireland. In their experience, the movements that began in the 1830s that equated Irishness with Catholicism and a Gaelic past marginalized their community and trivialized their deep connections to Ireland and their profound contributions to it. For more on Protestant experience in Northern Ireland, see Susan McKay, *Northern Protestants: An Unsettled People* (Belfast: Blackstaff Press, 2000), and Lee Smithey, *Unionists, Loyalists and Conflict Transformation in Northern Ireland* (Oxford: Oxford University Press, 2011).

16. "Creative destruction" is a term coined by Joseph Schumpeter, who utilized Marxian theory to describe the ways capitalist economic development arises out of the destruction of some prior economic order. See Joseph Schumpeter, *Capitalism, Socialism, and Democracy* (New York: Harper, 1942).

17. Richard English, *Irish Freedom: The History of Nationalism in Ireland* (New York: Macmillan, 2006), 368.

18. See Marianne Elliott, *The Catholics of Ulster: A History* (New York: Basic Books, 2001), see, esp., chap. 11, "Catholics in Northern Ireland 1920–2000." More recently, Christopher Norton has picked up this trope to describe Northern Catholics in Norton, *The Politics of Constitutional Nationalism in Northern Ireland, 1932–1970: Between Grievance and Reconciliation* (New York: Manchester University Press, 2014).

19. This argument has been made most eloquently by Roy Foster. See Foster, *The Irish Story: Telling Tales and Making It Up in Ireland* (New York: Oxford University Press, 2002), xi.

20. George Bernard Shaw, "Preface for Politicians," in *John Bull's Other Island* (London: Constable and Co., 1907), 33.

21. This notion of a "hidden Ireland" was first raised with Daniel Corkery's 1924 book of the same title. In it, he constructed a Gaelic Irish worldview, which

he argued had been preserved within poetic and bardic traditions for 2,000 years. His assertion that it persisted, while remaining invisible in Anglo-Irish histories, has yielded much work on the perpetuations of Gaelic Irish culture and also on the need to interrogate the silences and avoidances that arise within Irish history. Daniel Corkery, *The Hidden Ireland: A Study of Gaelic Munster in the Eighteenth Century* (Dublin: Gill & Son, 1924).

22. Joep Leerssen, *Hidden Ireland, Public Sphere* (Galway: Arlen House for the Centre of Irish Studies, 2002), 14–15.

23. Tom Garvin, *The Evolution of Irish Nationalist Politics* (Ann Arbor: University of Michigan Press, 1981).

24. Mary Daly, "David Beers Quinn and Ireland," Oral Address to the Hakluyt Society, Warburg Institute, London, March 13, 2003. http://www.hakluyt .com/hak-soc-tributes-daly.htm.

25. R. F. Foster, *Modern Ireland, 1600–1972* (New York: Penguin, 1988), 3.

26. Nancy Curtin, "'Varieties of Irishness': Historical Revisionism, Irish Style," *Journal of British Studies* 35, no. 2 (1996): 211.

27. Ibid.

28. John Regan, *Myth and the Irish State* (Kildare: Irish Academic Press, 2013), 7.

29. See Steven Ellis, "Historiographical Debate: Representations of the Past in Ireland: Whose Past and Whose Present?," *Irish Historical Studies* 27, no. 108 (1991); Ciaran Brady, ed., *Interpreting Irish History: The Debate on Historical Revisionism, 1938–1994* (Dublin: Irish Academic Press, 1999); English, *Irish Freedom*.

30. Brendan Bradshaw, "Nationalism and Historical Scholarship in Modern Ireland," in Brady, ed., *Interpreting Irish History*, 210.

31. Ibid.

32. Guy Beiner, *Remembering the Year of the French: Irish Folk History and Social Memory* (Madison: University of Wisconsin Press, 2007); William Kellheher, *The Troubles in Ballybogoin* (Ann Arbor: University of Michigan Press, 2004); Glassie, *Passing the Time in Ballymenone*.

33. John Bodnar, *Remaking America: Public Memory, Commemoration and Patriotism in the Twentieth Century* (Princeton, NJ: Princeton University Press, 1993).

34. See William Hinton, *Fanshen: A Documentary of Revolution in a Chinese Village* (New York: Random House, 1966); Charles Payne, *I've Got the Light of Freedom: The Organizing Tradition and the Mississippi Freedom Struggle* (Berkeley: University of California Press, 2007).

35. For more on this, see Brian Dooley, *Black and Green: The Struggle for Civil Rights in Northern Ireland and Black America* (London: Pluto Press, 1998).

36. Ibid., 6.

37. Norton, *The Politics of Constitutional Nationalism*, 1.

38. For more on this, see Michel-Rolph Truillot, *Silencing the Past: Power and the Production of History* (Boston: Beacon Press, 1997).

39. Luke Gibbons, *Transformations in Irish Culture* (Notre Dame, IN: University of Notre Dame Press, 1996), 17.

40. Joan Tumblety, ed., *Memory and History: Understanding Memory as Source and Subject* (New York: Routledge, 2013), 2.

41. Maurice Halbwachs, *On Collective Memory*, ed. and trans. Lewis A. Coser (Chicago: University of Chicago Press, 1991), 38.

42. Edward Casey, "Public Memory in Place and Time," in *Framing Public Memory*, ed. Kendall R. Phillips (Tuscaloosa: University of Alabama Press, 1992), 21.

43. Glassie, *Passing the Time in Ballymenone*, 48.

44. Pierre Nora, "Between Memory and History: Les Lieux de Mémoire," *Representations* 26 (Spring 1989): 8.

45. Elena Ferrante, *The Story of the Lost Child* (New York: Europa, 2015), 310–11.

46. The scholarship on memory and identity is vast and includes the following works: Francis Yates, *The Art of Memory* (Chicago: University of Chicago Press, 1966); Eric Hobsbawm and Terence Ranger, *The Invention of Tradition* (New York: Cambridge University Press, 1983); Natalie Zemon Davis and Randolph Starn, eds., "Memory and Counter Memory," special issue, *Representations* 26 (1989); Maurice Halbwachs, *On Collective Memory* (Chicago: University of Chicago Press, 1991); Benedict Anderson, *Imagined Communities: Reflections on the Origin and Spread of Nationalism*, rev. ed. (New York: Verso, 1991 [1983]); John Gillis, ed., *Commemorations: The Politics of National Identity* (Princeton, NJ: Princeton University Press, 1994); Eric Hobsbawm, "The Historian between the Quest for the Universal and the Quest for Identity," *Diogenes* 168 (1994): 51–64; Paul Ricoeur, *Time and Narrative*, trans. K. Blamey and D. Pellauer (Chicago: University of Chicago Press, 1994); Susan Crane, "Writing the Individual Back into Collective Memory," *American Historical Review* 102, no. 5 (1997): 1372–85; Alon Confino, *The Nation as a Local Metaphor: Wurttemberg, Imperial Germany, and National Memory, 1871–1918* (Chapel Hill: University of North Carolina Press, 1997); Alon Confino, "Collective Memory and Cultural History: Problems of Method," *American Historical Review* 102, no. 5 (1997): 1386–1403; Niamh Moore and Yvonne Whelan, ed., *Heritage, Memory and the Politics of Identity: New Perspectives on the Cultural Landscape* (Aldershot: Ashgate, 2007).

47. Kevin Whelan, *The Tree of Liberty: Radicalism, Catholicism and the Construction of Irish Identity, 1760–1830* (Notre Dame, IN: University of Notre Dame Press, 1996), 133.

48. For more on this, see Marguerite Corporaal, Christopher Cusack, and Ruud van den Beuken, eds., *Irish Studies and the Dynamics of Memory: Transitions and Transformations* (Bern: Peter Lang, 2017).

49. Simon Prince, "The Global Revolt of 1968 and Northern Ireland," *The Historical Journal* 49, no. 3 (2006): 875; *Violence and Civil Disturbances in Northern Ireland in 1969: Report of the Tribunal of Inquiry*, volumes 1–2 (London: Her Majesty's Stationary Office, 1972), 14.

50. David McKittrick and David McVea, *Making Sense of the Troubles: The Story of the Conflict in Northern Ireland* (Lanham, MD: Rowman and Littlefield, 2002), 1.

51. Peter Taylor, *Families at War: Voices from the Troubles* (London: BBC Publications, 1991).

52. In republican ideology, the Irish state was considered illegitimate because it was not the thirty-two county Republic called into being in 1916. As a result, Sinn Féin had maintained a policy of political abstention in the Republic until 1969. At this time, two-thirds of the IRA membership voted that republicans, if elected, should sit in British, Republic of Ireland, and Northern Ireland parliaments.

53. Taylor, *Families at War*.

54. Marie Breen Smyth, "Presentation to the Management Committee of Towards Understanding and Healing," Derry, July 2005, http://www.thejunction -ni.org/Conference-TUH.htm (accessed July 2, 2007).

55. Ibid.

56. Elizabeth Crooke, "Giving Voice to Silences: Harnessing the Performative in Two Memory Projects in Northern Ireland," *Liminalities: A Journal of Performance Studies* 14, no. 3 (2018): 122.

57. See *Radharc in Derry*, Radharc Films (1964), documentary presented by Patrick Cunningham, https://www.rte.ie/archives/exhibitions/1378-radharc/355 627-radharc-in-derry/. I have relied on "Catholic" and "Protestant" as terms that represent confessional and political identities because I have found that they resonate historically and colloquially. They also underscore the mutually constitutive nature of identity in Northern Ireland. Faith traditions, language, cultural practices, community experience, and political identity are imbricated in and through history. Radharc was a division of Telefís Éireann, established in 1961 as Ireland's national television station. In 1964, a film crew came to Derry to examine sectarian tensions in the city generally and discrimination against Catholics specifically. See chapter 5 for more on Radharc and the film itself.

58. Journalists in Northern Ireland use these terms regularly to discuss competitive victimhood on the one hand and palliative but unsubstantial *bon mots* on the other. A search on the award-winning website Slugger O'Toole yields many examples: https://sluggerotoole.com.

59. Steve Bradley, "Why Is Derry So Poor and Why Is Nothing Being Done about It? (Part I)," https://sluggerotoole.com/2018/03/09/why-is-derry-so-poor-and-why-is-nothing-being-done-about-it-part-i/.

60. Nora, "Between Memory and History."

61. For more on traditional depictions of the nationalist community in Northern Ireland, see the following sources: Desmond Murphy, *Derry, Donegal and Modern Ulster, 1790–1921* (Derry: Aileach Press, 1981); Foster, *Modern Ireland*, 227; Sabine Wichert, "Nationalism in the Northern Ireland Conflict," *History of European Ideas* 16, no. 1-3 (1993): 110–11; Elliott, *The Catholics of Ulster*, see, esp., chap. 12, "A Resentful Belonging: Catholic Identity in the Twentieth Century."

62. Hume was referring to William Craig, Northern Ireland's minister for home affairs. For more on these issues, see chapter 4.

63. "The Maiden City and the Municipal Franchise," *Derry Journal*, January 1, 1897.

64. For an example, see "A Ban and Its Official Reason," *Derry Journal*, March 16, 1953.

65. Seamus Deane, "Why Bogside?," *Honest Ulsterman*, no. 27 (1971): 2.

Chapter One. Situating the Past in Derry

1. The Roman historian Tacitus refers to Galgacus in 89 CE leading Celts against the Romans in a battle in Scotland, which may be Calgach; Tacitus, *Agricola and Germania* (New York: Penguin Classics, 2010), 29–32.

2. Brian Lacey, *Siege City* (Belfast: Blackstaff Press, 1990), 77.

3. The Flight of the Earls has been looked to as a turning point in Irish history. For recent scholarship and a historiographical review of the cause, event consequences, and commemorations of the Gaelic nobility's departure from Ulster, see David Finnegan, Éamonn Ó Ciardha, and Marie-Claire Peters, ed., *The Flight of the Earls: Imeacht na nIarlaí* (Derry: Guildhall Press, 2011).

4. Edward Daly and Kieran Devlin, *Clergy of the Diocese of Derry* (Dublin: Four Courts Press, 2009), 18.

5. Lacey, *Siege City*, 88–89.

6. William Kelly, "The Plantation and Its Impact on the Bogside," in *From Columba to Conflict: The Early Years of the Bogside, Brandywell, and Lower Bishop Street*, ed. Mickey Cooper (Derry: Gaslight Press, 2012), 56.

7. In 1984, the city council voted to change the name of their governing body to Derry City Council. In fact, the debate over the name Derry versus Londonderry has been in play since at least 1885 and supports the supposition that the

city was rarely called "Londonderry" in vernacular speech by anyone in the north of Ireland or Northern Ireland until the Troubles broke out. In a discussion in the House of Commons in 1885, Frank O'Donnell (who represented Galway and Dungarvan) proposed an amendment changing "Londonderry" to "Derry" on the name of the parliamentary division between the north and south of the county on the election registers. O'Donnell stated that since the London Companies "were despairing of retaining their hold upon Derry," it might be a good time to make the change. He went on to say that "the Amendment would be welcomed in the North of Ireland, where the county in question was always spoken of as Derry, and not as Londonderry." The amendment passed in the House of Commons, with Thackeray's use of "Derry" in his writings on the city's history used as evidence that sectarian divides were not at play (*Hansard, HC Deb*, vol. 298, cc 37–91, 8 May 1885, http://hansard.millbanksystems.com/commons/1885/may/08/seventh -schedule#S3V0298P0_18850508_HOC_427). In 2003, the council passed a resolution stating, "In keeping with the principle of equality the name Londonderry should no longer be singularly imposed as the official or legal name of the city in its citizens, the majority of whom use and prefer the name Derry." The official name of the city is still a matter of debate, with a petition to change the city's name officially to Derry currently sitting before the Queen's Privy Council. For more on the current debate, see "Name Change Meeting Adjourned as a Mark of Respect," *Londonderry Sentinel*, February 25, 2010; "Council Efforts to Change Londonderry Name to Derry Condemned," BBC News, https://www.bbc.com /news/uk-northern-ireland-foyle-west-33647867, July 24, 2015. For an interesting discussion on how the city's name was pronounced, see Alan Ross, *How to Pronounce It* (London: Hamilton, 1970).

    8. "St. Patrick's Day in Derry," *Belfast News Letter*, March 6, 1884.

    9. Hugh Dorian, *The Outer Edge of Ulster: A Memoir of Social Life in Nineteenth-Century Donegal*, ed. Breandan Mac Suibhne and David Dickson (Notre Dame, IN: University of Notre Dame Press, 2001), 1.

    10. Ibid.

    11. There is ample discussion of the effects of the Ulster Plantation on the native population. See T. W. Moody, "The Treatment of the Native Population under the Scheme for the Plantation of Ulster," *Irish Historical Studies* 1 (1938): 51–63; Jane Ohlmeyer, "Seventeenth-Century Ireland and the New British and Atlantic Histories," *The American Historical Review*, 104, no. 2, April 1999, 446–62; Aidan Clarke, "The Irish Economy 1600–60," in *A New History of Ireland*, ed. T. W. Moody, F. X. Martin, F. J. Byrne (Oxford: Clarendon, 1976), 1:168–86; R. F. Foster, *Modern Ireland: 1600–1972* (New York: Penguin Books, 1988); R. A. Butlin, "Land and People 1600," in Moody et al., ed., *A New History of Ireland*,

1:142–67; Michelle O'Riordan, "The Native Ulster Mentalité as Revealed in Gaelic Sources 1600–50," in *Ulster 1641: Aspects of the Rising*, ed. Brian Mac Caurta, SJ (Belfast: Queens University, 1993), 32.

12. Daly and Devlin, *Clergy of the Diocese of Derry*, 25.

13. James Steven Curl, *The Honourable The Irish Society and the Plantation of Ulster, 1608–2000: The City of London and the Colonisation of County Londonderry in the Province of Ulster in Ireland. A History and Critique* (Chichester: Phillimore, 2000), 112.

14. John Mitchel, *The History of Ireland, from the treaty of Limerick to the present time: Being a continuation of the history of the Abbé Macgeoghegan* (Glasgow: Cameron and Ferguson, 1869), 51.

15. "Protestant and Catholic in Ireland," *Londonderry Sentinel*, March 10, 1904, 6.

16. Derry's first modern Catholic church, the Long Tower, was completed in 1788; prior to that, Catholics worshipped in the residence of the bishop or, according to tradition, under the hawthorn tree on the grounds of what became the Long Tower.

17. Daly and Devlin, *Clergy of the Diocese of Derry*, 25.

18. Bernard Canning, *By Columb's Footsteps Trod: The Long Tower's Holy Dead, 1784–1984* (Ballyshannon: Donegal Democrat, 1984), 118.

19. Charles Gallagher, *Acorns and Oak Leaves: A Derry Childhood, Growing Up in Derry, 1920–1945* (Derry: Dubh Regles Books, 1982), 18. Further, it is interesting to note that it was not until Catholic Emancipation that Catholic churches proliferated throughout Ireland.

20. See James Murphy, *Ireland: A Social, Cultural and Literary History, 1791–1891* (Dublin: Four Courts Press, 2003).

21. See Ian McBride, *Scripture Politics: Ulster Presbyterians and Irish Radicalism in the Late Eighteenth Century* (Oxford: Clarendon, 1998).

22. Ibid., 194 (emphasis original).

23. "Advances of Popery," *Londonderry Sentinel*, April 3, 1841, 2.

24. "Popery in Derry," *Derry Standard*, April 7, 1841; "Wheaten idol" refers to the Eucharistic host, raising doctrinal differences, specifically the Catholic belief in transubstantiation.

25. The convent was linked to the Playhouse Theater building in Artillery Street by a courtyard. The sisters and the convent moved to Thornhill in 1932.

26. See James Johnson, "The Population of Londonderry during the Great Irish Famine," *The Economic History Review*, n.s., 10, no. 2 (1957): 275.

27. Andrew Holmes, "The Development of Unionism Before 1912," Irish History Live, https://www.qub.ac.uk/sites/irishhistorylive/IrishHistoryResources /ArticlesandlecturesbyourteachingstafF/Thedevelopmentof Unionismbefore1912/.

28. "Municipal Franchise Bill (Ireland)," 12 June 1895, *Hansard Parliamentary Debates*, vol. 35, cols. 62–74.

29. "City of Derry Catholic Registration Association," *Derry Journal*, December 15, 1876, 2.

30. Neil Jarman and Dominic Bryan, *From Riots to Rights: Nationalist Parades in the North of Ireland* (Coleraine: Centre for the Study of Conflict at the University of Ulster, 1998), 11.

31. Lacey, *Siege City*, 184.

32. Ibid., 186.

33. Sean McMahon, "The Diocesan Seminary," in *Seeking the Kingdom: St. Columb's College, 1879–2004*, ed. Finbar Madden and Thomas Bailey (Derry: St. Columb's College, 2005), 3.

34. St. Eugene's Cathedral, *St. Eugene's Cathedral Derry Souvenir 1843–1936 Consecration* (Derry: Derry Journal, 1936).

35. "Catholic Church Dedication," *Derry Journal*, May 5, 1873, 2.

36. Quotation taken from "The Story of Saint Eugene's Cathedral," from the Cathedral's website, http://www.steugenescathedral.com/storyofsteugenes.htm.

37. "St. Eugene's Cathedral: The New Chimes," *Derry Journal*, n.d., Derry City Council Archives Scrapbook 1896–1910, bay 2, shelf 7, row 2a.

38. The Angelus is a prayer of intercession involving three recitations of the Hail Mary, interspersed with a depiction of God's call to Mary via Gabriel to become the mother of Jesus: "The angel of the Lord announced unto Mary. And she conceived by the Holy Spirit. . . . Behold the handmaid of the Lord. Be it done to me according to Thy word. . . . And the Word was made flesh. And dwelt among us."

39. Local lore has it that the guides who showed tourists around the city walls would point to St. Eugene's and say, "That is the Roman Catholic Cathedral that never was finished and never will be"; from "Derry Colmcille Peeps into Its Past," *Derry Journal*, n.d., clipping from unsorted materials, Irish Collection, Magee Library, circa 1941.

40. In 2000, James Steven Curl wrote, in his history of the fifty-five London livery companies who founded the Plantation city of Londonderry, that in the post-Famine period Derry saw Catholics flaunting their faith and growing strength. According to Curl, "The triumphalism of 19th-century Roman Catholicism" in Derry was expressed in the construction of St. Eugene's Cathedral, because the steeple was designed to be much taller than the Church of Ireland's St. Columb's Cathedral (see Curl, *The Honourable The Irish Society*, 176).

41. Ireland Census Office, *Census of Ireland 1901* (Dublin: Printed for Her Majesty's Stationery Office by Cahill & Co., 1902).

42. Desmond Murphy, *Derry, Donegal, and Modern Ulster: 1790–1921* (Derry: Aileach Press, 1981).

43. Travelers' accounts can be found in Sean McMahon, ed., *The Derry Anthology* (Belfast: Blackstaff Press, 2002); wherein see, for example, William Bulfin's account from "Rambles in Erin, 1907," 160; Stephen Gwynn's account from "The Famous Cities of Ireland, 1915," 156; and Marie Anne de Bovet's reflections in "Trois Mois en Irlande 1891," 178.

44. Alice Milligan, "A Journey to Cloudland: Rambling Reminiscences," in *Shan Van Vocht* (Belfast: P. W. Boyd, 1897), 4:37.

45. "Murder of a Police Constable in Derry," *Freeman's Journal*, December 30, 1874, 7.

46. William Makepeace Thackeray, "The Irish Sketchbook," in McMahon, ed., *The Derry Anthology*, 9.

47. *Census of Ireland 1901*, H.C. 1902 CXXVi. Belfast had pronouncedly better sectarian relations for all of the eighteenth century and a fair bit of the nineteenth. This may have had something to do with demography—a smaller Catholic population may have been understood to be either more easily assimilated or simply the grounds for accommodation across differences.

48. Walter Gallagher, "People, Work, Space and Social Structure in Edwardian Derry, 1901–1911" (PhD diss., University of Ulster, 1994), 136.

49. Gallagher reports (ibid., 128) that Catholics were not allowed to live inside the walls until 1793.

50. Ibid., 136.

51. Ibid., 163.

52. Gallagher, the only person to have studied residential patterns in the city at this time in any depth, argues that memories of sectarian violence in the 1860s led to increased segregation based on religious and political identity. He does not try to determine whether increased sectarianism was the cause or effect of segregation (see ibid.). Urban geography of early twentieth-century Derry is important to consider in the context of what might be considered nostalgia in the 1900s for a Derry unburdened by sectarianism. Geographic mobility in Derry was simultaneously a cause and effect of stricter sectarian identities in the city.

53. Ibid., 121.

54. "Tractarian Developments," *Londonderry Sentinel*, September 2, 1859.

55. "Special Correspondent from the Daily News," *Derry Journal*, January 20, 1913.

56. "Derry Town Tenants' Association," *Derry Journal*, December 18, 1903, 2.

57. "Housing Report," *Londonderry Sentinel*, May 4, 1901.

58. William Gailey, *Gailey's Guide to Derry and Its Suburbs* (Derry: William Gailey, 1892), 42.

59. Ibid., 44.

60. Arthur Bennett, *John Bull and His Other Island* (London: Simpkin, 1890), quoted in McMahon, ed., *The Derry Anthology*, 88 (my emphasis).

61. "Open Spaces and Other Things: A Visitor's Impressions," *Derry Journal*, April 7, 1897, 3.

62. "Meeting in St. Columb's Hall," *Derry Journal*, January 22, 1896, 8.

63. Bennett, *John Bull and His Other Island*. Moreover, in less flattering, but no less persuasive language, Methodist evangelist Andrew Jordan wrote in 1855 about his efforts to convert the "poor, deluded souls" of Derry from their Catholic faith to Protestantism. Rebuked roundly by Derry Catholics, Jordan concluded that "their hearts are as invulnerable to the truth as the walls of Pampeluna were to Britain's heaviest artillery." Although he worried over their eternal salvation, Jordan found that Catholics' insistence on their own religious observance, sometimes translated as rudeness or derision, depressing. This was not fruitful ground for conversions.

64. John O'Doherty, quoted from the opening of the hall, November 21, 1888, in Frank Curran, "St Columb's Hall: A Piece of Derry's History," *Derry Journal*, June 28, 1983.

65. "Meeting in St. Columb's Hall," *Derry Journal*, January 22, 1896, 8.

66. Christian Brothers, *Christian Brothers Souvenir and Prospectus* (Derry: Christian Brothers, 1902), 34.

67. "St Columb's Total Abstinence Society," *Derry Journal*, November 7, 1898, 5.

68. "The Emancipation of Derry," *Derry Journal*, January 1, 1897, 7.

69. "Memories of Old Derry," *Derry Journal*, February 22, 1955, 2.

70. "Memories of Old Derry," *Derry Journal*, November 17, 1954, 5. Brian Boru is known as the greatest of the Irish high kings and in 1004 was recognized as the supreme ruler of Ireland. In 1013, at the battle of Clontarf, he was attacked by an alliance of Norsemen and Leinstermen. Patrick Sarsfield was an Irish Jacobite and a hero in the Irish national tradition.

71. "St. Patrick's Day," *Belfast Newsletter*, March 19, 1877, 3.

72. Marianne Elliott points to this period as an important moment in Catholic and Protestant relations in Derry: "The various riots suggest that a definite territorial battle was in train" (Elliott, *The Catholics of Ulster*, 360).

73. "The Late Riots in Londonderry," *Freeman's Journal*, May 4, 1869. *Freeman's Journal* was understood to be a Catholic newspaper.

74. Marie Anne de Bovet, *Three Months' Tour in Ireland* (London: Chapman and Hall, 1891), 263.

75. John Poyntz, Earl of Spencer, *A Report of Londonderry Riot Commission, 1884* (London: The Queen's Printer, 1884), iv.

76. Edgar S. Shrubsole, *Londonderry and the North of Ireland: The Tourist's and Sportsman's Guide* (Belfast: Baird, 1909), 17.

77. Ibid. Thomas Witherow and Thomas Babington Macaulay both wrote narrative histories of the Siege of Derry in the nineteenth century.

78. Alistair Rowan, "The Buildings of Ireland: North West Ulster, 1979," in McMahon, ed., *The Derry Anthology*, 11.

79. Alistair Coey Architects, *Derry City Walls Conservation Plan* (March 26, 2009), https://www.communities-ni.gov.uk/publications/derry-city-walls -conservation-plan.

80. "The Governour Honoured," *Londonderry Sentinel*, July 30, 1909.

81. The issue of Catholic involvement with Orange parades has long engaged local historians. According to Fr. Willie Doherty, the history went like this: "Dr. Philip McDevitt was then Bishop. Happening to be in Derry on the 12st of August, 1789, he was going along the street with one of the priests, when at the corner, they came upon the municipal procession proceeding to the Protestant cathedral. Lord Bristol immediately recognised him and commenced a conversation. Unwilling to block the onward march of the processionists, Dr. McDevitt and his companion turned and proceeded with Lord Bristol as far as St. Columb's Court. This chanced to catch the eye of the 'Journal' reporter, and in the next issue he labeled the Bishop and priest as taking part in the procession. The *Ordnance* memoir copied from the Journal and thus the libel has been perpetuated. The real facts, as I give them, were gleaned from an eyewitness (Mrs. Hasson) by very reliable authorities and have been fully corroborated from various streams of tradition"; Long Tower Church, *Derry Columbkille: Souvenir of the Centenary Celebrations in Honour of St. Columba in the Long Tower Church, Derry 1897–99* (Dublin: Brown and Nolan Printers, 1899). A more recent interpretation comes from Bishop Edward Daly: "Appearing to be walking in an Orange parade, the bishop had stopped to talk to the Anglican bishop, walked a bit with him and thus appeared to be participating in the parade" (Daly, interview with author, August 23, 2008).

82. Great Britain, Commission of Inquiry, Belfast Riots, *Reports from Commissioners on the Riots in Londonderry and Belfast and on Magisterial and Police Jurisdiction, with Minutes of Evidence and Appendices, 1857–70* (Shannon: Irish University Press, 1970), x.

83. "Derry Defence Fund: Sympathizers Meeting in Glasgow: Address by Mr. Knox, MP and Local Delegates," *Derry Journal*, June 14, 1897, 5.

84. "State of Ireland," *Londonderry Sentinel*, March 21, 1885, 4.

85. "City of Derry Catholic Registration Association," *Londonderry Sentinel*, November 19, 1878, 2.

86. The terms "Catholic" and "nationalist" are used virtually interchangeably throughout this work. There were certainly Protestant nationalists, and even Catholic unionists, but the general assumption that all Catholics were indeed nationalist was summed up in 1906 by Fr. Willie Doherty, prelate of the Long Tower Church: "If registration in Derry was to be more than a name, more than a plaything, it should be the registration of all Nationalists, and that meant all Catholics in the city" ("Lecture in Saint Columb's Hall," *Derry Journal*, February 7, 1906). Eddie McAteer stated this more explicitly in 1964: "Whether the political theorists like it or dislike it, these terms (Catholic and nationalist and Protestant and unionist) are interchangeable ninety-nine point all the nines you like to mention"; *Radharc in Derry*, Radharc Films (1964), documentary presented by Patrick Cunningham, https://www.rte.ie/archives/exhibitions/1378-radharc/355627 -radharc-in-derry/.

Chapter Two. From under the Heel of the Minority

1. "Proposed Catholic Registration Association for Ulster," *Derry Journal*, February 18, 1876, 2.

2. Thomas Macaulay, *History of England from the Accession of James the Second* (Philadelphia: Butler and Co., 1861), 71.

3. "The Coronation," *Derry Standard*, August 11, 1902.

4. "Derry Commercial and Literary Debate Society," *Derry Journal*, January 15, 1897, 4.

5. The useful notion that there is an important distinction between "successful failures" and "failed failures" is developed by Eve Weinbaum in her exploration of the struggle to stop plant closings in Tennessee. See Eve S. Weinbaum, *To Move a Mountain: Fighting the Global Economy in Appalachia* (New York: The New Press, 2004).

6. They were lowered from £10 to £4.

7. Census data from the 1901 census suggests that Catholic adults outnumbered Protestant adults, but a disproportionate number of Catholics in Derry City at this time were too young to vote.

8. *Freeman's Journal*, July 20, 1895. A Parnellite is a supporter of the Irish nationalist politician Charles Stewart Parnell, the leader of the Irish Parliamentary Party (1882–91), which fought for Irish Home Rule.

9. "The Nationalist Position in Derry," *Freeman's Journal*, December 12, 1896.

10. *Hansard Parliamentary Debates*, 12 June 1895, vol. 34, col. 966–1016.

11. Had the Improvement Bill not been proposed in 1896, the English municipal voting system would have been in effect. This would have resulted in two-thirds of Derry's municipal seats going to Catholics. The Registration Association had proposed a compromise bill, which would increase the wards from three to six, as opposed to the five proposed by the Corporation. The difference was in the district lines; under the compromise bill, three wards would be likely to return Catholic councillors, the other three wards Protestant. See *Parliamentary Debates* XLLII, June-July 1896, London, Great Britain Parliament, 775.

12. Edward Vesey Knox, Speech, *Hansard Parliamentary Debates*, 25 February 1896, vol. 37, cols. 1054–55.

13. Edward Vesey Knox, Speech, *Hansard Parliamentary Debates*, 10 March 1896, vol. 38, cols. 543–63.

14. "The Corporation Bill," *Derry Journal*, January 22, 1896, 7.

15. Ibid., 8. As scholars have pointed out, for many residents of colonies of the British Empire, political consciousness and ideas about what constituted "rights" were inherited from British political philosophers and British legal institutions themselves. Simultaneously, critiques of global imperialism shaped the Home Rule movement. See Paul Townend, *The Road to Home Rule: Anti-Imperialism and the Irish National Movement* (Madison: University of Wisconsin Press, 2016).

16. "The Corporation Bill," *Derry Journal*, January 22, 1896.

17. Donations for Derry's efforts to stop the gerrymander came from Cardinal Logue and the bishops of Clogher, Cashel, and Kilmore in December 1896 ("Defence of Derry," *Freeman's Journal*, December 21, 1896).

18. "The Corporation Bill," *Derry Journal*, June 24, 1896, 5.

19. "The Maiden City and the Municipal Franchise," *Derry Journal*, January 1, 1897, 7.

20. "The Walls of Derry and How Preserved," *Derry Journal*, April 16, 1897, 5.

21. "Subcommittee Meeting," *Derry Journal*, April 8, 1897, 5.

22. "The Walls of Derry and How Preserved," 5.

23. "Defending Derry's Walls," *Derry Journal*, April 30, 1897, 5.

24. William O'Doherty's Diary, unpublished, 1893–94 Derry Diocesan Archives, Diocesan Priests, O'Doherty, William.

25. Ibid.

26. Taken from various *Derry Journal* accounts of the lecture evenings between 1896 and 1908.

27. "Odds and Ends," *Derry Journal*, January 13, 1897.

28. Ironically, local historians have leveled heavy criticism on Father Willie's interest in the "home-grown" saint; they have accorded something approaching

fanaticism to the local priest's interest in Derry's Catholic and Irish history and his commitment to celebrating it publicly and formally. According to Colm Fox, Father Willie "single-handedly helped to re-create the potent symbolism of the Columban settlement in Doire Columcille . . . to reinforce a local sense of Catholic and Nationalist identity and was to be a symbolic counterbalance with the Protestant myth of the siege"; see Fox, *The Making of a Minority: Political Developments in Derry and the North, 1912–1925* (Derry: Guildhall Press, 1997), 23, https://cain .ulster.ac.uk/othelem/fox.htm. Brian Lacey asserts that Father Doherty was not only "one of the most enthusiastic advocates of the traditional Columban association with Derry," but that he manipulated extremely vague evidence of the sainted presence in Derry, "masterminding" events to reshape history to suit local needs, despite limited evidence to support his claims. Further, Lacey asserts that Father Willie created a material culture out of myth, rebuilding the Long Tower Church and reshaping its landscape to create a monument to St. Columba and "a translation into architecture of the ancient legend . . . and the traditional account of the original monastery at Derry" (see Lacey, *Siege City*, 19–20). What Lacey and Fox ignore in their analysis is the enthusiasm that accompanied these celebrations and the scale at which local Catholics embraced them and the history they echoed.

29. This method of analysis of the Columban celebrations, as with much of my analysis of popular religion in Catholic Derry, has emerged from Robert Orsi's study of Italian Harlem in New York City from the late nineteenth century until the 1950s. Orsi defined people's religion as "the totality of their ultimate values, their most deeply held ethical convictions, their efforts to order their reality, their cosmology. This could be called their 'ground of being,' but only if this is understood in a very concrete, social historical way, not as a reality beyond their lives, but as the *reason* that, consciously or unconsciously, structured and was expressed by their actions and reflections. More simply stated, religion here means 'what matters'"; see Robert Orsi, *The Madonna of 115th Street: Faith and Community in Italian Harlem, 1880–1950* (New Haven, CT: Yale University Press, 1985), xliii.

30. Carmel McCaffrey and Leo Eaton, *In Search of Ancient Ireland: The Origins of the Irish from Neolithic Times to the Coming of the English* (Chicago: New Amsterdam Books, 2002).

31. "Feast of Saint Columba," *Derry Journal*, June 10, 1898.

32. "Ballad Derry," in *Derry Columbkille: Souvenir of the Centenary Celebrations in Honour of St. Columba in the Long Tower Church, Derry, 1897–99* (Dublin: Brown and Nolan Printers, 1899), 21.

33. "The Centenary of St. Columba in Derry," *Derry Journal*, June 11, 1897, 6.

34. Ibid.

35. "Derry Columbkille," *Derry Journal*, June 2, 1899, 5.

36. "The Centenary of St. Columba," *Derry Journal*, June 11, 1897, 6.

37. Reverend William Doherty, "Derry Columbkille: Read Aloud July 28, 1902," typed manuscript, Derry Central Library, Subject File "St. Columb's Wells."

38. "St. Columba's Stone," *Londonderry Sentinel*, June 12, 1897, 3.

39. Doherty, *Derry Columbkille*, 159.

40. Ibid.

41. Philip Cunningham, *Derry Memories* (Derry: Guildhall Press, 2007), 55.

42. "Centenary of St. Columba," *Derry Journal*, June 11, 1897, 6.

43. "Columba," *Londonderry Sentinel*, June 15, 1897.

44. "Derry Colum-cille," *Derry Journal*, June 10, 1898, 4–5.

45. Ibid.

46. Ibid.

47. "St. Columba's Day," *Derry Journal*, June 13, 1910, 4.

48. Ibid.

49. "Derry City," *The Shan Van Vocht*, April 4, 1898, 78.

50. Theobald Wolfe Tone, in John MacCormack, *The Irish Rebellion of 1798 with Numerous Historical Sketches* (Dublin: James MacCormack, 1844), 231.

51. "Eire Og Ceilidhe," *Derry Journal*, March 20, 1905, 6.

52. Unionists actually were not all in step about using tax dollars for the Jubilee. An alderman and a city councillor got into a fist fight while the Corporation debated the issue. On the one side, unionists insisted that every loyal town and village would honor the queen, but Alderman Fleming argued that the city "shouldn't sell ourselves to royalty for a bit of pomposity." Alderman Fleming took a swing at Councillor Bible when the latter stood up and cut him off. Both men had to be restrained ("Londonderry and the Jubilee," *Londonderry Sentinel*, June 24, 1897).

53. "Rebel Cork and Loyal Derry," *The Shan Van Vocht*, May 3, 1897, 96.

54. "Londonderry and the Jubilee," 7.

55. It remains the tradition for the Mitchelburne Club to march out of Bishop's Gate while drumming at midnight of the 12th and again on midnight August 13.

56. Jarman and Bryan, *From Riots to Rights*.

57. "Rioting in Derry," *Londonderry Sentinel*, August 15, 1899, 8.

58. Ibid.

59. "Orange Riots in the City," *Derry Journal*, August 16, 1899, 5.

60. The *Sentinel* reported that boys hurled the stones, but that the factory girls hurled stones first. The *Derry Journal* wrote that it was men, not the boys, from Bigger's throwing stones at the women. The *Londonderry Standard*, which at that time probably had the most balanced coverage, reported that boys hurled rocks unprovoked by the factory workers.

61. The Apprentice Boys' flag was crimson.

62. "State of the City Yesterday," *Londonderry Sentinel*, August 17, 1899, 5.

63. *Derry Standard*, August 16, 1899, cited in T. H. Mullin, *Derry-Londonderry: Ulster's Historic City* (Coleraine: Coleraine Bookshop, 1986), 146.

64. "Special Meeting," *Derry Journal*, June 4, 1902, 4.

65. Ibid.

66. "No Change Likely in King Edward's Oath," *New York Times*, August 6, 1901.

67. "Special Meeting."

68. Ibid.

69. Ibid.

70. Phillip Donnelly, "Bishop Charles McHugh of Derry Diocese (1856–1926)," *Seanchas Ardmhacha: Journal of the Armagh Diocesan Historical Society* 20, no. 2 (2005): 226.

71. John Redmond, "Ireland and the Coronation," *World's Greatest Orations, 1775–1902*, Vol. 6, *Ireland*, ed. William Jennings Bryan (New York: Funk & Wagnalls, 1906), https://en.wikisource.org/wiki/The_World%27s_Famous_Orations /Volume_6.

72. "Historic Spectacle, Brilliant Pageant," *Londonderry Sentinel*, August 12, 1902, 7.

73. In his examination of the pomp and circumstance that accompanied the 1911 coronation of King George V, Ellis says that "royal festivals became the major patriotic celebrations of a modernizing Britain. The declining political power of the monarchy corresponded to the rise of its symbolic power. Through royal celebrations, the British nation was imagined and unified; see John Ellis, "Reconciling the Celt: British National Identity, Empire, and the 1911 Investiture of the Prince of Wales," *The Journal of British Studies* 37, no. 4 (1998): 392.

74. "Monday's Orange Displays in Derry: Protests by Alderman McCarter and Councilor Crampsey," *Derry Journal*, August 16, 1901, 5.

75. "Register of Orders Granting Use of Guildhall Premises 1890–1924: CC/11/," Derry City Council Archives, row 6a, bay 5, shelf 3.

76. Ibid.

77. Ibid.

78. Ibid.

79. It is interesting that twenty years later, Irish national flags and emblems would come to be seen as incendiary.

80. "Register of Orders."

81. Ibid.

82. Ibid.

272 Notes to Pages 68–74

272 Notes to Pages 68–74

83. "A Disgrace to Derry," *Derry Journal,* July 14, 1902, 4–5.

84. Ibid.

85. Ibid.

86. "Letters," *Derry Journal,* July 18, 1902, 4.

87. "Tuesday, July 15, 1902," *Londonderry Sentinel,* July 15, 1902, 5.

88. "Letter to the Editor," *Derry Journal,* July 20, 1902, 5.

89. "A Priest Mobbed Going to Call on the Dying," *Londonderry Sentinel,* July 15, 1902, 4–5.

90. Ibid.

91. Murphy, *Derry, Donegal,* 163.

92. Christian Brothers, "The Story of Derry," in *Souvenir and Prospectus: Brow of the Hill* (Belfast, 1927), 100.

93. Thomas Macaulay, quoted in William Thomas, *The Quarrel of Macaulay and Croker: Politics and History in the Age of Reform* (New York: Oxford University Press, 2000), 286.

94. George Douglas, ed., *Derriana: A Collection of Papers Relative to the Siege of Derry, and Illustrative of the Revolution of 1688* (Derry: G. Douglas, 1794), ii.

95. More on O'Donovan, Petrie, and O'Curry can be found in Patrick MacSweeney, *A Group of Nation Builders: O'Donovan, O'Curry, Petrie* (Dublin: Catholic Truth Society of Ireland, 1913). More recently, David Harvey has argued that O'Donovan, O'Curry, and Petrie were less avid nation builders than MacSweeney claimed, that their interests and avocations were more ambiguous than posited in *A Group of Nation Builders.* For this perspective, see David Harvey, "'National' Identities and the Politics of Ancient Heritage: Continuity and Change at Ancient Sites in Britain and Ireland, c. 1675–1850," *Transactions of the Institute of British Geographers* 28 (2003): 473–87.

96. MacSweeney, foreword to *A Group of Nation Builders,* n.p.

97. John Keys O'Doherty, *Derriana* (Dublin: Sealy, Bryars & Walker, 1904), 25.

98. Ibid., 83.

99. Ibid., 84.

100. Ibid., 85.

101. Speech given by Walter Bernard, "The Ruin of the Grianan of Aileach," *Proceedings of the Royal Irish Academy, 1878,* Derry Central Library, Subject File "Grianan."

102. "Excursion," *Derry Journal,* August 18, 1897, 3.

103. "Meeting in Glasgow," *Derry Journal,* June 18, 1897, 3. The plea worked; in August 1897, the Derry Defense Fund sent £20 to be used for registration work in the city (see "Derry and the Nationalists of Scotland," *Derry Journal,* August 27, 1897, 4).

104. "Aileach of the Kings," *Derry Journal*, October 5, 1906, 2–3.

105. "Onlooker," *Derry Journal*, May 11, 1954, 5.

106. "Historic Sites," *Derry Journal*, July 12, 1915, 3.

107. "Sunday Night's Lecture by Mr. F. J. Bigger, M.R.I.A." *Derry Journal*, December 8, 1916.

108. "The Real Objects of Nationalists," *Londonderry Sentinel*, January 25, 1913.

109. "Home Rule: Notes on the Campaign," *Derry Journal*, March 13, 1914.

110. "Remembered," *Irish Press*, July 12, 1962, 10.

111. "The Coal Fund," *Londonderry Sentinel*, December 23, 1911, 5.

112. "The Coal Fund," *Londonderry Sentinel*, December 19, 1911, 6.

113. "Ancient Order of Hibernians," *Derry Journal*, August 17, 1906, 6; "Ancient Order of Hibernians," *Derry Journal*, September 1, 1915, 3.

114. "Ancient Order of Hibernians," *Derry Journal*, January 31, 1906, 5.

115. "Registration in Derry: The Duty of Nationalists, Practical Suggestions by Reverend William Doherty, ADM," *Derry Journal*, February 7, 1906, 5.

116. "Year in Review," *Derry Standard*, January 4, 1911.

117. "A Welcome and Something More," *Derry Journal*, June 29, 1910, 4–5.

118. Ibid.

119. Ibid.

120. Ibid.

121. Ibid.

122. Liam Brady, "Derry's Part in the War for Irish Independence," *Derry Journal*, May 1, 1953, 7.

123. Douglas Goldring, *A Stranger in Ireland* (Dublin: Tablot Press, 1918), 58.

124. Ibid., 58.

125. Ibid., 57.

126. Ibid., 68–69.

127. Ibid., 69.

128. Eamon Phoenix, *Northern Nationalism: Nationalist Politics, Partition, and the Catholic Minority of Northern Ireland, 1890–1940* (Belfast: Ulster Historical Foundation, 1994), 27.

129. Ibid., 49.

130. "Triumph in Derry," *Derry Journal*, December 25, 1918, 5.

131. "National Volunteers," *Derry Journal*, March 15, 1915, 3–4.

132. Dennis Kennedy, *The Widenirg Gulf: Northern Attitudes to the Independent Irish State, 1919–49* (Belfast: Blackstaff Press, 1998), 44.

133. Ibid., 31.

134. Fox, *The Making of a Minority*. Fox illustrates the dangers of general and literal analysis: "This particular incident serves to show the extent to which religion

and politics had become inextricably linked in Ireland, since the relationship between the Assumption of the Blessed Virgin and Derry Walls can only be at best, tenuous."

135. Ronald MacNeill, *Ulster's Stand for Union*, quoted in Phoenix, *Northern Nationalism*, 74.

136. "Historic Triumph," *Derry Journal*, January 21, 1920, 3.

137. Phoenix, *Northern Nationalism*, 74.

138. For more on this, see A. C. Hepburn, *Catholic Belfast and Nationalist Northern Ireland in the Era of Joe Devlin, 1871–1934* (New York: Oxford University Press, 2008).

139. Christian Brothers, "The First Catholic Mayor of Derry," in *Souvenir Magazine: Christian Brothers School Brow O'-the-Hill Anniversary*, Derry, June 1927.

140. Ibid.

141. Ibid.

142. Ibid.

143. Quoted in Fox, *The Making of a Minority*.

144. Jonathan Bardon, *A History of Ulster* (Belfast: Blackstaff Press, 1992), 469.

145. Ronan Gallagher, *Violence and Nationalist Politics in Derry City, 1920–1923* (Dublin: Four Courts Press, 2003).

146. Charles McHugh, quoted in Phoenix, *Northern Nationalism*, 11.

147. Phoenix, *Northern Nationalism*, 157.

148. "To the Editor of the Derry Journal," *Derry Journal*, July 12, 1920, 4.

Chapter Three.   Against the Wishes of the Inhabitants

1. Phoenix, *Northern Nationalism*, 27.

2. Clare O'Halloran, *Partition and the Limits of Irish Nationalism: An Ideology under Stress* (Atlantic Highlands, NJ: Humanities, 1987), 56.

3. In Derry, one train line leaving the city crossed into the Free State and back seventeen times, according to Brian Lacey (see Lacey, *Siege City*, 232).

4. Northern Ireland was referred to as "Carsonia" in the *Derry Journal*, August 17, 1922, but it wasn't the only paper to do so. "Carsonia" was used regularly to refer to the six counties of Northern Ireland.

5. Marianne Elliott popularized the notion of an Ulster Catholic "culture of grievance" that emerged during the battles for Home Rule and evolved despite

gradual improvements in housing, health, and employment (see Elliott, *Catholics of Ulster*, 476).

6. "Catholics and the Corporation," *Derry Journal*, January 5, 1931.

7. Abstention in Derry reflected a broader policy of republican abstention across the Free State, the result of disillusionment with the compromise Partition represented.

8. "Derry's New Rate," *Derry Journal*, February 22, 1922, 4.

9. Fred Woods, *The Derry Quays* (Derry: Guildhall Press, 2004), 32.

10. Bardon, *A History of Ulster*, 494.

11. "Growth of Derry," *Londonderry Sentinel*, July 8, 1937, 5.

12. Quotation is from World War II remembrances collected by Derry City Council Museum Services for their "Their Past, Your Future" project on World War II memories, http://www.secondworldwarni.org/.

13. "Articles of Agreement for a Treaty between Great Britain and Ireland, 6 December 1921," Royal Irish Academy, *Documents on Irish Foreign Policy*, Vol. 1 (Dublin: Royal Irish Academy/National Archives of Ireland, 1998), doc. no. 214.

14. Phoenix, *Northern Nationalism*, 158.

15. See Dennis Kennedy, "Politics of North–South Relations in Post-Partition Ireland," in *The Northern Ireland Question: Nationalism, Unionism and Partition*, ed. Patrick Roche and Brian Barton (Turnbridge Wells: Wordsworth Publishing, 2014).

16. Phoenix, *Northern Nationalism*, 168.

17. "Free State and the Dáil," *Derry Journal*, January 11, 1922, 3–4. Gransha was the name of the local insane asylum.

18. Phoenix, *Northern Nationalism*, 180.

19. The "northwest liberties" included the parts of County Londonderry that fell on the west side of the Foyle. Liberties were rural tracts of land adjacent to the city.

20. The last census had been taken in 1911, at which point the population had split 56.2 percent to 43.8 percent. The Commission stated that the proportion of Catholics had increased since World War I, but they did not have definite figures. See Geoffrey Hand, ed., *Report of the Irish Boundary Commission, 1925* (Dublin: Irish University Press, 1969), 79.

21. "Letter for the Editor," *Derry Journal*, January 3, 1923.

22. Hand, ed., *Report of the Irish Boundary Commission, 1925*, 81.

23. Ibid.

24. Geoffrey Hand, "MacNeill and the Boundary Commission," in *The Scholar Revolutionary: Eóin MacNeill and the Making of the New Ireland, 1867–1945*, ed. F. J. Byrne and F. X. Martin (Dublin: Irish University Press, 1973),

201–75. Note: In Derry, local lore played less kindly towards MacNeill. In his treatment of the subject, Brian Lacey suggested that locally people said that he was more interested in archeology than in supporting Derry's case for inclusion in the Free State (see Lacey, *Siege City*, 222).

25. Lacey, *Siege City*, 87.

26. Ibid., 88.

27. Gillian McIntosh, *The Force of Culture: Unionist Identities in Twentieth-Century Ireland* (Cork: Cork University Press, 1999), 29.

28. Ernest Hamilton, quoted in McIntosh, *The Force of Culture*, 28.

29. Laura Donahue, "Regulating Northern Ireland: The Special Powers Acts," *The Historical Journal* 41, no. 4 (1998): 1090.

30. Ibid.

31. Ibid.

32. "The Fifteenth of August in Derry," *Derry Journal*, August 17, 1932, 3.

33. Interview with John Maultsaid, Ulster Folk and Transport Museum Oral History Interview, interviewer Tony Morrow, April 29, 1988, tape number 72, side B.

34. "Josef Locke, 82, Irish Tenor Who Inspired Tears, Is Dead," *New York Times*, October 16, 1999.

35. "In Time's Eye," *Derry News*, December 20, 2001.

36. Finbar Madden and Thomas Bradley, "The Diocese of Derry in the Twentieth Century, c. 1900–1974," in *History of the Derry Diocese from the Earliest Times*, ed. Henry Jeffries and Kieran Devlin (Dublin: Four Courts Press, 1999), 247.

37. Féis Committee, *75th Anniversary of Féis Doire Colmcille Souvenir Book* (Derry: Féis Committee, 1999), 25.

38. Phoenix, *Northern Nationalism*, 215.

39. Statement dated April 26, 1922, Bishops' Annual Meeting, Derry Diocesan Archive, Folder: Bishops of Derry, 1905–1974, #37.

40. Dennis Kennedy, *The Widening Gulf: Northern Attitiudes to the Independent Irish State, 1919–49* (Belfast: Blackstaff Press, 1988), 116.

41. "Féis Doire Colmcille," *Derry Journal*, June 28, 1922, 2.

42. Madden and Bradley, "The Diocese of Derry," 248.

43. St. Eugene's priest, Fr. John McGettigan, with the support of local music teacher Mrs. E. H. O'Doherty, started the féis. The Londonderry Féis had been established by Ambrose Ricardo and Mrs. A. McStewart at the turn of the twentieth century, but it moved away from its interests in things Gaelic during the Home Rule battles. By the 1920s, the Londonderry Féis had become a British festival; it prohibited Irish-language events and highlighted talents, such as classical music, sight-reading, and elocution.

44. Interview with Maultsaid.

45. Bishop Charles McHugh, quoted in Madden and Bradley, "The Diocese of Derry," 248.

46. "Gaelic in Music, Song and Story," *Derry Journal*, June 28, 1922, 2.

47. "Féis Doire Colmcille."

48. Ibid.

49. Ibid.

50. "Féis Doire Colmcille: Concluding Competitions," *Derry Journal*, July 3, 1922.

51. Ibid.

52. "Féis Medal," in *Féis Doire Colmcille Souvenir Book*, in McMahon, ed., *A Derry Anthology*, 140.

53. Ibid.

54. Ibid.

55. "Conclusion of Derry Féis."

56. Interview with Sister Kathleen, n.d., Ulster Folk and Transport Museum Oral History Interview, interviewer Tony Morrow, tape 69a, p. 2.

57. Interview with John Maultsaid.

58. Charles Gallagher, *Acorns and Oak Leaves: A Derry Childhood, Growing Up in Derry, 1920–1945* (Derry: Dubh Regles Books, 1982), 92.

59. Interview with John Maultsaid.

60. Interview with Lillian O'More, March 16, 1988, Ulster Folk and Transport Museum, Audio Summary, tape number 72A, transcript p. 2.

61. Christian Brothers, "The Story of Derry," in *Souvenir and Prospectus: Brow of the Hill* (Belfast, 1927), n.p.

62. "Story of Derry," *Derry Journal*, June 29, 1927.

63. "Chronicle and Comment," *Derry Journal*, June 27, 1927, 8.

64. "Story," *Derry Journal*, June 29, 1927.

65. "Placing the Responsibility," *Derry Journal*, July 4, 1927.

66. "Letter to the Editor," *Derry Journal*, July 1, 1927.

67. "Tours with Our Tame Historian," *Derry Journal*, July 4, 1927.

68. "Placing the Responsibility."

69. Madden and Bradley, *Seeking the Kingdom*, vi.

70. "A Glimpse of Old Derry: Archbishop Colton's Visitation," *Derry Standard*, April 23, 1925, 7.

71. Gillian McIntosh makes a similar argument for unionists' engagements with the coronation of Queen Elizabeth II.

72. "High Mass in St. Eugene's Cathedral," *Derry Journal*, November 6, 1929.

73. Ibid.

74. "The Corridor in the Old Wing of the College," *Derry Journal*, November 6, 1929.

75. "St. Columb's College," *Derry Journal*, June 27, 1927, 8.

76. Madden and Bradley, *Seeking the Kingdom*, 114.

77. "St. Columb's College Union," *Derry Journal*, January 7, 1931.

78. "St. Columb's College Jubilee Celebrations," *Derry Journal*, November 8, 1929, 5.

79. Ibid.

80. Ibid.

81. Daniel Corkery, *The Hidden Ireland: A Study of Gaelic Munster in the Eighteenth Century* (Dublin: Gill & Son, 1924).

82. See Gillian McIntosh, "Acts of National Communion," in *Ireland in the 1930s: New Perspectives*, ed. Joost Augusteijn (Dublin: Four Courts Press, 1999), 82.

83. Dennis Kennedy, *The Widening Gulf*, 166.

84. "A Savings Movement in Derry City," *Derry Journal*, September 25, 1931.

85. Gallagher, *Acorns and Oak Leaves*, 92.

86. Neil Jarman, "The Orange Arch: Creating Tradition in Ulster," *Folklore* 112, no. 1 (2001): 9.

87. Gallagher, *Acorns and Oak Leaves*, 27.

88. *The Irish Times*, n.d., as quoted in Dermot Keogh, *Ireland and the Vatican: The Politics and Diplomacy of Church-State Relations, 1922–1960* (Cork: Cork University Press, 1995), 97.

89. Ibid.

90. Public Records Office of Northern Ireland (PRONI), D2953/1/2/1.

91. McIntosh, *The Force of Culture*, 42.

92. Alvin Jackson, *Home Rule: An Irish History, 1800–2000* (New York: Oxford University Press, 2003), 230.

93. Donahue, "Regulating Northern Ireland," 1096.

94. "The Consecration," in *Souvenir: 1843–1936: St. Eugene's Cathedral Derry* (Derry: St. Eugene's Cathedral, 1936), 4.

95. Ibid., 41.

96. Ibid., 17.

97. The groups represented included the St. Vincent de Paul Society, the St. Columb's Temperance Society, the Gaelic Athletic Association, the John Mitchel Club, the United Irish League, the Ancient Order of Hibernians, the Irish Foresters, and Clan na Gael.

98. "The Consecration," 17.

99. Ibid.

100. "Cardinal MacRory in Derry," *Londonderry Sentinel*, April 28, 1936.

101. Alan Megahey, *The Irish Protestant Churches in the Twentieth Century* (New York: Springer, 2000), 98.

102. "Cardinal's Speech Provocative of Bitterness," *Londonderry Sentinel*, April 28, 1936.

103. "The Consecration," 49.

104. He was referring to Gilla Macleag, who succeeded St. Malachy as abbot of Armagh; he was abbot of the monastery at Doire.

105. "The Consecration," 54.

106. Ibid.

107. Ibid.

108. These celebrations reflect the Catholic Church as a unifying and benevolent force, but the history of the Church in community life in Derry has its flip side. Its successes at fundraising, for example, came in part from an organized campaign that publicly acknowledged generosity and shamed those who did not, or could not, give money to the Church. (This gave rise to criticisms of families that gave considerable funds, presumably to gain the favor of the priests; they were referred to as "the fur coats, no knickers brigade.") Families' donations to the Catholic churches were recorded, and on one Sunday a year, priests read out the contributions, name by name. Also, those who chose to marry outside of the Catholic Church were "read off the altar," publicly kicked out of the Church for their choice. Although these strategies were successful at sustaining the Church and the Catholic community, it would be worthwhile to explore how these practices shaped Catholic consciousness in Derry.

109. "The Calvary and the Resurrection of Catholic Derry," *Derry Journal*, April 27, 1936.

110. Ibid.

111. Ibid. Note: The article didn't mention that The Honourable The Irish Society contributed a small sum for the construction of the Long Tower.

112. "Cardinal MacRory in Derry," *Londonderry Sentinel*, April 28, 1936.

113. "South Ward Victory," *Derry Journal*, January 19, 1931.

114. Ibid.

115. Nationalists abstained for eight years from local politics.

116. St. Eugene's Cathedral, *St. Eugene's Cathedral Derry Souvenir 1843–1936 Consecration* (Derry: Derry Journal, 1936), 33.

117. Patrick Buckland, *The Factory of Grievances: Devolved Government in Northern Ireland, 1921–39* (Dublin: Gill and Macmillan, 1979), 244.

118. PRONI, HA/51/4, Londonderry Gerrymandering.

119. The Ulster Covenant, signed by approximately 500,000 people, was a document protesting the Third Home Rule Bill and the establishment of home

rule, or devolved government within the UK, in Ireland. It galvanized unionists, who made signing the document a spectacle and a statement.

120. Derry Diocesan Archives, Derry Catholic Registration Committee, Folder: 1931–1958.

121. "The Reason for Gerrymanders," *Derry Journal*, February 2, 1938, 6.

122. "Proposed Derry Gerrymander," *Derry Journal*, October 9, 1936, 6.

123. Reprint of the Ministry's letter in Frank Curran, *Ireland's Fascist City* (Derry: Derry Journal, Ltd., 1946), 46.

124. Ibid., 48.

125. Editorial, *Derry Journal*, September 16, 1927.

126. Common Irish saying. The first date it appears in the context of this study is in 1897, by William O'Doherty, nationalist councillor. It has, however, long been attributed to nationalist leader Eddie McAteer.

127. Interview with Paddy "Bogside" Doherty, Ulster Folk and Transport Museum Oral History Interview, interviewer Tony Morrow, n.d.

128. "Derry Town Planning Scheme," *Derry Journal*, October 13, 1943.

129. Seamus Heaney, "The North: Silent Awareness" (interview with Monie Begley), in Begley, *Rambles in Ireland and a County-by-County Guide for Discriminating Travelers* (Old Greenwich, CT: Devin-Adair, 1977), 161.

130. For more on these ideas about processes of memory, see Pierre Nora, "Between Memory and History: Les Lieux de Mémoire," *Representations* 25 (1989): 7–25.

131. Diana Taylor, *The Archive and the Repertoire: Performing Cultural Memory in the Americas* (Durham, NC: Duke University Press, 2003), 1.

132. Matthew Barlow argues for a similar role for memory work in Montreal's Irish neighborhood, Griffintown. See Barlow, *Griffintown: Identity and Memory in an Irish Diaspora Neighborhood* (Vancouver: University of British Columbia Press, 2017), 140–55.

133. Michel de Certeau, *The Practice of Everyday Life* (Chicago: University of Chicago Press, 1984), 37.

134. "Memories of Old Derry," *Derry Journal*, October 29, 1954, 8. The evidence of the important role women played in memory work is corroborated in a photo of a "Penal Day Rosary" the *Derry Journal* printed in June 1950. The caption read, "Derry family's cherished heirloom— handed down from mother to daughter for over two hundred years" ("Penal Day Rosary," *Derry Journal*, June 28, 1950, 4).

135. De Certeau, *The Practice of Everyday Life*, 36–37.

136. "St. Brigid's Eve in the Donegal Gaeltacht," *Derry Journal*, February 1, 1957.

137. The Free State ceased to exist in 1937, with the passage of de Valera's constitution. Éire became the Republic of Ireland in 1949, though Éire remains the Irish-language name for Ireland.

138. Philip Cunningham, *Derry: Down the Days* (Derry: Guildhall Press, 2010), 117. The tradition has remained relevant. According to a 2010 article in the *Derry Journal*, a campaign to educate young people in Derry about responsible decision-making around alcohol consumption at the St. Patrick's Day holiday was called "Don't Drown with Your Shamrock" ("Don't Drown with Your Shamrock," *Derry Journal*, March 15, 2010).

139. "Chronicle and Comment," *Derry Journal*, March 16, 1953, 4.

140. "St. Patrick's Day," *Derry Journal*, March 16, 1931.

141. "Chronicle and Comment."

142. Bernard Canning, *The Street That Is Gone but Lives On* (Limavady, NI: Limavady Printing Company, 2001), 72.

143. Seamus Deane, *Reading in the Dark* (New York: Random House, 1996), 33.

144. Shane Conway, "Three Hallow Eve Poems," *Derry Journal*, October 29, 1954, 10.

145. "The Street That Is Gone but Lives On," *Derry Journal*, April 7, 2000.

146. Canning, *The Street That Is Gone but Lives On*, 71–72.

147. Cunningham, *Derry: Down the Days*, 25.

148. "The Coming of May," *Derry Journal*, May 7, 1928, 8.

149. It seems that the author was describing the Londonderry Academical Institution in Academy Road, which later merged with Foyle College to become Foyle and Londonderry.

150. A. R. Foster, "This Was William Street . . . before Derry Made It Famous," *Belfast Telegraph*, 1972 (circular files, Derry Central Library, Local History Collection).

151. Ibid.

152. Ibid.

153. Angela Bourke, *The Burning of Bridget Cleary* (New York: Penguin, 1999), 34.

154. Glassie, *Passing the Time in Ballymenone*, suggests something very similar: "Ballymenone's story texts record one person's attempt to coordinate multiple responsibilities to time, to the past event, the present situation and the future of the community. Social effect does not postdate texts, it organizes them" (48).

155. Micí Sheáin Néill Ó Baoill, "Taibhse Dhoire: A Derry Ghost," in McMahon, ed., *The Derry Anthology*, 398–409.

156. It is difficult to get an exact chronology of the first haunting from the story itself.

157. Ó Baoill, "Taibhse Dhoire," 395.

158. "The Devil and the Long Tower Gamblers" was retold by local Derry storytellers and transcribed as part of a local history and folklore project; find it at http://www.derryghosts.com/.

159. Ibid.

160. "The Great-Grandmother's Warning," http://www.derryghosts.com/.

161. "The Haunting on Wellington Street," http://www.derryghosts.com /welling.htm.

162. Cunningham, *Derry: Down the Days*, 38.

163. Ibid.

164. Ibid., 123.

165. Philip Cunningham, *Derry Memories* (Derry: Guildhall Press, 2007), 115.

166. Ibid., 120.

167. Madeleine McCully, interview with author, June 13, 2014.

168. Ibid.

169. Glassie, *Passing the Time*, 48.

170. Ibid.

Chapter Four.   Tickling the Lion's Tale, 1945–1962

1. "Thanksgiving by a City," *Catholic Standard*, September 14, 1945, 1.

2. "Moving Scenes at Lecky Road Grotto," *Derry Journal*, August 1, 1952, 1.

3. "Thanksgiving by a City."

4. Ibid.

5. Ibid.

6. Ibid.

7. Robbie Crockett, "Robbie Crockett's End of War Memories," Second World War: Online Learning Resource for Northern Ireland, http://www.second worldwarni.org/default.aspx?id=8&themeid=11.

8. "Victory Celebrations in Derry," *Londonderry Sentinel*, May 12, 1945, 8.

9. Brian Barton, *Northern Ireland and the Second World War* (Belfast: Ulster Historical Foundation, 1995), 139.

10. "Derry Celebrates," *Londonderry Sentinel*, August 16, 1945, 2.

11. "'Up the Rebels' Shouted," *Londonderry Sentinel*, August 30, 1945, 6.

12. Claire Wills, *That Neutral Island: A Cultural History of Ireland during the Second World War* (London: Faber and Faber, 2007), 422.

13. "Derry's New Freeman," *Londonderry Sentinel*, September 15, 1945, 1.

14. Ibid.

15. Editorial, *Londonderry Sentinel*, September 18, 1945, 1.

16. For more on the censorship issues related to the *Derry Journal*, see Freya McClements, "Press Censorship and Emergency Rule in Ireland: The Ban on the *Derry Journal*, 1932 and 1940" (Master's thesis, University of Ulster, 2005).

17. In fact, as Gillian McIntosh explains, de Valera's statement in the 1937 Éire constitution, laying claim to all of Ireland, which came on the heels of his 1936 removal of the king from the constitution, led to fears that the foundations of the partition agreement had been weakened (McIntosh, *The Force of Culture*, 145).

18. Bardon, *History of Ulster*, 585.

19. George Bernard Shaw, quoted in "Review: *That Neutral Island: A Cultural History of Ireland During the Second World War*," *Sunday Times*, August 19, 2007, 17.

20. *Belfast News Letter*, May 18, 1945, quoted in Barton, *Northern Ireland*, 135.

21. Claire Wills, *That Neutral Island*.

22. "Black Saturday Showed Growing Strength," *Londonderry Sentinel*, August 29, 1950, 2.

23. The term "dissident minority" first appears in the *Derry Journal* in 1927, when it wrote about measures "that will reduce Catholic voters will crush the same dissident minorities which are beginning to make ominous rents in the seamless robes of Ulster unionism" ("The Cause of the Delay," *Derry Journal*, August 29, 1927), 6. The same phrase was used to discuss Northern Irish nationalists in the *Belfast News Letter*, the *Scotsman*, and the *Western Daily Press* between 1925 and 1940.

24. Paddy Maxwell, nationalist City Corporation councillor and founding member of the Anti-Partition League, described Derry in this way: "During recent years they had been on the defensive. Now they had gone over to the offensive" ("Against Partition," *Irish News*, July 27, 1945), quoted in Brendan Lynn, "Nationalist Politics in Derry, 1945–1969," in *Derry & Londonderry: History and Society: Interdisciplinary Essays on the History of an Irish County*, ed. Gerard O'Brien and William Nolan (Dublin: Geography Publications, 1999), 20.

25. "Annual Report of the Executive Council," 1945, Derry Diocesan Archives, Derry Catholic Registration Committee, Folder: 1931–1958.

26. The Anti-Partition League also represented the first attempt since Partition to develop common ground between Northern republicans and their constitutionalist brethren.

27. "The Irish Anti-Partition League: Constitution and Rules," quoted in Lynn, "Nationalist Politics in Derry," 2. The effort was somewhat fruitful. A search through ProQuest's historic newspaper database reveals that no major U.S.

newspapers appear to have written about Curran or McAteer's postwar writings, but Mayor O'Dwyer of New York did call for full Irish independence and claimed that the nation "was too small to be divided and too big to stand for any partition" ("Unified Ireland Backed," *New York Times*, November 17, 1949, 10).

28. Eddie McAteer, foreword to *Ireland's Fascist City* by Frank Curran (Derry: Derry Journal Press, 1946), ii.

29. Interview with Frank Curran, January 11, 2008.

30. Curran, *Ireland's Fascist City*, 1.

31. Ibid., 5.

32. Ibid.

33. Ibid., 6.

34. Ibid., 7.

35. The pervasive image of Ulster's native Irish as lawless and unseemly emerged out of accounts like this one, reputedly written by a sixteenth-century survivor of the wrecked Spanish Armada: "The habit of those savages is to live like brutes in the mountains . . . they are great walkers and stand much work and by continually fighting they keep the Queen's English soldiers out of their country, which is nothing but bog. . . . Their great delight is robbing one another, so that no day passes without fighting . . . there is no order nor justice in the country and everyone does that which is right in their own eyes"; "The Natives of Donegal in Elizabethan Days," quoted in Amy Young, *Three Hundred Years in Inishowen* (Belfast, 1924), reprinted in *Acorn*, November, 1963.

36. Curran, *Ireland's Fascist City*, 10.

37. Ibid.

38. Oliver MacDonagh, *States of Mind: A Study of Anglo-Irish Conflict, 1780–1980* (Boston: Allen and Unwin, 1983), 14.

39. Ibid., 49.

40. Curran, *Ireland's Fascist City*, 11.

41. See details of the bill in chapter 1.

42. Curran, *Ireland's Fascist City*, 22.

43. Ibid.

44. Ibid., 49.

45. Ibid.

46. Eddie McAteer, *100 Hours of Nationalism or Irish Made Too Easy: Written for Those Who Are Too Lazy, Too Old, Only Mildly Interested, Too Busy* (Derry: Derry Journal, 1945).

47. Kennedy, *The Widening Gulf*, 182.

48. Eddie McAteer, *Irish Action: New Thoughts on an Old Subject* (Ballyshannon: Donegal Democrat, 1948), reprinted in McAteer, *Irish Action* (Belfast: Athol Books, 1979), 51.

49. Caroline Kennedy-Pipe, *The Origins of the Present Troubles in Northern Ireland* (New York: Longman, 1997), 27.

50. "Nationalist Strife," *Londonderry Sentinel*, February 16, 1954, 2.

51. McAteer, *Irish Action*, 53.

52. Saul Alinsky, *Reveille for Radicals* (Chicago: University of Chicago Press, 1946). Alinsky was a labor organizer in the 1930s and began doing general community organizing in 1939. McAteer and other Derry nationalists took some of these tactics to heart; they refused to stand for the queen's toast at Londonderry Corporation functions, for example, and stayed noticeably quiet when "God Save the Queen" was sung.

53. In 1880, Charles Stewart Parnell called attention to Charles Boycott, the estate agent to the Lord of Erne, a County Mayo landlord. Boycott was so loyal to his employer that he evicted tenants who had petitioned for lower rents. Following Parnell's suggestion, members of the Land League movement enacted a campaign of social ostracism.

54. McAteer, *Irish Action*, 55.

55. Ibid., 56.

56. Ibid., 57. McAteer himself stopped paying taxes on his residential property and was sued by the city in 1951.

57. Ibid., 58.

58. Marianne Elliott refers to this kind of identification with Ireland as a "necessary crutch" for northerners who had no choice, upon rejecting the Northern state, but to look southwards towards a cultural home (see Elliott, *The Catholics of Ulster*, 399). Her argument minimizes the depth of nationalist identification with Éire.

59. Jenni Doherty and Alex Carlin, *History of the Foyle Fisheries* (Derry: Guildhall Press, 1996).

60. "'Irish Action' in New Garb," *Londonderry Sentinel*, November 6, 1948, 6.

61. Eddie McAteer, in *Radharc in Derry*, Radharc Films (1964).

62. Victor Griffin, *Mark of Protest* (Dublin: Gill and McMillan, 1993), 76. Of course, it is fascinating that, looking back in 1993, Griffin would associate Derry Catholics with the Irish language and sports like Gaelic football and hurling. That Griffin, a Dubliner not seeking out or expecting divided communities, found them upon his arrival to Derry speaks to the boundaries between Catholics and Protestants.

63. Ibid.

64. *Radharc in Derry*.

65. For a more extensive discussion of this, see McIntosh, *The Force of Culture*, 103.

66. Brendan Lynn, *Holding the Ground: The Nationalist Party in Northern Ireland, 1945–1972* (New York: Routledge, 1997), 67.

67. See chapter 3 for a discussion of the development of Northern Ireland's education system(s).

68. Bardon, *History of Ulster*, 594.

69. "Amazing Scenes at Unionist Headquarters: Education Minister Heckled," *Northern Whig*, November 11, 1946, 1.

70. Ibid. Hall-Thompson did have an advocate in the audience, Mrs. Martin Wallace, LLB, who wanted to know how many people in the room went to church and had their children attend church and Sunday school. She argued that if children were learning religion at home, religious instruction in school would not be such a pressing issue.

71. "Employment in Derry," *Londonderry Sentinel*, May 28, 1948, 2.

72. Ibid.

73. Quietly nervous about the implications of this "revenge of the cradle," Derry's unionist leaders continued to bear down on expressions and symbols of Irishness. The "*revanche du berceau*," or "revenge of the cradle," was an idea Québecois nationalists coined in the early twentieth century, the notion being that a higher birth rate would eventually change political dynamics.

74. "Derry: City of Silence, Patient Men and Police," *Irish Press*, March 20, 1948. The italics were in the original article.

75. Extract of letter from the Mitchelburne Club Apprentice Boys of Derry to the Minister of Home Affairs, March 13, 1948, quoted in Laura Donahue, "Regulating Northern Ireland: The Special Powers Acts," *The Historical Journal* 41, no. 4 (1998): 1101.

76. "Derry Anti-Partition Parade," *Belfast News Letter*, March 3, 1948, 5.

77. In Irish stick-fighting, trailing the coat was daring the opposing team to step on it and seen as aggressively provocative.

78. "Derry Anti-Partition Parade," *Belfast News Letter*, March 3, 1948, 1.

79. *Irish News*, May 31, 1948, quoted in Lynn, *Holding the Ground*, 42.

80. H. C. McSparran, Deb (NI) v. 32 c. 501, quoted in Lynn, *Holding the Ground*, 79.

81. "Derry: City of Silence, Patient Men—And Police," *Irish Press*, March 20, 1948, 7.

82. Ibid.

83. Thomas Haljkowski, *The BBC and National Identity in Britain, 1922–1953* (New York: Oxford University Press, 2017), 223.

84. "Lillibulero," *Londonderry Sentinel*, March 18, 1948, 3.

85. "Three Anti-Partitionists Arrested: Police Use Batons," *Derry Journal*, March 19, 1951.

86. Ibid.

87. Ibid.

88. "Dublin A.P.'s Association Letter to Corporation," *Derry Journal*, March 21, 1951.

89. Description based on photograph in *Derry Journal*, March 21, 1951.

90. "Dublin A.P.'s Association Letter to Corporation."

91. Ibid.

92. "The Attack on the Tricolour," *Derry Journal*, March 19, 1951, 4.

93. "Dublin A.P.'s Association Letter to Corporation."

94. "National Flag Flies from Walker's Pillar," *Derry Journal*, March 28, 1951.

95. "Chronicle and Comment," *Derry Journal*, April 2, 1951, 4.

96. Ibid.

97. Ibid.

98. The *Sentinel* refers to the incident in an article about insidious enemies in their midst ("Protestant Repealers," *Londonderry Sentinel*, July 1, 1848).

99. "Chronicle and Comment." The phrase "to spike a cannon" meant to disable it by driving a tapered wrought iron plug, or spike, down the touch hole with a hammer until it was level and firmly embedded.

100. See *Londonderry Sentinel*, "Londonderry," December 12, 1829, 2; "To the Editor," July 20, 1833, 2; and "Derry Conservative Society," January 21, 1837, 2–3, for examples of the language used to anthropomorphize the cannon.

101. A tailor's goose was an iron with a wooden handle, used for ironing clothes.

102. "Chronicle and Comment."

103. "Derry's Greatest Easter Week Commemoration," *Derry Journal*, March 28, 1951, 1.

104. Ibid.

105. Ibid.

106. Ibid.

107. "Protest by Defence," *The Irish Press*, November 6, 1951.

108. Ibid.

109. "Monday's Derry Incidents," *Derry Journal*, March 19, 1952, 4.

110. "Ex-British Soldier's Court Declaration," *Derry Journal*, May 28, 1952, 2.

111. The 1953 and 1954 St. Patrick's Day processions in Derry were banned.

112. "St. Patrick's Day Was Quiet in the City of the Ban," *Derry Journal*, March 18, 1953, 1.

113. "The Constitutional Kinks of the Carsonites," *Derry Journal*, May 23, 1953, 5.

114. Hugh Shearman, quoted in McIntosh, *Force of Culture*, 105.

115. McIntosh, *Force of Culture*, 129.

116. Ibid., 113.

117. *Northern Hansard*, vol. xxxiv, 28 February 1950, quoted in McIntosh, *Force of Culture*, 131.

118. "First Details of Derry's 1951 Festival Plans Released," *Londonderry Sentinel*, September 21, 1950, 2.

119. "Derry and the Festival of Britain," *Londonderry Sentinel*, November 30, 1950, 2. "Shoneenism" is a term for Anglophile snobbery.

120. "Great Welcome Awaits Mr. De Valera," *Derry Journal*, June 29, 1951, 1.

121. "Stormont Bill Tramples on Derry Majority's Rights," *Derry Journal*, June 11, 1951, 1.

122. "Ulster's Indebtedness to the Orange Order and Its Steadfast Resistance to Its Enemies," *Ballymena Observer*, July 20, 1951, 7.

123. "Derry Gives De Valera a Rapturous Reception," *Derry Journal*, July 7, 1951.

124. Ibid.

125. Ibid.

126. Ibid.

127. Ibid.

128. "De Valera's 1924 Visit to Derry," *Derry Journal*, July 4, 1951.

129. See Andrew Sanders, *Inside the IRA: Dissident Republicans and the War for Legitimacy* (Edinburgh: Edinburgh University Press, 2011).

130. Richard English, *Armed Struggle: The History of the IRA* (New York: Oxford University Press, 2003), 75.

131. Ibid.

132. Bardon, *History of Ulster*, 608.

133. "Outlook Is Bright in North Ireland: A Special to *The New York Times*," *New York Times*, January 8, 1957, 15.

134. Northern Ireland Civil Rights Association, "'We Shall Overcome': The History of the Struggle for Civil Rights in Northern Ireland, 1968–1978" (1978), http://cain.ulst.ac.uk/events/crights/nicra/nicra781.htm.

135. By 1959, more than 200 men from Northern Ireland were being held in Irish prisons in connection with the Border War.

136. Charles Early, "Reader's Views," *Derry Journal*, April 29, 1957, 5.

137. Ibid.

138. Liam Brady, "Derry's Part in the War for Irish Independence," *Derry Journal*, May 1, 1953, 7.

139. "Continued from Wednesday," *Derry Journal*, May 6, 1953.

140. Brady, "Derry's Part in the Irish War for Independence."

141. Ibid.

142. "Continued," *Derry Journal*, May 4, 1953, 5.

143. Ibid.

144. "Continued from Wednesday," *Derry Journal*, May 8, 1953, 7.

145. "Continued from Friday," *Derry Journal*, May 11, 1953, 5.

146. "Continued from Wednesday," *Derry Journal*, May 13, 1953, 5.

147. The argument that the IRA was moved to protect Catholics during the 1920 troubles came directly out of evidence that loyalist paramilitaries were armed by the British army.

148. "Continued," *Derry Journal*, May 13, 1953, 5.

149. Anyone familiar with the more recent history of Derry will undoubtedly see the parallel between this remembered event and the image of Bishop Edward Daly, then a parish priest, waving a white handkerchief as he headed into the fray on Bloody Sunday.

150. "Continued."

151. "Continued from Friday," *Derry Journal*, May 15, 1953, 7.

152. Ibid.

153. Hill Sixty was a battle in Ypres in November 1914.

154. "Continued from Wednesday," *Derry Journal*, May 20, 1953, 5.

155. "Continued from Monday," *Derry Journal*, May 27, 1953, 5.

156. "Continued from Wednesday," *Derry Journal*, June 1, 1953, 5.

157. "Continued from Friday," *Derry Journal*, June 5, 1953, 6.

158. "The Late John Fox," *Derry Journal*, October 8, 1952, 1.

159. The Redmonite split refers to nationalist leader John Redmond's appeal to nationalists to enlist in the Allied forces in World War I via the National Volunteers. The Irish Volunteers split off from the National Volunteers in opposition to Redmond and to safeguard Home Rule.

160. "Veteran Derry Republican Bereaved," *Derry Journal*, June 20, 1952, 1. It is interesting to note that the article itself ran on the anniversary of the troubles in 1920.

161. "Death of Eamon MacDermott," *Derry Journal*, March 4, 1957.

162. Ibid.

163. Ibid.

164. Ibid.

165. "The Late Mr. P. Shiels, Derry," *Derry Journal*, April 13, 1957. See chapter 2 for a lengthier discussion of the violence that overtook the city in 1920.

166. Ibid.

167. "Death of Richard Doherty, Derry: Gave Lifetime's Service to the AOH," *Derry Journal*, April 12, 1957.

168. "Three Great Derrymen Gone," *Derry Journal*, April 29, 1957.

169. Ibid.

170. Ibid.

171. Ibid.

172. "Onlooker," *Derry Journal*, February 4, 1957.

173. "Onlooker," *Derry Journal*, March 25, 1957, 5. The only problem with it, according to the reporter, was that it weakened its ultimate argument by calling for a dual monarchy in England and Ireland.

174. "The Facts and Principles of Irish Nationality," *Derry Journal*, June 5, 1907, 6–7.

175. "Onlooker," *Derry Journal*, March 11, 1957, 5.

176. "Onlooker," *Derry Journal*, February 11, 1957, 5.

177. "A Famous Arch," *Derry Journal*, April 1, 1957.

178. Ibid.

179. Ibid.

180. Ibid.

181. Ibid.

182. "Memories of Old Derry," *Derry Journal*, February 23, 1955, 5.

183. "A Famous Arch." The picture was published with the article.

184. Dermot Quinn, personal correspondence to author, March 3, 2018.

185. "Onlooker," *Derry Journal*, March 4, 1957, 3.

186. Ibid., 5.

187. "From a Derryman in New York," *Derry Journal*, March 2, 1955, 6.

188. "From Another Derryman," *Derry Journal*, March 18, 1957, 8.

189. "Exile's Letter," *Derry Journal*, March 25, 1957, 5.

190. Ibid.

191. On the subject of nostalgia, the late Svetlana Boym argued that it is not something to be either overlooked or patronized by historians. In examining communist nostalgia in the former Eastern bloc, she discovered that nostalgia is neither facile nor merely kitschy. Instead, it is "a sentiment of loss and displacement, but it is also a romance of one's own fantasy"; Svetlana Boym, *The Future of Nostalgia* (New York: Basic Books, 2001), xiii.

192. For more on uses of nostalgia by the Irish and members of the Irish diaspora, see Matthew Barlow, *Griffintown*, 149–52.

193. "Bishop's Residence," *Derry Journal*, March 11, 1957, 5.

194. Ibid.

195. "Letters," *Derry Journal*, April 8, 1957, 7.

196. The burning of Lundy's effigy was transferred in the 1980s to the Fountain housing estate, the only Protestant subsidized housing scheme on the "cityside," a mainly Catholic part of Derry. Until about 2000, unionists were free to march where they wanted to in the city on their festival days that celebrated Derry's ascendance as a Protestant city, and King William of Orange's 1689–90 victory over Catholic King James. These events have long been considered by nationalists to be triumphalist. July 12, August 12, and December 18 have historically been those of most public violence in the Derry calendar.

197. "Letters," *Derry Journal*, April 8, 1957, 7.

198. "Onlooker," *Derry Journal*, March 11, 1957, 5.

199. "Onlooker," *Derry Journal*, April 11, 1957, 6.

200. "Onlooker," April 11, 1957, 6.

201. "Two categories of voters were formed to ensure Protestant dominance at the polls: (1) the 'ratepayers,' primary occupiers of a household as either tenants or owners, and (2) persons who owned commercial property valued at £10 or more per year. As only two people per house were allowed to vote, the ratepayer category effectively excluded lodgers or adult children living at home. Both lodgers and adult children living at home tended to be Catholics due to their lower overall economic status and larger families; thus, Catholic franchise was restricted. People in the second category, that is, owners of commercial property, were allowed to nominate special voters for each £10 of value of their property, up to a maximum of six voters. Since over 90 per cent of the commercial property in Northern Ireland was Protestant owned, this provision expanded their voting franchise and, along with the ratepayer category, extended Unionist control over the ballot box and the government" (Landon Hancock, "Northern Ireland: Troubles Brewing," http://cain .ulst.ac.uk/othelem/landon.htm).

202. "Onlooker," February 18, 1957, 5.

203. Ibid.

204. Ibid.

205. "Onlooker," *Derry Journal*, March 4, 1957, 5.

206. "Onlooker," *Derry Journal*, March 25, 1957, 8.

207. "Readers' Views," *Derry Journal*, March 25, 1957, 7.

Chapter Five.   Sulphur in the Air, 1963–1968

1. Paddy "Bogside" Doherty, "A History of Community Development in Derry," Bridget Bond Papers, Derry City Archives.

2. Simon Prince, "The Global Revolt of 1968 and Northern Ireland," *The Historical Journal* 49, no. 3 (2006), 875.

3. John Lee, "Rioting Reopens Old Wounds in Northern Ireland," *New York Times*, October 8, 1968, 3. Lee wrote in his exposé that "televisions open a window on a world where Derry's communal traditions seem as obsolete as dinosaurs."

4. Bardon, *History of Ulster*, 648. For much of the twentieth century, Northern Ireland had the highest unemployment rate of any UK region.

5. Government of Northern Ireland, *Census of the Population, 1966: General Report* (Belfast: Her Majesty's Stationery Office), 1966.

6. "Derry's Population Confined and Choked, Corporation Told," *Derry Journal*, March 3, 1967.

7. These events are discussed more fully in chapter 4.

8. "Pastoral Letter," Derry Diocesan Archives, Folder: Bishops of Derry, 1905–1974, Bishop Neil Farren.

9. The Bann River, which runs on a roughly south–north axis, has long been used to demarcate the east and west of the province. Catholics have been a majority west of the Bann and Protestants a majority to the east of the river since Partition.

10. Bardon, *History of Ulster*, 624.

11. Michael Bannon, ed., *Planning: The Irish Experience, 1920–1988* (Dublin: Wolfhound Press, 1988), 105.

12. Paul Bew, Peter Gibbon, and Henry Patterson, *The State in Northern Ireland, 1921–72: Political Forces and Social Classes* (Manchester: Manchester University Press, 1979), 152.

13. Ibid.

14. "Derry's Population Confined and Choked, Corporation Told."

15. For more on this, see Brian Eggins, *The History of Hope* (Stroud, UK: The History Press, 2015).

16. Victor Griffin, *Mark of Protest* (Dublin: Gill and McMillan, 1993), 97.

17. Ibid., 96.

18. Radharc is pronounced "rye-arc."

19. "History of RTÉ—Telefís Éireann, Ireland's National Television Station, Goes On Air: 31 December 1961," https://www.rte.ie/archives/exhibitions/681 -history-of-rte/704-rte-1960s/.

20. Maeve Casserly, "Dead Air: Radharc and the Irish Broadcast Censor," unpublished paper, https://www.academia.edu/8872035/Dead_Air_Radharc_and _the_Irish_broadcast_censor.

21. Paddy Friel was the father of writer Brian Friel, who also appeared briefly in the film.

22. John Bowman, *Window and Mirror: RTÉ Television: 1961–2001* (Cork: University of Cork Press, 2011), 127.

23. Lance Petit, *Screening Ireland: Film and Television Representation* (Manchester: Manchester University Press, 2000), 84.

24. *Radharc in Derry*, https://www.rte.ie/archives/exhibitions/1378-radharc/355627-radharc-in-derry/.

25. Cunningham, *Derry Memories.*

26. Eddie McAteer, in *Radharc in Derry.*

27. Ibid.

28. Cunningham, *Derry Memories.*

29. Frank McAuley, in *Radharc in Derry.*

30. McAteer, in *Radharc in Derry.*

31. Ibid.

32. Ibid.

33. Paddy Friel, in *Radharc in Derry.*

34. McAteer, in *Radharc in Derry.*

35. McAuley, in *Radharc in Derry.*

36. Cunningham, *Derry Memories.*

37. McAteer, in *Radharc in Derry.*

38. Ibid.

39. Cunningham, *Derry Memories.*

40. Ibid.

41. Ibid.

42. McAuley, in *Radharc in Derry.*

43. "Derry Must Have Will and Space to Develop," *Derry Journal*, January 18, 1966, 1.

44. Not only were there housing problems in Derry dating back to the World War I era, but there were corresponding grassroots efforts to ameliorate them. As early as 1903, there is evidence of a Derry Town Tenants' Association; the group held open-air protest meetings to object to arbitrary rent increases and lobby for repair of their dilapidated houses. The group had 200 members in 1915 ("Derry Town Tenants' Association," *Derry Journal*, November 26, 1915, 3–4).

45. Bannon, ed. *Planning.*

46. Alan Murie, W. D. Birrell, P. A. R. Hillyard, and D. J. D. Roche, "Developments in Housing Policy and Administration in Northern Ireland since 1945," *Social Policy & Administration* 6, no. 1 (2007): 44–58.

47. Ibid., 45.

48. Michael McGuiness and Garbhán Downey, *Creggan: More Than a History* (Derry: Guildhall Press, 2000), i.

49. Murie et al., "Developments," 55.

50. Ibid.

51. Bardon, *History of Ulster*, 642.

52. The Campaign for Social Justice in Northern Ireland, *Londonderry: One Man, No Vote* (Dungannon, 1965), http://cain.ulst.ac.uk/events/crights/pdfs/csj84.pdf.

53. Murie et al., "Developments," 63.

54. "Housing Sub-Committee Minutes," February 23, 1953, Derry City Council Archives, Council Meeting Minutes, Housing Sub-Committee Minutes, Bound Volumes, 1952–1957.

55. "Housing Sub-Committee Minutes," December 1, 1955, in ibid.

56. Figures are based on the 1961 census; see Bardon, *History of Ulster*, 647.

57. Bardon, *History of Ulster*, 647.

58. Ibid., 648.

59. Frank Curran, *Derry: Countdown to Disaster* (London: Gill and Macmillan, 1986), 66.

60. "Pigs Can't Hold Up Housing Scheme," *Derry Journal*, February 17, 1967.

61. Paddy "Bogside" Doherty, "My Own Story," Ulster Folk and Transport Museum Oral History Interview, n.d., 14.

62. Ibid.

63. Margo Shea, "There Were Streets: Urban Renewal and the Early Troubles in London/Derry, Northern Ireland," in *Spatializing Politics: Essays on Power and Place*, ed. Delia Wendel and Fallon Samuels (Cambridge, MA: Harvard University Press, 2015), 19–48.

64. Alderman McCartney expressed the general unionist attitude held regarding the Catholic community in June 1967: "There may be a shortage of houses, but they certainly have not been neglected. Must they all get houses built for them? Could they not look about houses themselves? Do they expect the rest of the community to build houses continually for them?" ("Corporation Meeting," *Derry Journal*, June 2, 1967).

65. Derry Diocesan Archives, Folder: Catholic Community Social Service Centre, Various, 1947–1953.

66. "Oak Leaf Building Society Comes of Age with Record Year," *Derry Journal*, April 8, 1966.

67. Ibid.

68. Paddy "Bogside" Doherty, "My Story," Heritage Library Talks, 14, Local History Collection, Derry Central Library.

69. "Profiteers in Human Need Condemned," *Derry Journal*, February 16, 1967.

70. Michael Canavan, interview, Ulster Folk and Transport Museum Oral History Interview, interviewer Tony Morrow, October 13, 1988, tape 084, ref no. 941.062, Q&A section, unmarked pages.

71. Ibid.

72. "Letters to the Editor: A Young Mother's Housing Plea," *Derry Journal*, February 20, 1968.

73. "A Young Mother's Housing Plea," *Derry Journal*, March 5, 1968.

74. "Nearly 10,000 Houses Needed in the Next 13 Years," *Derry Journal*, March 5, 1968.

75. "Derry at the Bottom of the List Again," *Derry Journal*, January 17, 1967.

76. The DHAC appealed the decision to the Ministry of Development in March 1968, but the appeal was dismissed in May 1968 on the grounds that the Pennyburn site lacked services and amenities required for residential areas.

77. Curran, *Derry: Countdown to Disaster*, 61.

78. "Derry at the Bottom of the List Again."

79. "Housing Decisions that Deeply Disturb," *Derry Journal*, June 18, 1968.

80. "Nearly 10,000 Houses Needed."

81. "Civil Rights Chant Echoes through Derry Guildhall," *Derry Journal*, November 1, 1969.

82. Curran, *Derry: Countdown to Disaster*, 63.

83. "Housing Action Group Calls for Crash Building Programme," *Derry Journal*, May 3, 1968.

84. "Rotten Political System Governs Derry Planning," *Derry Journal*, July 2, 1968. The interface area in question lay between Catholic and Protestant neighborhoods in the Foyle Road.

85. "Caravan Dweller Who Can't Get Housing Accommodation," *Derry Journal*, April 26, 1968.

86. Ibid.

87. That same week, two dozen tenants who lived in condemned houses in the area of St. Columb's Wells, Nelson Street, and Wellington Street threatened a sit-in strike after they were told that they had to vacate their homes and would not qualify for resettlement grants. As subtenants without rent books, they were considered ineligible by the Northern Ireland Housing Trust for assistance. Charles Quigley, one of the tenants, explained that all of the tenants had been moved out of other properties slated for demolition into the area that was now up for redevelopment; they had spent money making their homes inhabitable and were being treated unfairly (see "Derry Tenants Threaten Sit-In Strike," *Derry Journal*, June 18, 1968).

88. Flynn denied this when asked about it under cross-examination at the prosecutions of members of the DHAC (see "Corporation Flayed in Caravan Protest Case," *Derry Journal*, July 5, 1968).

89. Eamonn McCann, *War in an Irish Town*, 3rd ed. (London: Pluto Press, 1993), 83.

90. "Multi-Story Flat Tenants to Challenge Post Office Ruling," *Derry Journal*, February 23, 1968.

91. *The New Reality: Organ of the Derry Civil Rights Association*, n.d., Derry City Council Archives, Bridget Bond Papers: Derry Civil Rights Association.

92. Simon Prince has argued that organizers planned the Duke Street march in order to force the police to overreact and thereby shift public opinion. He reached his conclusion through McCann's account of the march in *War in an Irish Town* (see Simon Prince, "The Global Revolt of 1968"). McCann himself alludes to the fact that even at the scene of the march, leaders disagreed about violence. Seamus Heaney, writing in October 1968, suggests that some of the spokespeople for nonviolence were at the forefront of the march: "Eyewitnesses have attested to the irony of the occasion: the eventual victims of the law were anxious to keep the police calm, urging them as they confronted the cordon to stay calm and in control of themselves" (Seamus Heaney, "Old Derry Walls," *The Listener*, October 24, 1968, 521–23).

93. McCann, *War in an Irish Town*.

94. Nominally, the Derry Labour Party, the Derry Labour Party Young Socialists, the Derry Housing Action Committee (DHAC), the Derry City Republican Club, and the James Connolly Society were all involved in organizing the events for the 5th, but two men, Eamonn McCann and Eamon Melaugh, did most of the work.

95. McCann attacked McAteer in December 1969: "McAteer was browned off even before he feasted on O'Neill's half a loaf. He opposed the 5 October march and spent some time trying to get the organizers to call it off. However when it was decided to go ahead McAteer took up a place at the head of the procession—a sordid little twist that illustrated perfectly the nature of Nationalist leadership" (from Curran, *Derry: Countdown to Disaster*, 105).

96. Paddy Doherty, "Speech to the Meeting of Community Associations of Northern Ireland, May 16th and 17th, 1975," Bridget Bond Papers, Derry City Archives.

97. Poor housing conditions represented an issue that Protestants in Northern Ireland could back, in part because the concrete problem faced both working-class Protestants and Catholics. Also, the issue offered those Protestants and moderate unionists who did want to see political change in Northern Ireland a

safer way into politics. This was well understood at the time. In "Old Derry Walls," Heaney described the Protestant presence at the Duke Street march: "Mr Fred Taggart, one of the leaders of the march, declared, 'I am a Protestant, and to any Protestant Unionist who sees no need for reform I say there is something wrong with your Unionism or there is something wrong with your Protestantism'" (Seamus Heaney, "Old Derry Walls," *The Listener*, October 24, 1968, 522).

98. Fionnbarra Ó Dochartaigh, *Ulster's White Negroes: From Civil Rights to Insurrection* (Edinburgh: AK Press, 1994), 44.

99. McCann, *War in an Irish Town*, 84–85.

100. Ó Dochartaigh, *Ulster's White Negroes*, 46.

101. Eamon Melaugh explained in an interview that the route was chosen precisely because it was the traditional Orange march route; organizers were sure it would be banned because of this alone, and intended to defy the ban (Eamon Melaugh, interview, Ulster Folk and Transport Museum Oral History Interview, interviewer Tony Morrow, tape 050 A & B, recorded June 25, 1987, tape reference number 941.62, 11).

102. "Callaghan and Craig: What A Difference," *Derry Journal*, October 29, 1968.

103. Melaugh, interview, 11.

104. Eddie McAteer has been roundly castigated by the '68ers as the epitome of accommodationism. I disagree with that assessment, as of course did McAteer. Once, when called a Green Tory by some of the younger generation, he said "the definition of a Green Tory is a Roman Catholic who works for his living" ("Meeting Eddie McAteer," *Irish Press*, April 5, 1971, 8).

105. Lord Cameron, *Disturbances in Northern Ireland: Report of the Commission Appointed by the Governor of Northern Ireland: Presented to Parliament by Command of His Excellency the Governor of Northern Ireland, September 1969* (Belfast: Her Majesty's Printing Office, 1969), 28.

106. McCann, *War in an Irish Town*, 84–85.

107. "Callaghan and Craig: What a Difference."

108. Gerard McMenamin, "King Street," in The Waterside Book 1996, quoted in McMahon, ed., *The Derry Anthology*, 354.

109. Seamus Deane, "Why Bogside?," *Honest Ulsterman*, no. 27 (1971): 7. This reminiscence may be a conflation of the events of 1951 and 1952. In 1951, the nationalist councillors were batoned badly; in 1952, a much larger group of Catholics and nationalists were beaten.

110. Just as the Easter Rising was viewed as a foolhardy and miscalculated event until its suppression and retribution galvanized many Irish people, the

relatively small numbers of participants in the Duke Street protest paled in comparison to the multitudes who were disgusted by the police's response.

111. McCann, *War in an Irish Town*, 103. Obviously, this was to the detriment to, if not the antithesis of, the original goals McCann, Melaugh, and others had set out to attain.

112. Curran, *Derry: Countdown to Disaster*, 88.

113. Edward Daly, *Mister, Are You a Priest? Jottings by Bishop Edward Daly* (Dublin: Four Courts Press, 2000), 131.

114. Paddy "Bogside" Doherty, interview, Ulster Folk and Transport Museum Oral History Interview, interviewer Tony Morrow, n.d., 20.

115. "Civil Rights Marchers Establish Long-Denied Right," *Derry Journal*, November 5, 1968.

116. Ibid.

117. "Civil Rights Chant Echoes through Derry Guildhall," *Derry Journal*, November 1, 1969.

118. Ibid.

119. "Craig Gives His Reasons," *Belfast News Letter*, November 15, 1968, 2.

120. Curran, *Countdown*, 92. McAteer's initial efforts to encourage his party to think imaginatively were short-lived. On October 15, the Nationalist Party withdrew from its role as "official" opposition at Stormont, a position they had agreed to hold in 1965. McAteer did not take his seat in Stormont until the end of November. The party ceased to exist after the elections of February 1969, when a new generation of nationalist politicians were overwhelmingly voted into office.

121. "Letters to the Editor," *Derry Journal*, November 19, 1968, 5.

122. Paddy "Bogside" Doherty, interview, 21.

123. Ibid.

124. Daly, *Mister, Are You a Priest?*, 132.

125. "15,000 Civil Rights Marchers Smash Craig's Ban," *Derry Journal*, November 19, 1968, 1.

126. Paddy "Bogside" Doherty, interview, 22.

127. Curran, *Countdown*, 98.

128. Ibid.

129. Ibid.

130. "The End of Apathy," *Derry Journal*, November 19, 1968.

131. Canavan, interview, 6.

132. "Report," *Irish News*, November 19, 1968.

133. "Letters to the Editor," *Derry Journal*, November 19, 1968.

134. Ibid.

135. Michael Canavan, interview.

136. "Derry Commission Will Have Total Powers," *Derry Journal*, November 26, 1968, 1.

137. Ibid.

138. Melaugh, interview, 10.

139. Ibid.

Chapter Six.   Old Derry's Last Stand, 1969

1. The adult Catholic population of Derry was 20,102 in 1966. According to these figures, close to 85 percent of Catholic adults in the city attended.

2. The original coroner's report declared that Devenny died of "natural causes" and denied any link between the assault by police officers and his death, but a 2001 report by a lawyer hired as part of the Northern Ireland peace process to investigate police actions concluded that the police beating had killed Devenny. Police ombudsman Nuala O'Loan based her findings on the Drury report, a 1970 investigation carried out by the Metropolitan Police (Scotland Yard). In November 1970, RUC chief constable Arthur Young had issued a statement saying that none of the officers involved in the beating that led to Devenny's death had been identified: "I trust that this serious misconduct on the part of a small number of members of the Force will be considered in relation to all that the Force as a whole has subsequently achieved to become a non-aggressive, non-retaliatory police service resolved to win the respect and confidence of all members of the community" (from the "Samuel Devenny Enquiry," Pat Finucane Centre, http://www.patfinu canecentre.org/state-violence/appendix-1-document-2-samuel-devenny-enquiry; and http://www.patfinucanecentre.org/state-violence/appendix-1-document-1 -samuel-devenny-enquiry).

3. Madeleine McCully, interview with author, June 13, 2014.

4. Eamon Melaugh, quoted in *Battle of the Bogside*, dir. Vinny Cunningham (Derry: Perfect Cousin Productions, 2004), https://vimeo.com/32340356.

5. Paramilitary groups initially included both the official and provisional branches of the Irish Republican Army (IRA), the Irish National Liberation Army (INLA), the Ulster Volunteer Force (UVF), the Ulster Freedom Fighters (UFF), and the Ulster Defense Association (UDA). The official IRA called a cease-fire in 1972, with some members joining the Provos and others founding the INLA.

6. Deane, "Why Bogside?," 7.

7. Ibid.

8. Nationalists insist that Free Derry was autonomous during its short life, but unionists point out that it continued to rely heavily on the infrastructure of

the British state for postal delivery, access to telephone service, electricity, and medical assistance.

9. "Government Suggests Push for Derry Area Plan," *Derry Journal*, November 19, 1968.

10. "Commission Will Have Total Power," *Derry Journal*, November 26, 1968. The idea that they held back industry coming was a recent one, the argument being that the protests had turned away potential business investment in the city.

11. Burntollet, perhaps more than any other event of the Northern Ireland civil rights movement, echoes the experiences in U.S. cities such as Selma, Alabama, which saw civil rights protestors attacked by racists and armed police while they were on their way to Montgomery on March 7, 1965. This event also came to be known as Bloody Sunday.

12. Lord Cameron, *Disturbances in Northern Ireland: Report of the Commission Appointed by the Governor of Northern Ireland* (Belfast: Her Majesty's Printing Office, 1969).

13. The *Derry Journal* published a fascinating article about the provenance of "Free Derry" Corner on the anniversary of the November 16 march: "A Silent and Powerful Witness to Troubled Times," *Derry Journal*, November 16, 2009, https://www.derryjournal.com/news/a-silent-and-powerful-witness-to-troubled-times-1-2142120. The story of recognition of Liam Hillen as the original painter of the Free Derry slogan can be found here: "'You Are Now Entering Free Derry' Wall Painter Liam Hillen Dies Aged 69," https://www.thejournal.ie/free-derry-artist-liam-hillen-dies-4415244-Dec2018/.

14. Phil Cunningham, "Phil Cunningham's Battle of Fox's Corner," YouTube, https://www.youtube.com/watch?v=zW3l0i7FbKk.

15. Neil Farren, written statement, "Cameron Report, May 1, 1969," Public Records of Northern Ireland (PRONI), File GOV/2/1/116.

16. Russell Stetler, *Battle of the Bogside* (London: Steed and Ward, 1970).

17. Paddy "Bogside" Doherty, quoted in the film *Battle of the Bogside*.

18. Myra Canning, interview August 12, 2008.

19. Raymond McClean, quoted in the film *Battle of the Bogside*.

20. Nell McCafferty, quoted in the film *Battle of the Bogside*. McCafferty also suggested that the rumor provided the opportunity for middle-class residents of the area to justify joining the fray.

21. Ivan Cooper, quoted on RTÉ News, "Rioting Reaches Peak," August 13, 1969; search for at http://www.rte.ie/laweb/ll/ll_t18_main.html.

22. Ibid.

23. Nell McCafferty, quoted in the film *Battle of the Bogside*.

24. Frank Doran, quoted in the film *Battle of the Bogside*. Historians, journalists, eyewitnesses, and participants tend to offer similar accounts of the Battle of the Bogside, many of which corroborate these reminiscences of community spirit, but there remains a widely divergent interpretation of the events of August 12–14, 1969. For those who participated in the Apprentice Boys march that day, the Bogsiders were considered to be aggressive and assaultive.

To commemorate the fortieth anniversary of the event, DUP representative and MP for East Londonderry Gregory Campbell accepted an invitation to share his recollections. In a speech he gave, he offered this account:

> When I made my way to William Street seeing Police Officers sitting propped up against the wall many of them exhausted as both the riot and their duty had been going on for probably a day and a half at this stage. I was angry, angry at the rioters and those who seemed intent on creating mayhem and insurrection. As soon as I and a few others arrived I clearly recall a rioter hurling abuse at us as well as missiles. The attacks went on as I walked around the edge of the Bog to see what was going on. It had all the hallmarks of an open-ended rebellion against the rule of law. At night I came back, this time to Great James Street to see the Presbyterian Church coming under attack. . . . Over those few days I was witnessing the start of what few of us could have foreseen was a thirty-year onslaught of murder.
> (from Slugger O'Toole, "Gregory Campbell on the Battle of the Bogside," July 27, 2009, https://sluggerotoole.com/2009/07/27/gregory-campbell-on-the-battle-of-the-bogside/)

It also is relevant to note that local people have questioned some of Nell McCafferty's reminiscences of the "battle," stating with some consistency that "Nell never lets the truth get in the way of a good story." However, there is photographic documentation of middle-aged women in dresses and heels bent over making petrol bombs, so it can be inferred that at least some women participated in this part of the battle.

25. James Coyle Wray, interview, Ulster Folk and Transport Museum Oral History Interview, interviewer Tony Morrow, May 30, 1989, tape no. 123 A&B, tape reference no 941.62, 3.

26. Eddie McAteer, quoted in "Rioting Reaches Peak."

27. Kevin McCallion, quoted in the film *Battle of the Bogside*.

28. Tommy Makem, quoted in the film *Battle of the Bogside*.

29. McCallion, quoted in the film *Battle of the Bogside*.

30. Makem, quoted in the film *Battle of the Bogside*.

302   Notes to Pages 245–250

31. "Sunday Interview," *Derry Journal*, July 9, 2009.

32. Neil Jarman and Dominic Bryan, *From Riots to Rights: Nationalist Parades in the North of Ireland* (Coleraine: Centre for the Study of Conflict at the University of Ulster, 1998), 1–79, come to a very different conclusion. They argue:

> After persistent clashes between the police and the residents of predominantly Catholic areas there was a greater emphasis within the Catholic community to try and assert control of the areas in which they lived. This appears particularly clearly in the Bogside where there was a concerted attempt to exclude the security forces and the area proclaimed "Free Derry." Symbolically members of that community were beginning to attempt to shut the state out of their areas, rather than marching in to areas perceived as Protestant to demand their rights within the state. This shift reflects a political move away from a civil rights agenda towards a nationalist and republican agenda; a shift from the politics of NICRA to that of the IRA. (48)

My evidence suggests that the IRA presence was minimal during the Battle of the Bogside and that moderate community leaders continued to hold sway in decision-making processes during the tenure of the no-go zone. I would argue that residents *were* acting out of community pride, fear of police and loyalist rioters, and a profound exhaustion with the status quo. There seems little to suggest that they were convinced, or indeed manipulated, by the IRA.

33. Seamus Deane, foreword to *Beyond Hate: Living with Our Differences*, ed. Eamon Deane and Carol Ritner (Derry: Guildhall Press, 1994), xiii.

34. Melaugh, interview.

35. Arthur McVeigh, "Thoughts on the Derry Riots," *Community Forum* 2 (1974): 23.

36. Deane, "Why Bogside?," 2.

Conclusion

1. For more on this, see Gerald McSheffrey, *Planning Derry: Planning and Politics in Northern Ireland* (Liverpool: Liverpool University Press, 2000).

2. This was before the Tricolour had been designed.

3. "The Green Flag Flies in Derry," *Derry Journal*, February 24, 1896, 5.

4. David Glassberg developed the idea of a sense of history as a way to describe the accretive and dialogic relationships between identity and historical consciousness. See Glassberg, *Sense of History: The Place of the Past in American Life* (Amherst: University of Massachusetts Press, 2001).

5. Tom Maguire, "Curating Hatred: The Joe McWilliams's Controversy at the Ulster Museum," special issue, "Hate and Heritage," *Journal of Hate Studies* 13, no. 1 (2017): 62.

6. For more on heritage in Northern Ireland, see Elizabeth Crooke, "The Politics of Community Heritage: Motivations, Authority and Control," *International Journal of Heritage Studies* 16, no. 1-2 (2010): 17; Nuala Johnson, "The Contours of Memory in Post-Conflict Societies: Enacting Public Remembrance of the Bomb in Omagh, Northern Ireland," *Cultural Geographies* 19, no. 2 (2012), 237–58. Brian Graham, Greg Ashworth, and J. E. Turnbridge, *Pluralising Pasts: Heritage, Identity and Place in Multicultural Societies* (Chicago: Pluto Press, 2007).

BIBLIOGRAPHY

ARCHIVAL SOURCES

Derry City Council Archives

Bridget Bond Collection: Folder, Community Associations,
    Bogside Community Association
Bridget Bond Collection: Derry Civil Rights Association
Bridget Bond Collection: Paddy "Bogside" Doherty
Clippings Scrapbook, 1896–1910
Clippings Scrapbook, 1935–1943
Council Meeting Minutes, Housing Sub-Committee Minutes, 1952–1957
Register of Orders Granting Use of Guildhall Premises, 1890–1924

Derry Central Library

Local History Collection

Derry Diocesan Archives

Folder: Bishops: Neil Farren
Folder: Bishops of Derry, 1905–1974
Folder: Priests: O'Doherty, William
Folder: Derry Catholic Registration Committee, 1931–1958
Folder: Catholic Community Social Service Centre, Various, 1947–1953

Museum of Free Derry

Folder BB/61: *The Starry Plough: Derry's Own Republican Newspaper*

Public Records Office of Northern Ireland (PRONI)

File GOV/2/1/116: "Disturbances in Northern Ireland: A Report of the Commission Appointed by the Governor of Northern Ireland," May 1, 1969
File HA/51/4, Londonderry Gerrymandering
File D2953/1/2/1, Papers of the Derry Catholic Registration Association

University of Ulster, Magee Library, Derry

Irish Collection

Newspapers

Ballymena Observer
Belfast News Letter
Belfast Telegraph
Catholic Standard
Derry Journal
Derry News
Derry Standard
Freeman's Journal
Irish News
Irish Press
Irish Times
Londonderry Sentinel
New York Times
Northern Whig
The Times (London)
Time magazine

ORAL HISTORY INTERVIEWS

By the Author

Frank Curran, January 11, 2008
Bishop Edward Daly, August 23, 2008
Madeleine McCully, June 13, 2014
Myra Canning, August 12, 2008

Ulster Folk and Transport Museum Oral History Interview, interviewer Tony Morrow

Michael Canavan, October 13, 1988, tape nos. 84, 88b
Paddy "Bogside" Doherty, n.d., no tape no.
John Maultsaid, April 29, 1988, tape nos. 72b–73b
Eamon Melaugh, June 25, 1987, tape no. 50a-b
Lillian O'More, March 16, 1988, tape no. 72a
Sister Kathleen, n.d., tape no. 69a
James Coyle Wray, May 30, 1989, tape no. 123a-b

PUBLISHED PRIMARY SOURCES

Alistair Coey Architects. *Derry City Walls Conservation Plan, 2009.* https://www.communities-ni.gov.uk/publications/derry-city-walls-conservation-plan.

Appendix to Parliamentary Papers, 1883, Great Britain Parliament. London: House of Commons/The Queen's Printing Office, 1883.

Christian Brothers. "The First Catholic Mayor of Derry." In *Souvenir Magazine: Christian Brothers School Brow O'-the-Hill Anniversary.* Derry: Christian Brothers, 1927.

———. *Christian Brothers Souvenir and Prospectus.* Derry: Christian Brothers, 1902.

Gailey, William. *Gailey's Guide to Derry and Its Suburbs.* Derry: William Gailey, 1892.

Government of Northern Ireland. *Census of the Population, 1966: General Report.* Belfast: Her Majesty's Stationary Office, 1966.

Great Britain. Commission of Inquiry, Belfast Riots, *Reports from Commissioners on the Riots in Londonderry and Belfast and on Magisterial and Police Jurisdiction, with Minutes of Evidence and Appendices, 1857–70.* Shannon: Irish University Press, 1970.

Hansard Parliamentary Debates, 12 June 1895, vol. 34, cols. 966–1016.

Ireland Census Office. *Census of Ireland 1901.* Dublin: Printed for Her Majesty's Stationery Office by Cahill & Co., 1902.

Long Tower Church. *Derry Columbkille: Souvenir of the Centenary Celebrations in Honour of St. Columba in the Long Tower Church, Derry 1897–99.* Dublin: Brown & Nolan Printers, 1899.

Lord Cameron. *Disturbances in Northern Ireland: Report of the Commission Appointed by the Governor of Northern Ireland: Presented to Parliament by Command of His Excellency the Governor of Northern Ireland, September 1969.* Belfast: Her Majesty's Printing Office, 1969.

Milligan, Alice. "A Journey to Cloudland: Rambling Reminiscences." In *Shan Van Vocht*, 4:33–38. Belfast: P. W. Boyd, 1897.

"Municipal Franchise Bill (Ireland)." *Hansard Parliamentary Debates*, 12 June 1895, vol. 35, cols. 62–74.

Northern Ireland Civil Rights Association. "'We Shall Overcome': The History of the Struggle for Civil Rights in Northern Ireland, 1968–1978." http://cain .ulst.ac.uk/events/crights/nicra/nicra781.htm.

Poyntz, John, Earl of Spencer. *A Report of Londonderry Riot Commission*, 1884, S.l.: s.n. H.C., 1884, col. 3954.

Report of a Commission appointed to inquire into certain Disturbances which took place in the City of Londonderry on the 1st November 1883; together with the Evidence taken before the Commission. Dublin: Alex Thom. and Co., The Queen's Printing Office, 1884.

Royal Irish Academy. *Documents on Irish Foreign Policy.* Vol. 1. Dublin: Royal Irish Academy/National Archives of Ireland, 1998.

St. Eugene's Cathedral. *St. Eugene's Cathedral Derry Souvenir 1843–1936 Consecration.* Derry: Derry Journal, 1936.

Vesey Knox, Edward. Speech in *Hansard Parliamentary Debates*, 10 March 1896, vol. 38, cols. 543–63.

———. Speech in *Hansard Parliamentary Debates*, 25 February 1896, vol. 37, cols. 1054–55.

Violence and Civil Disturbances in Northern Ireland in 1969: Report of the Tribunal of Inquiry. Vols. 1–2. London: Her Majesty's Stationary Office, 1972.

PUBLIC SPEECHES

Bernard, Walter. "The Ruin of the Grianan of Aileach." In *Proceedings of the Royal Irish Academy, 1878.* Dublin: Royal Irish Academy, 1878.

Daly, Mary. "David Beers Quinn and Ireland." Address to Hakluyt Society. http:// www.hakluyt.com/hak-soc-tributes-daly.htm.

Doherty, Reverend William. "Derry Columbkille: Read Aloud July 28, 1902." Typed manuscript, Derry Central Library, Subject File "St. Columb's Wells."

Smyth, Marie Breen. "Presentation to the Management Committee of Towards Understanding and Healing, July 2005."

FILMS/VIDEO/SOUND RECORDING SOURCES

Battle of the Bogside. Directed by Vinny Cunningham. Derry: Perfect Cousin Productions, 2004.
Radharc in Derry (1964). Dublin: Radharc Films, 1989.

ONLINE SOURCES

Campaign for Social Justice in Northern Ireland. *Londonderry: One Man, No Vote.* Dungannon, 1965. http://cain.ulst.ac.uk/events/crights/pdfs/csj84.pdf.
Crockett, Robbie. "Robbie Crockett's End of War Memories." Second World War: Online Learning Resource for Northern Ireland. http://www.secondworldwarni.org/default.aspx?id=8&themeid=11.
Cunningham, Phil. "Phil Cunningham's Battle of Fox's Corner." YouTube. https://www.youtube.com/watch?v=v%3D%3Dz.
Derry City Council Museum. Services for their "Their Past, Your Future" project on World War II Memories. http://www.derrycity.gov.uk/ww2/index.htm.
Derry Ghosts (Online folklore project). http://www.derryghosts.com.
    Stories: "The Devil and the Gamblers"; "The Great-Grandmother's Warning"; "The Haunting on Wellington Street."
RTÉ News. "Rioting Reaches Peak." August 13, 1969. http://www.rte.ie/laweb/ll/ll_tl18_main.html.
———. "History of RTÉ—Telefís Éireann, Ireland's National Television Station, Goes On Air: 31 December 1961." http://www.rte.ie/archives/exhibitions/681-history-of-rte/704-rte-1960s/.
Slugger O'Toole. "Gregory Campbell on the Battle of the Bogside," July 27, 2009. https://sluggerotoole.com/2009/07/27/gregory-campbell-on-the-battle-of-the-bogside/.
"The Story of Saint Eugene's Cathedral." http://www.steugenescathedral.com/storyofsteugenes.htm.

ARTICLES AND MONOGRAPHS

Alinsky, Saul. *Reveille for Radicals.* Chicago: University of Chicago Press, 1946.
Anderson, Benedict. *Imagined Communities.* Rev. ed. New York: Verso, 1991.
Bannon, Michael, ed. *Planning: The Irish Experience, 1920–1988.* Dublin: Wolfhound Press, 1988.

Bardon, Jonathan. *A History of Ulster.* Belfast: Blackstaff Press, 1992.

Barlow, Matthew. *Griffintown: Identity and Memory in an Irish Diaspora Neighborhood.* Vancouver: University of British Columbia Press, 2017.

Barton, Brian. *Northern Ireland and the Second World War.* Belfast: Ulster Historical Foundation, 1995.

Beiner, Guy. *Remembering the Year of the French: Irish Folk History and Social Memory.* Madison: University of Wisconsin Press, 2007.

Bennett, Arthur. *John Bull and His Other Island.* London: Simpkin, 1890.

Bew, Paul, Peter Gibbon, and Henry Patterson. *The State in Northern Ireland, 1921–72: Political Forces and Social Classes.* Manchester: Manchester University Press, 1979.

Bourke, Angela. *The Burning of Bridget Cleary.* New York: Penguin, 1999.

Bowman, John. *Window and Mirror: RTÉ Television, 1961–2001.* Cork: University of Cork Press, 2011.

Boym, Svetlana. *The Future of Nostalgia.* New York: Basic Books, 2001.

Bradshaw, Brendan. "Nationalism and Historical Scholarship in Modern Ireland." In *Interpreting Irish History: The Debate on Historical Revisionism, 1938–1994,* edited by Ciaran Brady, 191–216. Portland, OR: Irish Academic Press, 1994.

Buckland, Patrick. *The Factory of Grievances: Devolved Government in Northern Ireland, 1921–39.* Dublin: Gill and Macmillan, 1979.

Bulfin, William. "Rambles in Erin, 1907." In *The Derry Anthology,* edited by Sean McMahon, 159–60. Belfast: Blackstaff Press, 2002.

Butlin, R. A. "Land and People, 1600." In *A New History of Ireland,* edited by T. W. Moody, F. X. Martin, and F. J. Byrne, 3:142–67. New York: The Clarendon Press, 1976.

Canning, Bernard. *By Columb's Footsteps Trod: The Long Tower's Holy Dead, 1784–1984.* Ballyshannon: Donegal Democrat, 1984.

———. *The Street That Is Gone but Lives On.* Limavady, NI: Limavady Printing Company, 2001.

Casey, Edward. "Public Memory in Place and Time." In *Framing Public Memory,* edited by Kendall R. Phillips, 17–44. Tuscaloosa: University of Alabama Press, 1992.

Casserly, Maeve. "Dead Air: Radharc and the Irish Broadcast Censor." Unpublished paper. http://www.academia.edu/8872035/Dead_Air_Radharc_and_the_Irish_broadcast_censor.

Christian Brothers. "The Story of Derry." In *Souvenir and Prospectus: Brow of the Hill.* Belfast, 1927.

Clarke, Aidan. "The Irish Economy, 1600–60." In Moody et al., ed., *A New History of Ireland,* 3:168–86.

Confino, Alon. "Collective Memory and Cultural History: Problems of Method." *American Historical Review* 102, no. 5 (1997): 1386–1403.

———. *The Nation as a Local Metaphor: Wurttemberg, Imperial Germany, and National Memory, 1871–1918.* Chapel Hill: University of North Carolina Press, 1997.

Corkery, Daniel. *The Hidden Ireland: A Study of Gaelic Munster in the Eighteenth Century.* Dublin: Gill & Son, 1924.

Corporaal, Marguerite, Christopher Cusack, and Ruud van den Beuken, eds. *Irish Studies and the Dynamics of Memory: Transitions and Transformations.* Bern: Peter Lang, 2017.

Crane, Susan. "Writing the Individual Back into Collective Memory." *American Historical Review* 102, no. 5 (1997): 1372–85.

Crooke, Elizabeth. "The Politics of Community Heritage: Motivations, Authority and Control." *International Journal of Heritage Studies* 16, no. 1-2 (2010): 16–29.

Cunningham, Philip. *Derry: Down the Days.* Derry: Guildhall Press, 2010.

———. *Derry Memories.* Derry: Guildhall Press, 2007.

Curl, James Steven. *The Honourable The Irish Society and the Plantation of Ulster, 1608–2000: The City of London and the Colonisation of County Londonderry in the Province of Ulster in Ireland. A History and Critique.* Chichester, UK: Phillimore, 2000.

Curran, Frank. *Derry: ountdown to Disaster.* London: Gill and Macmillan, 1986.

———. *Ireland's Fascist City.* Derry: Derry Journal, Ltd., 1946.

Curtin, Nancy. "'Varieties of Irishness': Historical Revisionism, Irish Style." *Journal of British Studies* 35, no. 2 (1996): 195–219.

Daly, Edward. *Mister, Are You a Priest? Jottings by Bishop Edward Daly.* Dublin: Four Courts Press, 2000.

Daly, Edward, and Kieran Devlin. *Clergy of the Diocese of Derry.* Dublin: Four Courts Press, 2009.

Davis, Natalie Zemon, and Randolph Starn, eds. "Memory and Counter Memory." Special issue, *Representations* 26 (1989).

Deane, Eamon, and Carol Ritner, ed. *Beyond Hate: Living with Our Deepest Differences.* Derry: Guildhall Press, 1994.

Deane, Seamus. *Reading in the Dark.* New York: Random House, 1996.

———. "Why Bogside?" *Honest Ulsterman* 27 (1971): 1–8.

De Bovet, Marie Anne. *Three Months' Tour in Ireland.* London: Chapman and Hall, 1891.

De Certeau, Michel. *The Practice of Everyday Life.* Chicago: University of Chicago Press, 1984.

Doherty, Jenni, and Alex Carlin. *History of the Foyle Fisheries.* Derry: Guildhall Press, 1996.

Donahue, Laura. "Regulating Northern Ireland: The Special Powers Acts." *The Historical Journal* 41, no. 4 (1998): 1089–1120.

Donnelly, Phillip. "Bishop Charles McHugh of Derry Diocese (1856–1926)." *Seanchas Ardmhacha: Journal of the Armagh Diocesan Historical Society* 20, no. 2 (2005): 212–44.

Dorian, Hugh. *The Outer Edge of Ulster: A Memoir of Social Life in Nineteenth-Century Donegal.* Edited by Breandan Mac Suibhne and David Dickson. Notre Dame, IN: University of Notre Dame Press, 2001.

Douglas, George, ed. *Derriana: A Collection of Papers Relative to the Siege of Derry, and Illustrative of the Revolution of 1688.* Derry: G. Douglas, 1794.

Eggins, Brian. *The History of Hope.* Stroud, UK: The History Press, 2015.

Elliott, Marianne. *The Catholics of Ulster: A History.* New York: Basic Books, 2001.

Ellis, John. "Reconciling the Celt: British National Identity, Empire, and the 1911 Investiture of the Prince of Wales." *The Journal of British Studies* 37, no. 4 (1998): 391–418.

Ellis, Steven. "Historiographical Debate: Representations of the Past in Ireland: Whose Past and Whose Present?" *Irish Historical Studies* 27, no. 108 (1991): 289–308.

English, Richard. *Armed Struggle: The History of the IRA.* New York: Oxford University Press, 2003.

———. *Irish Freedom: The History of Nationalism in Ireland.* New York: Macmillan, 2006.

Féis Committee. *75th Anniversary of Féis Doire Colmcille Souvenir Book.* Derry: Féis Committee, 1999.

Ferrante, Elena. *The Story of the Lost Child.* New York: Europa, 2015.

Finnegan, David, Éamonn Ó Ciardha, and Marie-Claire Peters, eds. *The Flight of the Earls: Imeacht na nIarlai.* Derry: Guildhall Press, 2011.

Foster, R. F. *The Irish Story: Telling Tales and Making It Up in Ireland.* New York: Oxford University Press, 2002.

———. *Modern Ireland: 1600–1972.* New York: Penguin, 1988.

Gallagher, Charles. *Acorns and Oak Leaves: A Derry Childhood, Growing Up in Derry, 1920–1945.* Derry: Dubh Regles Books, 1982.

Gallagher, Ronan. *Violence and Nationalist Politics in Derry City, 1920–1923.* Dublin: Four Courts Press, 2003.

Garvin, Tom. *The Evolution of Irish Nationalist Politics.* Ann Arbor: University of Michigan Press, 1981.

Gibbons, Luke. *Transformations in Irish Culture.* Notre Dame, IN: University of Notre Dame Press, 1996.

Gillespie, Paul. "Can Powersharing Lead to Place of Through-otherness?" *The Irish Times*, May 12, 2007. https://www.irishtimes.com/opinion/can-powersharing -lead-to-place-of-through-otherness-1.1205599.

Gillis, John, ed. *Commemorations: The Politics of National Identity.* Princeton, NJ: Princeton University Press, 1994.

Glassberg, David. *Sense of History: The Place of the Past in American Life.* Amherst: University of Massachusetts Press, 2001.

Glassie, Henry. *Passing the Time in Ballymenone.* Philadelphia: University of Pennsylvania Press, 1982.

Goldring, Douglas. *A Stranger in Ireland.* Dublin: Talbot Press, 1918.

Graham, Brian. "Heritage as Knowledge: Capital or Culture?" *Urban Studies* 39, no. 5/6 (2002): 1003–17.

Graham, Brian, Greg Ashworth, and J. E. Turnbridge. *Pluralising Pasts: Heritage, Identity and Place in Multicultural Societies.* Chicago: Pluto Press, 2007.

Griffin, Victor. *Mark of Protest.* Dublin: Gill and McMillan, 1993.

Gwynn, Stephen. "The Famous Cities of Ireland, 1915." In McMahon, ed., *The Derry Anthology*, 176.

Halbwachs, Maurice. *On Collective Memory.* Translated and edited by Lewis A. Coser. Chicago: University of Chicago Press, 1991.

Haljkowski, Thomas. *The BBC and National Identity in Britain, 1922–1953.* New York: Oxford University Press, 2017.

Hancock, Landon. "Northern Ireland: Troubles Brewing." http://cain.ulst.ac.uk /othelem/landon.htm.

Hand, Geoffrey, ed. *Report of the Irish Boundary Commission, 1925.* Dublin: Irish University Press, 1969.

———. "MacNeill and the Boundary Commission." In *The Scholar Revolutionary: Eóin MacNeill and the Making of the New Ireland, 1867–1945*, edited by F. J. Byrne and F. X. Martin, 201–75. Dublin: Irish University Press, 1973.

Harvey, David. "'National' Identities and the Politics of Ancient Heritage: Continuity and Change at Ancient Sites in Britain and Ireland, c. 1675–1850." *Transactions of the Institute of British Geographers* 28 (2003): 473–87.

Heaney, Seamus. "The North: Silent Awareness" (interview with Monie Begley). In Monie Begley, *Rambles in Ireland and a County-by-County Guide for Discriminating Travelers*, 161. Old Greenwich, CT: Devin-Adair, 1977.

———. "Old Derry Walls." *The Listener*, October 24, 1968, 521–23.

Hepburn, A. C. *Catholic Belfast and Nationalist Northern Ireland in the Era of Joe Devlin, 1871–1934.* New York: Oxford University Press, 2008.

Hobsbawm, Eric. "The Historian between the Quest for the Universal and the Quest for Identity." *Diogenes* 168 (1994): 51–64.

Hobsbawm, Eric, and Terence Ranger, eds. *The Invention of Tradition.* New York: Cambridge University Press, 1983.

Holmes, Andrew. "The Development of Unionism before 1912." Irish History Live. https://www.qub.ac.uk/sites/irishhistorylive/IrishHistoryResources/Articlesandlecturesbyourteachingstaff/ThedevelopmentofUnionismbefore1912/.

Jackson, Alvin. *Home Rule: An Irish History, 1800–2000.* New York: Oxford University Press, 2003.

Jarman, Neil. "The Orange Arch: Creating Tradition in Ulster." *Folklore* 112, no. 1 (2001): 1–21.

Jarman, Neil, and Dominic Bryan. *From Riots to Rights: Nationalist Parades in the North of Ireland.* Coleraine: Centre for the Study of Conflict, University of Ulster, 1998.

Johnson, Nuala. "The Contours of Memory in Post-Conflict Societies: Enacting Public Remembrance of the Bomb in Omagh, Northern Ireland." *Cultural Geographies* 19, no. 2 (2012): 237–58.

Keenan, Brian. Introduction to *Beyond Hate: Living with Our Deepest Differences,* edited by Eamon Deane and Carol Ritner. Derry: Guildhall Press, 1994.

Kelly, William. "The Plantation and Its Impact on the Bogside." In *From Columba to Conflict: The Early Years of the Bogside, Brandywell, and Lower Bishop Street,* edited by Mickey Cooper, 53–63. Derry: Gaslight Press, 2012.

Kennedy, Dennis. *The Widening Gulf: Northern Attitudes to the Independent Irish State, 1919–49.* Belfast: Blackstaff Press, 1998.

Kennedy-Pipe, Caroline. *The Origins of the Present Troubles in Northern Ireland.* New York: Longman, 1997.

Keogh, Dermot, *Ireland and the Vatican: The Politics and Diplomacy of Church-State Relations, 1922–1960.* Cork: Cork University Press, 1995.

Kuhn, Annette. *Family Secrets: Acts of Memory and Imagination.* New York: Verso, 1995.

Lacey, Brian. *Siege City.* Belfast: Blackstaff Press, 1990.

Leerssen, Joep. *Hidden Ireland, Public Sphere.* Galway: Arlen House for the Centre of Irish Studies, 2002.

Lynn, Brendan. *Holding the Ground: The Nationalist Party in Northern Ireland, 1945–1972.* New York: Routledge, 1997.

———. "Nationalist Politics in Derry, 1945–1969." In *Derry & Londonderry: History and Society: Interdisciplinary Essays on the History of an Irish County,* edited by Gerard O'Brien and William Nolan, 601–47. Dublin: Geography Publications, 1999.

Macaulay, Thomas. *History of England from the Accession of James the Second.* Philadelphia: Butler & Co., 1861.

MacCormack, John. *The Irish Rebellion of 1798 with Numerous Historical Sketches.* Dublin: James MacCormack, 1844.

MacDonagh, Oliver. *States of Mind: A Study of Anglo-Irish Conflict, 1780–1980.* Boston: Allen and Unwin, 1983.

MacKnight, Thomas. *Ulster As It Is, or Twenty-Eight Years' Experience as an Irish Editor.* Vol. 2. London: Macmillan and Co., 1896.

MacSweeney, Patrick. *A Group of Nation Builders: O'Donovan, O'Curry, Petrie.* Dublin: Catholic Truth Society of Ireland, 1913.

Madden, Finbar, and Thomas Bradley. "The Diocese of Derry in the Twentieth Century, c. 1900–1974." In *History of the Derry Diocese from the Earliest Times*, edited by Henry Jeffries and Kieran Devlin, 240–58. Dublin: Four Courts Press, 1999.

———. *Seeking the Kingdom: St. Columb's College 1879–2004.* Derry: St. Columb's College, 2004.

Maguire, Tom. "Curating Hatred: The Joe McWilliams's Controversy at the Ulster Museum." Special issue, "Hate and Heritage," *Journal of Hate Studies* 13, no. 1 (2017): 61–83.

McAteer, Eddie. *100 Hours of Nationalism or Irish Made Too Easy: Written for Those Who Are Too Lazy, Too Old, Only Mildly Interested, Too Busy.* Derry: Derry Journal, 1945.

———. Foreword to *Ireland's Fascist City* by Frank Curran. Derry: Derry Journal Press, 1946.

———. *Irish Action: New Thoughts on an Old Subject.* Belfast: Athol Books, 1979.

McBride, Ian, ed. *History and Memory in Modern Ireland.* New York: Cambridge University Press, 2001.

———. *The Siege of Derry in Ulster Protestant Mythology.* Dublin: Four Courts Press, 1997.

McCafferty, Carmel, and Leo Eaton. *In Search of Ancient Ireland: The Origins of the Irish from Neolithic Times to the Coming of the English.* Chicago: New Amsterdam Books, 2002.

McCann, Eamonn. *War in an Irish Town.* 3rd ed. London: Pluto Press, 1993.

McCann, Eamonn, and Maureen Shields, eds. *Bloody Sunday in Derry: What Really Happened.* Dingle: Brandon Books, 1992.

McCarthy, Mark. "Historico-Geographical Explorations of Ireland's Heritages: Towards a Critical Understanding of the Nature of Memory and Identity." In

Ireland's Heritages: Critical Perspectives on Memory and Identity, edited by Mark McCarthy, 3–51. Aldershot: Ashgate, 2005.

McEvoy, Kieran, ed. *Making Peace with the Past: Options for Truth Recovery Regarding the Conflict in and about Northern Ireland.* Belfast: Healing Through Remembering, 2006.

McGuinness, Michael, and Garbhán Downy. *Creggan: More Than a History.* Derry: Guildhall Press, 2000.

McIntosh, Gillian. "Acts of National Communion." In *Ireland in the 1930s: New Perspectives,* edited by Joost Augusteijn, 95–113. Dublin: Four Courts Press, 1999.

———. *The Force of Culture: Unionist Identities in Twentieth Century Ulster.* Cork: Cork University Press, 1999.

McKittrick, David, and David McVea. *More Than the Troubles: The Story of the Conflict in Northern Ireland.* Lanham, MD: Rowman & Littlefield, 2002.

McMahon, Sean, ed. *The Derry Anthology.* Belfast: Blackstaff Press, 2002.

———. "The Diocesan Seminary." In *Seeking the Kingdom: St. Columb's College, 1879–2004,* edited by Finbar Madden and Thomas Bailey, 1–53. Derry: St. Columb's College, 2005.

McMonagle, Barney. *No Go: A Photographic Record of Free Derry.* Edited by Adrian Kerr. Derry: Guildhall Press, 1997.

McSheffrey, Gerald, *Planning Derry: Planning and Politics in Northern Ireland.* Liverpool: Liverpool University Press, 2000.

McVeigh, Arthur. "Thoughts on the Derry Riots." *Community Forum* 2 (1974): 17.

Megahey, Alan. *The Irish Protestant Churches in the Twentieth Century.* New York: Springer, 2000.

Melaugh, Martin. "Interment: Summary and Main Events." http://cain.ulst.ac.uk/events/intern/sum.htm.

Mitchel, John. *The History of Ireland, from the treaty of Limerick to the present time: Being a continuation of the history of the Abbé Macgeoghegan.* Glasgow: Cameron and Ferguson, 1869.

Moody, T. W. "The Treatment of the Native Population under the Scheme for the Plantation of Ulster." *Irish Historical Studies* 1, no. 1 (1938): 51–63.

Moore, Niamh, and Yvonne Whelan, eds. *Heritage, Memory and the Politics of Identity: New Perspectives on the Cultural Landscape.* Aldershot: Ashgate, 2007.

Mullin, T. H. *Derry-Londonderry: Ulster's Historic City.* Coleraine: Coleraine Bookshop, 1986.

Murie, Alan, W. D. Birrell, P. A. R. Hillyard, and D. J. D. Roche. "Developments in Housing Policy and Administration in Northern Ireland since 1945." *Social Policy & Administration* 6, no. 1 (2007): 44–58.

Murphy, Desmond. *Derry, Donegal, and Modern Ulster, 1790–1921.* Derry: Aileach Press, 1981.

Nora, Pierre. "Between Memory and History: Les Lieux de Mémoire." *Representations* 26 (Spring 1989): 7–25.

Norton, Christopher. *The Politics of Constitutional Nationalism in Northern Ireland, 1932–1970: Beyond Grievance and Reconciliation.* New York: Manchester University Press, 2014.

Ó Baoill, Mící Sheáin Néill, trans. "Taibhse Dhoire: A Derry Ghost." In McMahon, ed., *The Derry Anthology*, 398.

Ó Dochartaigh, Fionnbarra. *Ulster's White Negroes: From Civil Rights to Insurrection.* Edinburgh: AK Press, 1994.

O'Doherty, John Keys. *Derriana.* Dublin: Sealy, Bryars & Walker, 1904.

O'Halloran, Clare. *Partition and the Limits of Irish Nationalism: An Ideology under Stress.* Atlantic Highlands, NJ: Humanities, 1987.

Ohlmeyer, Jane. "Seventeenth-Century Ireland and the New British and Atlantic Histories." *The American Historical Review* 104, no. 2, April 1999, 446–62.

O'Riordan, Michelle. "The Native Ulster Mentalité as Revealed in Gaelic Sources 1600–50." In *Ulster 1641: Aspects of the Rising*, edited by Brian Mac Caurta, SJ, 61–92. Belfast: Queens University Press, 1993.

Orsi, Robert. *The Madonna of 115th Street: Faith and Community in Italian Harlem, 1880–1950.* New Haven, CT: Yale University Press, 1985.

Payne, Charles. *I've Got the Light of Freedom: The Organizing Tradition and the Mississippi Freedom Struggle.* Berkeley: University of California Press, 2007.

Petit, Lance. *Screening Ireland: Film and Television Representation.* Manchester: Manchester University Press, 2000.

Phoenix, Eamon. *Northern Nationalism: Nationalist Politics, Partition and the Catholic Minority in Northern Ireland, 1890–1940.* Belfast: Ulster Historical Foundation, 1994.

Potter, Simon. "Review: The Eternal Paddy." *Reviews in History* 501 (2006). https://reviews.history.ac.uk/review/501.

Prince, Simon. "The Global Revolt of 1968 and Northern Ireland." *The Historical Journal* 49, no. 3 (2006): 851–75.

———. *Northern Ireland's '68: Civil Rights, Global Revolt and the Origins of the Troubles.* Dublin: Irish Academic Press, 2007.

Rafferty, Barry. *Pagan Celtic Ireland: The Enigma of the Irish Iron Age.* London: Thames and Hudson, 1994.

Redmond, John. "Ireland and the Coronation." In *World's Greatest Orations, 1775–1902.* Vol. 6, *Ireland*, edited by William Jennings Bryan. New York: Funk and

Wagnalls, 1906. https://en.wikisource.org/wiki/The_World%27s_Famous _Orations/Volume_6.

Ricoeur, Paul. *Time and Narrative.* Translated by K. Blamey and D. Pellauer. Chicago: University of Chicago Press, 1994.

Robinson, Alan, and Raymond Johnston. "The Ballyarnett/Shantallow Recreation Center." *Community Forum* 2 (1974): 16.

Ross, Alan. *How to Pronounce It.* London: Hamilton, 1970.

Rowan, Alistair, "The Buildings of Ireland: North West Ulster, 1979." In McMahon, ed., *The Derry Anthology,* 11.

Schumpeter, Joseph. *Capitalism, Socialism and Democracy.* New York: Harper, 1942.

Shaw, George Bernard. "Preface for Politicians." In *John Bull's Other Island,* v–xxxiii. London: Constable and Co., 1907.

Shea, Margo. "There Were Streets: Urban Renewal and the Early Troubles in London/Derry, Northern Ireland." In *Spatializing Politics: Essays on Power and Place,* edited by Delia Wendel and Fallon Samuels, 19–48. Cambridge, MA: Harvard University Press, 2015.

Shrubsole, Edgar S. *Londonderry and the North of Ireland: The Tourist's and Sportsman's Guide.* Belfast: Baird, 1909.

Smyth, Marie Breen, and Mike Morrissey. *Northern Ireland after the Good Friday Agreement: Victims, Grievance and Blame.* London: Pluto, 2002.

Staunton, Enda. *The Nationalists of Northern Ireland.* Dublin: Columba Press, 2001.

Stetler, Russell. *Battle of the Bogside.* London: Steed and Ward, 1970.

Tacitus. *Agricola and Germania.* New York: Penguin Classics, 2010.

Taylor, Diana. *The Archive and the Repertoire: Performing Cultural Memory in the Americas.* Durham, NC: Duke University Press, 2003.

Taylor, Peter. *Families at War: Voices from the Troubles.* London: BBC Publications, 1991.

Thomas, William. *The Quarrel of Macaulay and Croker: Politics and History in the Age of Reform.* New York: Oxford University Press, 2000.

Townend, Paul. *The Road to Home Rule: Anti-Imperialism and the Irish National Movement.* Madison: University of Wisconsin Press, 2016.

Tumblety, Joan, ed. *Memory and History: Understanding Memory as Source and Subject.* New York: Routledge, 2013.

Weinbaum, Eve S. *To Move a Mountain: Fighting the Global Economy in Appalachia.* New York: The New Press, 2004.

Whelan, Kevin. *The Tree of Liberty: Radicalism, Catholicism and the Construction of Irish Identity, 1760–1830.* Notre Dame, IN: University of Notre Dame Press, 1996.

Wichert, Sabine. "Nationalism in the Northern Ireland Conflict." *History of European Ideas* 16, no. 1-3 (1993): 109–14.

Wills, Claire. *That Neutral Island: A Cultural History of Ireland during the Second World War.* London: Faber and Faber, 2007.

Woods, Fred. *The Derry Quays.* Derry: Guildhall Press, 2004.

Yates, Francis. *The Art of Memory.* Chicago: University of Chicago Press, 1966.

Young, Amy. *Three Hundred Years in Inishowen.* Belfast, 1924.

THESES AND DISSERTATIONS

Gallagher, Walter. "People, Work, Space and Social Structure in Edwardian Derry, 1901–1911." PhD diss., University of Ulster, 1994.

McClements, Freya. "Press Censorship and Emergency Rule in Ireland: The Ban on the *Derry Journal*, 1932 and 1940." Master's Thesis, University of Ulster, 2005.

INDEX

abstention from political participation, 15, 21, 48, 88–89, 94, 118, 144, 149, 275n7, 279n115; and resumption of political roles, 118, 147, 149

"Aggro Corner," 231

alcohol, 138, 281n138; and abstention from, 37–38, 181, 189, 278n97. *See also* St. Columb's Total Abstinence Society

Alinsky, Saul, 155, 285n52

All Souls' Day, 126, 129–30

Altnagelvin hospital, 197

Ancient Order of Hibernians (AOH), 60, 77–79, 85, 95, 114, 181

Anglo-Irish Treaty, 85, 92, 178

anti-Catholicism, 30, 33; attitudes, 47, 63, 67, 116, 128, 191, 251; in employment, 113, 158–61, 201

anti-Partition movement, 95, 147, 149, 154–63, 166

Apprentice Boys, 42, 51–52, 60, 65, 116, 152, 164, 190, 200, 218, 223, 232, 239, 271n61, 301n24; Apprentice Boys Hall, 164

archaeology, 71–73

arches, 57–58, 60–62, 64–65, 110–14, 128, 185–86

Atlee, Clement, 147, 149

B Specials, 85, 98, 140; Derry presence in the 1920s, 85, 171, 178; Derry presence in 1969, 1, 218–19, 236, 239, 242, 244

bands, 38–39, 60, 73, 99, 170–71, 186, 242–44. *See also* Féis Doire Colmcille; music

Bates, Richard Dawson, 118

battle for the flag, 161–67; bystanders and, 163; nationalist political leaders and, 162; police and, 162

Battle of the Atlantic, 90, 145. *See also* World War II

Battle of the Bogside, 1, 23, 231–44; and community solidarities, 247–53; and end of "old Derry," 244–47, 302n32. *See also* Bogside

Battle of the Boyne, 28, 39, 68, 105, 164, 201

Bealtaine, 126, 131

Belfast, 18, 28, 33, 34, 39, 59, 63, 97–98, 99, 104, 108, 112, 113,

McCarroll, Frank, 162
McCarter, Alderman, 63, 67
McGee, Thomas D'Arcy, 164–65
McGettigan, John, Fr., 276n43
McHugh, Charles, Bishop, 64, 81, 85,
    87, 91, 97
McVeigh, Arthur, 246
Meenan Park, 165
Melaugh, Eamon, 214–16, 229, 245,
    296n94, 297n101, 298n111
memory: community and, 2, 3, 10,
    12, 14, 15, 19, 20, 22, 46, 88, 116,
    125, 141, 147, 178, 182, 187, 194,
    217; as a concept, 7, 11, 12, 13–19;
    construction of the past and, 13,
    18, 19, 73, 251; contestation of, 7,
    45, 46, 59, 62, 65, 150–52, 192;
    countermemories, 8, 70–76, 149;
    cultural, 2, 7, 52, 58, 75, 94, 96,
    103, 108, 109; cultural national-
    ism and, 18, 54, 61, 69, 70, 71,
    75, 78, 95, 96, 100, 101, 103, 107,
    127, 166, 167, 180; expressions
    of, 2, 5, 18, 20, 22, 78, 79, 125,
    126, 142, 189; generational, 151,
    182, 183; historical consciousness
    of injustice and, 12, 65, 67, 89,
    149, 196, 209, 219–20, 225, 231,
    243; Home Rule and, 46, 69, 70,
    75–86; identity and, 2, 3, 5, 6,
    7, 13, 14, 15, 16, 17–22, 62, 76,
    88, 89, 92, 94, 103, 108, 109, 125,
    126, 127, 128, 147, 159, 161, 167,
    174, 182, 191, 192, 194, 201, 243,
    245, 251, 252, 258n46, 280n132;
    invented traditions and, 54, 55,
    58, 252; iterative nature of, 13,
    18; landscape and, 1,4, 19, 28,
    40, 70, 71, 76, 80, 100, 132, 171,
    186, 188, 229, 252, 268–69n28;
    memory work, 3–4, 7, 10, 12, 13,
    16, 18, 19, 21, 46, 76, 80, 88, 89,
    114, 147, 172–79, 193, 219, 229,
    251; oral tradition and, 18, 19, 72,
    125, 141; parallel, 16–17, 21, 45,
    52, 97, 168, 186, 289n149; per-
    formance of, 18, 22, 23, 55, 125,
    141, 189, 196, 232; public, 46;
    republicanism and, 9, 10, 16; and
    ritual, 2, 3, 4, 8, 20, 22, 46, 89,
    96, 111, 124–31, 140, 141, 142,
    186, 194, 244, 247, 252; social
    frameworks and, 12; source and
    subject, 12; strategic, 13, 16; trans-
    mission of, 125; traumatic events
    and, 5, 219–20; urban space and,
    40, 41, 43, 44, 59, 109, 161, 162,
    166, 170, 216, 219, 220, 224
Ministry for Home Affairs, 118, 121,
    160–61, 168, 213, 218, 260n62
Montgomery, Bernard Law ("Monty"),
    145
Moody, Theo, 157
Mulvey, Anthony, Fr., 209
Muncie Partnership, 206, 212
municipal government, and ward con-
    struction, 31, 43, 48–49, 117–23,
    206–8
Municipal Improvement Bill, 43–44,
    48
music, 60, 97–98, 100–101, 128, 143,
    156, 160, 166, 169, 185, 191–92,
    243, 252, 276n43. *See also* bands;
    Féis Doire Colmcille

nationalism, 6, 7, 8, 9, 15, 18, 22, 36,
    43, 55, 80, 118, 133, 148, 151, 153,
    154, 156, 158, 161, 171, 173, 179,

taries, 249; and republicanism, 144, 178, 224–25, 240–42, 270n60, 301n24; sectarianism and, 61–62, 69, 159, 163, 176, 178, 190–91

World War I, 33, 76, 79–80, 90, 177, 241, 289n159, 293n44

World War II, 21–22, 130–31, 143, 193, 244; conscription and military personnel in Derry, 90; effects on politics of sectarianism, 22, 146–47; end of, 142, 143, 244; instructive use of propaganda and censorship, 148; Irish neutrality, 90, 146. *See also* Battle of the Atlantic

worries and preoccupations of, 136–39

Wray, James Coyle, 241–42

Young Ireland movement, 58, 71, 162, 165

MARGO SHEA is an assistant professor of history at Salem State University.

Printed in the USA
CPSIA information can be obtained
at www.ICGtesting.com
CBHW072217041224
18470CB00004B/126

9 780268 107932